CHICKEN SOUP FOR THE GOLFER'S SOUL COLLECTION

Stories of Insight, Inspiration and Laughter on the Links

Jack Canfield
Mark Victor Hansen
Jeff Aubery
Mark & Chrissy Donnelly

Health Communications, Inc.
Deerfield Beach, Florida

www.hcibooks.com
www.chickensoup.com

We would like to acknowledge the following publishers and individuals for permission to reprint the following material. (Note: The stories that were penned anonymously, that are in the public domain, or that were written by Jack Canfield, Mark Victor Hansen, Jeff Aubery, Mark Donnelly or Chrissy Donnelly are not included in this listing.)

Only One. Reprinted by permission of J. G. Nursall. ©1998 J. G. Nursall. Originally appeared in *Golf Journal.*

Lost and Found. Reprinted by permission of Greg R. Bernard. ©1998 Greg R. Bernard.

The U.S. Open. Reprinted by permission of Bill Pelham. ©1998 Bill Pelham.

In the Pink. Reprinted by permission of Ernie Witham. ©1998 Ernie Witham.

The Golf Maniac. Reprinted by permission of Nancy N. Winthrop (copyright holder for Stephen Leacock). ©1998 Nancy N. Winthrop.

(Continued on page 535)

Library of Congress Cataloging-in-Publication Data is available at the Library of Congress.

©2006 Jack Canfield and Mark Victor Hansen
ISBN 0-7573-0540-7 (hardcover)

Publisher: Health Communications, Inc.
3201 S.W. 15th Street
Deerfield Beach, FL 33442-8190

Cover design by Andrea Perrine Brower
Inside book re-formatting by Lawna Patterson Oldfield

With love we dedicate *Chicken Soup for the Golfer's Soul* to the millions of golfers around the world. Your passion and spirit for the game help keep golf and all its history alive for generations to come. We also dedicate this book to Patty Aubery, vice president of Chicken Soup for the Soul Enterprises. We are so grateful to have you in our lives and are thankful for all that you have done to help with this project. Your uncanny ability to see only the good in people and your willingness to care inspire us all to be better human beings. We love you!

Contents

v

2. GOING FOR THE GREEN

3. SPECIAL MOMENTS

4. GOLFMANSHIP

5. GOLF LINKS A FAMILY TOGETHER

6. OUT OF THE ROUGH

7. THE NINETEENTH HOLE

1

THE
FIRST TEE

Only One

Norma Halstead was a slender fifteen-year-old in the summer of 1941. Her father, Grant, was the professional at the new Fresno Municipal Course located on the banks of the San Joaquin River. She and her parents lived on the second floor of the clubhouse, high on a hilltop overlooking the river and the first fairway. It was a simple time and Norma's life was filled with many things, but especially her love of golf.

Summer days in Fresno can be unmercifully hot. Norma would frequently rise before the sun, complete her chores, and then tote her canvas bag off to the first tee for a solitary nine. In the early morning a fine mist often rose off the river. The first hole, which plunged down the hillside from the clubhouse, appeared milky white. Norma was relatively new to the game, but her father's instruction was evident when she cracked a drive off the first tee and watched as it carried out and down into the mist over the fairway below. Norma loved the game and her life at the river's edge.

On one particular July morning Norma set out for her round with no more than the mere expectation of a good walk in the country. As she teed up one of the three Dunlop balls given to her by her father, she remembered his admonition, "a good golfer never loses a ball." Her father's word on matters of golf was gospel, and Norma dreaded the thought of ever asking him for more golf balls. But this morning her drive bore true through the mist and landed well down the first fairway.

Billy Bell designed the course. Grant Halstead convinced the city fathers that Bell was the man to draw up their first public course, and Bell's execution was flawless. It soon became known as the "big Muni" and was the site of many exciting city championships. The real challenge for Bell was in designing the first three holes in the limited space available. The first hole, a long par-4, stretched down the hill from the clubhouse and out along the riverbank. The second was a short, well-bunkered par-3 running up a hillside to a bowl-shaped green. The third hole paralleled the first, with its green chiseled into the steep embankment looming over the river. The design of these three holes, now obvious for its simplistic elegance, was considered impossible. But Bell's talent for the simple yet elegant solution was evident throughout the course.

As Norma approached her ball in the first fairway she could hear the distant whistle of an early morning freight train. The tracks ran the eastern length of the course and at the river's edge crossed a great trestle. Soon the train would be rumbling by the second hole, clattering north to Modesto, Stockton and Sacramento. It took Norma three strong shots to reach the first green, and she holed out with two putts for a personal par.

On the second tee she selected a long iron. Her father's simple wisdom told her never to fear any club. Swing them all the same. But most of all, he would say, "Trust your swing." As she took a practice swing, she thought only of mimicking her father's graceful style. He often said to her, "Imagine someone is taking your picture. Try to look pretty." It was easy for the young girl.

The train was just rumbling past the wooden fence posts lining the edge of the course. Norma's concentration was complete as she rocked into the ball. To her delight it soared swiftly on a line for the round green. Norma hoped for par on the short holes and tried extra hard to reach the putting surface. She was a good putter and could often get down in two. This looked like a good shot, landing at the front of the green, right on line with the flag. She picked up her bag and began climbing up the hill to the green.

On hot days players would often dawdle at the back of the second hole, where two big pine trees spread their limbs and offered momentary shade. The bowl-shaped green easily collected shots, but because it was a small green any tee shot more than ten degrees off line would ricochet off the hillside. Accuracy was rewarded. Norma knew the secret to this hole was to take plenty of club— and trust your swing.

As Norma reached the top of the hill she was unable to see her ball. The train, now well down the track and over the trestle, sounded three short hoots of its great whistle. Norma looked to the back of the green, expecting to see her ball nestled against the collar. It wasn't there. She laid down her bag and began looking closely at the ribbon of rough at the back of the green. Slightly exasperated, the realization began to sink in that she may have lost her first golf ball. She imagined her father's brow creased with wrinkles of incredulity, mouth gaping, dumbstruck by his only child's shameful loss.

It must be here somewhere, Norma thought. She began to walk to the front of the green on the chance the ball had not bounced forward as she had first thought. Then, as she walked past the hole, she looked down and there it was. A hole-in-one!

Though she was only a novice, she knew that a hole-in-one was a terrific golfing feat. She knew her father would be delighted. His broad smile and gleaming eyes filled her thoughts as she reached into the cup and extracted her ball. She wished her father had seen it. She wished her mother had seen it. She wished anyone had seen it.

She finished her round of nine and walked to the steps of the clubhouse, now washed with the warming rays of the morning sun. She looked up to the porch and saw the face of her mother. Not wanting to sound too excited, she said coyly, "Oh, Mom, I hit a really good shot today." Her mother, having been saturated with stories of golf from the time of her first meeting Grant, was prepared to patiently attend to yet another exploit on the field of glory.

Suitably braced to receive the laurels of her triumph, Norma announced, "Yes, on the second I hit a shot right into the hole."

Her mother scanned the horizon, looking out across the course as if she were taking inventory of the young trees sprouting along the fairways. Her mind was on the baking of pies, cakes and chili for the day's customers. While Grant ran the golf shop and taught lessons on the range, Norma's mother ran the coffee shop. Everything was fresh.

She turned and looked at Norma's shoulder-length brown curls, and noticed beads of sweat at her temples. Finally she said, "That's very good, dear. Be sure to tell your father. Now come inside and get out of the sun."

Norma was somewhat disappointed with her mother's reaction. Certainly there was meant to be something more to this. She must have announced it wrong. Trailing after her mother as they walked into the coffee shop, Norma said, "No, Mother, I mean I hit the ball into the hole with only one shot. A hole-in-one!"

Norma's mother put her arms across her young daughter's shoulders and guided her through the coffee shop, and then gently sent her off in the general direction of the golf shop. "Yes, dear, that's very good," she repeated. "Be sure you tell your father."

Norma's frustration only grew when she announced her triumph to her father. They stood alone in the golf shop. The slight fifteen-year-old was dwarfed by the muscled pro. Grant's most impressive features were his massive hands and bald head. His steady gaze could be stern, but most often his eyes sparkled with the spirit of Christmas.

In a solemn tone Grant said to his child, "That's very good, Norma, but you have to understand something. It's not really sporting to say you've scored an ace while playing alone. You see, without a witness . . . well . . . we'd have jokers coming off the course every day claiming to have done one thing or another." Grant then wrapped his arms around his daughter, gave her a gentle hug, and said, "Just remember—trust your swing and you'll do fine."

In days to come, parents would ponder the psychological injury such a disappointing reception might inflict upon the young willow. But 1941 was a more realistic time, and in some ways parents were not so concerned with sheltering their children from the harshness of the world. They were more intent on preparing them to live in a world of both evil and good.

Norma thought little more of her triumph. She had learned that in addition to the Rules of Golf taught to her by her father, there were other rules. Rules that were only learned by experience.

Two weeks later a postcard, addressed only to "Head Pro," arrived at the clubhouse. Grant received the card and his thunderous laughter could be heard throughout the clubhouse. The card read simply, "Congratulations to that young lady who aced the second hole. What a beautiful shot." The card was signed, "J. C. Wade, Engineer, Southern Pacific Railroad."

When Norma heard the ruckus in the shop below, she came down the staircase from her bedroom and was greeted by her father and four members of the men's club. Her father's booming voice proclaimed his daughter's victory as Norma read and reread the postcard in disbelief. She smiled broadly, and with due modesty finally accepted the conqueror's wreath.

She was about to go back up to her room when her father spoke. "Now dear, fetch your piggy bank. You owe us all a drink."

Norma sensed she was about to learn one more of golf's unwritten rules.

J. G. Nursall

Lost and Found

*They say golf is like life, but don't believe them.
Golf is more complicated than that.*

Gardner Dickinson

From the satchel on my office desk, forty ungraded compositions whispered at me in grammatically incorrect urgency. But after two days of torrential rainfall, a radiant sun enveloped the local greens in a golden Sunday embrace. After a quick shower, I was off for a lone round before trading in my pitching wedge for the proverbial red pen.

The attendant at the clubhouse greeted me with an only slightly disgruntled countenance; rising early to watch others play golf is apparently not without its limitations. The sign-in sheet indicated only one other gentleman had begun his round. Good. The golf would be quick, private and unhurried.

After sticking my wedding ring in my front pocket for safekeeping (it causes blisters if I leave it on), I astounded myself with my first drive, a sweet whistle down the center of the fairway. I lovingly replaced the head cover on my driver.

By the sixth hole, it was becoming increasingly apparent, even given my poor math skills, that I was having the round of my life. Not that Tiger Woods has to worry just yet; after five holes I was one under, thanks in part to holing a slippery twenty-footer.

Addressing my ball, I peered down the sixth fairway, a beautifully designed par-5 that loped around a kidney-shaped pond fronted with flowering water plants and cattails. Poking around with his ball retriever was Mr. Early. This is what I dubbed him, unable to recall his name from the logbook I had hastily scribbled my signature into less than an hour ago. Hair whiter than a freshly opened pair of tube socks, with a posture that suggested firsthand recollections of the birth of the game, he did not notice my growing impatience on the tee box. Finally, rationalizing that I was playing too well this morning to actually hit him (and feeling the ever-increasing weight of those essays bearing down on the remaining hours of my shortened weekend), I teed off with a shank that would make Sir Murphy and his Book of Laws proud.

Old fart, I grumbled to myself, thrusting the ill-fitting head cover over my driver. Eager to make the turn alone, I promised myself not to engage this feeble duffer in conversation. Trouble is, in my disgust over the missed hit, I had failed to track my ball with any degree of precision. All I knew is that it had sculled somewhere near where Mr. Early was still searching.

"Quite the morning, isn't it?" he asked as I approached.

"Yeah," I said, avoiding direct eye contact. Old folks are like animals, I reasoned, they can see the weakness in your eyes.

"We seem to have lost ourselves in here somewhere," he said, waving his ball remover over the tangled grass in which we waded.

Just as it seemed I was destined to spend my Sunday

morning chaperoning a member of the geriatric unit
around the links, I spied a dimpled sphere buried deep in
the rough.

"Here I am," I said, reaching for the first thing in my
bag. A rotten stick would have done.

"Are you sure?" he asked. "I was hitting a Titleist."

"Me too," I said, rolling my eyes in exasperation. Or
was it a Top-Flite? Who cares, I finally decided. The ball
was mine.

And I was gone.

But the image of the old man staring at me as I made
my way around the lake kept me from concentrating. My
game suffered. I grew angrier and angrier.

Following another chunked drive, I slammed my driver
into the bag, resolved never to grip its evilness again.

My iron game left me as well, literally. On the thirteenth hole, I went to my bag to retrieve my 7-iron, only
to find it was not there. I groaned, realizing what I would
be forced to endure. Mr. Early was still behind me, and
most likely in possession of my club.

Unfortunately, he was gone. Apparently, nine was
enough for him this fine Sunday morning. Probably off to
church, I steamed, heading for the clubhouse, my round
destroyed.

The clubhouse was still empty as I entered, the over-
head fan doing little to cool me off. The attendant gazed at
me with that same sleepy boredom with which he had
greeted me earlier.

"Did anyone else come in here?" I asked.

"Older guy? Head of white hair?" he asked, yawning.

"Yeah," I said. "Did he leave anything behind?"

"Yup. Said you'd be looking for it. He set everything
over on the bar."

"Everything?" I asked.

"Look, it's on the bar. That's all I know," he said.

I walked over to the mahogany counter, the clicking of the cleats ringing in my ears. There on the bar was the cover to my driver, my 7-iron and a golf ball. Reaching for the ball, I felt my face flush red. Top-Flite. It even had my personalized markings, three dots with a permanent red pen. Then I noticed a drink napkin amidst my returned equipment. Set in the middle, shining as bright as the day on which my wife had slipped it on my finger, was my wedding ring. It had fallen out of my pocket somewhere on the golf course. A miracle itself that he had found it. Even more astonishing that he had somehow known it was mine and to return it, with everything else. My throat tightened as I raced for the parking lot.

Mr. Early was just pulling out as I skidded to a halt in front of his car. I slowly made my way to the driver's-side window, which he was already rolling down.

"My stuff," I said. "You returned my stuff. Even after . . . the ball . . . your ball . . . I stole your ball."

"Let me see it," he said, gazing up at me.

I almost ripped my pants digging for that ball I still had in my front pocket. With shaking fingers, I slipped it into his palm.

He peered at the ball, turned it in his gnarled hands and sucked on his teeth. After a long moment, he reached the ball back out the window and said, "Nope. This isn't mine. I was hitting a Titleist 3. This here is a Titleist 1. You keep it, son. You found it."

In a daze, I retrieved the ball from his hand. "But my stuff, you found all the stuff I lost," I stammered.

"Not everything," he replied with a slight smile. "Not everything."

"What do you mean?" I asked.

He put his car in gear and eased it forward. As he rolled up his window, he said, "You lost the one thing even I can't get back for you, son. Go read the napkin on the bar."

And then he was gone.

Back in the clubhouse, I made my way to the bar. Turning the napkin over, I read in Mr. Early's scrawled handwriting the following words:

YOUR TEMPER

Greg R. Bernard

The U.S. Open

How would you like to meet the top 143 people at what you do each week in order to survive?

Bruce Crampton

When I was seven, my dad introduced me to golf by taking me to Houston's Memorial Park Golf Course to watch the gentle giant who strolled the fairways of professional golf. It was there that I first laid eyes on Arnold Palmer and his swashbuckling style of playing golf. I was mesmerized by his charisma. I told my father that I wanted to be just like him! My dad saw that I had every chance to succeed, and twenty years later I was blessed with the fulfillment of that dream.

But as good as I was, I wasn't nearly good enough to be an unqualified success. I struggled and persevered, but fell short time and time again. More than anything, I wanted to play in a major championship and experience what that was like. It took me eleven attempts, and ten straight years of disappointment, before I finally qualified for my first U.S. Open Championship in 1979.

Qualifying was a rigorous test of thirty-six holes in one

day, usually played in one-hundred-degree heat, with only a couple of players from a very strong field advancing to the championship. For every golfer who ever dreamed of playing golf against the greats of the game, competing in a U.S. Open was always the pinnacle.

After so many failures, simply qualifying to play one Open was almost more than I could anticipate. Expectations ran high and hope eternal. I couldn't wait to get on the plane, fly to Toledo and drive to the course. When we finally drove through the gates of Inverness Country Club, the relief and the emotions of the moment brought my family and I to tears.

I played well in practice, but once the Championship began, my game deserted me when I felt pressure the most. I started poorly and finished even worse to miss the 36-hole cut by only two shots. My wife and parents both walked every step of the way, in some ways living my dream vicariously. It was a huge disappointment to come up short, because we knew that I might never have another chance to play in a U.S. Open.

On Sunday, while waiting in Chicago's O'Hare Airport for our connecting flight home, we saw the opening moments of ABC-TV's national broadcast. Jim McKay's opening oratory was so stirring that I saw my father moved to tears. He turned to me, almost embarrassed by his emotions, and said, "Next time, make the cut for me for Father's Day." The moment was particularly poignant because it was Father's Day and the U.S. Open historically ended on Father's Day every year. "I promise I will next time, Dad," I assured him, holding my breath and hoping against hope that I would have one more chance. Deep in my heart, I knew it was a long shot.

Despite my retirement from full-time competition the next year, my prayers were answered in 1981. I qualified to play at Merion Golf Club in Ardmore, Pennsylvania, for my second (and last) U.S. Open. Once again, my family joined me to share in this special experience, and I brought along my best friend, Sam Irwin, to caddie for me. My expectations were low, and more than anything I was just hoping to play well and have a great time.

McKay described Merion as a lovely old dowager. It was a traditional course, built in the early 1900s, relatively short by today's Tour standards, but laced with thick rough, deep bunkers and lightning-fast greens. She was a mighty test despite her length. But most intriguing to me was the history of the great course. It had hosted other championships, including the U.S. Amateur Championship where Bobby Jones had defeated Gene Homans to win the final leg of the Grand Slam.

This time I started well, shooting a solid round of 73, despite a triple bogey at the fifth hole and bogies on 17 and 18. My score had placed me in a position to make the cut, yet none of us dared speak about it for fear that it would play too much into my psyche the next day. I had not competed in almost nine months, and my nerves and confidence were just too fragile. Besides, I was having fun for the first time in years, just playing for the pure enjoyment and not to put food on the table!

The second round started well, too. I played the front nine in even par before bogeying 11 and 12. As I came to Merion's brutal finishing holes, I knew that I would be tested like never before. I was hovering near the cut line, and one bad shot could end any hopes of playing the weekend. I managed to par 14 and 15 without difficulty. A good drive and a 6-iron to the green at 16 left me with a monstrous forty-foot putt with more than five feet of break. All I wanted to do was get close enough to two-putt and go to the next hole. To my surprise, my putt wandered and curled its way across the green and into the cup for a birdie! Even a bogey at the difficult seventeenth "Quarry

Hole" left me thinking a bogey at the last would afford me the 36-hole cut I wanted so badly.

I played the eighteenth hole—a long 470-yard, dogleg-left par-4—more conservatively than usual. I used a 3-wood off the tee to clear the quarry wall and to better shape the tee shot so that I could easily make the fairway. However, I was left with a very long iron shot to the green, which I left considerably short. My pitch came to rest fifteen excruciating feet from the hole. I only had to get down in two putts now, but the speed of the greens was so fast that I had to be careful—very careful. When I struck the putt, I knew instinctively that it was struck too hard. My heart leapt to my throat as I looked up to see where the ball would finish. To my relief and almost disbelief, it hit the back of the cup and dropped in the hole for a par-4!

I almost danced to the scorers' tent to sign my card. I knew that my score was good enough to make the 36-hole cut, but I didn't think my father knew. He knew that I had played well and that it would be close, but he didn't dare raise his hopes. I had missed too many cuts in the past by one or two shots; it was difficult for anyone in my family to expect good fortune.

After I finished signing my card and shaking my fellow competitors' hands, I walked outside the tent to see my dad standing only a few yards away. As I walked toward him, I could tell he was obviously pleased that I had played well. He said, "Way to go, Punkins," my nickname since childhood. I could hardly contain myself as I hugged my dad tighter than I ever had. All the years of support and encouragement had finally reaped its just reward. "Happy Father's Day, Dad," I said proudly, two days early. I didn't need to say anything more. At that very moment he realized that "we" had made the cut in the U.S. Open.

Bill Pelham

In the Pink

Laughter is the best communion of all.

Robert Fulghum

I had several choices on Saturday. Clean the garage, wash the car or go to the golf store and waste hours looking at a bunch of stuff I couldn't afford.

It was crowded at the golf store. I like it when it's that way. The salespeople are too busy to pester you, and you can play with the putters all day long. I have won many imaginary tournaments on that little carpeted green.

I was heading to the front of the store to forage in the "experienced" golf ball jar when I saw three familiar kids—mine—coming in the front door. At first I assumed my wife sent them on a search party and that I'd have to clean the garage after all. Then I saw the sign over the checkout stand, "Ask About Our Father's Day Specials." They were here to buy me a gift! Not another Three Stooges tie. Not another Handy Mitt, the greatest car-washing aid since water, but a golf gift. Cool.

I ducked down behind the shoe mirror as they headed toward the golf ball section. Would they buy the Tour

Edition Titleists? Probably not without help. I dashed down the club display aisle and slipped behind the mountain of shimmering red and gold boxes.

"What about these yellow balls?" I heard my youngest child ask.

"Or these orange ones?" my daughter added.

I poked until a box of Titleists fell on the floor a few feet from them.

"Whoa, dude. This whole thing could fall," said my older son.

"Yeah. Let's look somewhere else."

Darn. I followed in a crouched position as they walked slowly by the golf bags and over to the glove display. Perfect. One of those double-thick, imported gloves with the removable ball marker. They walked right by. Okay. Maybe they'll pick out one of those electronic distance calculators or a six-pack holder. They ambled on.

Finally, they entered the clothing section and headed for a rack full of Ralph Lauren Polo shirts. Yes! I could already picture myself standing in the fairway, contemplating my approach shot, while the others in my group commented on my impeccable taste.

"Hey. Look over here." The enthusiasm in my daughter's voice meant they had found the perfect gift. I felt bad that they were going to spend all that money, but who was I to question their immeasurable affection?

"Cool. And they're cheap, too."

Cheap? I peeked through some women's sweaters. My daughter was holding up a pair of pink polyester pants that had been on the clearance rack since day one.

"And we could get this to go with it." My older son held up a lime-green mesh shirt.

I gasped audibly. They looked in my direction, so I slipped further back into women's wear, bumping into the store manager.

"Just browsing," I whispered.

He looked at me strangely and I realized I was holding a pair of extra large women's shorts and an athletic bra. Behind me I heard, "Look. The final touch."

I got down on all fours and stuck my head out. My youngest son was holding up a hat that said "Tee-riffic Golfer" in type large enough to see four blocks away.

"But it's red," my younger son said. "Does that matter?"

"Naw," said my daughter. "Golfers always dress weird."

I watched them walk toward the front, then I turned and looked at the manager. "I don't suppose . . . ?"

"Nope. All sales final. Besides, you'd break their hearts."

I slept in on Sunday. At about nine they marched into the room, placed a package on my chest and said, "Happy Father's Day."

I tore the wrapping slowly, hoping I could muster up enough excitement when I held up that hat. But the package contained only a note.

"Look beside you," it said.

I turned slowly and there on the pillow was one of my favorite putters from the golf store.

"I don't understand," I said.

"Dude," said my older son. "We, like, knew you were there. Your car was parked out front."

"Are you disappointed?" my daughter asked.

"No! This is perfect." I stroked my new putter lovingly. "So," I laughed. "Guess they let you take those dreadful pink pants back, huh?"

Just then my wife entered the bedroom carrying a carefully wrapped package.

"Ahhh. Not exactly . . ."

Ernie Witham

The Golf Maniac

We rode in and out pretty often together, he and I, on a suburban train.

That's how I came to talk to him. "Fine morning," I said as I sat down beside him and opened a newspaper.

"Great!" he answered. "The grass is drying out fast now and the greens will soon be all right to play."

"Yes," I said, "the sun is getting higher and the days are decidedly lengthening."

"For the matter of that," said my friend, "a man could begin to play at six in the morning easily. In fact, I've often wondered why there's so little golf played before break-fast. We happened to be talking about golf, a few of us last night—I don't know how it came up—and we were say-ing that it seems a pity that some of the best part of the day, say from five o'clock to seven-thirty, is never used."

"That's true," I answered. Then, to shift the subject, I said, looking out the window, "It's a pretty bit of country just here, isn't it?"

"It is," he replied, "but seems a shame they make no use of it—just a few market gardens and things like that. Why, I noticed along here acres and acres of just glass—some kind of houses for plants or something—and whole fields full of lettuce and things like that. It's a pity they don't make something of it. I was remarking only the other day in the train to a friend of mine that you could easily lay out an 18-hole course here."

"Could you?" I said.

"Oh, yes. This ground you know, is an excellent light soil to shovel up into bunkers. You could drive some big ditches through it and make one or two deep holes. In fact, improve it to any extent."

I glanced at my morning paper. "Look at this," I said, pointing to a headline, "'United States Navy Ordered Again to Nicaragua.' Looks like more trouble, doesn't it?"

"Did you see in the paper a while back," said my companion, "that the United States Navy is now making golf compulsory at the training school in Annapolis? That's progressive, isn't it? I suppose it will have to mean shorter cruises at sea; in fact, probably lessen the use of the navy for sea purposes. But it will raise the standard."

"I suppose so," I answered. "Did you read this article about the extraordinary murder case on Long Island?"

"No," he said. "I never read murder cases. They don't interest me. In fact, I think this whole continent is really getting over-preoccupied with them—"

"Yes, but this one had such odd features—"

"Oh, they all have," he replied, with an air of weariness. "Each one is just boomed by the papers to make a sensation—"

"I know, but in this case it seems that the man was killed with a blow from a golf club."

"What's that? Eh, what's that? Killed him with a blow from a golf club!"

"Yes, some kind of club—"

"I wonder if it was an iron—let me see the paper—though, for that matter, I imagine a blow with even a wooden driver. Where does it say it? It only just says 'a blow with a golf club.' It's a pity the papers don't write these things up with more detail, isn't it?"

"Have you played golf much?" I inquired. I saw it was no use to talk of anything else.

"No," answered my companion, "I am sorry to say I haven't. You see, I began late. I've only played twenty years, twenty-one if you count the year that's beginning in May. I don't know what I was doing. I wasted half my life. In fact, it wasn't until I was well over thirty that I caught on to the game. I suppose a lot of us look back over our lives that way and realize what we have lost.

"And even as it is," he continued, "I don't get much chance to play. At best I can only manage about four afternoons a week, though of course I get most of Saturday and all Sunday. I get my holiday in the summer, but it's only a month, and that's nothing. In winter I manage to take a run south for a game once or twice, perhaps a little swack at it around Easter, but only a week at a time. I'm too busy—that's the plain truth of it." He sighed. "It's hard to leave the office before two. Something always turns up."

And after that he went on to tell me something of the technique of the game, illustrate it with a golf ball on the seat of the car, and the peculiar mental poise needed for driving, and the neat, quick action of the wrist (he showed me how it worked) that is needed to undercut a ball so that it flies straight up in the air. He explained to me how you can do practically anything with a golf ball, provided you keep your mind absolutely poised and your eye in shape, and your body a trained machine.

So, later in the day, meeting someone in my club who was a person of authority on such things, I made an inquiry about my friend. "I rode into town with Llewellyn Smith," I said. "I think he belongs to your golf club. He's a great player, isn't he?"

"A great player!" laughed the expert. "Llewellyn Smith?

Why, he can hardly hit a ball! And anyway, he's only played for about twenty years."

Stephen Leacock

A Day at The Tradition

Blessed is he who has learned how to laugh at himself, for he shall never cease to be entertained.

John Bowell

Several years ago I was diagnosed with cancer. It was the most difficult time I have ever faced. I think it was my sense of humor that allowed me to hold onto my sanity. Like many people who have gone through chemo-therapy, I lost all of my hair and I was bald as a cue ball. I always had enjoyed wearing hats, so when my hair deserted me, I ordered several special hats with the hair already attached. It was easy and I never had to worry about how my hair looked.

I have always been a big golf fan. In fact, I have been to twenty-three straight U.S. Opens. At one point during my cancer treatments, my husband John and I decided to get away from the cold Minnesota winter and took a trip to Scottsdale, Arizona. There was a Senior PGA Tour event called The Tradition being played, and that seemed like just the ticket to lift my spirits.

The first day of the tournament brought out a huge gallery. It was a beautiful day, and I was in heaven. I was standing just off the third tee, behind the fairway ropes, watching my three favorite golfers in the world approach the tee box: Jack Nicklaus, Raymond Floyd and Tom Weiskopf.

Just as they arrived at the tee, the unimaginable happened. A huge gust of wind came up from out of nowhere and blew my hat and hair right off my head and into the middle of the fairway! The thousands of spectators lining the fairway fell into an awkward silence, all eyes on me. Even my golf idols were watching me, as my hair was in their flight path. I was mortified! Embarrassed as I was, I knew I couldn't just stand there. Someone had to do something to get things moving again.

So I took a deep breath, went under the ropes and out into the middle of the fairway. I grabbed my hat and hair, nestled them back on my head as best I could. Then I turned to the golfers and loudly announced, "Gentlemen, the wind is blowing from left to right."

They say the laughter could be heard all the way to the nineteenth hole.

Christine Clifford

I Hate Golf—I Love Golf!

*I have often been gratefully aware of the heroic
efforts of my opponents not to laugh at me.*

Bernard Darwin

I used to be an 11-handicap golfer. That was before "slope indices," before "soft spikes," before golf carts even.

Today, fully equipped with the latest technology, I am a 22-handicapper going south.

Yes, way back then my woods, crazy though it may seem, had wooden heads. The shafts were of shiny metal. No titanium, no matched graphite, no range of flexes.

The golf balls would smile back when you mishit a wedge shot or topped a 6-iron. Slice a 4-iron and you could see the seemingly endless rubber band that wrapped around the ball's rubber core.

I could hit the ball a ton back then. I could get out of sand traps and two-putt greens, too. I have happy memories.

In 1947 I even defeated Chad Brown, a friend at the post office. In the tournament I beat Chad 8 and 7, finishing him off with a fearless, curling fifteen-foot birdie putt. I admit I caught bon vivant Chad on an Excedrin day.

Back then I played in the high 70s.

Today, though I try to play a fair amount, things are different. Chad Brown would kill me. Everyone else does.

I slice off the tee, losing distance in the process. My long irons sting my hands. The ball is seldom airborne. Nor can I chip. Putting? Forget it.

It's not the equipment, for I have the latest in technology. I have four Tight Lies, but mine go straight up. I have great Titleist DCI irons—Black Cats, too. I have Cobras given to me by Hale Irwin himself. I have a big 975 Titanium Titleist driver, also a Taylor Made bubble driver and the biggest Bertha ever made. My high-performance wedges run the gamut—fifty-six degrees, fifty-eight degrees, sixty degrees. I have 'em all. I even have an "Alien."

My golf balls are high-tech. Zylin Covered XLs, Tour Distance-Wound 90s, the Slazenger 420s. You name the kind of ball you like, I've got it.

Sometimes I play with a guy worse than me. He's into all this high-tech stuff. He goes, "I sure like the feel of these new balatas," or "This new baffled 3-wood really works for me." Or "The only putter that makes any sense at all is the Scotty Cameron—that Tel3 is so true. Talk about center cut. I have three of them Scottys—I love the Microstep and the Teryilium insert."

The poor son-of-a-gun hasn't gotten a wedge off the ground in the last three outings and his baffled 3-wood emerges from the fairway carrying a divot the size of an adult toupee. The last time he two-putted a green was when I gave him a four-footer.

He goes, "This new Maxfli Multi-layered Revolution lands quiet. I can just feel the difference on my wedge shots—on my putting, too." Sure, right!

High tech is great. Don't get me wrong. Look at Davis, Tiger and Freddie; but let's face it—high tech hasn't solved my web of problems.

Practice is my main problem. I hate it. I am allergic. I break out in a rash if I go out and hit practice balls. I can't help it.

Putting is the worst part of my game, followed closely by sand play and chipping. A good friend, a guy who supported me as president and was respectful back then, put it rather succinctly last week when he said, "George, you stink."

Anyway, a couple of weeks ago out at Muirfield—a course on which a guy like me should be forbidden to play—I invoked the "no-laughing rule."

My playing partners agreed—"Okay, no laughing."

I put them to the test. In one sand trap I flailed away four times, before going in the pocket. I found brooks and eddies that Jack Nicklaus didn't even know existed when he laid out this monster.

Things were dragging for me. I was thinking, "Why do I need this? I am seventy-four. I have a boat and a nice wife—why this torture?"

But then on the sixteenth I hit a perfect 9-iron—long and straight with a lot of spin on it. It stopped but six feet from the hole. My partners were ecstatic. "You're back!" "What an effort!" "You pureed that one."

But then came my turn to putt. I admit my attitude was negative as I lined up for my downhill putt. I pushed it off to the left. It gathered speed as it ripped past the cup, stopping about six feet away. But I had another six-footer to make coming back.

I jabbed my second putt. It took off like a cruise missile. The direction was great. The speed was wrong. It lipped the cup and was whiplashed violently off course. Four and a half feet still to go for putt number three.

I froze over the ball, my long putter wagging like a vaulter's pole. I came back slowly, and then literally shanked the putt. As it careened off to the right, the "no-laughing rule" was broken. They didn't mean to hurt my feelings—for fifteen dreadful holes they had been careful not to. My partner knocked away my remaining four-footer. "A gimme!" he says.

As I have done several times before, I decided right then and there to give up golf. I hate it.

But after a two-week moratorium I was back.

Playing with our Cape Arundel pro, Ken Raynor, I felt inspired.

The first nine was bad—the chipping and putting betraying me.

Then came the magic. On the par-4 eleventh, my drive was fine. I then topped my 5-wood shot—a scorching grounder that stopped sixty yards short of the green.

I pulled out my fifty-six-degree Cleveland Classic-588. My swing was surprisingly smooth. The "True Temper" shaft gave me that velvet feeling. I felt the grooves gently spin the ball. I felt the "touch" of my Tour Distance-90. It feathered on to the green—landing like a butterfly. Breaking gently to the right, it meandered sixteen feet, right into the hole.

Golf? I hate it, sure, but I really love it.

I'll be on the first tee tomorrow at 6:50 A.M.

George Bush

A Candle in the Wind

There's a lot of levity and joy that goes with being a professional golfer, not to mention the many privileges afforded those who achieve success at the top levels of the sport.

But it would be misrepresenting the whole experience of the PGA Tour to imply that the men who compete out here are somehow exempt from the pain and sorrow of everyday living. Like all the players, I'm reminded from time to time that what we do every day—often with the solemn demeanor of heart surgeons—is nothing more than a game, and that the genuine business of life takes place outside the ropes, far removed from all the lights and cameras. This story is about the real world.

Peter and Paul: the two names are linked together all the way back to the Bible, and when brothers just two years apart are given those names, comparisons are inevitable. As much as every parent aspires to equal treatment of all their children in a good-sized family, it's impossible to ensure that each child gets his full share of attention. In Paul's case, I think it was difficult, because he had two very active older brothers to follow and to be compared against. David and I were both athletic, and involved in golf and other sports. We were both sports editors of the high school paper and took part in a number of other school activities. We made friends easily and had a relatively carefree time of it.

Paul, on the other hand, didn't care much for sports and was more introverted by nature. He had to listen to friends and teachers constantly asking, "Why aren't you like your older brothers?"

As the third boy in the Jacobsen family a lot was expected of Paul, and he just couldn't or didn't want to live up to it. So he went his own way, and, as too often happens these days, he eventually fell into problems with drugs.

As we got older, Paul and I drifted apart. We still loved each other and stayed in contact, and I would hear from his friends that he was proud of what I had done in my career, but it was difficult for him to express that pride directly to me. It was very important to Paul that he establish his own identity. He didn't want to stay in Portland and have to be pestered with questions about being Peter's brother, and why Peter missed that five-footer on television last week, and all the other burdens that David and Susie, my sister, put up with all the time.

So he moved to Los Angeles and got a job as a graphic artist, and did some modeling on the side. In Southern California he could be just Paul Jacobsen and have his own life. I thought it was a courageous thing to do, and I admired him for it.

However, there was a certain tension between Paul and the rest of the family that wouldn't go away. When my wife Jan and I would go to Los Angeles each year for the L.A. Open, it seemed that Paul was usually too busy to come out to the course to watch me play. It was his way of telling me that his life was much more important than coming to a golf tournament, and I understood. We would always talk on the phone when I was in town, but that was about it.

When Paul was twenty-six, he just blurted something out in a phone conversation with me. "You know I'm gay, don't you?" he said.

And I told him that, of course, I knew, and that it was no big deal to me. Although I was surprised that he had told me so suddenly, I was glad for him that he could get it off his chest. It meant he was coming to grips with his life and facing who he was.

Paul's problems with drugs and alcohol grew worse through the years, and it was not uncommon for us to get phone calls from him at three or four in the morning. These would start out normally enough, with "Hi, how ya doin'," then quickly deteriorate into bouts of ranting at us about all the problems in his life. He would get irrational and start calling us names. Mom and Dad would get the calls, or David or Susie, or whomever he could reach on the phone. He was using a lot of cocaine during the day, and drinking vodka at night to come down from it, and just hurling himself around on this emotional roller-coaster.

It got so bad in late 1987 that we checked him into the Betty Ford Clinic in Palm Springs. Thankfully, through the good work of the people there, Paul got clean. He seemed to be getting his life back on track in 1988, when I got the phone call that changed everything.

It was August 24, the day after the Fred Meyer Challenge. Mom called to say that Paul had been admitted to the hospital with pneumonia. Jan and I were immediately concerned that he might have AIDS. I called Paul and he sounded upbeat and said he thought he'd been living on too fast a track and needed to slow down and rest. He even talked about moving back to the Northwest. However, by the next week, when I was in

Toronto for the Canadian Open, the news was all bad. Paul did, in fact, have AIDS and had been admitted to the intensive care unit at Cedars Sinai Hospital. I was worthless in Canada, and withdrew after shooting a first-round 79. My mind had never been further from a golf course than it was that day.

I flew back to Portland, and Jan and I caught the first flight to Los Angeles to be with Paul.

I had heard from friends that Paul's weight was down, and that he had not been in good health for a while, but seeing him in the hospital was a shock. I hadn't seen him since we'd checked him into the Betty Ford Center eight months before, and it was obvious that his condition was critical. He had lost a lot of weight and was extremely gaunt. In hindsight, I think Paul had known he was seriously ill for months before he was tested, but his fear of learning the truth was so great that he put off going to the doctor. By the time he was examined, he had full-blown AIDS.

Despite his drug problem, Paul had always stayed in shape with regular exercise, but now he was so thin and pale. He had lost more than thirty pounds off a slight frame. It broke my heart to see him. I told Jan that we better put all our plans on hold, because we really needed to be with Paul.

An especially vivid memory is of walking into his room and seeing him hooked up to a respirator. He looked up at me with terror in his eyes. Then he wrote something on a pad and handed it to me. It said, "Peter, you can do anything. Please make this go away."

My eyes filled with tears, then Paul put his arms around me and hugged me real tight. It was the most powerless feeling I'd ever had. Here, my kid brother was telling me I could do anything, but there wasn't a damn thing I could do to help him when he most needed it. I couldn't find anything to say, and I started to cry. I finally choked out something like, "Paul, we'll do everything we can for you."

The poor guy was just so scared and desperate. I'll never forget that look in his eyes.

I stayed in his room for several hours at a time, and we all took turns being with him. Then we'd return to the hotel, catch a nap and go back. Just the third day after we'd arrived, Paul took a horrible turn for the worse. He'd been fighting the respirator, which, of course, he needed to keep breathing, and the doctors had just started using a paralyzing drug on him so that his body would relax and he'd be better able to fight the pneumonia. Then he suddenly slipped into a coma.

We went home that evening, aware that the end was near. It was September 5, just twelve days after I'd been told of Paul's illness and only a week since he'd been diagnosed. I was sound asleep when something unusual happened. At exactly one-thirty in the morning, I woke up suddenly and felt a fluttering movement inside my body. I asked Jan to turn on the light, and I told her that Paul was with us.

I said, "He's inside of me."

"Are you all right?" she asked.

I was oddly at peace. I told her that Paul had come there to tell me everything was okay, and that he was fine. I also told her I just wanted to lie there for a moment and feel the spirit of my brother, because that's exactly what it was. Paul's spirit was with me, and it was comforting.

I remember the fluttering movement didn't go away—it was almost like butterflies inside of me—and then I faded off to sleep. When I awoke the next morning, Jan asked if I remembered waking up the previous night, and I recalled it all perfectly. I told her Paul had come to visit me, and that he was finally out of his pain, but that he had left something with me.

That morning I called one of Paul's close friends, who lives on a farm in the state of Washington, and before she heard my experience she told me that she had been awakened the previous night by an owl that had flown down and landed on her open windowsill and started to hoot into the room. An owl is universally regarded as a sign of death. I asked her what time it had happened, and she said one-thirty.

Later in the day, I talked to Paul's roommate, and he said that the dog and cat had been going crazy all week without Paul there, and that the animals had been keeping him awake at night. But at one-thirty in the morning, they had suddenly calmed down. He said he felt Paul's spirit had been with them.

It's extraordinary that three different people who were close to my brother—one of them a thousand miles away—felt his presence at the same time.

When we went to the hospital, one of Paul's nurses told me that his vital signs had dropped sharply at one-thirty in the morning. "In my opinion, he has left us," she said.

Paul never came out of his coma, and he died peacefully later that day. He was thirty-two years old.

The sorrow of his death was eased for me by the certain knowledge that he'd visited me. Paul had said something to me that night that I remember distinctly. "Peter, you're okay just the way you are," he said. "Be nice to people and don't let anything get you down." And then he said, "Go out there and win. Just go out there and win."

Our family struggled for quite a while after Paul's death to make sense of what had happened. I knew that all I could do was try to honor his life by carrying forward with the message he'd given me: just to be myself and go out and win.

While I hadn't won on the PGA Tour since 1984, I had been close on several occasions. I'd had something like seven runner-up finishes in the past five years. But I won the Isuzu Kapalua International in November 1989, and then, in a victory that was extra special, I won the Bob Hope Chrysler Classic two months later, playing the final round on the PGA West/Palmer Course. Coincidentally, the last round of golf I'd ever played with Paul was sixteen months before on that very course. My dad was also with us.

I struggled with that realization the entire last round. I was paired with Steve Elkington and Mike Reid, and had a two-shot lead, but I was also wrestling with vivid memories of playing the Palmer course with Paul and Dad. Every time my mind would wander and I would think about Paul, I'd hear him say, "Don't think about me. I'm fine. Just go out and win." That thought carried me all day.

When I birdied the last hole to win, David, who had come to Palm Springs for the week, gave me a big hug, and I said, "I sure wish Dad and Paul were here to see this."

And David said, "Paul saw every shot. I think he helped you keep that last 3-iron on line."

Peter Jacobsen
with Jack Sheehan

Turning Back the Clock

Golf dispels the myth that the older Americans have to be less active or competitive. Ask any middle-aged golfer who's been bested by someone his parents' age. I speak from experience; on the links, youth offers no advantages.

Dan Quayle

The bounce has been missing from my dad's step. Illness has invaded his body and spirit. He is eighty. Yet, this seems so sudden. Now I know the ache of the thought: If only I could turn back the clock, just for a day.

Besides his family, my dad has always loved a good joke, the San Francisco 49ers, playing cards and, "best of all," golf. His swing is one of his better jokes—a marvel of mistakes he makes work. "I really synchronized my jerks that time!" he says.

Searching through the misty barriers of age and gender, fathers and daughters sometimes catch only a glimpse of one another. Not us. The morning I quit piano lessons, my mother—the daughter of a music teacher—cried right into a box of Cheerios. She could only watch as I grew more like my father every day. Relatives say when I play cards I even tap my fingers on the table exactly as he does. When I was little, we had "our song." He would sing it, and we'd laugh ourselves silly:

"We belong

To a mutuaaaalllll

Ad-mir-a-tion So-ci-e-ty,

My buddy and me."

Now we are a thousand miles apart in geography, politics and much else. But we are still buddies. We share the most enduring bond of all.

We are golf buddies.

A little more than a year ago, my dad experienced the first of many setbacks in his battle against cancer. All of us wondered if the end was near.

Shortly thereafter, I flew to San Francisco and talked him into a leisurely round at the Olympic Club. I thought just being out on the course would boost his spirits. And there was this other motive: I was playing the best golf of my life, breaking 90 the first time just two weeks earlier.

Once a steady 80s/90s player, Dad had never seen me play this well. I was wild to take his money and win his approval. With the same predatory DNA swirling in our cells, we always played for money. Over the years I'd lost nearly enough Nassaus to reimburse my college tuition. My dad says of this, "Want to earn forty thousand dollars the hard way?"

He delighted in being my mentor as well as my cut-throat opponent. I am convinced his parting words to me will be "Pull down with your left!"

That day at Olympic, I would have to give him strokes. What a proud day it would be for us both, I thought.

Well, he wasn't nearly as excited as I thought he'd be. Our golf date fell on his seventy-ninth birthday. But neither that, my newfound handicap nor a sunny San

Francisco day could summon a smile. We began the round chatting sorrowfully about how his treatment sapped his strength, how he hated never breaking 100 anymore. Then it appeared to me he got down to business. He had 1-putt par on the first hole, while I gasped away with an 8. After that, he started holing out from everywhere. I'd never seen him putt better.

While my score was rising, his jerks were synchronizing. Time after time, he flailed his driver straight up in the air, his body shaking in every direction like Jell-O molds. Before I could even venture a laugh at the sight, THWACK, he'd look up and laugh at himself.

He began trotting back to the cart, urging me to do the same before I'd even completed my swing—just like when I was twelve. "Never up, never in!" he chirped for the hundred-millionth time as I dabbed a dainty putt four feet short. From some unknown place, a laugh rose up out of me.

With an all-too-familiar glow on his face, he totaled up the damage. A 96 for him; 114 for me.

It was exactly like twenty years ago.

Later, above the clouds on a plane to Seattle, I thought of my dad's deteriorating health. I wondered, for the first time, if I'd ever see him again. Then I recalled our game, how bizarre it was that he played so well—and I so poorly—and how much fun it had been. Suddenly, it was as clear as the sky in front of me. On the golf course, on his seventy-ninth birthday, we were given a magical gift. Someone let us turn back the clock, just for a day.

Betty Cuniberti

The Promise Keeper

He is an old man in golf at age twenty-four, has reached his peak and can't get any better. It's a question of how long this boy can hold what he has.

Sam Snead—on Jack Nicklaus, 1965

You know what the coolest thing was about Tiger Woods's streak?

Nah, not the six straight wins, one of the top-ten feats in modern sports history.

Not the way he almost made it seven, even after losing his swing somewhere among the hang gliders and moon-doggies and nude beachers at Torrey Pines Golf Club outside San Diego.

Not that during those seven tournaments he fricasseed 623 other golfers, tied one and lost to one.

Not that he earned just cab fare less than $5 million over those seven weeks, or did enough ads to make people actually believe he drives a Buick, or that he went from seventeenth on the career PGA Tour money list to first.

Not that during that stretch he passed Ralph Guldahl,

Tommy Bolt, Ken Venturi, Tom Weiskopf, Fred Couples, David Duval, Paul Azinger, Mark O'Meara, Davis Love III, Phil Mickelson, Corey Pavin and Nick Price in career wins even though he still isn't old enough to rent a car in most places.

Not that he beat the nastiest sticks from all over the world while tromping through ten time zones and being herded daily through last-day-of-Saigon mobs, Watergate press conferences and lobbies full of get-a-life autograph hounds, including one at 5:50 one morning at the Torrey Pines Hilton.

Not that he had done all this when no other Tour golfer had even won four in a row since the '50s. And not that after losing at Torrey Pines to Mickelson he wasn't relieved as any sane human would be, but was genuinely pissed at what he called "finishing second" to Byron Nelson's antiquated, not-even-comparable streak of eleven in 1945 against a whole lot of Jug McSpadens in Miami Four Balls.

Not even that last Saturday night somebody actually asked, "Tiger, would you be surprised if one of these guys makes a run at you?" and Woods was trailing by six at the time.

No, the coolest thing about the Tiger Woods streak was that when he was hotter than a six-dollar pistol, in a publicity boiler, he kept a promise he'd made to a junior high school buddy three months before and let him caddie in San Diego.

Can you believe that?

Woods benched his regular caddie, Steve Williams, in favor of a gangly twenty-four-year-old childhood friend, Bryon Bell, who was trying to earn a little money for med school.

Wouldn't you have said, "Look, B, I'll catch you sometime when I'm not trying to climb Annapurna." Or, "Yo, B, can I front you the cash instead?"

"If it were me in a situation this big," said one longtime

Tour caddie, "I wouldn't have let anybody but my regular guy within a mile of that bag."

But as Tiger's mother, Tida, said on Saturday night, "My son has changed completely. He's all grown up now." It's true. He laughs more, glares less, looks you in the eye more, storms out less, breaks out in grins more, breaks shafts less, makes bogey more, triple bogey less and, maybe because of all that, has become the most thrilling athlete in the world.

He's the kind of man who risked the streak in the madness of Pebble Beach to play with his best college buddy, Jerry Chang. He's the kind of man who would put Bell, a 10-handicap Pacific Bell planning engineer, on the hottest set of tools this side of Bob Vila's—just to be true.

Of course Woods did much of the caddying himself. He double-checked every yardage B gave him. B read fewer of Tiger's putts than the guy from *The Des Moines Register*. Sometimes B would throw some grass to check the wind, and Woods would reach down and throw some, too. No offense, of course. None taken.

"I was a little worried about screwing up," said the bespectacled Bell, who's known Woods since the seventh grade and played No. 2 to him on Anaheim's Western High golf team, "but we've had a great time." Profitable, too. Figuring Woods's usual fat caddie fees, Bell made upward of $25,000, which is about half what he makes a year at Pac Bell. Med school, here we come.

Nurse, which way does this break?

Yeah, Tiger can make a driver scream in fluent titanium, or get balata up and down out of Sing Sing, or make twenty-year vets turn Maalox-white and pull over at the sight of him in their rearview mirrors, but all that's the outdoor pool-shark stuff.

What's cool now is what's *inside*.

Rick Reilly

Augusta Heaven

I started to shake with anticipation as I hung up the phone. Could it really be true that I would be playing a round of golf at the hallowed ground of Augusta National?

The generous offer had been extended by my friend, Frank Christian, a world-renowned golf course photographer and the official photographer of Augusta National for the last thirty years. Each year Augusta allows selected employees to invite two guests to play the course. Our date was to be just two weeks after the Masters.

I brought along my friend Tim Townley. Tim and I have been friends forever, but I have since found myself constantly reminding him that he will be indebted to me for just as long a period of time. Needless to say, the weeks leading up to our date seemed like an eternity. We talked every five minutes, sharing some nuance of Augusta history.

Frank Christian has a way to make people feel special and make his friends' trip to Augusta a once-in-a-lifetime experience. So it was when we arrived in Augusta.

Frank has a long-standing tradition that he invites you to partake the night before you play. You see, when the great Bobby Jones died, Frank was in charge of cleaning out Bobby's locker. In it he found a bottle of 1908 Old Rye Whiskey some three-quarters full. With permission, Frank cradled home his prize. Frank's preround ceremony consists of each member of the foursome taking a sip of whiskey from Bobby Jones's bottle. To this day, I get the chills thinking back on it.

I awoke before dawn the next morning in anticipation of the day that lay ahead. Finally the hour of our departure arrived, and we headed out to the course.

On approach, I had my first glimpse of the famed gate and the magnolia-lined drive. Just outside the gate stood a man and his young son craning their necks to get a peek inside. The young boy was attired in knickers and a tam o'shanter, just like Payne Stewart. Clearly golf was a passion the father had passed on to his son and now was being jointly shared. If I had the ability to let them inside the gates I would have, but alas, as we passed, I wished them luck in their efforts.

Everything was perfect, just the way I had always imagined it would be. Every blade of grass was perfectly cut, the gardens were brilliant and every shrub was precisely manicured. The golf course was very different than it appears on television. Namely, the course is distinguished by deep and numerous undulations and hills. Although the difficulties of the greens are well documented, I believe they are even tougher in person.

I have played St. Andrews, Royal Troon, Muirfield, Pebble Beach and many others, but Augusta National was without a doubt the best overall golfing experience I have ever enjoyed.

I have my own tradition whenever I play one of these great courses. I collect a small vial of sand from one of the bunkers and display it alongside its distinguished brethren. I pinched some sand from the famous bunker alongside the 18th of Augusta as my keepsake.

Arriving at the airport for my return home I spotted the father and son I had seen at the gate to Augusta. I asked the little boy, whose name was Max, if he had a good time in Augusta, and he gave me a reluctant "yes." His dad mentioned to me that Max was really disappointed because he could not get in the gates of Augusta National to get a souvenir. Well, here I was just fresh from a round at Augusta wearing my new Augusta shirt and my new Augusta hat, and this little boy had nothing.

At that point I took off my hat and put it on his little head. I then reached into my bag and grabbed my vial of sand from the 18th hole and explained to Max what it was and how I got it. I told Max that this would be a great start for a new collection for him.

The look on his face was absolutely priceless.

As great as my golfing experience was at Augusta National, my most memorable moment was the look on Max's face.

Jeff Aubery

The One Hundred Greatest
Golf Courses

A golfer called the Chicago Golf Club and explained
that he was playing the "One Hundred Greatest Courses"
and desperately needed to add the club to his list. The
club was very private but reluctantly agreed to allow him
to play under these special circumstances.

After the round, a member asked the man, "By the way,
how many do you have left to complete the One Hundred
Greatest?"

"Ninety-nine," he replied.

Bruce Nash and Allan Zullo

Daddy Tees Off

All children find chaos congenial.

George F. Will

If James Joyce was right about our errors being portals of discovery, then a miniature golf course—the Poconos Putt-o-Rama—was the door to Saint Basil's Cathedral. I made a honey of a mistake there, and on the 11th hole (dogleg left, up a ramp, through an alligator to an elevated plywood green) I made one major discovery about children.

It was Rebecca's sixth birthday. The plan was to simulate the PGA championship: cake and juice and miniature golf for everybody. According to the log at Putt-o-Rama, my wife Jody paid green fees for eighteen.

Even before we teed off, there were bad omens. The kids battled over who would play with what color ball. Brenda complained that green didn't match her shorts. Julian hated yellow.

Sensing chaos, I jumped into the breach with parental authority. "Rule number one: Any dispute over the color of your golf ball," I said, choosing order over good cheer, "will result in immediate disqualification."

I looked over at Sean, who had Joey in a chokehold with the midget putter.

"Rule number two," I went on, "no player shall at any time hold his club against the trachea of another player."

"What's a traker?" Brendan asked.

"It's my neck," Joey gasped.

"Close enough," I said.

While the kids were choosing clubs, Jeffrey claimed to have won the world miniature golf championship. His twin brother, Mark, in an attempt to publicly humiliate his clone, shouted, "He's never even played miniature golf before."

Nice, I thought, *very nice.*

"Shut up, Mark. I have too played golf."

"Oh, yeah? When?"

"Uh, uh . . . I . . . I . . . ," Jeffrey stammered, paralyzed by the fact that he and the Grand Inquisitor not only had identical DNA packages but identical life histories. "I played once when you were asleep."

My heart broke for the little liar.

But before I could even say anything in his defense, Jeff lunged past me and stabbed his brother in the belly with the business end of his putter. When I stepped between them, I took a club head in the kneecap.

I should have enjoyed it more; it was the high point of my day.

On the tee at No. 1, the first foursome argued about who should tee it up first. I gaily suggested the birthday girl should have the honor and then we go in birthday order. Mark said that was unfair to kids born nine minutes after their stupid-head brother. He teed up his ball in protest. Another boy—Brian, I think—kicked it into a wishing well on the 9th fairway.

I wrapped five or six of the kids in a big old Daddy hug—or was it a threatening headlock?—and gave a quick little speech about how if there were sportsmanship we would all have a wonderful time. Absent cooperation, I went on, our memories of Becky's birthday would be full of recrimination.

"Rule number three," I had to announce a few minutes later, "no player shall help another player count his shots."

"Eleven . . . twelve . . . ," said Jill in gleeful play-by-play on Beth's first dozen strokes.

"Three," Beth chirruped as her ball clunked into the hole. There was mayhem in the air.

I did a quick count of the children. Came up one short.

"Jody, give me a count, will ya?" I yelled through the clamor to Mom.

"I make us minus one," she shouted back, apparently unconcerned since both of the kids to whom she had given birth were accounted for.

I grew frantic. There's nothing I hate more than having to tell a parent I lost a child somewhere on the front nine. "Lock the front gate," I shouted to the kid in charge.

"Hey, I don't do security, pal," he replied. "I do lessons."

I grabbed a perfectly calm little girl—Wendy, I later learned her name was—by her shoulders and said with panic in my voice, "We've got to find somebody."

"Who?" she asked.

"I don't know. Who's missing?" I answered.

"I think Jonathan's in the windmill," she said, clearly worried I was exactly the type of man her parents had warned her never to talk to.

I raced across to the windmill and found a little boy cowering inside. He was holding a rather large hunk of devil's food, which appeared to have been ripped from the birthday cake we had left in the pro shop "for later."

"Are you with the Becky O'Neill party?" I asked.

"Yes," he confessed, trying to hide the fistfuls of cake behind his back.

By the 5th hole everybody was hitting golf balls simultaneously. Orange and blue and green golf balls were whirring around Putt-o-Rama, like mesons in a particle accelerator. Becky's friend Jessica hit a shot that would have done Tom Kite proud—a low boring liner that ricocheted off Sneezy's foot into Josh's chin.

"Hey, mister, there's a liability ceiling of ten grand," said the teenage manager.

By the 10th hole, kids were actually dueling with their putters. There was dental work in the air.

The kids were no longer playing golf but some variation of hockey, pushing their balls toward the hole, a la Gretzky swooping the puck across the neutral zone. Every one of them claimed to have a hole-in-one on every hole. Believe it or not, when we got to the 11th hole—the seven-yard dogleg left through the alligator—things got worse.

Brendan, who was—may God hold him in the hollow of his hand—the only child still actually *striking* his ball, rolled a handsome putt up the ramp and cleanly into the alligator's throat. It did not, however, come out the other side.

"Becky's Dad," he said sweetly, "my ball got stuck." He actually appeared to think I could help him, that maybe a grown-up knew something a six-year-old didn't. I loved him for that.

I got on my hands and knees and peered down the reptile gullet into darkness. There was no light at the end of this tunnel. But I could see Brendan's ball stuck near the papier-mâché reptile larynx.

I stretched out on my stomach across the fairway and reached down the gator's throat. The ball, needless to say, was just out of my reach.

I stretched still more.

I grazed the ball with my fingertips, tried to poke it out the other side. No luck. I strained. I could feel the ball's dimples.

"Can you get it, Becky's Dad?" asked the only child in the world I cared about at all.

"Almost, Brendan . . . ," I croaked.

"Fore," I heard from behind the castle.

Brendan turned at the sound.

A golf ball whizzed past his knee.

And hit my temple with a fleshy clomp.

"Aaarrrgggghhhhh . . . ," I opined, rolling over on my stomach, in the process twisting my arm in the alligator's throat. When I tried to pull it free, I couldn't budge.

"Brendan," I said with fake calm in the manner of Timmy telling Lassie to go get help, "go find Becky's Mommy." I cast a fearful sidelong glance at the tiny four-some up ahead. They could sense weakness. If they knew I was helpless, they'd pounce.

Mark looked back at me, prone and pinned. He smiled a carnivorous smile. He said something to his brother, who turned to look at me but then decided to whack his brother with his putter again. I remember the sound of cast iron against anklebone.

The last thing I remember clearly is Jody arriving at my side. I remember resting my head in her lap.

What was the lesson I learned? Actually, I learned two lessons—one practical, one philosophical.

The practical parent lesson was never to give eighteen six-year-olds clubs, projectiles and large doses of sugar at the same time.

The philosophical lesson was that children are the opposite of golf. Golf is a liturgy of etiquette and manners. Golf is manicured, refined and disciplined. Golf is self-control. Children are none of those things. Children are—what's the word?—wild.

"In wildness is the preservation of the world," wrote Thoreau. He never wrote a word about minigolf.

Hugh O'Neill

The Man with the Perfect Swing

You must work very hard to become a natural golfer.

Gary Player

On a warm morning at a country club near Orlando, a stocky gentleman with wispy gray hair makes his way past the crowd gathered for today's exhibition. To those who don't know better, the impish old fellow could be just another sunburned senior dreaming of bogey golf.

He wears a black turtleneck despite the heat. The left pocket of his neon-lime slacks bulges, as always, with two golf balls—never more, never fewer. All three watches on his left wrist are set to the same time.

Taking his position at the tee, he quickly lofts a few short wedge shots about 70 yards. At first the spectators seem unimpressed. Then they notice that the balls are landing on top of one another. "Every shot same as the last," chirps the golfer, as if to himself. "Same as the last."

Moving to a longer club, a 7-iron, he smoothly launches two dozen balls, which soar 150 yards and come to rest so close to each other you could cover them with a bedspread.

He then pulls out his driver and sends a hail of balls 250 yards away—all clustered on a patch of grass the size of a two-car garage.

Astonished laughter erupts from the crowd. "Perfectly straight," says the golfer in a singsong voice. "There it goes. Perfectly straight."

People who have followed Moe Norman's career are no longer surprised by his uncanny displays of accuracy. Many professionals and avid players consider the seventy-year-old Canadian a near-mythical figure. But few outside the sport have ever heard his name. Fewer still know the story of his struggle to find acceptance in the only world he understands.

One cold January morning in 1935, five-year-old Murray Norman was sledding double with a friend on an ice-packed hillside near his home in Kitchener, Ontario. Speeding downhill, the sled hurtled into the street and skidded under a passing car.

Both boys survived and ran home crying. But the car's right rear tire had rolled over Moe's head, pushing up the cheekbone on one side of his face. His parents, unable to afford medical care, could only pray he did not suffer serious brain injury.

As Moe grew older, he developed odd behavioral quirks and a repetitive, staccato speech pattern. His older brother Ron noticed that Moe seemed unusually frightened of unfamiliar situations. At night, Ron often heard his little brother sobbing in bed, devastated by some real or imagined slight.

At school Moe felt glaringly out of place among other kids. Desperate for friends and acceptance, he tried to be playful, but his efforts often backfired—pinching people too hard or bear hugging them until they pushed him away. He heaped ridicule on himself and even coined his own nickname: Moe the Schmoe.

He became known as a slow student in every subject—except one. At math no one could touch Moe Norman. He astounded his classmates by memorizing complicated problems and multiplying two-digit numbers in his head almost instantly.

When he wasn't acting the clown, Moe walled himself off from others. Over time he plunged deeper into isolation, and yet, ironically, loneliness led him to his greatest happiness.

In the years following his accident, Moe spent hours atop that same winter sledding hill, hacking around an old golf ball with a rusty, wood-shafted 5-iron he found at home. Here in the solitary and magical world of golf, he found a reason to wake up each morning.

Kitchener, Ontario, in the 1940s was a gritty factory town where working-class teenagers had little desire or money to play the "sissy," upper-class game of golf. But Moe was spellbound, often skipping meals, school and chores to head off by himself in a field to hit balls—five hundred or more a day. He practiced until dark, sometimes until the blood from his hands made the club too slippery to hold.

In his early teens Moe landed a job as a caddie at a country club—only to be fired when he hurled the clubs of a low-tipping local mogul into some trees. Soon he gave up caddying to concentrate on playing, honing his skills at a nearby public golf course. He quit school in tenth grade, and by the time he was nineteen, he knew he was blessed with a rare talent: He could hit a golf ball wherever he wanted it to go.

Moe left home in his early twenties, hitching rides to compete in amateur golf tournaments all over Canada, supporting himself with a succession of low-paying jobs. At his first few tournaments in the late 1940s, fans didn't know what to make of the odd little fellow with the garish, mismatched outfits, strawlike red hair and crooked teeth.

His manner was playful, almost childlike, his self-taught technique wildly unorthodox. Legs spread wide, he stood over the ball like a slugger at the plate, clutching the club not with his fingers, as most golfers are taught to do, but tightly in his palms, wrists cocked, as if he were holding a sledgehammer.

Many spectators dismissed him as an amusing sideshow. Some giggled when he stepped up to the tee. Soon, though, Moe Norman was turning heads for reasons other than his personal style.

Recognized as a gifted player who could hit a golf ball with breathtaking precision, he quickly became a sensation on the amateur golf circuit. In one year alone he shot 61 four times, set nine course records and won seventeen out of twenty-six tournaments.

Even as his fame grew, Moe remained painfully shy and could not shake the sense that he was undeserving of the attention. Rather than bask in the spotlight, he avoided it. In 1955, after winning the Canadian Amateur Open in Calgary, Moe failed to show for the awards ceremony. Friends later found him by the nearby Elbow River, cooling his feet.

That victory qualified Moe for one of golf's most prestigious events: the Masters. When the invitation to the tournament arrived, he was only twenty-six and spending his winters setting pins in a Kitchener bowling alley. The Masters was his chance not only to represent his country but to show skeptics he wasn't just some freak on a run of beginner's luck.

But his old demons would give him no rest. Moe felt like an intruder among some of golf's bright lights. He played miserably in the first round and even worse on day two. So he fled to a nearby driving range to practice.

While hitting balls Moe noticed someone behind him. "Mind if I give you a little tip?" asked Sam Snead. The

Hall-of-Famer merely suggested a slight change in his long-iron stroke.

But for Moe it was like Moses bringing the Eleventh Commandment down from the mountaintop.

Determined to put Snead's advice to good use, Moe stayed on the range until dark, hitting balls by the hundreds. His hands became raw and blistered. The next day, unable to hold a club, he withdrew from the Masters, humiliated.

But Moe climbed right back up the ladder to win the Canadian Amateur again a year later. A string of victories followed. In time, he had won so many tournaments and collected so many televisions, wristwatches and other prizes that he began selling off those he didn't want.

When the Royal Canadian Golf Association charged him with accepting donations for travel expenses, which was against regulations for amateurs, Moe decided to turn professional. His first move as a pro was to enter, and win, the Ontario Open.

As a newcomer to professional golf, Moe approached the game with the same impish lightheartedness of his amateur years. When people laughed, he played along by acting the clown. An extremely fast player, he'd set up and make his shot in about three seconds, then sometimes stretch out on the fairway and pretend to doze until the other players caught up.

Fans loved the show, but some of his fellow competitors on the U.S. PGA Tour did not. At the Los Angeles Open in 1959, a small group of players cornered Moe in the locker room. "Stop goofing off," they told him, demanding that he improve his technique as well as his wardrobe.

Friends say a shadow fell across Moe that day. Some believe the episode shattered his self-confidence and persuaded him to back out of the American tour, never to return. More than anything, Moe had wanted to be accepted by the players he so admired. But he was unlike the others, and now he was being punished for it.

The laughter suddenly seemed barbed and personal. No longer could he shrug it off when some jerk in the galleries mimicked his high-pitched voice or hitched up his waistline to mock Moe's too-short trousers.

Because Moe never dueled the likes of Americans Jack Nicklaus or Arnold Palmer, he achieved little recognition beyond Canada. At home, though, his success was staggering. On the Canadian PGA Tour and in smaller events in Florida, Moe won fifty-four tournaments and set thirty-three course records. While most world-class golfers count their lifetime holes-in-one on a few fingers, Moe has scored at least seventeen.

Despite his fame and the passing years, Moe was continually buffeted by the mood swings that tormented him in childhood. Even among friends he could be curt, sometimes embarrassingly rude.

At other times he was charming, lovable Moe, bear hugging friends and tossing golf balls to children like candy— the happy-go-lucky clown from his amateur days.

Through the 1960s and '70s, Moe racked up one tournament victory after another. But in the early 1980s his enthusiasm for competition began to wane. His winnings dwindled, and he slipped into depression. Not being wealthy, he seemed to care very little for money, lending thousands to aspiring golfers and never bothering to collect.

Broke and all but forgotten, he drifted from shabby apartments and boardinghouses to cut-rate roadside motels, often sleeping in his car. Had it not been for the generosity of friends—and a stroke of good luck—he might have faded entirely into obscurity.

Moe has never had a telephone, a credit card or owned a house. Few people know where he might be living on any given day, and he seldom talks to strangers. Little wonder it took Jack Kuykendall two years to track him down.

Kuykendall, founder of a company called Natural Golf Corp., finally caught up with him in Titusville, Florida. He told Moe that, trained in physics, he had worked for years to develop the perfect golf swing—only to discover that an old-timer from Canada had been using the same technique for forty years. He had to meet this man.

Moe agreed to demonstrate his swing at clinics sponsored by Natural Golf Corp. Word spread quickly through the golfing grapevine, and before long, sports magazines were trumpeting the mysterious genius with the killer swing.

Among those following Moe's story was Wally Uihlein, president of the golf-ball company Titleist and FootJoy Worldwide. Hoping to preserve one of golf's treasures, Uihlein announced in 1995 that his company was awarding Norman five thousand dollars a month for the rest of his life. Stunned, Moe asked what he had to do to earn the money. "Nothing," said Uihlein. "You've already done it."

Two weeks later, Moe Norman was elected to the Canadian Golf Hall of Fame. Even today, however, he remains largely unknown outside his native country except among true disciples of the game. For them, Moe is golf's greatest unsung hero, the enigmatic loner once described by golfer Lee Trevino as "the best ball-striker I ever saw come down the pike." Many agree with Jack Kuykendall—had someone given Moe a hand forty years ago, "we would know his name like we know Babe Ruth's."

In the parking lot of a Florida country club, Moe Norman is leaning into his gray Cadillac, fumbling through a pile of motivational tapes. He seems nervous and rushed, but as he slides behind the wheel, he pauses to reflect on his life, his family and his obsession.

Moe never had a real mentor or a trusted advisor. "Today's kids," he says, "are driven right up to the country club. Nice golf shoes, twenty-dollar gloves, nice pants. 'Have a nice day, Son.' I cry when I hear that. Oooh, if I'd ever heard that when I was growing up . . ."

He squints into the sun and cocks his head. "Everyone wanted me to be happy their way," he says. "But I did it my way. Now, every night I sit in the corner of my room in the dark before I go to bed and say, 'My life belongs to me. My life belongs to me.'"

With that, he shuts the door and rolls down the window just a crack. Asked where he's going, Moe brightens instantly, and a look of delight spreads across his face.

"Gone to hit balls," he says, pulling away. "Hit balls."

It is, and forever will be, the highlight of his day.

Bruce Selcraig

Common Ground

Growing up in Egypt, I never had a chance to play golf or even come close to being on a course, even though Egypt was (as a golfer once told me) "a big sand trap." Now, courses are sprouting everywhere in Egyptian resorts.

Golf is too much of an individualistic and disciplined game for someone who, for most of his life, played the undisciplined game of football (soccer), which is full of improvizations and creativity.

Golf is a sport found in a culture of abundance, where players usually bring their own balls, bags, shoes, umbrellas, raincoats, hats, carts, clubs and caddies. For years I subscribed to the notion that golf is an elitist game, where men with ugly pants go to strike business deals on the course away from women and minorities.

When I went to the course for the first time I found, to my surprise, mostly younger baby boomers with nice pants. And the only thing they cared to strike was the ball. The only business they talked about was the business of controlling this small ball and keeping it straight on the fairway.

I was alone and leery as a first-time golfer, equipped with only my golf bag and a few trips to the driving range, mostly wondering about the rules and the etiquette of this enigmatic game.

First, they lined me up at the clubhouse with three other men I had never met before. Very few sports do that. They asked if I could fill out a foursome. I wondered for a second if this had something to do with my handicap.

On the 1st hole, we were just men getting to know each other for the first time. On the 5th hole, we became associates. Once we strode off the 9th hole, we became drinking buddies (nonalcoholic, please). Golf is one of the few sports that you can play and drink at the same time—if you don't count bowling.

By the time we got to the 18th hole, we had become friends who had just spent more than half of the day away from work, families and wives. We were cut off from any sign of civilization, bonding together, surrounded by the primitive nature of the course.

What a refreshing experience and a wonderful treat for me as an Arab-American, surrounded by people who looked at me as one of them. I wasn't looked at as a hyphenated American, to be interrogated about Middle East affairs and asked to explain Saddam Hussein's complicated self-destructive behavior.

I was not asked to help find Osama bin Laden. All that was asked of me was to find the ball. The only jihad we had was to fight the course terrain and stay on the fairway. With this camaraderie, we were cut off from our ethnic roots, bias and prejudice. We were merely men against the course. We had transcended our race, color and ethnicity. The only color we saw was the color green. On the course, no cultural sensitivity or diversity training is required. I was just another golfer. Bad golfer I may be, but never a bad Arab.

The concentration and the exotic exhilaration of smashing this small ball onto the fairway overwhelmed our own stereotyping, racism and ethnocentricity. We were liberated men, free of all the societal burdens of accomplishing big tasks in life.

For Arab-Americans, our energy has been consumed for years by the long debate over the fate of a piece of divine real estate thousands of miles away that we can't do anything about. On the course, the only piece of divine real estate was the green before us. This game was our reality, and I was the only one who could do anything about it.

Golf anyone?

Ahmed Tharwat Abdelaal

Ladies, Is Golf for You?

Our minds need relaxation, and give way
Unless we mix with work a little play.

Moliére

I took up the game of golf eight years ago when I was at the age of . . . never mind. I became so addicted to the game, I didn't have time to do the laundry anymore. Soon after, my husband had a plaque made for me that says "Martha Stewart Used to Live Here." Sometimes I'd have to stop on my way home after a round of golf to buy him a pair of underwear for work the next day. He has two drawers full of BVDs. God forbid, but if he's ever in an accident, not only will he be wearing clean underwear, most likely it'll be brand-new.

Golf is great, but I can still remember what a frustrating experience it can be for the beginner. For the first three months, I wondered if golf was my punishment for the time I sneaked into Sister Mary Margaret's bedroom to see if she really had a poster of Bob Dylan hanging over her bed. That was the rumor around school. I cried so much as a beginning golfer, my husband suggested I have my hormone level checked. He couldn't believe it was just golf doing it. But I persevered and things became better, and so now I would like to share some tips and ideas that can make a woman's initial foray into golf a little smoother.

Whatever your reasons for taking up the game, whether it's to avoid listening to your son practice the French horn or to get away from your mother-in-law, ask yourself a few questions to see if this game is really your bag. You may be athletic, but there's more than skill involved here.

Temperament, for instance. If you have a hair-trigger kind of temper, occasionally coupled with a bad case of anxiety, a club in your hands that particular day can be dangerous. I once saw a woman do quite a number on the 150-yard marker, a pretty shrub in bloom, with her 7-iron just because her favorite pink ball went into the lake.

Vanity. Particularly in the summer. If you worry about your hair flopping on humid days, your foundation running until your face looks like it's melting, or your mascara making black tracks down your cheeks, stay at home and make pot holders.

Prudery. If you're the kind of person easily offended by less-than-ladylike words, forget it.

But before you spend a fortune on clubs and figure out six months later that what you really want to do is skydive, I suggest you borrow most, if not all, the essentials first. You'll need clubs (up to fourteen, eight of which look exactly alike, but in a few years you'll be able to tell the difference), a bag, shoes (the ones with plastic spikes for traction), balls, tees, a towel and a ball marker (a quarter will do, but don't forget to pick it up when you leave the green).

If your friends don't have a spare set of clubs to loan out, you can find used clubs at garage sales or pawn shops at reasonable prices. Buy something cheap for now. At this point, equipment doesn't matter much since you have no idea what you're doing.

Eventually, if you stick with the game, you'll find yourself buying a new driver all the time. Every time you hear about another that can help you hit the ball ten more yards, you'll go and buy it. I've noticed that no matter who the manufacturer is or what the club material, it's always "an extra ten yards." You'd think, out of all the clubmakers, one company would have an engineer smart enough to come up with a club that'll give us fifty extra yards and get it over with for a while.

I love drivers. They're all so different. They come in persimmon, graphite, titanium, with bubbles, without bubbles, large heads, extra-large heads, stiff and extra-stiff shafts—you name it.

Now once you have your equipment, you need an instructor. But ladies: Do not let your husband teach you. When was the last time you listened to him anyway? What makes you think you're going to start now? Sooner or later even his voice will start grating on your nerves. Trust me, it won't work. Find yourself a real pro. My guess is that the person who said sex is one of the main sources of disagreements between couples didn't teach his wife the game of golf.

One more piece of advice: While you're still a beginner, don't play in events for couples if the format is that of alternate shot. Heaven help if your shot lands directly behind a tree, on top of a root or in a bunker in a "fried egg" lie and now he has to play it. That's an argument waiting to happen. And it will happen.

Another thought to keep in mind for the sake of keeping peace at home: If you ever hit a hole-in-one, never mention it again after the day it happens. I've had two, and he hasn't even one. I love my husband too much to upset him, so I don't talk about them in his presence. But my plaques hang in the den, one on each side of the television, where he can see them every night. I also have a vanity license plate, 2-HOLS-N-1—and he washes my car every Saturday.

Golf's like fishing: There's always the one that got away. In golf there's always the putt that didn't fall. But there's more to golf than making good shots. Fun moments that don't have anything to do with the game can happen on the course. There was the time when my husband uncharacteristically threw his sand wedge after shanking a short chip. The grip hit the cart path first, propelling the club into a 360-degree rotation and directly into the golf bag. Eventually, you'll have your own stories to tell, and you'll remember them years from now.

Above all else, have fun, even on those days when you feel you should have stayed home making those pot holders instead of going to the course, accomplishing nothing more than achieving that dreaded tan line that makes your feet look like you're wearing bobby socks with high heels in your finest evening gown.

Golf can be played long after you start collecting your first Social Security check. When you reach that age, you can start making cute ball markers and tee holders to give your friends at Christmas. By the way, did you know the Senior Tour has players in their seventies? Ladies don't have a Senior Tour. They won't admit when they turn fifty. It's a woman thing.

Deisy Flood

Like Father, Like Son

Like many fathers and sons, Bob and Dave like to play an occasional round of golf together when they can find the time. Nothing serious: Ten bucks a hole; bonuses for birdies and "polies" (approach shots that come to rest within a flagstick-length of the hole); optional presses whenever you're steamed—pretty much the same kind of convivial game fathers and sons enjoy in every part of America. The competition is fun, sure. But it's the being together that really matters. Because of career commitments and travel and all the other complications of being two working stiffs, they don't have a chance to see each other as much as they like. Even though they're in the same line of work, both master practitioners of the same profession, Bob and Dave's paths cross with depressing rarity. Like so many fathers and sons in our increasingly turbocharged world, they communicate mostly electronically, over the phone or—and this is one of the benefits of doing what they do—the television.

So when these two fellows do come together on the links, every moment counts.

When they arrive at the golf course, filled with the same kind of heightened anticipation most dads and sons feel before they're about to display their game to the most important male in their life, the conversation usually goes something like this:

Dad: "How many strokes am I getting today?"

Son, scoffing: "None."

Dad: "All right, fine. What tees do you want me to play?"

Son, indicating the back markers: "The same as me, of course."

Dad, pleading: "You may not be aware of this, Son. But the old guys? We don't play these tees. We start a little closer to the hole."

Son, resting his hand on Dad's shoulder: "You got your freakin' name on your bag, don't you? Quit your crying, and play some golf."

These days, Bob, who is one of the longest hitters you've ever seen for a guy in his fifties, is about fifteen yards shorter than his son off the tee. But as old Pops likes to remind his precocious kid, the game of golf is not merely a driving distance contest. And every now and then he proves it to young Dave. "There are days I make him dig into the wallet," Bob says proudly. "And, man, he's as tight as can be. It kills him!"

Bob laughs heartily. "It doesn't happen all the time. I'm not ashamed to admit it: He's definitely got the best of me these days. But you know what?" he says, smiling contentedly. "It's pretty cool to be able to compete with the number-two player in the world. And to know he's your son."

Bob and David Duval are both touring professional golfers. They both crisscross the United States in search of birdies and the monster paychecks that accompany them. They are both winners on their respective Tours.

And they are father and son.

Fathers try to teach their sons well, and watch with

pride and contentment as their boys blossom into the men Dad hoped they would be.

Fathers serve as role models for their blooming off-spring, idealized examples of the fully realized adult man young sons hope to become. Fathers show the way, and sons try earnestly to follow.

Sons try to make their fathers proud. Sons try to learn their fathers' lessons well. Sons hope to live up to their fathers' guiding example.

Which is all to say that Bob Duval, professional golfer, Senior Tour champion, and, yes, father, is in the peculiar and enviable position of having a son who has become the man his old dad hoped he would. And then much more.

David Duval, PGA Tour superstar, is one of the most famous golfers on the planet, a stylish, enigmatic athlete who has at times been capable of dominating his sport more completely than anyone but Tiger Woods.

Bob Duval has finished in the magic Top-31 his last three campaigns on the Senior Tour.

David Duval earns multimillions in both prize money and product endorsements. He travels the country in a private jet. He cannot go anywhere near a golf course without being mobbed by autograph-seeking fans.

Bob Duval earns a healthy six-figure income. He flies commercially. Only friends and family members recognize him.

David Duval is Bob's son. But that's not how the world sees it.

"No, David used to be Bob's kid," Bob Duval tells me, chuckling at the thought. "Now I'm definitely David's dad." He thinks for a moment.

"Everything has sort of flipped around," Bob Duval says. "The father has become the son."

We're sitting on the back deck of Bob's Jacksonville Beach home. With Buddy, Bob's faithful dog patrolling for lizards and the ocean crashing into the shore just a wedge away, it's a perfect afternoon to reflect on what it means to be a dad. And not just any old dad—though dads of any sort are cherished by their sons—but a member of the Senior Tour dad, and the father of a PGA Tour superstar dad. "I remember when it happened," Bob recalls. "It was David's first time being in contention down the stretch as a pro on the PGA Tour—and my first cigarette in several years! I was so nervous. He was battling with Peter Jacobsen at Pebble Beach. I remember having an overwhelming sense of pride—and it just got bigger when the phone didn't stop ringing for two hours, even after he finished second. At that point, in the eyes of a lot of people, he stopped being my kid and I became 'David's Dad.'"

Bob Duval doesn't say this with even the faintest trace of bitterness or remorse. He says it like a proud papa.

"I mean, my son chose the same path, the same business, as old dad. I couldn't be prouder. I don't think any dad could be prouder," Bob Duval says, smiling.

As if on cue, the phone rings. It's David, who lives a little ways down the road, in Ponte Vedra. Wants to know what time they're meeting this afternoon, for a round of golf. And if they've got a tee time arranged.

For some reason this thought amuses me immensely: David and Bob Duval showing up at a nearby golf course, wondering if, perhaps if it wasn't too much trouble of course, if they might, you know, hop on to the 1st tee? And then I realize: Today they're just a father and son looking to have an impromptu round of golf together.

And that's pretty sweet.

Michael Konik

The Dying Light

I line up the six-foot putt. All is quiet, save for a few people talking quietly in the distance. Slowly, I take the putter back and stroke the ball. For a split-second, the ball rolls toward the hole, then slides decidedly off to the right, like a car exiting a freeway long before its destination.

"Maybe you'd like to try something else," says the young salesman, watching from beside the artificial-turf putting green.

For an instant, our eyes meet. I am standing in one of the West Coast's largest golf shops, and a young man twenty-five years my junior is telling me—behind his veneer of entrepreneurial etiquette—that I cannot putt.

After thirty-two years of golf frustration, it's time, I've decided, to face the reality that I can no longer blame my ineptness on my irons or woods. Instead, I've decided to blame it on my putter. So here I am shopping for a new one. After nine years, I am kissing my Northwestern Tour model good-bye for a younger, sleeker model.

I feel so cheap; alas, I am a desperate man. At forty-five, my golf game is going through a midlife crisis. And so emerges a belief, a hope, a desperate clinging to the idea that I can somehow buy my way back to respectability.

Long a believer that the swing, not the equipment, makes the golfer, I've scoffed at friends who plunk down hundreds of dollars to find "new and improved" clubs to help them once again hit the drives of their youth. I've chided them for seeing some pro win a tournament, then rushing out to buy the replica of the putter he used; after Jack Nicklaus's stunning Masters win in 1986, who can forget that rush on putters whose heads were roughly the size of bricks? The golfer makes the club, I've long insisted—not the other way around.

But in recent years, my game has gone so far south that even my putter talks with a twang. Blame it on a schedule where golf now makes only a rare guest appearance. After months of not playing, I usually prepare for a round like I prepare for a yearly dental checkup: by flossing the night before—i.e., hitting a bucket of balls—and hoping I can fool the hygienist. Of course, it never works—in the dental chair or on the golf course.

Blame it on a number of other excuses; the bottom line is that some sales kid who didn't even start shaving until after the invention of the Big Bertha driver is now trying to help save my golf game.

I look up at the kid with one of those don't-you-think-I know-what-I-need looks on my face, then put my pride on a leash. "Sure, let's try something else."

"If you'd like, you can go out on our real putting green and test them," says the young salesman.

The kid is nice—he's only trying to help, after all—but something about this situation just doesn't seem right. I take three putters, a couple of balls, and start walking toward the outdoor putting green.

"Uh, I'll need you to leave your driver's license," he says.

"I'll only be, like, two hundred feet away," I say.

"Store policy."

You gotta be kidding. What's he think I'm going to do—take three putters and a couple of Titleists and hop the first plane to Mexico?

"Seriously?" I say, thinking that my slight balking will probably waive the mandate.

"Sorry."

I look at the young man incredulously and say the only thing that's left to say.

"But I'm your *father*. Doesn't that count for something?"

"Sorry, store policy."

I pull out my driver's license and hand it to the kid who I once taught to drive. The kid I once taught to play golf. The kid who I haven't beaten on a golf course since he was a sophomore in high school.

I love this kid. I'm proud that, at age twenty, he's found himself a job that he likes and is good at. I think it's wonderful that he has developed into a near-scratch golfer who has shot 69, won back-to-back men's club championships, and posted an 84 at night, using a glow-in-the-dark ball.

But deep inside I have this tiny dream: to beat him just one last time, at anything: golf, home-run derby, or h-o-r-s-e on the backyard hoop. Like Nicklaus coming back to win the Masters at age forty-seven, I'd like one last hurrah to remind the world I'm still around.

It's not a vindictive thing at all. It's just a little pride thing. Not a chest-beating thing, but Pride Lite. Father-son pride. It's wanting to be the hero one last time. It's wanting to still be considered significant, like when you give your son a bit of advice about life itself and he tries it and it works and you think: I'm still needed. I still matter.

And one more thing: Weird as this may sound, fathers want their son's approval. In Ryan's journal, I wrote this about the first time we played golf together as a team. He was sixteen:

Going to the 18th, the two teams were all even. I nailed a 152-yard 7-iron to within two feet of the cup, sunk the putt for birdie and we won! But I was so nervous standing over that putt, more nervous than you'll ever know. (Until now.) Why? Because I wanted so badly to prove to you that I wasn't just this hacker of a dad. That I could pull through. That I could produce under pressure. Because I want you to be the same kind of guy, whether the venue is golf, marriage, work, whatever. I want you to pull through when you need to. Withstand the pressure.

"Do you wanna try one of these putters?" he asks, snapping me back to reality. "This is like the putter you bought me when I beat you for the first time."

I remember the day. He was fifteen. I shot 88. He shot 86. Though I'd done all I could to prevent it, I was glad he'd won, proud to have been outdueled by my own son. I wrote a mock newspaper article—"Ryan stuns Dad for first win!"—and made good on a promise to buy him the putter of his choice.

Since then, it's been his show. I've watched proudly from the edges of the fairway and learned what it must be like for a kid to grow up with high-achieving parents, because whenever I play now, people expect me to be good because Ryan is. And I'm not.

Not long after Ryan won his second men's club championship at a Eugene public course, I teed up my opening drive at the same place and promptly hit it out of bounds. It was like Einstein's father flunking Algebra I.

"So," said the starter, "you're Ryan Welch's father, huh?" As if he really wanted to say, "So much for that axiom about the acorn not falling far from the tree, huh?"

For the most part, I've accepted this role reversal. Twice now, Ryan has had me caddie for him in tournaments that brought together all the winners of club championships from around the state. And I've considered it one of the highest honors a father could be accorded: to be able to carry on my back the clubs of a son I used to carry in my arms.

But deep down, the instinct quietly gnaws at me to prove myself—to nobody else but myself.

Bob Welch

2

GOING FOR THE GREEN

Plimpton to the Fore

I should have known that the week of the Crosby Pro-Am tournament was going to be taxing when I checked in for the flight to California. The clerk had been very helpful tying the clubs together and encasing them in a plastic bag. It was when he tipped the bag over to see if the clubs were secure that the mouse nest fell out.

We stared at the small heap of shavings and string lying on the floor. "I see that you're ticketed through Monterey," he said. "Going to the Crosby?"

"That's right," I said. "I played it once, fourteen years ago. I'm going to take another crack at it."

"You've really been spending the years getting ready," he said, looking at the mouse nest.

In the first Bing Crosby National Pro-Am I played, in 1966, my golf bag was carried by a diminutive furniture mover named Abe—a somewhat elderly local who occasionally worked as a caddie at Pebble Beach, one of the Monterey Peninsula courses used for the tournament. To my astonishment Abe was waiting for me this time when I arrived to register. He had heard I was coming and hoped I would have him back to "pack" my bag. I was delighted.

Abe felt it would be a good idea if we walked the course, "to refresh our minds" on what the holes looked like.

We started off by following a foursome that included Jack Lemmon. Duffers hold Lemmon in particular affection for his difficulties on the final holes of Pebble Beach, all graphically caught by the television cameras the first time he played the Crosby more than a decade ago. I recalled with relish Lemmon's attempts to make a recovery shot up a steep slope. The ball bounced jauntily up the slope and, as if appalled by what it discovered at the top, turned and hurried back down. We could see the top of Lemmon's head as he shifted about to address the ball a second time. Exactly the same thing happened. The ball bobbed up to the top of the slope, then curled back down. We never saw much of Lemmon himself, just a great deal of his errant golf ball—it seemed to fill the screen with its antic behavior.

As we walked along, Lemmon reminisced about the experience. "The whole mess started when our foursome came into view of the television cameras for the first time. You'd think I'd be used to cameras by now, but when it comes to golf, I'm not. I think I averaged ten shots on each of these last five holes."

Lemmon said that on the eighteenth, as he lay 12 with his ball still thirty-five feet from the cup. He had an elderly caddie whose sense of dignity seemed overtaxed by what was going on. He kept sidling away. Lemmon, down on one knee on the green trying to sight his putt, had to call him out of the crowd for advice. The caddie moved reluctantly until, finally, Lemmon could hear him breathing behind him. "Which way does it break?" Lemmon had asked, over his shoulder. "Who cares?" the caddie muttered.

Now, on the same eighteenth, the famous ocean hole,

Lemmon hooked his drive down onto the smooth, wave-worn boulders at the foot of the seawall that curves along the length of the fairways. The ball remained in sight for an astonishing length of time, skipping and ricocheting hysterically from one rock to another. "Life is an irreplaceable divot," Lemmon said to me mysteriously as he stepped off the tee.

In the Crosby, one professional and one amateur play together as partners from start to finish. This means that even a rank amateur can play in front of the TV cameras on the final day, assuming he and his pro partner make the cut.

Not many golfers go through the stress of the first drive of a tournament in front of a large crowd. It is one thing to start off a country-club Labor Day tournament before two witnesses jiggling Bloody Marys in plastic cups, and quite another to bend down to set the ball on its tee, acutely aware that five hundred people are watching you. The blood rushes to the head. The ball falls off the tee. To start the swing takes almost a physical command of "Now!"

My first drive surprised me, a high slice down the fairway that managed to stay in bounds. I hurried after it, feeling almost palpable relief in getting away from the first tee and its witnesses. After the first round I went with Abe to the practice range to try to do something about my miserable showing. I had not scored a par and had not helped my professional partner, Jack Ferenz.

My second round, on the nearby Cypress Point course, was no better than the first. I spent a great deal of time searching with Abe for errant shots. I had played thirty-six holes without scoring a par. The next day we would be playing Spyglass Hill—one of the most difficult courses in the world. The thought was very much in my mind that I, not a bad athlete, with a golf swing worked on through the years by a bevy of pros, might not achieve even one par.

The round at Spyglass did not start propitiously. My drive moved out onto the fairway, hopping along nicely, but the second shot went off at a sharp angle, hit a pine, then another, and rolled back toward me, ending not more than eight yards away after a flight that might have totaled almost two hundred yards. I stared at the ball as if it were a smoking grenade.

On the next drive I tried to slow things down. The great golf writer, Bernard Darwin, said of Bobby Jones's swing that it had a "certain drowsy beauty." I thought of that on the tee, and slowly, too slowly, I brought the club back. Imperceptibly, like an ocean liner inching away from the pier, the club head slowly moved away from the ball, gradually lifting to the top of the swing. But at the summit everything went out of control. The club head faltered like a paper airplane stalling on the wind, and then it dashed earthward in a cruel whistling swipe. A cry erupted from my throat as the club pounded into the earth a foot behind the tee, bounced, and sent the ball perfectly straight down the fairway for about ninety yards.

"Straight as an arrow," Ferenz's caddie said helpfully.

On the twelfth, Matt Mitchell, the other amateur in our foursome, threw his ball into the water hazard. Of all the indignities that man tries to heap on inanimate objects, throwing a golf ball into the water is perhaps the most hapless. The lake accepts the ball with a slight ripple that disappears almost immediately, leaving the surface smooth, almost smug. "I suppose the thing to do is to think of the ball bloating down there," I said comfortingly to Matt. He stared at me furiously.

As if to make him feel better, on the last par-3 hole, my 8-iron shot described a high parabola and dropped into the water edging the green, stitching it with a little geyser.

"It'll be bloating any minute now," Mitchell said.

The par-4 eighteenth would be my last chance in the tournament to make a par. I hit an enormous hook into a grove of pines. "It's gone," Abe said gloomily.

I told Abe that we had to find the ball. It was my last chance. If we found it, I told him, I would take a tremendous swing and catch it to perfection, whatever its lie. The ball would rocket into the clear open air above the fairway and float gently toward the green. From where it landed, I would hit a delicate wedge onto the green, and then sink a long, curling putt for a par. I would tip my hat gracefully to the spectators. But there was no sign of the ball. My last chance was gone.

When I got back home, I called a place outside New York City called Golf-O-Rama. It has indoor driving ranges that simulate actual golf courses by flashing a picture of each hole on a screen while computers track the flight of the ball. The man said they had the Pebble Beach course. I made a reservation.

Norman Schaut, president of Golf-O-Rama, showed me around. One side of the hangar-like room was taken up with the "golf courses," lined up side to side, each with an elevated tee. The golfer hits the ball twenty feet or so into a nine-foot square screen on which can be seen a color-slide reproduction of the golf hole.

We stepped up on the Pebble Beach tee. "If the computer says you've driven the ball into a water hazard," Schaut said, "there'll be the sound of splash."

I said, "You should have the sound of the waves breaking and the seals barking out there in the Pacific."

Schaut switched on the course. The picture of the par-4, 482-yard first hole at Pebble Beach flashed on. "That's it!" I said. "The dogleg to the right." I remembered the names of the contestants being called out by the starting marshal, the patter of applause from the crowds by the tee and the dryness of my throat when I had bent down to set the tee into the grass—and even here, with the Muzak playing "Deep Purple," I felt my nerves tighten.

I teed up and swung. My drive, according to the computer, was an excellent one for me, 205 yards out. My second shot stopped fifty yards from the pin, and then I hit a lovely, easy wedge, which left me with a six-foot putt for my par. I stepped onto the Astroturf green with my putter. I stared down, brought the putter back, then forward, and watched the ball ease down the line and drop into the hole.

I had the urge to throw my putter into the air. Instead I turned and tried to look suave. Schaut came hurrying over. "Have you got something to say?" he asked, looking at my face, which had broken into a broad grin.

"Piece of cake," I said.

George Plimpton

There Is No "I" in Team

We rather than "I."

Charles Garfield

Bob and Tina Andrews work together like a well-oiled machine. She sets him up on the tee box, steps back, looks down the fairway and says, "Okay." He takes a deep breath and swings, and the ball sails down the left side of the first fairway at Killearn Country Club near their Tallahassee, Florida, home.

They display impressive teamwork. Bob Andrews is totally blind. Tina, his wife, is his "coach," and together they make up one of the best teams in the United States Blind Golf Association.

"The first thing you learn is that blind golf is a team sport," says Bob, fifty-one, who was blinded by a grenade in Vietnam in 1967. "Until you have a coach, you're not a blind golfer. You're just a blind person with some golf clubs."

Bob and Tina were married not long after he returned from Vietnam. He took up golf first for the exercise. "I tried running," he says with a laugh, "but you get tired of taking those falls."

He had played golf as a kid, but he was never serious about it until he became blind. He joined the USBGA, and in 1995 he became president.

Tina is his third coach. Andrews's father did it at first, but it got to be too much for him. Then, Andrews's son took a turn. But he soon went off to college. That left Tina, who isn't a golfer, but Bob actually thinks that's a plus because she doesn't overload him with information. All she does is point him in the right direction.

After they play a couple of holes, it's understood how they do what they do. Or so you think. "Ready to try it?" asks Bob.

You stammer for a few moments, then answer weakly, "Sure."

Until you've "coached" a blind golfer, you can't appreciate how hard it is—and how wonderful it is when things go right. You find that you've never been so interested in someone else's golf game.

Bob holds the club out in front of him, and the first thing the coach does is place the club firmly on the ground, right behind the ball, square to the target. This serves as an anchor. Next is the position of his feet, also square to the target. Then the shoulders. When everything is right, a simple "okay" is all he needs.

Andrews swings, and the ball takes off. "Little fade down the right side?" he asks, judging the ball's path by its feel.

"Yep. Little fade down the right side."

Later, Andrews has about 160 yards, of which about 140 is a carry over water. "What do we got?" he asks.

"About 160 yards, over water," you say.

"Oh, boy," he says. "Let's try a 7-wood." After he's set up, Andrews spends a little more time standing over this shot. He hits it a little fat and it splashes in the water. Your heart sinks. That wouldn't have happened if Tina were coaching. "See, I wouldn't have even told him about the water," she says. "No point in giving him one more thing to worry about. Take advantage of his disadvantage, know what I mean?"

After dropping, Andrews hits a nice pitching wedge over the water and onto the green. You lead Andrews by the arm to the spot where his ball rests, then walk with him to the flagstick. "Fourteen feet," he says. "A little left-to-right, slightly uphill."

Andrews reads his own putts, feeling the contour of the green through his shoes. This seems amazing. But when you step behind him to take a look, you come to the same conclusion: left-to-right, slightly uphill.

You set him up with the putter's face aiming just outside the left edge of the cup.

"How's that look?" he asks.

"Perfect," you say. But you cross your fingers. His putting stroke is smooth and sure, a perfect pendulum. On its final rotation, the ball ducks into the left side of the cup. Andrews hears the hollow sound of a holed putt. It is a sweet sound indeed.

"Hey," you say as you head to the next tee, "that was a great bogey you made back there."

"No," he says, "that was a great bogey we made."

Dave Sheinin

The Magoo Caper

A great handicap for some golfers is honesty.

Harvey Mackay

Long before con men were immortalized in *The Hustler* and *The Sting,* there was The Magoo Caper. They didn't make this one into a movie.

Here's why.

I started playing golf at about the same age that Tiger Woods did, with a cut-down set of clubs and a doting father to preside over my development. By the time I reached high school I was convinced I could "follow the sun" as a professional golfer.

When I got to the University of Minnesota, the similarities between the Tiger legend and the Mackay legend soon parted company. During my sophomore year, I competed at the NCAA Golf Championship at Purdue University in West Lafayette, Indiana. That weekend I learned that for every good northern golfer—who could practice maybe, at most, six months a year—there were equally talented Southern golfers—who could practice twelve months a year and become twice as good.

So I settled down and accepted my role as a respectable, if not spectacular, member of my college squad. Our coach believed in nicknames. Mine was "Magoo," a nice play on "Mackay," and an accurate take on the Coke-bottle horn-rimmed glasses I wore. My eyesight was so bad I couldn't follow the flight of the ball off the tee without them.

During Easter vacation my senior year, the eight-man squad traveled on their own to that warm-weather mecca, St. Louis, to get in a little practice before the short Minnesota golf season began.

After the first day's round, we all sat together at a beer joint.

"Magoo," said one of the members of my frolicking foursome, "We've got business to attend to. Let's set up the bets for the next day's play. Make it interesting."

Our usual wager was a big-time two bits a hole. But I had a proposition.

"Tell you what. Tomorrow I will play all of you for a buck a hole WITHOUT MY GLASSES. All you have to do is give me a mere eighteen strokes—a stroke a hole—plus, promise you'll point me in the direction of the hole."

A dollar a hole was big bucks then, but they couldn't get their money down fast enough.

Let the games begin.

The next morning we merged the two foursomes and we played an eightsome. No problem. We had the course to ourselves due to a light rain and big wind.

I miraculously parred the first hole. Impossible. The guys went nuts.

I parred the second hole. They went ballistic.

I parred the third hole. Berserko.

Standing on the fourth green, I needed two putts from ten feet to get my fourth par in a row.

"You guys are eyeballing me like a Las Vegas pit boss

studies a guy who has made three straight passes," I said as I lined up my putt.

Suddenly, a big gust of wind came up and I immediately let out a scream.

The wind had just blown one of the contact lenses out of my eyes.

Contact lenses? My teammates had never even heard of them. They had just been invented. I, of course, being Magoo, was the first kid on my block to get a pair.

Hey, I just said I would play without glasses. I didn't say anything about contact lenses.

No go. Hairsplitting legalisms didn't cut it. I shot the rest of the round sans glasses, sans contact lenses.

It was an expensive lesson.

After it was over and I took my licking, I paid off my bets, and we went back to the beer joint to review the day's festivities.

"Magoo, you were right. You were like the guy at the craps table," one of my jolly crew said. "Do you know what happened to him? Just when he was about to shoot his fourth consecutive pass, three dice rolled out of his sleeve. All sixes. That's when the pit boss reached over, pocketed one of the dice and said, 'Go ahead and shoot. Your point is eighteen.'"

And so it was.

Harvey Mackay

Beat the Pro

You hear that winning breeds winning. But no winners are bred from losing. They learn they don't like it.

Tom Watson

Sam Snead tells the story of a charity golf challenge he played years ago.

A pro was stationed at each hole, and threesomes would come up and bet against the pro individually. Sam was positioned at a par-3 hole and, with one shot to the green, whoever's ball was closest to the pin on the tee-off was the winner.

A threesome approached and the first man said, "Hello, Mr. Snead. I'd like to bet you five hundred dollars that I'll get closer to the pin than you do." Snead accepted the challenge. The golfer hit a good shot to the green. Snead hit it past the green and lost the bet.

The second golfer approached, saying, "It's great to meet you, Mr. Snead. I'm going to make the same bet as my friend. Five hundred dollars says that I'll hit the ball closer to the pin than you will." This time, Sam hit the ball twenty yards past the hole and lost the bet again. He just laughed. It was, after all, a charity event and the object was to raise money and have fun.

The last one of the threesome strolled up to Snead and, with a brash New Jersey accent, said, "You washed-up old man! You just don't have it anymore, do you? I'll bet thirty-five hundred dollars that I can beat you." Sam just smiled and quietly accepted the bet. The cocky golfer hit the ball four inches from the pin. "Now beat that, old man," he said. "You should have put down those clubs years ago." Again, Sam just smiled. He leaned over and positioned the ball, drew back, took a swing and made a hole-in-one. "Better luck next time," said Slammin' Sammy Snead.

Susan D. Brandenburg

Golf Balls

A few years ago I introduced a coworker, Roy, to the game of golf. I outfitted him with a set of my old clubs, including head covers, a bag, tees, ball markers, divot tools and two dozen new golf balls. I even provided him with a visor and a new glove. The only thing he had to buy for himself was a pair of golf shoes.

After a few lessons on the driving range, he played his first round of golf at a company-sponsored outing at Bay Valley Inn, Bay City, Michigan. This beautiful and challenging 18-hole course has water on thirteen holes and is constantly buffeted by winds sweeping in off Saginaw Bay. Not necessarily a good first choice for a beginning golfer, but Roy was bound and determined to play in the company outing.

After a typical beginner's horrendous first nine, Roy turned to me and said, "Sam, I'm out of balls. May I have some more?" I thought my generosity had already reached beyond normal expectations and I replied, "Roy, do you know how much golf balls cost?" Roy calmly replied, "Sam, if you can't afford the game, you shouldn't play."

Sam Murphy

Walter Won the Honors

If you ever felt that there is a wee touch of the spiritual in golf, like the famous book *Golf in the Kingdom* says, let me tell you a true story that may further the notion.

Last autumn, Walter Donoughe, one of my closest friends, was told by his doctors they couldn't cure his pancreatic cancer, but they thought treatments could extend his life and, yes, he could play a lot more golf. He and I were talking all about it a couple of days after he got his prognosis while we were playing the front nine as a twosome. As we sat in the cart waiting for the eighth green to clear, I asked Walter which he would prefer, three more years of golf, or a guarantee of eternity in heaven. He answered immediately that he would take the guarantee of heaven, but he smiled and said he hoped he could play golf there instead of harps. From other things Walter told me over the winter and last spring I knew he had a lock on membership in heaven's best golf club.

We also talked a lot about golf, and how a really sweet swing starts effortlessly, like somebody else takes it back, then brings it down on plane and you hear more than feel the click as the ball jumps off the club. We spent some great hours hitting 5-irons into the net in the bag room as we forgot the winter cold outside and tried for the sweet swing feeling.

Walter kept hanging in there fighting the cancer and was still swinging pretty well early in the spring when the golf committee decided to initiate for July a two-day tournament that each year would honor some member who has meant a lot to the club. They selected Walter as the first honoree. A great choice. He had worked many, many years as a board member and on every committee the club ever had. He won the handicap championship twice, numerous flight and senior championships, and he even won the annual gin tournament twice. A fine man, a good competitor and a great friend.

In the July 5–6 tournament honoring him, Walter and I would have been partners, as we usually were in team events, but he died on June 5. I was invited by, and played with, our club champion, Scott Arthur, who played well enough for us to win it all. But I made sure we didn't as I rolled the ball off the tee, heeled and toed fairway woods, scraped irons right and left, bladed and chili-dipped chips and pitches, and three- and four-putted my way to an agony of double and triple bogeys.

With only two holes left to play, as we headed to the par-3 thirteenth, I told Scott there had to be some lesson for me to learn from these humiliating two rounds, but I didn't think the lesson could be worth it. When we got on the thirteenth tee a hawk was circling high above the green. Scott said it was our last chance for a hole-in-one and he would like one because it was his fortieth birthday. For all the years he had been playing golf he said he had seen only one ace—hit by Walter Donoughe years ago when Scott caddied for him.

With zero enthusiasm I teed up the ball to hit and get it over with, then something strange happened. My 5-iron started back effortlessly like somebody else was swinging it back then bringing it down on plane, and I heard the click more than I felt it as the ball jumped off the club. My myopic eyes couldn't follow the ball but I knew it was hit by that sweet swing Walter always talked about, a swing that I felt only a few times before, at the practice net when he coached me.

Bill Kelley, Chris Vasiliades and Scott started to holler things like "Great swing.... Great shot.... Go in the hole!" There was a sudden hush, then, "It did! It did! It went in the hole!" Chris grabbed my hat, threw it towards the green, then picked me up and swung me around like a rag. I was thinking, *Please Chris, don't throw me after my hat.*

The screams kept up and were truly sky-splitting, but that hawk was undisturbed. Like the steady pilot Walter was when he earned his wings with the Air Force years ago, that hawk just kept calmly circling the green and was not surprised at all by the miracle that happened down below him.

Now, I don't know how Walter petitioned the Almighty for me, but I know he did. Perhaps he said his buddy down there was getting close to giving up the game, breaking the commandment, Thou Shalt Not Quit. So he took over during his tournament, and before it was too late he arranged to send his pal Frank a message about hanging in there—a hole-in-one. Thanks, Walter, for swinging it for me. Go in peace.

Frank J. Haller

A Special Rapport

They limp when they walk, as if the world is perpetually tilted. Sometimes for them, it is.

Casey Martin hits and rides, hits and rides. When he reaches the greens at Heatherwoode Golf Club, he limps from the golf cart to his ball. The pain in his right leg is throbbing and insistent.

Gina Homan limps. Sometimes, she hops on her good, right leg. When the pressure on her left leg is too much, she'll stand on her right, her hand grabbing the left leg at the knee.

What are the odds? Martin, the pro golfer, has Klippel Trenaunay Weber Syndrome, a rare circulatory disorder. Gina Homan, who is twelve, does, too. Until Martin sued the PGA for the right to use a golf cart in tournaments, Gina never knew anyone else with her disability.

This was somebody like her, doing exactly what he wanted to do, without fear of prejudice. This she had to see.

She came from Minster, Ohio, with her parents and her older sister, to watch Martin in the Nike Miami Valley Open. He spoke to her at the first tee, "How's the leg today, buddy?" and smiled at her frequently during the round.

"What a sweet kid," Martin marveled afterward. "What a trouper."

Gina Homan was quiet and beaming. She didn't say what the day meant, but you knew what was happening behind her eyes.

Here's a funny thing about people with disabilities and the people who love them: They count their blessings. They smell the roses. They know what good fortune is, because they've seen the flip side.

Gina's mother Eileen explained the bumps on her daughter's leg. "Clumps of blood vessels," she said. "We're lucky. She could have that on her face, or throughout her body."

What are the odds? The Homans noticed Gina's oversized leg when she was about six months old. They took her to doctors who checked her kidneys and heart. They took her to an arthritis specialist. Why is her leg so big? Nobody knew.

An x-ray technician finally made the correct diagnosis. The blood does not move efficiently from Gina's leg to her heart and back. It pools, causing the swelling. Martin shares her disability. He embodies her spirit.

And so Gina was out there waiting for him and following him for eighteen holes. They took a walk together, of a fashion.

The PGA thought the Casey Martin controversy was about carts and unfair advantages and the athleticism involved in putting one foot in front of the other. They didn't know.

It was about giving somebody a chance who deserved one.

Gina Homan might grow up to be a teacher. She's an A-student. She loves little children. She's patient and tolerant, and now she knows she's not alone.

"It slays me when kids stare" is what Eileen says. Gina

can't run or ride a bike. The left leg is noticeably bigger than the right; at the knee, it bows out.

Because her left foot is significantly smaller than her right, the Homans often buy Gina two pairs of shoes, to get one pair that fits. "I'm a little different physically," she says.

I ask Eileen Homan, "What do you wish for your daughter?" She says, "To grow up, find a job she likes and find a person she can be happy with."

At twenty-six, Casey Martin has grown up. He has found a job he likes. About the other, I don't know.

I know he did not ask for special treatment. People with disabilities rarely do. They want what we want, which is a fair shake. If you've watched Martin play, you understand. If you saw Gina Homan—limping, hopping and beaming, courageous—you'd empathize.

Eileen says, "She has a good heart. She's compassionate. She always strives to do her best."

After the round, Martin gave her a hug. If only we all were so disabled.

Paul Daugherty

Life on the Back Nine

*Don't get your knickers in a knot; nothing is
solved and it just makes you walk funny.*

Kathryn Carpenter

The first time I played golf—real golf where you keep
score and putt everything out and take it seriously—was
in a father-son tournament. I was ten. I remember thinking it would be cool to drive the golf cart. I was right. It
was very cool driving the golf cart. Did I already say I was
ten at the time? I think we shot about a 65 for nine holes,
which is all we played because the attention spans of
young golfers really don't allow for a full round.

The golf course I grew up playing, Meadowbrook
Country Club, has a 609-yard par-5 that wore us out. I
think we made a 12. But I was very proud of the fact that
I didn't whiff any shots. And I was hooked. My dad had
introduced me to a game that would forever be a part of
my life.

It would also test the boundaries of our bond.

By the following summer, I was playing golf every day,
which included sneaking onto the course on Mondays,

when it was officially closed, and squeezing in three holes on the front nine on Tuesdays before the Ladies Day crowd would make it around to the seventh tee.

I even found what would be the family dog on the golf course that summer. A stray collie mix met me on the third tee one morning and followed me for the rest of the front nine. After I fed her half my hot dog from the snack bar, she was mine.

By the time the next father-son tournament rolled around, I would have cried if I'd shot a 65 on my own ball. I had developed a strong short game and expected my dad's length off the tee to make up for my shortcomings. If he could get us within 135 yards on the par-4s, I could get us on the green. And one of the best things about Meadowbrook back then was there was hardly any water and—except for one par-3—you never had to carry a water hazard to reach a green.

We shot 48, and I was miffed. I rolled my eyes every time my dad mis-hit a shot. I grimaced when my putts didn't fall. I kicked at the grass and mumbled to myself. I had a miserable time. We finished third. I thought we should have won.

That afternoon and evening, I moped around the house like it was the end of the world. This pattern carried on for years because, although my dad and I were both accomplished players, we never learned how to play together. By the time I hit my mid-teens, I was regularly shooting in the 70s. I won the club junior championship when I was fifteen, and the members had to put up with a five-foot-nothing squirt playing in their club championship that summer because the junior champ got an automatic invite.

Life was good, except for when Dad and I would tee it up as a team. We could go out on Saturday and both shoot in the 70s—I remember both of us had 6 handicaps when I was sixteen—then turn around the following day in that hate-inducing alternate-shot format and fire an 85 in an event in which you were allowed to choose the better of two tee shots.

I was so disgusted one time that I putted the last three holes left-handed. Not a word was spoken on the ride home. The crazy thing was that we'd take this act on the road to play in the Tommy Galloway Father-Son at Hermitage Country Club, which was a big regional to-do. Winning the low gross in our age group was impossible because we were bound to make a couple of 7s. We'd always get to the sixteenth tee and one of us would say, "Well, there's always the net. If we shoot 82, they take away our two worst holes."

One time, we reached the par-4 seventeenth hole 7-over for the day and looked like we'd break 80 . . . until we both dunked it into the lake running down the right side of the fairway. It was negative on negative. The problem was, we couldn't learn to accept each other's faults. He sprayed drives and had a tendency to severely misclub himself. I was into go-for-broke golf. By the time I was sixteen and had hit a growth spurt, I figured there wasn't a par-5 I shouldn't reach in two. And I had turned into a terrible putter. My dad fretted over my jab stroke, which was either on fire or ice cold; I, meanwhile, fretted about his desire to play it safe.

By the time I was seventeen, we'd accepted the fact that we weren't much of a team. We were at the peaks of our games—my high school team won the 1981 state championship and I signed a golf scholarship with Virginia Commonwealth University. Dad was as consistent about shooting in the 70s as he'd ever be. But together we were mush.

I went off to school and lost myself in books and knowledge and a hunger to be a newspaper writer. And I lost my interest in playing competitive golf. After two seasons, I was through as a college golfer. There were some memorable rounds, but they were too few and far between.

Meanwhile, we had aged out of the father-son tournament. But a few years ago, Dad called and asked if I wanted to play in the father-son again. Turns out they'd changed the name to the politically correct parent-child and had created an over-eighteen age group.

Did we really want to put ourselves through that turmoil again?

I was playing rarely, and Dad had developed shoulder problems and was playing even less.

"Sure," I said. "Why not?"

A funny thing happens when you reach adulthood. All of a sudden, you can accept your dad's faults because you start to realize you have your own. And why in the world should four hours of golf with Dad be so stressful?

We hit a bucket of balls to warm up, and I don't think either of us hit more than three practice shots on the sweet spot. I would have hated to pick up the range that night; Team Radford had sprayed shots everywhere. But we must have left all the bad shots on the range. We birdied the first hole when I hit a wedge to about ten feet and Dad ran in the putt. Then we birdied the fourth hole, a par-5, when Dad hit a 200-yard 5-wood onto the front of the green, and we two-putted from forty-five feet. By the end of the round, we'd made four birdies. We had some ugly holes, too, but they weren't too ugly. And the amazing thing was that after an ugly hole, we always followed it with a chance for birdie. I remember laughing when I signed the scorecard.

Here were two hacks who had never played well together and they'd just shot 4-over 75 in an alternate-shot format. A lot of the guys I had grown up with, and who had always trounced us as a father-son tandem, had decided to play that Sunday. I scanned my age group's scores—81-77-85-76-82-90.

We'd won? Unbelievable. When we came home with the hardware, Mom also couldn't believe it. For years, she'd had to hear us trash each other for hours after every father-son event we played. Now she had to hear us gloat.

Suddenly, Dad's 220-yard drives into light rough were a thing of beauty. And just as suddenly, as long as my putts went into the hole, Dad didn't care what my awful stroke looked like. We laughed about the fifteen-inch putt he missed on the fifteenth hole, something I was constantly guilty of.

Two holes later, I air-mailed a par-3, something he was more prone to do in the past. The following year we shot 72. By the back nine, we weren't worried about beating the field, we were wondering if we could beat par.

All of that negative energy that had followed us for years had become positive power. For years, we had been in situations where we would ponder whether to play the ball out of the woods or the one that was buried under the lip in the bunker. Now, we were having to choose between a ten-foot downhill putt or a fifteen-footer uphill for birdie.

We haven't played in a parent-child tournament for a few years now. Dad's shoulder became so aggravating that he quit playing and gave up his membership at the club. But I was in the attic of my parents' house the other day looking for some old Batman comic books for my own son when I came across a box of old golf trophies. The first one I picked up was the first-place trophy for the 1989 Meadowbrook Country Club Parent-Child, unlimited age group. The second one was a third-place cup for the 1973 father-son, eleven-and-under. It took sixteen years to get it right. But finally we did.

Rich Radford

Living the Dream

The name jumped out at me from the list of tournament scores in a national golf publication. It was printed in teeny-tiny type, and I caught it only because I'm in the habit of scanning the mini-tour results for past and future tour stars.

I didn't expect to see his name in italics, and it stopped me in my tracks and made me smile.

Darryl Staszewski.

I stared at the letters until they blurred, feeling pangs of nostalgia as I thought about an old high school friend and the paths we chose in life. I felt admiration for Darryl, and maybe a little envy, too.

Staszewski, a graduate of St. Francis (Wisconsin) High School class of '74—my class, my friend—had tied for seventh place in an obscure mini-tour event somewhere in the Northwest. He won $216.

Big deal, you say?

It is, if you knew Darryl twenty-five years ago. As a high school freshman, he stood probably four-feet-ten-inches, and couldn't have weighed much more than seventy-five pounds. By his senior year, he had sprouted to five-feet-six-inches and tipped the scales at about 120, soaking wet.

Naturally, he got teased about his size. His buddies, especially, were relentless with their wisecracks. He took it in stride, mostly, but I'll never forget the day I snatched his driver's license out of his hand and loudly announced, with no small amount of glee, that Darryl was required to sit on a platform to see over the steering wheel.

In terms of teenage insults, I'd hit a 350-yard drive. Darryl laughed with the rest of us, but I noticed tears of humiliation welling in the corners of his eyes. It was the last time I ever teased him.

Darryl was a pretty good athlete, but he obviously was too small to play football, and after freshman basketball— he looks like a waif in the yearbook team photograph—he didn't make the squad as a sophomore.

So he turned to golf.

A left-hander, he swung in slow motion and barely managed to hit the ball out of his own shadow. He practically buckled under the weight of his golf bag. He didn't make the varsity team until he was a senior, and then only as the sixth man on a five-man squad, perhaps as a reward for his perseverance. Darryl played in few actual matches.

Back then, a few of us dreamed about becoming professional golfers, but we were eighteen and full of silly notions. Instead, we went off to college or to work, got married, had children. Ultimately, we fulfilled our destinies in golf: We became weekend hackers.

Except for Darryl Staszewski. He had the determination, the courage and the focus about which the rest of us only talked. Maybe the teasing he had endured made him tougher. Maybe he just wanted it more than we did. Maybe he just had more talent than we did, and it simply took a while to surface.

Not long after we graduated, Darryl moved to California to work on his game. Eventually, he became a club professional, and at some point in the late 1970s, I lost track of him.

Twenty years later, I was in the media tent at the Greater Milwaukee Open when somebody tapped me on the shoulder. I turned around and there was Darryl Staszewski—a lean, athletic six-footer.

He was living near Seattle, but was in town on vacation and had barely missed earning a spot in the GMO field in the Monday qualifier. We chatted for a while, and he gave me his phone number, saying it would be fun to get together and play a round if I ever got up to the Northwest.

And then I forgot about Darryl again until I found myself staring at his name in a golf magazine. It really doesn't matter whether he won $216 or $216,000, whether he finished seventh on the Cascade Tour or won the U.S. Open.

You see, Darryl is living the dream.

Gary D'Amato

Requiem for a Milkman

*God does not subtract from one's allotted time
the hours spent playing golf.*

Gerald O'Gara

This is the story of a retired milkman named Emil Kijek,
who wound up his life in the arms of a friend in the
middle of a fairway on a Thursday afternoon.

The setting is southeast Massachusetts, on the rim of
Narragansett Bay, where stories this small are usually
thrown back. Lizzie Borden hailed from Fall River, right
next door; Ishmael and Ahab sailed from New Bedford,
just down the road.

As a center of drama, Rehoboth is not quite in their class.

It's a pretty little town though. Driving through, you
might take it for hunting country if John Pellegrino
weren't there to set you straight. "Shoot my deer"
explained the owner of the Sun Valley Golf Club, "and I'll
shoot you."

Pellegrino's operation is similarly unvarnished. Starting
with the arrow sign on the highway, everything at Sun
Valley could stand some paint. The roof wouldn't mind a

little leveling. The clubhouse is mostly a bar. But the gray-haired men crisscrossing with pullcarts look well satisfied. The senior rate is thirteen dollars for eighteen holes.

Ron Collett, Morris Dumont, Jack Alexander and Emil Kijek were teamed up that Thursday in a tournament. Collett and Dumont were not Kijek's regular partners, although both knew "Ky" well. Everyone did. "He had a spirit about him, I tell you," said Dumont, a retired piano tuner. "Ky was the type who enjoyed the day better than the golf, who took the good shots and the bad shots as they came, always hoping the next one would be perfect."

Alexander, on the other hand, was Kijek's customary golfing crony and his closest friend. They served together in Hawaii during World War II, though they didn't know it at the time. Kijek had gone in and out of the Army before the war broke out. When it did, he came back as a Seabee, a builder, and eventually saw Saipan.

On Oahu, when Alexander only knew of him, Kijek was also a boxer, a middleweight. He was one of the staple attractions in the Friday night fights at Schofield Barracks, a model of that paradoxical gentleness you so often find in boxers.

His father was the same way. Back in Warsaw, Jacob Kijek had been a weaver's foreman preoccupied with keeping a certain loom operating, the one run by Caroline. Falling in love and emigrating to Pawtucket, Jacob and Caroline raised their boy in the weaving business. As he had been an only son, Emil grew up to have an only daughter, Sandra. Her childhood memories are of spontaneous picnics, Sunday rides and a father whose only rule was kindness.

It was in the early 1960s that he embraced golf, when a cardiologist's first warning gave him four months off. After he retired—especially after losing his wife, Mabel—the golf course became home. He was a good, straight hitter, an 11- or 12-handicapper who held to that number (even as his distance waned) with increasingly better putting. This phenomenon is unheard of in the pros but well known in places like Sun Valley.

As a cardplayer, Kijek was a scratch, a legend at gin but even more partial to "pitch," the working man's rhapsody of high, low, jack and game.

"Deal the cards, old man," Alexander would say. Kijek would smile like a handsome child, and everyone else would laugh. At seventy-five, Alexander was only four years younger, but lately they were telling years. Ky was losing his edge with the cards.

He could still putt. At the first hole that day, he made a twenty-footer for par. At the fourth, he knocked in another. "You're saving us, old man," Alexander said. The day looked bright.

The sixth hole at Sun Valley is a 155-yard par-3. Kijek took a 3-wood.

"He hit that thing so beautifully," Dumont would say later. "It had this amazing trajectory."

"Emil, I can't see the ball," Alexander murmured after a moment, "I think it went in."

"Naw," Kijek said. He'd never had a hole-in-one.

"Old man!" Alexander sang as they reached the green. "Come get your ball out of the cup!"

Dumont recalled, "Ky was really happy, but there was no jumping up and down. He was such a humble man."

After driving nicely at the seventh, Kijek wavered over his second shot. "Emil, let somebody else hit first," Alexander suggested gently. "No, no, I'm okay, Jack," he said.

In the next instant, Ky started to fall, and his friend caught him. They settled softly in the grass. As the others ran for help, Jack said, "Emil, squeeze my hand. Don't stop until I tell you to." But Ky gave him that smile again and let go.

Who was he? He was a man who enjoyed the day better than the golf, who took good shots and bad shots as they came, always hoping the next one would be perfect. And it was.

Tom Callahan

Golf and the Caddie at Royal Troon

If I ever think anybody is better than me, then I can never be the best. I always have to believe I'm the best.

Payne Stewart

My wife and I had planned our first trip to Scotland for more than a year. Working through Scottish Golfing Holidays, we started our week at Royal Troon. I was to play the course in the morning, then my wife would join me in the afternoon across the street on the Portland Course.

This was the first morning of the first day of my first golf in Scotland.

Two things happened that will remain with me forever.

First, we were delayed more than fifteen minutes waiting for Payne Stewart and his group to show up. Clad in uncustomary slacks and regular golf-style cap, Stewart and his group finally appeared and were escorted to the back, or "medal" tees, where they all teed off. Playing with Stewart were three others, the best of whom probably was no more than a 10 handicap. Having already been rebuffed from playing the back tees, I decided to give it another go. The starter, with whom I had been enjoying a long conversation waiting for Stewart's group to appear, said it was impossible—unless, of course, the club secretary gave his approval. He then volunteered to speak with the secretary on my behalf. Taking my letter of introduction, which said I was an honorable fellow from Nebraska who had played in several USGA events including Amateurs and Mid-Amateurs (I have never qualified, but that didn't stop me from trying) and currently holding a 2.4 index, he disappeared into the clubhouse. A few minutes later, a tall, respectable gentleman wearing a coat and tie came to the tee box. Colin Montgomery's father looked down at my five-feet-six-inches, from somewhere high above six feet, fixed me with a Scottish stare I would get to know over the coming week, and asked me directly, "Have you one to waste?" Being fully loaded with far too many golf balls to fit comfortably into my carry bag, I responded affirmatively.

He then said, "Hit your driver o'er that hillock," pointing to a tall mound between the first tee and the ocean. With slightly sweaty palms, and a crowd of twenty-five or so golfers watching, I managed to make a good swing and sent a fine drive directly over the hillock. Mr. Montgomery then turned to the starter and said, in a voice that carried clearly to the surrounding crowd, "Mr. Kahler is a fine amateur from the States and will be allowed to play the medal tees. Everyone else will play the regular tees." With that statement he turned and strode directly into the clubhouse. And I played Royal Troon from the medal tees.

The second event that day involved Payne Stewart. As we were teeing off on the seventh hole, a dogleg-right slightly downhill, the rain and wind simultaneously picked up. Stewart's group had moved off the fairway into two rain shelters on the left side of the hole. We hit our drives, then agreed to also seek shelter to allow the storm to pass. I had hit a great drive and was just a few yards behind another ball from the group in front of us. As we reached the shelter, our twosome was huddled in one shelter and Stewart's group in another. A few minutes later, Stewart's local caddie ran over to our shelter and said a few words to my caddie. My caddie then said to me, "Mr. Stewart would like to know if you would like a small wager: closest to the pin for a pound." I agreed. Not because I thought I could hit it closer than Payne Stewart, but I would have a great story to tell and it would only cost me a pound. Because we were a twosome, and more willing to brave the elements than Stewart's foursome, they invited us to play through as the rain and wind lessened. I hit a career shot, holding it into the wind, coming to rest within ten feet of the hole. As we walked to the green, Stewart's caddie came running out and handed my caddie a pound coin, which he, in turn, passed on to me.

I don't know whether Payne Stewart actually made the bet or provided the pound. The more I have learned about caddies in Scotland, the more likely it was the caddie himself who made and paid the bet. And I don't know how close Payne Stewart hit the ball to the hole; we went on to the famous Postage Stamp eighth hole before they resumed play. But I did leave a ball marker in the green where my ball had been on No. 7. And no one asked me for the pound back later. I use it to this day as my ball marker.

Jeff Kahler

The Day Mr. 59 Bottled Lightning

*If you hit a bad shot, just tell yourself it is great
to be alive, relaxing and walking around on a
beautiful golf course. The next shot will be better.*

Al Geiberger

Hundreds of men have run the mile in less than four
minutes, and a couple more no doubt just started their
finishing kicks as we speak. How many can you name?
And who is the current record-holder?

We remember Roger Bannister, who did it first and did
it for posterity. Talk about the four-minute barrier and
you talk about Roger Bannister.

It's the same with Al Geiberger. He became the first
player to break 60 on the PGA Tour, shooting a shocking
59 in the second round of the 1977 Memphis Classic.
Seven golfers shot 60 on tour before 1977, including Sam
Snead, but nobody plunged into the 50s until that one-
hundred-degree afternoon in Memphis. Only two players
have done it since, Chip Beck in 1991 at Las Vegas and
David Duval in 1999 at Palm Springs.

The supremely modest Geiberger is Mr. 59, a superla-
tive his agent alertly copyrighted. You can put it on his

tombstone. Tell Tiger Woods if he starts to run out of goals there's always the 59, which Geiberger shot on a 7,249-yard, par-72 Colonial Country Club course that ranked among *Golf Digest*'s One Hundred Greatest Courses.

The tempo king hit every fairway and every green. He made eleven birdies and an eagle, holing a thirty-yard wedge shot. He took but twenty-three putts, the longest from forty feet to start his round; an amateur mathematician reckoned that Geiberger sank 166 feet worth of birdie putts.

I remember Johnny Miller remarking afterward that he never thought anybody could putt that well on those greens. "They're Bermuda grass, which means you have to hit everything very firmly and truly," he says. "And Al had a late starting time, which means they were tracked up. You just don't make twelve putts longer than ten feet!"

The closest score to 59 was 65.

Yes, there's a caveat. The fairways were so patchy after a severe winter that players were permitted to lift and clean the ball. Nobody is quite clear how many times Geiberger improved his lie. Playing partner Dave Stockton remembers that on several shots Geiberger did not need to touch the ball. Geiberger recalls perhaps being helped on one shot, the holed wedge.

The turning point was a snack.

With the field split, Geiberger's round began on the tenth hole, and at the fourteenth events heated up, literally. A fire had broken out in a nearby parking lot, and fire trucks, sirens shrieking, were arriving as cars burned. Then, a friend of Geiberger's, who lived alongside the fourteenth brought him some crackers heaped with peanut butter. The gangly Geiberger fights a low blood-sugar count with frequent protein fixes, and peanut butter is his favorite.

"The heat was making me weak," he said. "I needed a picker-upper, and the peanut butter did it. I played the next seven holes in eight under par."

After he birdied the last four holes on his front nine,

Geiberger began thinking about the tour record for consecutive birdies, which is eight. Shooting 59 didn't occur to him until he birdied his fifteenth hole and his rapidly swelling gallery began to chant, "59! 59! 59!"

He needed to birdie two of the last three holes.

He birdied No. 7, a par-5, with a pitch shot and nine-foot putt, but parred the eighth, two-putting from twenty feet. So it was all riding on the last hole, a 403-yard dogleg-left with a bunker lurking at the corner. Geiberger was a short, left-to-right driver. But the crowd was goading him into breaking out of his conservative nature, and he aimed straight at the bunker . . . and carried it, which he'd never done. His resulting 9-iron shot finished eight feet from the cup.

Geiberger told himself to get the ball to the hole whatever else he did. The putt was left to right and uphill—the type that's easy to misread or think you are misreading.

Geiberger rammed it into the heart of the hole.

Stockton, Geiberger's close friend and winning partner in the old CBS Classic, said later, "Berger came the closest I've seen him to getting excited. He got his fist halfway clenched."

Since the 59, Geiberger's life has taken unexpected turns, some for the better, some for the worse. He has divorced and remarried, lost a child to a drowning accident, undergone major surgery almost regularly and battled financial problems. He's always in the middle of one comeback or another, and yet he's won ten times in ten years on the senior tour.

Today a fifty-nine would shoot his age. Despite a life that appears from the outside to have been dominated by hardship, Geiberger considers himself a lucky man. If that sounds like Lou Gehrig, Mr. 59 is made of much the same stuff.

Nick Seitz

A Mate's Memory of Payne's Open Victory at Pinehurst

It's great to win, but it's also great fun just to be in the thick of any truly well and hard-fought contest against opponents you respect, whatever the outcome.

Jack Nicklaus

Although Payne and I rarely talked during a round, he always wanted me to be there as often as possible, and he claimed to know exactly where I was on the course at all times.

"Aren't you supposed to be concentrating on your golf?" I'd tease.

"I am, but I always know where you are," he said.

The U.S. Open crowds at Pinehurst were so huge by Saturday that I knew I wouldn't be able to see Payne's shots. I told him, "I think I'm going to watch the round on television today. I'll be there, though, when you get done."

I stayed glued to the television most of the afternoon. I rarely played golf—tennis is more my game—but I had watched Payne play for twenty years, so I knew his game well. As I watched, I noticed that Payne was moving his head ever so slightly on his putts, forward and upward, as though he were trying to watch the ball go into the hole. I watched helplessly as one putt after another failed to drop. "Oh, Payne!" I cried aloud to the television screen. "Keep your head down!" He ended up shooting a 72, his worst round of the championship. Though he was still one stroke ahead of Phil Mickelson, it wasn't a comfortable lead to sleep on.

After his round, I headed to the golf course. "I'm going to go hit some balls," he said.

"Okay, I'll go with you," I said. "You need to spend some time on the putting green, too." Payne nodded in agreement. "You need to keep your head down," I continued quietly.

Payne looked surprised.

"Really?"

"You're trying to watch the ball go in, rather than keeping your head down."

After hitting balls, he spent forty-five minutes working on the practice green. He forced himself to keep his head still and not look up until the ball was well away from the putter. He got to the point where he was putting with his eyes closed and hitting the center of the cup on almost every stroke.

Later, we returned to the home we were renting. Because our daughter, Chelsea, was at a basketball camp, we couldn't talk to her, but Payne called our son, Aaron, at his friend's home.

"Aaron, I'm leading the U.S. Open again!" Payne said.

Aaron, ten, was unimpressed. "That's great, Dad," he replied. "Guess what! Conner got a long-board skateboard!"

Payne laughed. Unwittingly, our kids had a marvelous way of keeping Payne's feet on the ground, and he loved them all the more for it.

With the television blaring Sunday morning, and Payne on his cell phone, I went to take a shower. When I came out of the bedroom, I was shocked to see that Payne's eyes were puffy. He looked as if he had been crying.

"Luv'ie, what's wrong?" I asked. Payne wiped his eyes with his knuckle and motioned toward the television. "NBC just ran a Father's Day segment," he said. "It was about my dad and me." Payne had been unaware that NBC had planned to broadcast a segment concerning Bill Stewart—Payne's dad, who had died of cancer in 1985—and his influence upon Payne's life and career. Payne had been tuning in to watch the early tournament coverage. As he watched the video of himself and his dad, tears flooded his eyes.

Rather than being disconcerted, Payne drew strength from the piece, inspiring him to want to play his best Father's Day round ever.

Eventually the time came to head to the course. Because of the damp, chilly weather, Payne had donned a rain jacket, but when Payne began to warm up, he felt the sleeves of the rain jacket tugging at his arms. The sleeves were restricting Payne's long, fluid swing, yet because of the weather, he needed the warmth the raingear provided.

"Get me a pair of scissors, Mike," Payne asked his caddie, Mike Hicks. Mike found a pair in the golf shop, and Payne proceeded to cut the sleeves off the jacket, trimming the garment so that it covered his shoulders and about three inches down his arms. Although Payne was known for his sartorial splendor on the golf course, he was not concerned about appearances today. All that mattered was playing his best.

After the ups and downs of a final round, Phil Mickelson approached the green on the final hole facing a twenty-foot birdie putt. If Phil made it, Payne would have to make his fifteen-footer to force a playoff. For a moment, it looked as though Phil's putt was in, but then it rolled off and stopped a few inches to the right of the hole.

Now it was Payne's turn. He slowly went through his pre-putt routine, crouching low, eyeing every undulation in the putting surface, lining up the putt. Finally, he stood, pulled the putter back evenly, and brought it forward firmly but smoothly, aiming just to the left inside edge of the cup. The blade connected with the ball, sending it toward the hole. Payne did not move his head.

From my vantage point, I couldn't see the hole. I saw Payne's ball rolling as if in slow motion, bumping over the spike marks, each one a potential land mine that could knock the ball off course. On line, curving slightly, bending; the ball seemed suspended in time, the logo turning over and over, still rolling . . . and then, suddenly, the ball disappeared.

The huge crowd at Pinehurst exploded. It was one of the loudest—and best—responses that I'd ever heard. Payne picked his ball out of the cup, kissed it and slid it into his pocket. This was one ball he would want to keep.

On the side of the green, I pushed to the front of the crowd gathered inside the roped-off area where the players exit the green. Roger Maltbie, the NBC announcer and an old friend of Payne's and mine, spotted me and we hugged. We were both too choked up to speak, and the crowd noise was so loud, it's doubtful that we could have heard each other anyhow. But it didn't matter. Words were unnecessary. Awash in an incredible sense of relief, tears of joy seemed the only appropriate response.

Payne was walking toward me. Because of the throng, he didn't see me at first, and nearly walked right past.

He pulled me close, and we embraced on the green. With my head buried in his shoulder, I heard him say in my ear, "I did it. I kept my head down. All day . . . all day, I did it. I kept my head down."

Through my tears, I said, "I know you did, and I'm so proud of you!"

Many people were amazed at how Payne handled losing the 1998 U.S. Open and winning the 1999 Open with equal measures of grace. Members of the media and some of his fellow competitors were intrigued. Something was different about Payne Stewart. Oh, sure, he was still Payne—spontaneous, outspoken, extremely confident and always wearing his emotions on his sleeve. He still loved a good party, and he'd still tell you what he thought about a subject if you asked him—or even if you didn't. He still worked hard, played hard and loved passionately. Yet people who knew Payne well recognized that he had changed somehow for the better, if that were possible. He possessed a deeper, unusual sense of peace . . . a peace that hadn't always been there.

Tracey Stewart
with Ken Abraham

[EDITORS' NOTE: *Oct. 25, 1999—A runaway Learjet partly owned by golfing great Payne Stewart crashed in Edmunds County, South Dakota. Payne Stewart perished in the accident.*]

The Journey Before "the Putt"

*Golf is the hardest game in the world. There's no
way you can ever get it. Just when you think you
do, the game jumps up and puts you in your place.*

Ben Crenshaw

A bizarre putt at qualifying school symbolizes Joe
Daley's road to the PGA Tour.

On the fourth day of Q school, with two rounds to play,
Joe Daley was 16 under par and moving with the leaders.
"Cruisin' along," he says.

His 17th hole that day was a 158-yard par-3 into the
wind. When his playing partner's 8-iron shot dropped on
the green's front edge, Daley went up a club. "I wanted to
hit a smooth 7, but I came over it and pulled it into the
water," he says.

From the drop area, 72 yards away, he put a sand-
wedge shot 18 feet behind the hole.

His first putt rolled four feet past. The putt coming back
was simple. He thought, *Left center.*

The Journey

It was her birthday, in the spring of 1991, and the Atlantic Ocean moved over her feet, for after dinner they walked on the Virginia beach. Joe Daley had the ring in a box hidden in his sock.

"Come over here," he said to Carol, and he handed her the ring, and she said, "What does this mean?"

He said, "What do you mean, 'What does this mean'?"

She waited.

"Oh," he said, "I have to say it?"

She waited.

"Carol, will you marry me?"

"Yes."

He said, "But you do know, don't you, what I want to do?"

"Yes."

He wanted to chase the dream.

She wanted to chase it with him.

And what a dream at what a time. Some men his age had already given it up. He was thirty. He had been a wholesale credit manager since graduation from Old Dominion University in Norfolk, Virginia. He played golf, as he had in school, and now and then friends would remind him he could really play, as during a pro-am when he watched PGA Tour players.

"They'd ask, 'Why aren't you out here with these guys?'" Daley said.

So the newlyweds hit the road. They went to Florida, where she worked as a teacher and he worked on his game, moonlighting as a banquet waiter to help pay the bills. Slowly they saved fifty-five hundred dollars; they tried not to spend it quickly. "A big night out," Carol says, "was pizza once a week."

The Putt

If you're a professional golfer forty years old, as Joe Daley was on that day in December, you've knocked in tens of thousands of four-footers. Still, four days into Q school, you grind on those putts, because if you miss them you can be a dreamer, lover, husband and banquet waiter, but you cannot be a professional golfer.

Left Center

For years Daley carried with him a putting-practice gizmo, a cup liner that reduced the regulation hole opening by an inch. Heaven only knows how many hours on how many putting greens in how many countries he stood hunched over putts just like this four-footer.

Of 169 players in the final-stage field, 36 would qualify for the 2001 PGA Tour. The next 51 would go to the Buy.com Tour that, nice as it is—and it's maybe the third-best tour in the world—is the minor leagues.

It's the Dakota Dunes Open.

It's the dream deferred.

Daley had played well all week at La Quinta's PGA West Jack Nicklaus courses, starting with a 65. Now, a four-footer. Left center.

The Journey

Crisscrossing North America for two years and more, Joe Daley, six-foot-three and 159 pounds, folded himself into a tiny Nissan 200SX and drove 200,000 miles. The Canadian tour in 1992. Florida mini-tour events in '93.

Chile, South Africa, Bermuda, Jamaica in '94 and '95. "It's not nine-to-five, forty-eight weeks a year," Daley says. "I had that for ten years. I know what that's about. We could have that now. We could have the two jobs, the stability, the house. But this is a lot more fun and a lot more rewarding. It's the unknown. It's an adventure."

Says Carol: "My friends in teaching, when I told them I was going to Florida with Joe, said, 'What are you doing with your life?' Well, now they're still teaching, and I've been all over the world."

Twice he qualified for the PGA Tour, first in '96 and again two years later, but failed to play well enough long enough to stay. "Such commotion out there," he says. "So many people, so much happening." One journalist described Daley in those years as "a kid in a candy store," changing equipment, playing too many pro-ams, listening to too much well-intentioned advice.

Daley saw Tiger Woods make the first hole-in-one of his pro career. He shared a first-round lead with Greg Norman (a headline began, "Norman, unknown Joe Daley . . ."). He tied for sixth in the B.C. Open. In two years in the big leagues, Daley earned $138,379. He came to a harsh realization: "My swing needed work, big-time. I'd developed movement that I didn't need. It looked like Jim Furyk's."

While working with an Old Dominion teammate, John Hulbert, to reshape his swing, Daley lost even his Buy.com card. He already was an old man on a young man's journey. Asked by Toronto sportswriter John Gordon if he thought his time had come and gone, Daley said, "There's no quit in Joe Daley."

He made nine straight Buy.com cuts in 2000, had five top-five finishes and, with $151,233, finished twenty-third on the money list, good enough to earn a spot in the final PGA Tour Qualifying School.

The Putt

He needed to hit the four-foot putt firmly, left center. He hit it just that way on just that line. It was in. It disappeared.

Some images are processed by the brain so quickly that even as we move our eyes away, even before we can say what that image is, we realize we've seen something. Reflexively, our eyes leaving the image snap back to it. We want to know what that something is. Joe Daley saw something and looked again and knew what it was and had no idea how it could be his ball. But there it was, perched on the near edge, as if it had stopped there.

That couldn't be. He'd seen it roll over that very spot and disappear. It hadn't caught the lip and spun out. It fell over the front edge of the cup and into the darkness.

He'd made the putt. Hadn't he? Well, no.

"It came back out towards me," he says. He glared at the thing. He hurled his cap to the ground. "It was the damndest thing I had ever seen," Daley told reporters that day.

His ball had bounced out of the hole after hitting the top edge of the cup liner. By rule, the liner is to be set at least an inch beneath the green surface. In Daley's case, the liner sat crookedly in the hole, probably jerked away with the flagstick.

"I asked a tour official about it, but he said there was nothing he could do about it," Daley says. So he made a triple-bogey 6, one stroke lost to bad luck. He played the last thirty-seven holes 1 under par. Doing that good work under such pressure, the lost stroke couldn't hurt him that much.

Could it?

The Journey

It could. Thirty-six players at 417 or better qualified for the 2001 PGA Tour. Joe Daley shot 418. He'd rather have shot 417, but he's a grown-up and he knows things happen.

"It's the journey that matters, not one putt. Hey, on that same hole the last day, I made a thirty-foot downhiller with a foot-and-a-half break," he says. "I'm a lucky man. I'm doing what I want to do, my wife is traveling with me and we're having fun. That one putt is just a bump in the road."

Again this summer, then, Joe and Carol Daley will be on the Buy.com road, and if history suggests the future, there'll come a day when they're in the middle of nowhere, cruisin' along, and they'll answer to a voice that says . . .

Sky diving?

After Daley missed a Buy.com cut in 1999, he and his wife were en route from North Carolina to Virginia. "I thought we needed a diversion," Carol says. "So we stopped at a friend's who said, 'I know, how about I take you skydiving?'"

She'd been fly-fishing in Idaho, hiking in Colorado, dancing in Morocco, all with her dreamer who didn't know what to say on that Virginia beach. Now she has thrown herself from a plane and lived to laugh about it.

"Who knows," she says, "what's going to be next?"

Dave Kindred

Arnie's Army

Arnold Palmer is the biggest crowd pleaser since the invention of the portable sanitary facility.

Bob Hope

Arnie faced a near impossible shot, at least in the eyes of mere mortals. Two hundred yards separated his ball and Memorial Park's 4th hole. His ball rested on a crushed-shell maintenance path in the pocket of trees bordering the left side of the fairway, while the overhanging limb from a nearby oak tree restricted his powerful swing. Numerous swales in the fairway complicated his approach to the green, if he chose a low punch-and-run shot, and the canopy of tree foliage made a high-lofted shot unrealistic.

I had never seen or heard of Arnold Daniel Palmer in the spring of 1958. You see, I was just nine years old, a sandlot golfer since the age of seven, and totally unaware of the world of golf outside my own little world. Golf to me was still plastic golf balls, holes dug in the backyard and small tree branches with rags attached for flagsticks.

My father, God bless him, had decided today was the day to expose me to the masters of the fairways, and he drove us nearly an hour so that we could see the 1958 Houston Open. He, too, was anxious to see the man who had just won the Masters, and by the look of it, so was the entire golfing population of Houston.

A huge gallery surrounded Palmer and lined the fairways four deep. Around the green, they were six and seven deep, some using periscopes or stools, anything for a better vantage point to view their new hero. Arnie seemed unperturbed by the masses and more concerned with his very difficult shot. He took several practice swings in an effort to see just how much of a swing he could take without striking the tree limb. With each swing, his club struck the limb with a loud thump. The gallery muttered among themselves, assuming the worst. "What's he gonna do?" asked one man. "I don't know. Surely he'll just chip out," said the other. Apparently, neither man had ever witnessed Arnold Palmer in action.

Arnie took a drag from his cigarette and tossed it to the ground. He stared into his bag, then to the hole, trying to imagine which club would produce the shot he desperately needed. The crowd, which had been buzzing, fell silent. My father lifted me to his broad shoulders, and we both peered over the dozens of heads straining to see what would happen next.

Palmer took out a 3-iron and addressed the ball. His feet scratched at the shale like a mad bull, trying to get his footing. One more practice swing and he was ready. You could hear a pin drop.

Whack! Almost instantaneously, shouts of approval and applause rose from those lucky enough to be nearest Arnie. The rest of us could see nothing, only crane our heads in the direction of the distant green—hoping to catch a glimpse of the ball streaking toward its target.

What happened next was probably more thrilling than if I had hit the shot myself. I never did see the ball, but what I heard sent chills down my spine. The thousands that lined the fairway and green let us know just how the shot was progressing. As the ball danced toward the green, the shouts and applause grew in intensity until, finally, a prolonged roar came that seemed to last forever. The enormous pines and oak trees inhabiting Houston's Memorial Park echoed the thunderous applause tenfold across the fairways to the other spectators on the golf course. They seemed to trumpet the arrival of a new legend in the making—King Arnold.

When the crowd raced ahead of us toward the green, we could finally see where Arnie's ball finished—six inches from the cup! The arrow from Cupid's bow had been thrust deep into my heart! I can still see the smile and the joy on my father's face, as we shared a truly magical moment together—father and son. From that very moment, I knew I wanted to be a professional golfer.

I was to see Arnie many more times in my youth. Whenever he competed in the Houston area, I was there with my golfing buddies, sometimes carrying signs that said "Go Arnie!" and cheering at the top of my lungs. Eighteen years after my experience at Memorial Park, I fulfilled the dream he instilled in me as a nine-year-old and qualified to play on the PGA Tour. I can honestly say that, had it not been for the man we idolize today, I might never have achieved the dream of becoming a professional golfer.

But it wasn't just Arnie's instant inspiration that got me there. It was also my wonderful father who made sure that I played and worked hard on my game. He plodded every step of that arduous journey with me—encouraging me, challenging me, and most of all, loving me. In my heart and soul, he will always be "The King."

Bill Pelham

A Bright Light

Success in this game depends less on strength of body than strength of mind and character.

Arnold Palmer

It took a ravaging form of cancer to beat Heather Farr, the professional who died in 1993 at the age of twenty-eight.

Even against great odds, she was unaccustomed to defeat. Heather, the underdog, had always prevailed. Too short and too small, they said; couldn't hit it far enough.

But Heather, who barely topped five feet, ignored the common yardsticks. Tee shots had nothing to do with the size of her heart. In that, she was a giant.

At the age of eleven, she brought Lee Trevino home to dinner. At sixteen, when told that the first step to the Curtis Cup was winning the Girls' Junior, she won it the following week. At twenty, she refused all offers of sponsorship on the LPGA Tour. She had money to get to the first tournament and that, of course, would be enough.

From her first junior tee shot to her last professional putt, Heather Farr won ten state titles, a host of junior events, a couple of national championships and a million hearts.

"I don't think anyone ever loved the game more than Heather did," said Sharon Farr, her mother.

Heather was five when she first joined her father on his weekend rounds in Phoenix, Arizona. Equipped with coffee and a blanket, they lined up at 3 A.M. for a tee time at Papago Golf Course. For three years she simply tagged along, then begged, "Let me hit it! Let me hit it!"

Heather was nine when she announced that she had entered a tournament. On that momentous day, she headed for the 1st tee while her mother waited in the coffee shop, chatting with another mother.

A few hours later, Heather returned in the company of a small, tow-headed boy who addressed Mrs. Farr's companion. "Mom, you won't believe what happened to me," said the boy. "I got hit in the stomach by a golf ball. What's worse, it was hit by a girl!"

"I told him not to walk out in front of me when it was my turn to hit," Heather explained. "Finally, the only way I could play was to ignore him and go ahead and hit the ball. He turned around, and it hit him right in the stomach."

The boy, future U.S. Amateur champion Billy Mayfair, jerked up his shirt to reveal the dimpled imprint of a ball. "And this is how hard she hit it," he announced.

Despite the mishap, Heather's lifelong love of competition had begun.

"We had no idea what her capabilities or limitations were," Sharon said. "Only she knew that. We didn't know which courses she liked to play, so we told her to make her own schedule and we'd do our best to get her there."

Heather learned in victory, one memorable day winning a junior event in Phoenix in the morning and a Tucson tournament in the afternoon. And she learned the bitter lessons of defeat. Leading the ten-and-under division of the Junior World Championship, she was alarmed by the size of the gallery and five-putted the final green to finish fourth. It was simply a mistake, she said, one she would not repeat.

She lost so many balls that she was forced to borrow one on the final hole of the Orange Blossom Classic. The youngest, smallest player in the tournament, she suffered the added humiliation of finishing dead last.

"We were leaving the tournament, and Heather stood in front of the scoreboard for a long time while we waited for her," her mother remembered. "When she turned around she said, 'I'll tell you one thing—I'm never going to be last again.' And she never was."

At home in Phoenix, Heather signed up for a weight-training program at a local gym. She may have been smaller than the other players, but she could get stronger.

By this time, she was also under the tutelage of U.S. and British Open champion Lee Trevino. At the age of ten, with typical bravado, she had taken a newspaper clipping about herself to the Phoenix Open and asked the pros to sign it. Only Trevino paid serious attention to the tiny girl in tennis shoes, stopping to read the entire article, then offering encouragement.

That summer, Heather wrote a letter. "Dear Mr. Trevino, When you're in town next time, why don't you come over for dinner?"

At the next Phoenix Open, Trevino spotted her. "You wrote me that letter, didn't you?" he said. Trevino turned to Heather's mother and laughed, "That little sneak put her picture in it. Well, when's dinner?"

"Heather told him to pick a night," Sharon recalled, "and, bless his heart, he showed up when he said he would, walked into the house, grabbed a beer out of the refrigerator, and became just one of the family."

Over the years, Heather and Trevino visited often. He taught her shots, amazed at her ability to soak up his instruction.

"They had this wonderful, warm friendship," Sharon said. "He even taught her how to work on her clubs and change the grips, telling her to never let anyone do anything to her clubs if she didn't know what they were doing. When he gave her a 4½-wood, he said, 'Heather, you're going to do a lot of damage with this.' And she did."

One extraordinary winter day, Trevino telephoned, urging Heather to come to Dallas to play at Royal Oaks Country Club, a tight, tree-lined layout where he liked to practice.

"But Dallas is having an ice storm," Heather protested. "We can't play Royal Oaks."

"Come on down. We'll work it out," Trevino said.

Heather made the short flight to Dallas. In the bitter cold on a deserted Royal Oaks fairway, Trevino pulled out a pocket knife, cut out a square of sod, pulled it back from the bare dirt, and built a bonfire. Warmed by the fire, the great professional and the little girl laughed and talked, hitting golf balls to their hearts' content.

Little Heather was on her way to big things. At sixteen, she shared medalist honors in the 1981 U.S. Women's Amateur. She wasn't long, but she could smack a fairway wood closer to the hole than most players could hit a wedge. Thanks to Trevino, she had a great short game. Best of all, she believed in herself.

"Heather had a walk of confidence like nobody I've ever seen in my life," said Tom Meeks, a USGA official and long-time friend. "She walked like she knew exactly what she was trying to do and how she was going to do it. There wasn't any question in her mind that every time she went out to play she was going to have a successful round."

In 1982, she attended the Curtis Cup Match on her way to the U.S. Girls' Junior. Enthralled, she asked an official how to win a spot on the team. "Winning the Girls' Junior next week would be a good start," the official kindly replied.

Heather said only, "Okay." She may as well have said, "Done."

After that win, Heather finished as low amateur in the U.S. Women's Open the following summer. A berth on the 1984 Curtis Cup team was hers.

Her travel diary from that trip to Great Britain is the only written record Heather left behind. In rounded, youthful script, she recorded what she considered to be the greatest adventure of her life.

At Golf House, "P. J. Boatwright tells us not to be polite but to win as big as we can.

"June 3—Toured the R&A club. Actually got to see the whole thing! The upper balcony has the most awesome view . . . then ate lunch at the St. Rule Club. Glenna Collett Vare sat three people away.

". . . At dinner, received our Curtis Cup pins. Something so small means SO much."

Of a practice round at Muirfield, site of the match, she wrote, "The afternoon was so clear. Looking out over Muirfield was such an unbelievable experience. The course was out there waiting for us."

Perhaps exhaustion kept her from writing much about her opening foursomes match. She wrote simply that it was an exciting match that her team won, 1-up.

"Yes, Heather was full of beans and ready to play," said Tish Preuss, the 1984 Curtis Cup captain. "A little cocky, but that's good; that's just the way she was. She was happy-go-lucky. She knew she could play, and she proved it."

Preuss recalled that her team had only a one-point lead going into the final round.

"And on the 1st tee, Heather said, 'Don't worry about me, Captain. I'll win my point.'" She did, of course.

Judy Bell, former Curtis Cup team captain, saw Heather play many times. "Every inch of her was positive," said Bell. "Her golf swing was traditional, orthodox. She worked hard. She worked on her mechanics, but she had the extra stuff to go with it. She had this fiber.

"That whole team was a real enthusiastic bunch," Bell continued. "She just took to it. She had never played in Scotland in her life, but pretty soon she was wearing a tam. Those were the best of her golf days."

The U.S. team won the Curtis Cup match, and Heather cried at the closing ceremonies when Preuss quoted from Bob Ward:

"I wish you joy in all your days;

"I wish you sadness so that you may better measure joy."

Heather then flew to Rapid City, South Dakota, and won the Women's Amateur Public Links. Still happy and care-free, she joined Meeks and others on a victory ride down the rapids. Giggling in ecstasy, she floated down a creek on a huge inner tube. When the creek wound through the golf course and under a bridge, USGA committee members bombarded the new champion with water-filled balloons.

The best of her golf days, yes.

She turned professional and at twenty was the youngest player to emerge from the 1986 LPGA Qualifying School. With her little bankroll, she hit the tour. Heather was once again meeting her agenda. Life was so sweet and bright that she thought every month was May, never guessing that it was really November.

Heather Farr had a great short game and she could hit a driver from the fairway, pure and true. She had a small body, a great heart and a million friends. She had a short life, granted. But how it did shine.

Rhonda Glenn

Golf's Ace with Heart

It was another tournament town, another cardboard hotel room, another evening spent staring at the too-blue, too-orange television images atop the Formica-covered bureau. Juan "Chi Chi" Rodriquez, vying for the lead at the 1967 Texas Open in San Antonio, was practicing putts on the carpet and thinking about the birdies that slipped away that afternoon.

The drone of the evening news suddenly riveted his attention: a reporter was interviewing a distraught woman whose home in Illinois had been destroyed by a tornado. All she had left were the clothes she wore. Rodriguez was so moved that he made a pact with himself. If he bagged the trophy the following day, he would send the tornado relief fund five thousand dollars. The next day he won—and so did the tornado victims.

Across the country, dozens of people have benefited from the compassion of this pencil-thin Puerto Rican golf pro. While some professional athletes spend their spare time doing beer commercials, Rodriguez checks up on things like incurable diseases, child abuse and world hunger.

Everybody on tour knows about his big heart, even the caddies. After each of his eight tournament wins, he has staged a lavish dinner party for them. "Chi Chi makes us feel we really count," says veteran tour caddie Richard Holzer.

Rodriguez's benevolence has perhaps detracted from his golf game. For a man who once outdrove Jack Nicklaus by one hundred yards and is regarded by Ken Venturi as one of golf's finest shotmakers, there should be more than eight titles, and his career earnings should have soared beyond $1 million. But Rodriguez's mind was on other things.

"He'll never be as great a golfer as he is a human being," asserts pro Bill Kratzert. "Sometimes he worries more about what's happening in Asia than what's happening on the course. During practice he talks incessantly about poverty overseas."

At age forty-six in 1979, Rodriguez continued to play the PGA Tour nonstop while other pros his age were retiring. Although he hadn't won an event in three years, he zealously pursued a comeback. The reason: He planned to give his next winner's check to Mother Teresa for her leper colony in India.

Rodriguez came from a background riddled with the kind of despair he empathizes with today. He knows the feeling of a stomach aching with emptiness. Remembering is one of the things Chi Chi does best.

Rio Piedras is a poverty-scarred village just outside San Juan, Puerto Rico. Chickens and naked toddlers and skeletal dogs mingle around shacks alongside dirt roads where Chi Chi Rodriguez grew up.

One of six children, Chi Chi labored in the sugar-cane plantations with his father, from whom he learned sensitivity, goodness and hope. "My dad worked fourteen hours a day, every day of his life." Rodriguez recalls. "He would come home dead-tired and hungry, but if he saw a kid walk by with a big belly—the sign of malnutrition—

he'd give him his rice and beans. He did that so often I was concerned he wasn't getting enough to eat, but he always told me that God would supply him with strength."

Little time was available for recreation, but occasionally Chi Chi and his older brother would push each other down the highway in a cart. One day they crested a hill, rolled to the bottom—and discovered golf: "We saw this very green grass and men hitting tiny white balls with shiny steel sticks. I figured the guys who carried the bags for the players made money. It looked easier than being a waterboy at the plantation."

Rodriguez was only seven, but he marched across the stately fairways of Berwind Country Club and asked about a job lugging "those bags." The caddiemaster told him he was too small and suggested he start as a forecaddie, the person who marks the position of a player's ball and searches for errant golf balls. Chi Chi eagerly accepted.

Along the way he invented his own version of golf. For a club he attached a pipe to a guava limb, and for a ball he shaped a tin can into a sphere; then he dug a few holes to "play." Soon he could drive fifty to one hundred yards. All those swipes with guava limbs developed tremendous hand action, eventually making the 135-pound Rodriguez one of golf's longest hitters.

Caddies were prohibited from playing Berwind, but sometimes, just before nightfall, Chi Chi would sneak onto the turf with borrowed clubs and play eighteen holes in forty-five minutes. On occasion, he was trailed by an irate greenskeeper, who took potshots at him with a revolver. "I'd hit and run," Rodriguez remembers. (He is still one of pro golf's fastest players.) When he was only twelve, Chi Chi scored an astonishing 67 and knew golf was his future.

At the entrance of Berwind was an old Banyan tree that provided a perch for Rodriguez between shifts. There he watched the Cadillacs drive by and dreamed of the day he would be rich and waving to throngs of fans.

Rodriguez enlisted in the army at nineteen, making a name for himself in military golf tournaments during his two-year stint. After his discharge, he worked for a year as an aide at a psychiatric hospital in San Juan. He fed and bathed patients, played dominoes with them, calmed them when they became violent. The job was menial, paying eighty dollars a month, but Chi Chi calls it "the most rewarding work I've ever had. I was *giving*, and there's nothing more enjoyable than that."

He hadn't forgotten his dream, however, and he found the key to it in 1957, when the Dorado Beach Resort opened. Among its amenities was Puerto Rico's first pro-caliber golf course. Chi Chi headed there with a bundle of clippings about his army golf triumphs. Ed Dudley, the pro at the new course, was bringing a man from the states to assist him, but he grudgingly agreed that he and Chi Chi could play a game.

Rodriguez was so nervous that he shot an 89. "Mr. Dudley, I played awful today," he said, "but if you help me, I could become one of the best golfers in the world." Dudley looked off in the distance, then said, "Okay, you've got a job." And for the next three years Chi Chi worked for Dudley and Pete Cooper. Both men nurtured his potential, coaching him several hours a day.

When he was twenty-five, Rodriguez joined the Tour. From the start he made a comfortable income, and soon he was taking home trophies. He was a pacesetter when it came to injecting the bland pro-golf caravan with humor. "Americans are so hard-working," he explains, "and half of them don't enjoy their work. So I try to give them something to smile about when they come out to watch us."

As a successful golf pro, Rodriguez bought the big, shiny car he'd dreamed about in the Banyan tree, and a sprawling villa at Dorado Beach, too. But before he indulged in these trappings, he sent his brother through law school and bought homes for his mother and other family members. "This is the first house house we've had," says Iwalani, Chi Chi's Hawaiian-born wife. "Until three years ago, we lived out of suitcases. When he'd give away money to strangers, I'd think, 'We don't even have a place to call our own yet!'" Says Chi Chi, "When someone hurts, I hurt. It's tough being poor, and it's so easy to say, 'Well, I made it, so can everybody.' That just isn't true. Thousands of people don't have a chance."

Young people are more and more the focus of the golfer's generosity. The Chi Chi Rodriguez Youth Foundation, a nonprofit organization based in Clearwater, Florida, draws most of his charitable energies. Established to help troubled or abused youngsters, the foundation provides a program designed as a springboard into the free-enterprise system that also includes intensive academic tutoring and lots of golf instruction. They go on field trips to see how various businesses are run and to museums and sports events.

"Basically, these kids have been defeated all their lives," says Chi Chi. "So we're introducing them to challenges and positive competition, showing them that they can succeed."

During the 1979 J.C. Penney Golf Classic in Tampa, Florida, Rodriguez became interested in the project. Some youngsters from a juvenile detention center approached him for autographs. "The next thing I knew," recalls Bill Hayes, the counselor accompanying them, "Chi Chi was offering to come out and do a golf clinic. He arrived a few days later and hit balls over the prison walls. Afterward, he sat in the cells talking with the kids and ate dinner with them." That's when Hayes outlined to Rodriguez the plans for the Youth Foundation. Today 450 youngsters are enrolled.

Meanwhile, back home, Chi Chi's kind touch is felt by

the Children's Hospital of Puerto Rico, which his annual tournament—the Chi Chi Rodriguez International Festival of Golf—continues to benefit.

But it's not just the sweeping gestures Chi Chi is known for. "If someone is hurting," points out Bill Braddock, a longtime friend, "Chi Chi's going to try to help. It wouldn't surprise me at all if he gave up golf and started making house calls."

Jolee Edmondson

[EDITORS' NOTE: *Ranked fourth on the Senior Tour's all-time victory list, Chi Chi continues to devote his energies to his youth foundation, which currently serves over five hundred kids.*]

A Change of Heart

From somewhere in that sky, deliriously clogged with corks and hats and shirts and roar and glee came the best thing of all: a pair of dark, wraparound, screw-you sunglasses. That's how you knew that everything about American golf had changed.

What's weird was that up until Sunday it looked as if nothing had. The U.S. Ryder Cup team arrived in Boston with all the emotion of wilted arugula. No team spirit. No camaraderie. Just the same old story: twelve players, twelve Lears.

David Duval had called the Ryder Cup "another exhibition." Four players had wanted pay for play. At the opening ceremony, Tiger Woods chomped gum through "The Star-Spangled Banner" behind black sunglasses. The Americans got hate mail. They were heckled. Duval played part of a Thursday practice round by himself, prompting one fan to holler, "Hey, David, playing with all your friends?"

Well, just about. Coming in, Duval had about as many Tour pals as five-putts. Being shy, bookish and having dinner every night with the Marriott room-service guy doesn't help.

The European players, meanwhile, were breaking all of Bela Karolyi's hug records. They read each other's putts, kissed each other's wives, walked down fairways linked at the elbow.

But then an impossible, preposterous, wonderful thing began to happen. The twelve American CEOs in spikes started melting a little. They started acting like *people.* Better, they started becoming teammates. Maybe it was the team haircuts that registered 13 on the Stimpmeter. Maybe it was what Duval said when everybody was just about to leave a meeting on Thursday night. "You might have read I don't want to be here," he said through teary eyes. "I do. I am *passionate* about winning this." Maybe it was the way their captain, Ben Crenshaw, kept looking at them with those aching blue eyes and saying how much he admired them, even after they'd gone out and laid the worst opening-day egg for the United States in Ryder Cup history. Whatever it was, Crenshaw found a Super Glue.

Even though the United States was down 10–6 after two days, even though no team had ever come back from three points to win on the final day, forget four, the unheard-of notion of American togetherness started to spread like a sappy chain letter. In a Saturday night meeting, every player spoke and every player cried. "Every night I go to bed with a smile on my face," Woods said. "And every morning I wake up with a smile on my face, because I can't wait to come to the team room and be with my friends." His speech stunned and then touched his teammates.

Crazier still, the Americans went out the next morning and played as if they cared for each other. A guy would thump some outmatched Swede or a lost Frenchman and sprint off to find a teammate in trouble. Duval punched out Jesper Parnevik 5 and 4, then raced rabidly around the 14th green, pumping the crowd to ecstasy with his fists, exhorting the thousands lining the par-5 fairway to chant, "U! S! A!" Yes, *David Duval.*

Behind him, Justin Leonard trudged along the 10th fairway—three holes down to José María Olazábal, needing at least a tie for the United States to win the Cup—crying. Just then, teammate Davis Love III sidled up to him and said, "You can tell me to leave if you want, but I want you to know something: You can do this."

Leonard promptly lost 10 and after halving 11 was four down with seven holes to play. Still Love stayed with him. Suddenly, all heaven broke loose. Leonard started making a beanpot full of putts, winning four of the next five holes and then burying a forty-five-foot bomb at 17 that won the Cup and sent the Yanks into a fit of boorish, shameful and ridiculously emotional behavior. Wasn't it great?

"I've been around these guys for a long time," said Crenshaw's wife, Julie. "This week, they changed."

Apparently, when it suddenly hits you that one of the greatest thrills in golf doesn't necessarily come with an appearance fee, you lose yourself. When the national anthem was played at the closing ceremony, Woods chewed no gum, wore no sunglasses and put his hand over his heart. At one point in the post-putt pandemonium, family man Tom Lehman ripped off his shirt and flung it to the crowd. Fluff and Tiger, divorcees, embraced as if filming a Kodak ad.

High above them, from a champagne-soaked balcony overlooking thousands of joy-drunks, Duval, newly baptized, ripped off those hideous face-hiding sunglasses, reared back and heaved them into all those yesterdays.

Rick Reilly

Golf Nuts

Let's talk about golf nuts.

I'll start with the runny little sixty-eight-year-old combatant who always insists on playing from the gold tees.

He says you can't really see a golf course unless you play it from the tips.

He finds something terribly intriguing, as opposed to insane, about a seventy-two-hundred-yard golf course, particularly if it's infested with water, waste, sand, bulkheads, trees, moguls, deep rough, violent wind, severe pins and slick greens.

He would never improve a lie. He is greatly offended at the mere suggestion of a mulligan.

He loves playing a par-5 hole with driver, 3-wood, 5-wood, 7-wood, sand blast, pitch, chip, and four putts.

He is enthralled by a long, brutal par-4 hole that he can attack with driver, lateral, spoon, unplayable, 5-iron, boundary, 9-iron, cart path, pitch, and three putts.

He is fascinated with a killer par-3 hole that he can bring to its knees with driver, water, 5-wood, bulkhead, wedge, chip, and three putts.

One day he hopes to break 126.

"How did you play today, dear?" his wife asks.

"Great. I had a putt for a par and three chips at birdies."

Next, I give you the tireless gentleman who calls me every year or so to bring me up to date on the progress he's making in trying to play all of America's famous courses.

He has been at this for about twenty-five years, I guess.

In all of the phone calls over the past quarter of a century, he has asked me the same question.

Can I suggest anything that will help him get on Pine Valley, Augusta National, Merion, Seminole, Cypress Point, Oakmont, Los Angeles Country Club, Bel Air, Shinnecock Hills, Colonial, Winged Foot, Chicago Golf, Brook Hollow or Olympic?

I used to say, "Crawl over the fence and don't play the 1st hole or the 18th."

Now I say, "Steal a hundred million dollars from your company and put a hyphen in your name."

I give you this retired fellow I've stumbled upon who plays six times a week and makes all of his own clubs. They are rather crude-looking things, but he makes them in his workshop.

Although golf is obviously his life, he has been pleased to inform me that he has never attended a tournament, doesn't watch golf on television, doesn't read golf books, doesn't read golf magazines and doesn't even read the sports pages of the newspapers.

One day he asked what I did for a living. I said I was a writer.

"What do you mean?" he said, looking at me as if he had just heard of the most bizarre profession imaginable.

I said, "Well, among other things, I write articles for a golf magazine."

He looked at me for a long moment, and then he said, "Why?"

I excused myself hurriedly and went home and reported to my wife that I thought I had just met the mysterious sniper who fires at motorists from a freeway overpass.

Also in my neighborhood is this elderly man who only plays on weekends but spends the rest of the time hunting golf balls.

He's always out there during the week, creeping through the trees or poking around at the edge of lagoons.

It is rumored that he has over ten thousand golf balls in his garage, where he keeps them neatly arranged on shelves.

More than one person has told me I must visit this man's garage—his collection of golf balls is astounding.

"It's on my list," I say nicely.

As amazing as anyone I've heard about lately is the dentist. He is said to be a lifelong fan of Arnold Palmer. He is said to be such a fan of Arnold's, it borders on mental illness.

I don't know if it's true—I can only hope—but the dentist is purported to carry in his pocket a ball marker made from the gold that was extracted from Arnold's teeth.

This might not make him the biggest Arnold Palmer fan in the world, however.

There was a journalist in Great Britain whose unbounding hero worship of Palmer became a legend. He was never satisfied, one hears, with autographs, scrapbooks, photos, paintings or articles about Arnold.

One day he got the inspired idea to begin collecting the divots Palmer would take out of fairways in England and Scotland. Eventually, the entire lawn of his home near London was made out of Arnold Palmer divots.

Actually, if I were to follow through on a thought I had the other day, I think I could be exempt on the Golf Nut Tour myself.

You see, I have this habit of knocking balls into the woods when they betray me. I might add that it doesn't take much for me to feel betrayed. A four-foot putt that curls out, a pulled 7-wood that winds up in a bunker, a chip shot that races across the green and into the frog hair, a tee shot that defies its stern warning and seeks out the forest.

I've been leaving these balls in the woods, but I've come up with a better idea. A small cemetery in my yard. It could be fenced in by a variety of broken shafts. Call me the Mortician.

In this cemetery I will bury all of the golf balls that betray me, because if they can betray me once, they will certainly betray me again. Planted into the earth, however, they will have nothing to do but rot in eternal hell forever.

Never again will they be able to bring unwarranted grief and anguish to some innocent golfer, like myself, who never meant them any harm whatsoever.

It's what they deserve, I say. All I've ever asked of them is a simple string of bogeys.

Dan Jenkins

Drive and Determination

The more I practice, the luckier I get.

Gary Player

I have to admit that I have never played golf. In fact, the only golf course that I have ever been on ended with me trying to hit the ball into a clown's mouth. That's why it is so strange that the game of golf had such an impact on my life.

I was nineteen years old and had just started dating a young man that I had met at work. We seemed to have a chemistry together and both shared a love of competition. A lot of our time with each other was spent bowling or playing arcade games like pinball or Pac Man. Being a '70s kind of girl, I was determined to prove my capabilities and be an equal and worthy opponent. As it turned out, our skills were fairly evenly matched. We were both thoroughly enjoying our playful competitions.

One day, he came to my house dressed casually as always. Searching for something different to do he asked, "Have you ever been to a driving range?" I thought, *My God! A driving range? What does he want to do now, race cars?* He explained that he was talking about driving golf balls, not cars. Well, I had never tried it before, but surely it must be simple. After all, if I can hurl a fourteen-pound ball fifty feet down a lane and knock down ten sticklike pins at the far end, how difficult could it be to swing a club and hit a tiny ball perched right at my feet? I was confident that this little activity would not damage my athletic image, so off we went to the driving range.

We arrived at Bill's Golfland & Family Fun Park—a virtual megaplex of batting cages, arcades, go carts, mini-golf and, of course, our chosen destination, the driving range. After selecting our clubs, buying our balls and several embarrassing moments of scrambling to gather the bouncing balls that I spilled out of the top of the bucket, we were ready to start.

After brief instructions from my date, I then set out to prove my abilities. The first five or ten swings I took were either total misses or full-force collisions between my club and the rubber mat on the tee. I received more instruction from my teacher.

"Keep your eye on the ball."

"Bring the club back slowly."

Okay, there were a few more useless attempts and then . . . CONTACT! The ball took air and landed just shy of the fifty-yard marker, but it was a start! Over the next hour or so, it didn't get much better than that. Balls trickled off of their mount and rolled into the grass in front of my station. Several fell off of their tee, in a delayed reaction, caused by the wind from my swing passing its target. I admit it was pathetic, definitely not the piece of cake that I had imagined.

Each time that I turned to pick up a new ball from my bucket, I would catch the sight of onlookers (a crowd was beginning to gather) wearing Titleist caps and Spalding sun visors. There were heads shaking and eyes rolling.

Occasionally, I would hear a comment like, "Your feet are too far apart," or, "Bend your knees." I felt the pressure mounting. An audience formed behind me. To each side of me, a row of fellow golfers quested after swing perfection. In front of me, golf balls were flying through the air and landing at the 200-, 250- and even the 300-yard markers. At my feet the tiny white ball, which I thought would pose no challenge whatsoever, had grown fangs and horns. The sphere was sneering up at me, as if to say, "I showed you."

Snap out of it! I thought. *You have a brain; IT does not.* After all, the ball is just a lifeless piece of rubber that I command where to go. I felt a rush of determination come over me. I took a deep breath and repeated all of the directions to myself.

"Feet shoulder-width apart."

"Knees slightly bent."

"Bring the club back slowly."

"Keep your eye on the ball."

"Smooth and steady swing."

"Finish with your hands towards the target."

With an air of confidence, I approached the ball. I carefully acted out each mental step-by-step instruction. Before I knew it, I found myself following through with my swing with absolute perfection. My concentration was broken by the sound of *whack.* I raised my head to see the ball soaring through the air. I actually lost it in the sun's glare for a while, before it fell to earth somewhere around the 300-yard marker!

"Yes!" It was perfect! I jumped. I screamed. I rejoiced at my success.

I arrogantly turned to my date, "Did you see that? I knew I could do it!"

The laughter of my companion quickly dampened my celebration. He pointed to my tee, where my ball was still perched, tauntingly sticking its tongue out at me. The incredible 300-yard drive that I was claiming credit for actually belonged to the golfer on my left (who, by the way, was also laughing). The audience that had gathered began to chuckle, as did the range attendant. After taking several bows and curtsies, I quietly and humbly returned to my futile attempts at hitting a golf ball.

Needless to say, I never made it to the LPGA. The man who was my date that day became my husband and the father of my children. My determination, his patience and an ability to laugh at life, the very characteristics that we showed each other that day during the driving range episode, are qualities that have been the basis for a long, happy, strong and successful marriage. We occasionally return to the driving range with our two teenage sons. But now, when we go, it's not to prove anything or to compete with each other. It's strictly for the fun of it.

Darlene Daniels Eisenhuth

The Boys of Summer

On the last afternoon of the last major of the century, the players meet at the golf club at three. One drives up in his Volvo, two are dropped off by a mom on her way to the grocery store, the fourth rides his bike to the course. Quickly, it's decided that Mike and the Old Guy will play Rob and Ritchie in a four-ball match.

A tee is tossed in the air. Ritchie and Rob are up first. Ritchie is sixteen, a rising junior player with blond peach fuzz on his chin. He works part-time at Burger King but is thinking about quitting because it will interfere with his golf team practice, which begins tomorrow. He sets up and casually slugs a drive about 230 yards out to the first cut of rough. The Old Guy congratulates him and he grins, almost sheepishly, and says, "That's nothing. Wait till you see Rob and Mike."

Rob, fifteen, wears baggy gray cargo pants, unlaced Foot-Joys and braces on his teeth. His hero is Davis Love III. His stance seems unusually wide, but it must get results because in twenty-five state golf association junior tournaments, he's won six times and this year has finished no less than second or third in every event in which he's played. Last year, a three-putt cost Rob the state junior title.

Rob slams a beautiful drive 270 yards to the heart of the fairway.

"Whoa," thinks the Old Guy, idly massaging an elbow that's sore from planting crab-trees that morning. "These guys are good."

Mike is up next. He is almost two years younger and fifty pounds lighter, but he's Rob's best golf buddy. They met three years ago qualifying for the club junior championship and have been nearly inseparable ever since. You see them constantly talking game, shooting the breeze and making birdies.

Neither has a girlfriend but they do have golf, and for probably the last splendid summer of their lives neither even works a part-time job—though Mike allows that he mows a few lawns and umpires Little League games now and then to pick up movie money. His favorite all-time flick is *Shawshank Redemption,* and he seems a bit disappointed when you admit you haven't seen it.

Mike takes dead aim with his strong grip and beat-up War Bird driver. His battered Foot-Joy shoes look ancient—they turn out to be only four months old. His artfully faded Nike shirt is buttoned neatly to the top, David Duval style, and his khakis seem to hang on his slight frame the way clothes cling to a wire coat-hanger. In a driving rainstorm he might weigh ninety-eight pounds wringing wet. "Hey," he protests when you innocently mention this fact, "I'm exactly one hundred—a triple-digit guy." Mike is a freshman who will start his high school playing career tomorrow following in the footsteps of his older brother Pat, a rising senior. According to Rob, Mike is pound for pound probably the longest driver in the entire club. He also has an ace and several eagles on his resume. He coolly tees up and hurls all three digits into a shot that send his Maxfli SX Tour arching toward his best friend's ball, prompting Rob to turn and glare at him. "You better not outdrive me," he warns Mike, finally displaying some impressive mouth hardware that shows he's pleased.

The Old Guy hits his ball respectably and breathes a sigh of relief, watching the Boys of Summer shoulder their bags and bolt down the fairway. Mike and Rob walk together, bags slung low, talking sand wedges and Smashing Pumpkins, like young guns late for the shoot-out. The Old Guy almost has to lope in order to keep up with them and for a moment tries to remember what it feels like to be that young and that limber and so deeply drawn to chasing a game with your best friend.

Among American boys, golf is booming. According to the USGA, a record 4,508 competitors showed up at sixty-one sectional qualifying sites for this year's U.S. Junior Amateur Championship at York, Pennsylvania, which was won in August by seventeen-year-old Hunter Mahan of McKinney, Texas. For the seventh year in a row, the field of entries grew substantially—this year by a whopping 12 percent, a surge many attribute directly to the influence of Tiger Woods. Golf is not about greatness; it's about goodness—good shots, good friends, good times.

However, Tiger is popular with these particular northern Boys of Summer. "No question, the way he holds a lead, he'll win the PGA," Mike sagely asserts three hours before the verdict of the PGA Championship is formally recorded. "But you gotta like that Weir guy, the Canadian. He's a ballstriker. Solid . . ." So are Love and Justin Leonard and half a dozen others who, at this moment, seem as remote as rock stars.

To quote Mike, who whistles softly when he walks and cleans his grooves with the exactitude of a gum surgeon as he waits to hit, "Fame is kinda cool." But fathers and friendship probably have more to do with why Rob and Mike and Ritchie are so hopelessly smitten with the game and never seem to go home from the club except to take meals and sleep a bit.

Rob toddled onto his father Jim's homemade putting green at age four, and by ten he was being dropped off at a local nine-holer where he could play all he wanted till dark for a few bucks. Then a cousin gave him eleven hours of videotapes that included the swings of golf's greatest players, and he took a few free lessons from a pro at a driving range. That was sufficient to kill his basketball dreams.

A year later; he entered his first state junior event, shot 103 and realized he'd have to practice much more if he wanted to compete. This summer, he fell only a couple strokes shy of qualifying for the National Juniors at Essex County Club near Boston. He has three more years of eligibility and no shortage of golf dreams—hopes of a collegiate career "somewhere down south" and maybe the PGA Tour.

Mike's tale is different only in shades of ambition. Both his father and grandfather caddied and played the game, so it seemed only logical for him to at least "give golf a shot." He was a promising team player in soccer and basketball until his dad, a golf-loving forester named Kevin, began taking him to a local par-3 course.

Quickly, reading books and watching players on television, Mike essentially taught himself to play and graduated to the muni and finally the golf club. Now he has a deft putting touch that would impress Dave Pelz and talks of eventually studying medicine and "finding some kind of job—I don't care what—in the golf world."

He displays his surgical touch chipping in for birdie at a critical moment in the match on two consecutive holes, slicing Rob's and Ritchie's lead over him and the Old Guy to one with two to play. "He always does this," says Ritchie, rolling his eyes and then explaining that he followed Mike into golf primarily because they were school pals and promptly got hooked himself.

On the 17th hole, amused by the engaging teen banter about the Frenchman's Folly and the upcoming Ryder Cup selections, the Old Guy finally contributes a birdie putt to the cause and the match is suddenly all square with one to play. The players fall silent, adjusting grips and grinding thoughts. Faraway Medinah, at this moment, holds no more magic than this tiny scene of high drama played out on an almost empty northern golf course where autumn seems imminent. Mike's tee ball catches the hazard and the Old Guy scrambles for par but it isn't good enough—both Rob and Ritchie close with birdies to win.

They shake hands and the Old Guy thanks them for allowing him to tag along, noticing as he does that the northern thistle is in bloom and the goldenrod is almost over—a sure sign, as locals say, that first frost is just six weeks away.

For the record, the Boys of Summer have real last names—*Rob McDonough, Mike Doran* and *Ritchie Thibeault.* You may hear a lot about them someday. Or nary a peep again. In a way, it doesn't matter. These guys are eternal, with their homemade swings and small-town dreams. The reason the game keeps going.

After a five-minute pause for Rob to phone home, the Boys decide to go another loop before darkness catches them. They shoulder their bags, wave politely, speed off on Softspikes worn to nubs. Six weeks till first frost, thinks the Old Guy, rubbing his sore elbow and shaking his head as he heads for the Volvo.

Summer ends far too soon. Not to mention youth.

James Dodson

A Hole in "How Many"?

I try to use a method I call the positive-negative approach. I positively identify the negatives and work from there.

Bob Murphy

Two golfers were on the green of the 3rd hole at Bethpage Golf Course, when all of a sudden a golf ball came from nowhere and rolled right up to the cup. One of the golfers said, "Let's put the ball in the cup and give the guy a hole-in-one."

All of a sudden a golfer came out of the woods and said, "Did any of you see a golf ball around here?"

One of the golfers on the green said, "Yes, it landed right in the cup."

"Good," said the man who hit the "hole-in-one," "that gives me a 13 for this hole."

Steven Schockett

3

SPECIAL MOMENTS

All the Good Things
Any Man Should Be

*Golf puts a man's character on the anvil and his
richest qualities—patience, poise and restraint—
to the flame.*

Billy Casper

I have to tell you honestly that I never believed Squeek
wouldn't be back carrying my bag. Not for one minute.
Not until the very end, when he was so sick he couldn't
even open his eyes to say good-bye. It's selfish, I guess,
but that's what it's like when you lose a friend.

He was diligent and conscientious and humble and
simple and honest and all the good things any man
should be.

I remember often I would invite him in to share our
success, to set the clubs down for a minute and drink a
victory beer in the locker room. "Don't worry, Squeek,
come on in," I'd tell him when he hesitated. "If there's a
fine, I'll pay it."

We shared dinner often, but there were other times I
would offer and he would decline politely, saying he had

other plans. But I knew he really didn't. It was just his way of stepping back, never trying to take too much.

On the road, I think he was more content to baby-sit my kids and order a pizza. He loved to sit and play with them, and I know they loved him, too. They don't understand why he's gone now, anymore than I do.

For him, the rewards were more private. It was enough for him to get the flag from the eighteenth hole after a win and tack it up on his wall at home.

Doing the job well, doing it thoroughly, that was paramount for Squeek. In our six years together, I think I questioned a yardage only once. Once. That's unheard of.

He was no expert on the golf swing, but he learned what to look for in my swing. "Watch that right elbow," he would say when I was getting frustrated on the practice range.

In tournament play, he always had a knack for knowing the right thing to say, even when that meant saying nothing at all. And he understood the nuances of competition as well as anyone I'd ever met. He would always check the leader boards, and he could see a player struggling long before I would.

"He's feeling the pressure, Nick," he'd say as we headed down the last few holes, convincing me that a tournament still could be won.

He'd never let me get negative. At Turnberry in 1994, I had two terrible days of practice, but he never lost confidence in me. When I said, "Aww, I'm not swinging so well," immediately he pulled me up on it. "How can you expect me to be positive when you start talking like that?" he would demand.

When I asked Squeek at the end of 1990 to come work for me, he said Tom Watson had just asked him the same thing. A few days later, he came to me and said I was his choice. I sometimes wonder how different things might have been for me had that decision gone the other way.

We had one hell of a time together, I know that. I might have won without him, but it wouldn't have been nearly as often or nearly as fun.

The moment that stands out most for me was winning the Open at Turnberry. Squeek cheered me on through all the doubts of that final round. When I had to hit that last shot to clinch it, Squeek was never more positive, giving me the exact yardage and telling me to split the "D" in the big yellow sign behind the eighteenth green. When I had hit the shot and started up toward the green, the walk of a champion with the great crowd cheering, Squeek lingered behind humbly, typically, not wanting to intrude. I stopped for a moment and looked back at him.

"C'mon, Squeek," I said. "Let's enjoy this together. I don't know when we'll get the opportunity again."

If I never win again, I will always have the memory of that walk, shared with a friend.

Nick Price
with Mike Stachura

Ike, Mamie, Spiro and Me

I've never been to heaven and, thinkin' back on my life, I probably won't get a chance to go. I guess the Masters is as close as I'm going to get.

Fuzzy Zoeller

As every player knows, each round of golf is subject to small miracles, moments when probability upends itself in glorious fashion and a thing occurs that shouldn't, according to the odds.

I've had my share of golf miracles, certainly—some good and some bad. I once had a hole-in-one on an unfamiliar course, wearing cowboy boots and playing with borrowed clubs and a range ball. I once came within inches of a double eagle on a shot that hit a concrete drainage pipe in a water hazard. On at least three occasions I have putted out-of-bounds, and twice I've putted into water hazards. Once I even lost a ball on a putt— which I still take to be a true milestone of statistical improbability.

But all these things pale before the astronomical odds of my most unlikely golf experience, one that had nothing to do with the rub of the green or the skill of any shot. When I was nineteen years old, I was the beneficiary of a happy chain of events involving tree surgery, the Civil War and the U.S. Secret Service, all of which culminated, weirdly enough, in my playing two rounds at the Augusta National Golf Club during the week of the 1971 Masters.

It started in the spring of my junior year of high school, when I was able to parlay my considerable employment experience in odd jobs into a better, more responsible position: I became the tree trimmer for the double-decker-bus tours in Gettysburg, Pennsylvania, that bastion of Civil War tourism. My role was to ride the upper deck on the fifteen-mile route and cut back any branches that might poke a tourist in the eye.

A few weeks later, something even better opened up: The Secret Service had been authorized to hire a yard boy/gardener to mow the grass and tend the flower beds on the Eisenhower farm—as well as to care for the General's backyard putting green.

General Dwight D. Eisenhower had retired to Gettysburg after his presidency, partly because of its distinction as a shrine of military history, but partly for sentimental reasons—he had been stationed there at Camp Colt early in his career.

On those days when you ended up standing around with him in the golf shop or chatting on the first tee, he was always a genial, accessible guy who loved to talk golf with golfers. Two of his Secret Service agents, in fact, were picked specifically because they shared his love of the game.

Well, it seemed to me that my bus-tour duties could pass for gardening experience, and I sure knew what a putting green was supposed to look like. I figured I was a natural for the job. So I talked to the Secret Service agents about it, and Herb Dixon, the Special Agent in Charge, hired me immediately. He was clearly impressed by my background in high-level plant defoliation.

Okay, it might have helped a little that my father was one of the agents on the Eisenhower detail and was the General's primary golf partner. But in any case, I got the job. The pay was two dollars an hour. I was in heaven.

Every day there would be stretches of free time, and that's when I would get out my golf clubs and practice chip shots to the putting green. The Eisenhowers didn't seem to mind. On the hotter afternoons, they would even send out lemonade.

The General passed away early one spring, and I stayed on as the yard boy to the end of the summer. September brought new priorities, and I had to quit the farm to focus on my schoolwork. Journalism was my main academic interest, though in the end academics played no role at all in my choice of college. I applied to Wake Forest University because it was the most prominent golf school I knew.

I soon found there was no shortage of golfers around campus. You couldn't throw a 9-iron without beaning some scratch handicapper. Lanny Wadkins was there, and Jim Simons, and later Jay Haas, Scott Hoch, Curtis Strange and a dozen others who could play the game like no kids I had ever seen before. Any one of them seemed to stand an infinitely better chance of being invited to play at Augusta than I did.

However.

I got the call from my father on the weekend before the Masters. Even though the General was gone, Mrs. Eisenhower still maintained their yearly schedule. Springtime always included a stay at the Augusta National Golf Club, in a house near the eighteenth green.

Mrs. Eisenhower didn't have any interest in the game, but she remembered that I did—probably from all the divots I had left in her yard. It had occurred to her, my father reported, that maybe I would like to visit for a few days before the tournament. She had noticed that the course was almost always deserted, so she saw no reason why I couldn't just stop in and play a few rounds. She said I could bunk with the Secret Service agents in her basement.

There were other factors for me to consider, of course. The timing couldn't have been worse. It was midterm, and I had tests to take and research papers to type. I had no choice but to decline the invitation.

Yeah, right.

Ten minutes after I hung up the phone I was in my car heading south. I drove straight through to Augusta.

I arrived on Sunday afternoon and was ushered through the front gate by a guard who found my name on a list. The parking area near the clubhouse had only a scattering of cars, but they were all shiny Jaguars, Mercedes and BMWs—plus a few others so exotic I didn't even know their names. The only Bentley I've ever seen was in that lot, and the only Aston-Martin, outside a James Bond movie. Mine was the only Ford Maverick.

After checking in with my father and Mrs. Eisenhower, I asked about the possibility of rushing out for a round before dark. Here was a setback: Hadn't I noticed it was pouring rain? The course was closed for the afternoon.

But rain or no rain, I knew there must be a practice area somewhere, so I shouldered my clubs and my shag bag and went out to find it.

Only one other golfer was practice-hungry enough to be out that day—a big, sturdy fellow virtually cocooned in rain gear—and I joined him in one of the bunkers. For twenty minutes we alternated shots to the pin, blasting ball after ball until our side of the practice green was white with trails of wet sand.

He finished before I did, but as a matter of etiquette I stopped hitting shots and walked onto the green to help separate the balls. That turned out to be an easy enough chore: most of his were right by the pin.

"You're pretty good with that sand wedge," I told him.

He looked up and smiled.

"Thanks," he said.

It was Jack Nicklaus.

I tried, of course, to remain cool, but it was useless. There was no way I could go on casually hitting practice balls with him, not without risking total golf humiliation.

So I opted for a simpler form of humiliation, pestering him with awestruck idle chatter until at last I drove him from the practice green. Yes, I alone succeeded where thunder and lightning had failed.

I slept fitfully that night, but when morning came I was up with the sun—and the sun, thank God, was indeed up. That morning there were only two groups scheduled to go off: former U.S. Amateur champion Steve Melnyk had a 10 o'clock tee time; I was to follow at 10:15 with my father and another Secret Service agent.

But at 9:45, I experienced one of the most bizarre episodes of my life.

Just as I was walking out the rear basement door, one of the younger agents—a nongolfer—stopped me with the news that Mrs. Eisenhower wanted to see me upstairs. My timetable was suddenly in jeopardy. Still, what choice did I have? I stepped out of my golf shoes and walked up the basement steps into the living room, where a window overlooked the eighteenth green and, beyond that, the first tee.

Mrs. Eisenhower was standing by the window in a big, flowery dress. A man in a suit stood next to her, gazing at the lush, empty course. I hesitated in the doorway, but she saw me at once and called out, "Come in, come in.

There's someone here you have to meet."

The man in the business suit turned from the window smiling, and shook my hand in a very solid, professional way.

"This is Mr. Agnew, dear," she said. "He's the vice president."

I don't remember much of the conversation that followed. I do recall apologizing for not wearing any shoes. I also recall that he talked about the country's need for more young Republicans like me. That struck me as odd, since I wasn't a Republican. I mean, I wasn't anything. I was just a golfer.

I do know he had a lot to say about the grave state of American youth and how we could fix it—hard work was part of it, I think he said, and respect for one's elders, fewer Beatles songs, a less liberal press—but most of the details were lost on me because the longer he talked, the more I wondered why he didn't have anything to say about golf. Didn't he know where he was?

Then came the moment when I failed my generation.

"What's your view on all this?" Mr. Agnew finally asked.

If only I could have told him some inspiring story, maybe offered some brilliant insight into the American psyche that would have set him thinking along some bright new path. At the very least I could have suggested he might want to glance through the Constitution one more time before launching any new projects. After all, Watergate was more than a year away, there was still time to head off disaster; no one yet needed to go to jail or resign in disgrace. But at that very moment, through that glaring picture window my only view was of Steve Melnyk hooking his drive into trees on the left side of the first fairway.

"I'm really sorry, Mr. Vice President," I said, "but I'm next on the tee." By the time Melnyk had found his ball and hit his approach shot, I was back in my golf shoes, shaking hands with George, my caddie.

Caddies were required at Augusta, and they wore uniforms slung with various belts and pouches containing grass seed, fertilizer and soil. You don't replace your divots at Augusta; instead, your caddie re-landscapes after each shot. This was intimidating—I kept topping the ball so George wouldn't have to clean up after me. George talked me through that crisis, and countless others. He didn't keep me out of trouble—no one could have done that—but in eighteen holes he never mis-clubbed me. If everybody in the workforce were as skilled and conscientious on the job as the Augusta caddies, there would be a worldwide Golden Age.

Of course, I was skeptical at first. After I hit my drive on the first hole, George handed me a 6-iron before I had left the tee box.

"How do you know I'll need a 6-iron?" I asked him.

He shrugged as he slid my driver back into the bag. "Tell from your swing," he said matter-of-factly.

"But you've only seen me hit one shot," I pointed out.

He shrugged again and started down the fairway. I followed him to my ball and saw that he was right: A 6-iron was indeed the club.

I was impressed enough to start asking questions—not about my shots, but about George. I couldn't help but be nosy. Here was a true insider.

George had been at Augusta for fifteen years, he told me, and had caddied in fourteen Masters.

"Who's the best golfer you've ever caddied for?" I asked, hoping to get a few juicy stories.

"Best is hard," he said. "Best comes and goes. Right now the man I put my money on is Mr. Charles Coody."

Charles Coody? This was a pretty disappointing answer. Charles Coody was essentially a rank-and-file pro.

"Mr. Coody was my man last year," George went on.
"We were right in it, too. Could have won it if he'd done a
couple more things I told him to." George shook his head
and smiled. "But this year—you just watch. Me and Mr.
Coody. That's the team."

I decided not to argue, though it would have been easy
enough to rattle off a long list of more likely candidates for
that year's green coat. Instead, I asked George what he
could predict for a player like me on this course.

"Low 90s," he said without hesitation. "That's the best I
can do."

"But I'm a 2-handicapper," I protested.

George nodded his head as if he had already figured
that into the equation.

"I'm bound to break 90," I insisted.

"Next round, maybe," he said. "Not today. Not off
championship tees. Couple good holes, though. Maybe a
couple birdies."

Much of that round, I regret to say, has faded from
memory. But certain moments remain. The greens were
fast as linoleum, and I shook over every putt. On the 205-
yard fourth hole, I hit the green in regulation, then took a
triple bogey with a five-putt. On other holes, I found
pathways to destruction: I hit into the creek on the
twelfth and lost two balls in the azaleas on the thirteenth.
But I came back with birdies on the fifteenth and sixteenth, which, even without TV cameras, was the
pinnacle of my golf life.

I shot a 92.

The next day I had another crack at it, and managed an
88.

High scores notwithstanding, this was an idyllic stretch
of days. I hung around the clubhouse with Phil Walil, the
club manager. I walked Augusta's Par-3 Course, favored
by General Eisenhower. I met the stern-faced Cliff Roberts,

a cofounder of the Augusta National with Bobby Jones, and of whom everyone was afraid. ("Don't annoy this guy," my father warned me. "He'd kick us all out in a heartbeat.")

Then, as suddenly as it had begun, it ended: just one sunny day before the opening round of that year's Masters, I had to pack up and leave. Mrs. Eisenhower, as I said, had no particular interest in golf. For her the tournament was an inconvenient interruption in her routine, a time when her lawn would be overrun by tourists, golfers and television crews. So she had the Secret Service load up, and they all set out for Palm Springs.

I had no choice but to buy a couple of souvenirs and hit the road myself. Everything about the experience had been wonderful. Standing by my car, looking one last time at that stately clubhouse, I was keenly aware I would never play there again, not if I lived to be two hundred.

And for a quarter of a century, that prediction has held true. But oddly enough, I'm not as pessimistic about my chances for a comeback. Something happened that Masters weekend that made me realize just about anything could come true. This revelation came to me while I was sitting alone in my dorm room watching the final-round coverage on a twelve-inch black-and-white television set. The golf world was shocked that year—I was, too—by one more Augusta miracle: A middling pro playing the rounds of his life had somehow walked off with the title.

The Masters' champion that year, some of us will recall, was Mr. Charles Coody.

Clint McCown

The Day I Met the King

I'll always remember how I first met him. It was in my rookie year of 1977. Coincidentally, it occurred at a tournament that has become very special to me through the years, the Bing Crosby Pro-Am. We had the Monday qualifying system back then, and I had missed the first two qualifiers at Phoenix and Tucson. I had finally made it into my first official PGA Tour event at the Crosby and was out playing a practice round at Monterey Peninsula Country Club, one of the courses used in the rotation at the time.

It was late Tuesday afternoon before the tournament, and I had played the front nine and was somewhere on the back side when I noticed a large cloud of dust billowing up in the distance. It was like in the old cowboy movies when there's a cattle drive or the posse's ridin' up on the bad guys, and I knew something important was happening. But I went about my business and, sensing I didn't have time to finish all eighteen holes, I cut over to the sixteenth tee.

As this was my first time on the course, I really didn't know the layout of the holes. I just knew I had about half an hour of sunlight left. So I hit a couple drives off the sixteenth, when all of a sudden, out of nowhere, an incredible throng of spectators emerged over the rise behind me and surrounded the back of the tee.

It was like when the entire Bolivian army encircled Butch Cassidy and the Sundance Kid and aimed their rifles at them. These people weren't armed and dangerous, but they were sure looking at me with expressions that said:

Who is this kid, and what's he doing out here?

And then the Red Sea parted, and who should walk through it but Arnold Palmer himself, The King. He couldn't have been more regal had he been wearing a robe and carrying a staff.

I felt a chill come over me. I was shocked and embarrassed. I mean, here was my boyhood idol, and I'd just cut right in front of him, and hit two balls no less. I wanted to crawl into the ball-washer and disappear. But true to his character, Palmer walked up to me, shook my hand, introduced himself and said, "How are you?"

I managed to squeak out a "fine," although I wasn't. And he said, "Could we join you?"

Now that was the first thing he ever said to me, and it struck me so funny because I was thinking, "Can *you* join *me*?" What I wanted to say was, "Can I have your permission to crawl under a rock and stay there for a day as penance for getting in your way?"

But, of course, I acted cool, considered his request for a long second, and said, "Sure, love to have you," like it was no big deal.

This was gut-check time, even if there was no money on the line, because in addition to meeting my idol for the first time, I also met Mark McCormack, who was Palmer's amateur partner. McCormack was head of IMG, with whom I had signed just a few weeks before, but I wasn't sure he even knew who I was.

Nevertheless, I was determined not to let the situation intimidate me, or worry about embarrassing myself. I've always loved the challenge of golf, whatever it may be, so I looked on this as just another challenge, and a darned good preparation for the coming week. After all, this was just a practice round, so I couldn't worry about future endorsements, or impressing these guys. My goal at that point in my career was simple survival. All I wanted to do was make some cuts, make some money and keep my playing privileges. I was recently married and I wanted to be able to make it to that Christmas and have enough money to buy my wife a nice present.

But back to the sixteenth hole. Arnold hit a nice drive, and I remember feeling good that both of my drives were past his. If I felt a moment of cockiness, however, it quickly evaporated when I snap-hooked a 7-iron into the bunker. Fortunately, I got it up and down, and that eased my nerves. On the next tee, Arnold asked me what kind of ball I was playing, and I told him it was a Titleist.

He said, "You ought to try one of these good balls," and tossed me a Palmer ball. I hit it and liked it, so he tossed me a three-pack and said, "As a rookie starting out, you need good equipment, and these might help you along the way." He was sincerely trying to be helpful, because it wasn't as if he needed the endorsement of an unknown kid from Oregon playing his golf balls.

As abruptly as the experience of playing golf with Arnold Palmer had begun, so it ended. After holing out at 18, Palmer thanked me, wished me luck in my career and disappeared into the madding crowd. When I looked up a few seconds after shaking his hand, everyone was gone. I mean everyone. There was no more Arnie's Army, only Peter's Poltergeists. I had to shake my head to make certain it had really happened.

Peter Jacobsen
with Jack Sheehan

The Price of Success

Success came late for golf pro Harvey Penick. His first golf book, *Harvey Penick's Little Red Book*, has sold more than a million copies, which makes it one of the biggest things in the history of sports books. His second book, *And If You Play Golf, You're My Friend*, has already sold nearly three-quarters of a million copies. But anyone who imagines that Penick wrote the books to make money didn't know the man.

In the 1920s Penick bought a red spiral notebook and began jotting down observations about golf. He never showed the book to anyone except his son until 1991, when he shared it with a local writer, Bud Shrake, and asked if he thought it was worth publishing. Shrake read it and told him yes. He left word with Penick's wife the next evening that Simon & Schuster had agreed to an advance of ninety thousand dollars.

When Shrake saw Penick later, the old man seemed troubled. Finally Penick came clean. With all his medical bills, he said, there was just no way he could advance Simon & Schuster that much money. The writer had to explain that Penick would be the one to receive the ninety thousand dollars.

Terry Todd

My Best Friend

The agony of the final round set in off the first tee. It wasn't Sunday. There was no tournament. It was just me and Matt, my golf partner of three years, not to mention my best friend since the third grade.

We had entered the world of golf as two youngsters with cheap clubs, inspired by our fathers' stories of birdies, three-hundred-yard drives, and near-holes-in-one. For some reason these tales failed to hold true when we played with them.

Expecting to go out and conquer the game, Matt and I were quite surprised (not to mention angry) when we found ourselves humbled by a little white ball. Over time though, our swings became more controlled, good shots became more frequent, scores lower and our friendship stronger.

That summer, we entered a junior golf tour. We soon realized how much we had to learn, and how much we wanted to win. We had been in the game for two years already, and we figured all we needed was some fine-tuning to give our game the extra edge.

We played almost every day after school that year with the hope that the hard work would pay off with victory on the tour next summer. Then we got the news.

"Andrew, my dad's being transferred to Charlotte right after school," Matt said when he broke the news to me. He was moving away following our freshman year and right before the golf season would start. We had only a month left together, so we decided to make the most of it. Golf was the only way we knew how to enjoy ourselves without facing the sorrow of separation. No matter what is going on, golf helps you forget by making you concentrate on the task at hand—beating the guy you're playing with—and that was good enough for us.

We played and the time flew, and soon we found ourselves in what we realized was our final round together. We had tried to ignore it for so long, but now it hung over us. The only way to shake it was to continue the eighteen.

When all was said and done, we finished the game. Our scores were average. He beat me by three strokes.

Matt had to be home so he could wake up early in the morning and head out. We stood at the practice green waiting for his mother to come get him. Finally, she arrived.

"It was a pleasure playing with you." I held out my hand. He shook, and then I half-hugged him, like boys do when they want to be men. I saw him off the next morning.

He played on a tour at his new home, and I competed also. One day, I received a letter in the mail. It was a scorecard and a picture of the leader board. Matt was atop it. He finally won.

Over the years, I received many scorecards from Matt (unfortunately more than I sent him). I keep them in my golf bag for good luck.

I guess the magic of golf isn't the course, or the swing, or the sound you hear when you hit a solid 3-iron. It's the feeling you get when you beat your best friend, or lose to him, for that matter.

And sooner or later you realize that you didn't play every week because you were golfers, you played because you were friends.

Andrew Galanopulos

Butterscotch

It isn't the big pleasures that count the most; it's making a great deal out of the little ones.

Jean Webster

My father did not start playing golf until he was in his sixties. He used to practice putting balls into plastic cups and coffee mugs on the rug in his family room while watching the Sunday tournaments on television. He used to boast about how he had sunk fifteen of these putts in a row. I used to watch him perform these putting exercises and watched his concentrated eye focusing on the mug at the end of the room, taking two or three practice strokes, and then following through with mechanical precision, making only minor adjustments to his swing when the balls would career off the edges of the mug. I did see him make about four or five in a row at one point, but unfortunately not fifteen.

My father did not have the best all-around golf game, but he did have an acute eye for putting. If he had started a little earlier in life, he may have even become a better and more complete player. But, his love of being outside in the sun and the long walks for exercise and the competition we shared on the course, that was what really made him enjoy this game. Nonetheless he would reward himself for any minor victory on the golf course with a piece of butterscotch candy. The candies were not only rewards for him, but for myself or anybody else who played a hole nicely. If someone sank the tough ten-footer from the rough or even just the two-footer to win the match, a butterscotch candy was his way of saying "Nice job." As long as something was done on the course that impressed him, a butterscotch candy was the victor's spoils.

When my father reached his early seventies he developed Alzheimer's disease. His world and my family's were suddenly turned upside down. His concept of time had been wiped out, his memory was fleeting at best and his independent life was soon coming to a close.

In the beginning stages of his sickness, we would still make the occasional trek to the golf course. I did not know exactly what to expect at this point and really just characterized the memory lapses and spatial imperfections as symptomatic of old age. The frustrations of my father's illness combined with the challenge of the game made it a very tough morning.

"Dad, Dad, Dad! This way!" That's all I seemed to be yelling as my father in the midst of disorientation would face the opposite direction of the holes and begin to tee up. I had to physically grab him and turn him in the right direction at some holes. When I put my hands on his waist and turned him around I could feel how lost this man had become and how dependent on me he was. It felt at times like I was playing with a small child who had never stepped on the golf course before in his life.

I remember watching him walk, or better yet shuffle, around the fairway in a half-hearted attempt to find his ball, truth being he had no idea where it was. "Dad, it's over there!" I would yell and point, simultaneously waving ahead another foursome that was playing behind us.

The afternoon seemed to drag along more and more. The fifteenth hole was upon us and I had finally reached the green in about six and was prepared to putt. I had dropped a ball for my father in front of the approach just to speed up our play and let him poke it onto the green. I stood behind my ball waiting for him to chip. He had three weak digs at the ball before it finally scooted onto the green about six inches directly in front of my ball! He wore a little smile as he awkwardly shuffled around the green and waited for me to putt.

We stood and looked at each other almost comically for a few seconds—then I lost it. "Dad, mark your ball!" He still wore a face of delusion and disorientation as he meekly patted his pockets for a marker. He pulled out tees and balls—but no marker. He sensed my frustration mounting and I started to let my impatience seep into my expression.

Eventually he pulled something out of his pocket. I watched him reach down and pick up his ball and replace it with one of his butterscotch candies. He put it down and did not have the slightest clue what he had just done. The candy stood right in my putting line, the circular candy only a little bit smaller than the ball itself, its shiny gold cellophane wrapper reflecting sun and sitting so stupidly on the green.

I looked up at him and he was not even looking back at me. He was just looking around at the trees, at other golfers, wherever. I looked at him and started to laugh. I laughed hard. He looked back at me, then he looked at the candy sitting on the green. He laughed too.

The last three holes we played that day were some of the most memorable ones I have had playing this game. We both still played lousy the rest of the day, but we had fun, and my father and I would both have small awakenings amidst the green. He was freed from the delusions and disorientation of Alzheimer's for a couple of hours, and I was freed from the grasp of taking this game way too seriously.

That would be the last time I would ever play golf with my father, but it was the best time. The game became simple and fun for me again and he gave me that. Now, there are no more temptations to throw clubs or curse out loud or come home after a weekend of golfing upset because "I lost my swing." From now on, I take my time and I have fun—in all aspects of life. I carry a butterscotch candy on me whenever I play golf and even when I realize I am getting terribly frustrated with this game, I reach in my pocket for the butterscotch and remember that day on the course with my father—and laugh. I now enjoy golf and I am better at it. I am a pretty good putter now, too. I sank fifteen in a row in the coffee mug just a couple of days ago. Really, I did.

A. J. Daulerio

Babe in the Woods

*If I don't celebrate the exquisiteness of each
day, I've lost something I will never get back.*

Sally P. Karioth

A large crowd had gathered around the first tee by the
time Babe Ruth shambled out of the golf shop at the
Poland Springs, Maine, resort in the summer of 1940. He
was a moderately heavy man, deeply tanned, with alert
dark eyes and sloping shoulders. He was immaculately
dressed; a woman's fancy bobby pin held his forelock in
place. I was a teenager at the resort's caddie camp, made
up mostly of boys off the streets of Boston's South End.
The Babe had just finished a charity golf match near
Boston and had come to Maine for some private time. I
had been chosen to be his caddie.

He approached me and handed me a small, square,
unlabeled bottle filled with a brown liquid. "This is medicine," he said. "Be careful of it." I tucked the bottle into the
golf bag between some clean woolen socks, and we
walked onto the first tee.

The crowd and photographers backed off, and the Babe

smashed a booming drive that almost reached the green over three hundred yards away. Throughout the afternoon the Babe, a lefty, hit towering arcs off every tee. But with almost every shot, he let loose a string of profanities in the most unexpected sequence. He was wild. Dangerously wild. We spent a lot of time in the woods and in the rough looking for his rockets. Even then, I lost three balls.

On the fourth hole, we were crashing through the woods alone when he asked for his medicine. I handed him the bottle, and he took a long swig. I sniffed it; it smelled suspiciously of rum.

At the eleventh hole's refreshment stand, an entourage awaited us, including Ruth's wife, Claire. She pranced around waving a lengthy cigarette holder and bussed Ruth with a big show-biz hug. Ruth bought soft drinks for everyone, including the four caddies. He summoned me for more medicine to mix with his Coke.

At the twelfth hole, I stood near his drive in the rough, waiting for the rest of the foursome. Ruth looked out at the distant mountains, the nearby lake and the flag flying atop the antique hotel. His huge face softened, and he leaned close, within six inches. "Gee," he whispered in that gravelly voice. "This is beautiful. So peaceful and quiet. Isn't it wonderful?"

That was the last respite. At the thirteenth hole, the crowds reappeared, and we were once again in the center ring. I'm not certain of the Babe's final score, though I think he finished in the mid-80s with a few "gimme" putts. And I don't recall exactly what he paid me for the caddie fee. In those days, seventy-five cents was the going rate. I do recall that despite the three lost balls, Babe tipped me five dollars, a monumental sum. Then he gave me a short wave good-bye and disappeared into the clubhouse.

An hour later I saw him at the baseball field near the hotel, posing for the cameras with some players. The crowd stood back, clapping, as flashbulbs popped. A small smile was fixed on his muffin face; the mighty Bambino was back on stage, performing for his public. The quiet moment we'd shared at the twelfth hole seemed far off and forgotten. Then he spotted me in the crowd and winked.

Tom Turley

The Lunar Golf Shot

Have you ever thought about hitting a driver 1500 yards or a 6-iron 900 yards? Or watching a white ball against a black sky with a time of flight of twenty-five to thirty seconds? What golfer even dares dream of these things?

I thought about these things during *Apollo 14* in 1971. You see, the moon has one-sixth the gravity of Earth. That means with the same clubhead speed, the ball will go six times as far and stay in the air (or in this case the vacuum) six times as long!

Actually, Bob Hope gave me the idea of playing golf on the moon, although he didn't know about it until months after the flight. He was visiting NASA one day—Deke Slayton and I were showing him around—and he had an old driver that he was swinging as we walked around the campus. We hooked him up in a moon walker and as he was bouncing up and down on his toes, he used the driver for balance! That's when I said, only to myself, I had to find a way to hit a ball on the moon.

Perhaps people on Earth watching me on television thought it was spontaneous and unauthorized, but it was well-rehearsed and all approved before we launched.

I had planned to use a collapsible aluminum handle, which we normally used to scoop up dust samples, since we really couldn't bend over in a pressurized suit. And then I had a golf pro design a clubhead to snap on the handle, replacing the small scoop. It was a number 6-iron since the handle was about as long as a normal 6-iron shaft. I planned to take the clubhead and two ordinary golf balls in my suit pocket—at no expense to the taxpayers!

I practiced before the flight several times in the suit-training room to be sure I could swing safely. The pressurized suit is cumbersome and I couldn't get both hands on the club; still I could make a half swing with one hand. And, finally, I checked with the "boss" and told him my plan to hit two golf balls at the very end of the lunar stay, only if everything went perfectly up to that point. He agreed.

Fortunately, although we had some problems earlier, everything went just right while we were on the surface. Consequently, just before climbing up the ladder to come home, I prepared to tee off! When I dropped the first ball, it took about three seconds to land, and bounced a couple of times in the gray dust. Then, I improved my lie of course (winter rules in February) and made my best slow-motion, one-handed half-swing. Making a full swing in a space suit is impossible. I made good contact and the ball, which would have gone thirty to forty yards on Earth, went over 200 yards. The ball stayed up in the black sky almost thirty seconds. I was so excited I swung harder on the second one, which I shanked about forty yards into a nearby crater! I decided to call that a hole-in-one, even if the hole was several miles in diameter.

So I folded up the golf club and climbed up the ladder to take off. The two golf balls are still there and ready to be reclaimed and reused—after all, they were new. But the club resides in a place of honor at the U.S. Golf

Association in Far Hills, New Jersey, where all who see it can imagine, as did I, what a 1500-yard tee shot would really be like!

Alan Shepard
As told to Carol Mann

[EDITORS' NOTE: *Alan Shepard was the first American launched in space, in 1961. Ten years later, he commanded* Apollo 14 *and became the fifth man to walk on the moon—and the first to play golf there.*]

Every Golfer's Dream

Imagine that you are an avid golfer who has discovered the "Secret of Golf." The U.S. Open is being played at your home golf course and you successfully qualify.

We see you in the first round
It's early, wet and cold,
You finish strongly for a 74
You were playing fairly bold.

Will you make the cut after two?
You wonder but aren't scared,
A 66 in the second round
You are very well prepared!

You make the cut by a solid amount
You're off the lead by 5.
You are confident, cool and talented
And very much alive.

After eight holes in the third round
Your friends begin to roar,
Three under par at this point
At the tenth you go to 4.

Eleven, twelve and thirteen, however,
Are way out of whack,
Bogey, bogey, double bogey
You're playing like a hack.

But you're two under par on the next five holes
Seventy for the day,
Three strokes behind the leader
Eighteen holes left to play.

The final round you're paired with a man
Whom everyone respects,
He hits it long and putts with touch
He is for sure the best.

The pressure mounts as the time draws near
It's no help looking back,
You can't sleep too well the night before
Because you're paired with Jack!

You start with birdie—birdie
Your friends just can't believe,
One ahead of Jack
Two strokes from the lead.

You make the turn at 33
Three under par,
You know that you can win it all
The lead isn't far.

Two ahead of you
Five up on the rest of the field,
He's making it look like a walk in the park
Could he possibly yield?

At the fifteenth you both take par
At sixteen you make a mistake,
On this tricky 5 par
Your drive goes splashing in a lake.

Jack with an easy birdie
You with a scrambling par,
Three strokes behind, two holes to play
The lead looks so far.

The seventeenth, a long par 3
Jack hits it in the sand,
You know what you must do
And you can hardly stand.

Your fairway wood on this par 3
Goes zooming at the hole
It's long enough, straight enough,
Oh, wow, it hit the pole!

It crashes, rattles, spins and rips
Electricity is in the air,
You aren't sure if the ball is in
Because of all the glare.

The people jump, hug and scream
Where will the ball finally rest?
It's in the cup, a hole in one
On this amazing quest.

You think you're dreaming
The people can't be controlled,
The thunderous applause is deafening
As you run up to the hole.

You take out the ball and give it a kiss
No doubt The Greatest Ace,
Jack bogeys, you're tied for the lead
The eighteenth hole to face.

You hit your drives on eighteen
Straight down the track,
In your hands a three wood,
A wedge in mighty Jack's.

The 3-wood stops within twelve feet
Fifteen for the pro,
If Jack misses and you make it
To the top you're sure to go.

Jack looks it over, studies, strokes it
But not too pure,
He pulls it to the left of the hole
A par he has secured.

If you could stroke it smoothly
And the ball goes in,
Publicity, fame, wealth and happiness
A new life would begin.

You can't believe it
You make the golf ball roll,
As you raise your arm to show your joy
The ball is in the hole!

You made the putt, you've won the Open
As everyone has seen,
I hope that you've enjoyed it
Every golfer's dream.

Jay Golden

The Brand New Golfer

It does look like a very good exercise. But what is the little white ball for?

Ulysses S. Grant

The first hole at the Mobile, Alabama, Municipal Golf Course was something to behold on that beautiful spring day several years ago. The tee sat atop a hill, looking down a narrow fairway, and the hole ended at a postage-stamp-sized green, surrounded at the back side by water. It was a hole that did not appear to be very forgiving to the careless or inexperienced golfer.

It was a busy Saturday morning, and my foursome was waiting to tee off, as were several others. As the golfers in front of us stepped to the tee, I noticed one man in particular. He was in his early thirties, slightly pudgy, wearing a spotless shirt, trousers, shoes and every other golfing accessory his charge card could buy. Even his golf clubs, bag and pull cart fairly sparkled with "newness."

As we watched, the other three men made decent shots, and then waited as their fourth, the new golfer, stepped forward and teed up his ball. The man looked down the fairway, then carefully addressed his ball, made his back-swing and swung mightily, missing the ball completely. His face reddened somewhat, but he did not look up as he again addressed his ball. His second attempt made a noisy *whooshing* sound, but missed his ball by an even wider margin. No one made any comment, and his three embarrassed friends simply looked away and cleared their throats.

For the third time, the new golfer addressed his ball, taking great care to place his feet, position his grip and waggle his club several times. Finally, he executed a careful and extremely slow backswing, followed by a vicious downswing of his club that barely topped his ball, which fell from the tee and rolled forward about four inches. For a moment he stood perfectly still, reddened face pointed to the ground. He finally looked up at the large group of waiting golfers, and with a perfectly straight face said, "This is the toughest darn hole I ever played!"

I have never laughed so hard, nor heard so much laughter on any golf course, before or since.

Stan Reynolds

Playing Through

*Laughter is the sensation of feeling good all over
but showing it principally in one spot.*

Josh Billings

Parachuting from a helicopter over a drop zone inside
Camp Dawson, West Virginia, a lieutenant colonel from
the Special Forces Group Airborne found himself doing
battle with a sudden twenty-two-knot wind, which forced
him onto a nearby golf course. On landing, the Green
Beret fumbled for the release but another gust drove the
chute and its struggling captive down the fairway, catching the attention of three players about to tee off. "Can we
help?" shouted the golfers.

Sliding by them, the officer clung to his sense of humor
as well as his pride. "No, thanks," he called out. "I'll just
play through."

Sondra Sue Ward Elder

Rub-a-Dub-Dub

Rub of the green. This idiom, in the parlance of golf, conjures the karma of the fairways, the luck of the links. A flubbed shot ricochets off a tree. Onto the green. Toward the flag. Into the hole. *Ker-plunk.* Or a flawless drive kicks into the rough. Down a slope. Toward a pond. Into the water. *Ker-plop.* Rub of the green.

I am well acquainted with the capriciousness of the gods of golf, the sudden confrontations with miracles and mortifications. My most poignant memories do not concern my exploits as a player, but rather as a caddie, and how that life came to such an astonishing end.

The scene: Acacia Country Club near Cleveland, Ohio. The time: the summer of '65. The protagonist: me, a high school kid.

Acacia divided all caddies into an A list and a B list. Caddie ranking was ruled by a ritual as intricate as the minuet: length of tenure counted. So did consistency of signing in, predawn, at the caddieshack. So did the grading cards golfers filled out at the end of a round. But a caddie's fate was also inexorably linked to the whims of the caddiemaster.

Our caddiemaster was a red-headed wise guy in his

early twenties. I had always given him a wide berth, respectful but not sycophantic. By the summer of '65, my fifth year at Acacia, I had ascended to the near pinnacle of the A list—A-5. Tote early and tote often, that was my mantra. On good days I caddied three loops. Popular with the players, I offered sage golfing advice, which was reciprocated by generous tips.

Then came my rub of the green. Early one morning, trekking up a steep hill toward the caddieshack, my head in the clouds, I heard a smash of glass, followed by a shout of profanity; I hurried to investigate, only to find shards of a whiskey bottle outside the shack. Without a tincture of savvy, I picked up some glass, finding myself face-to-face with the caddiemaster, wisps of smoke seemingly curling out his ears. Though I didn't break the bottle, I spoke incoherently. A one-minute trial took place. Guilty, I was sentenced to demotion: from the top of the A's to the tail end of the B's. Like a golf ball rolling downhill, I was ineluctably on my way to the bottom.

An abundance of free time was mine that summer as I awaited the possibility of an early evening loop. I read voraciously. Given my lingering mood of nihilism, I turned to the French existentialists. Camus. Sartre. At Acacia Country Club, I was a stranger with no exit.

Came early September and the club championships, and I received a reprieve from caddie purgatory. Mrs. Silverman insisted I tote her clubs. The caddiemaster could hardly refuse; she was outlandishly wealthy.

Mrs. Silverman, who bore a striking resemblance to Eleanor Roosevelt, was always attired in the dowdiest of golf outfits: paisley blouses, black orthopedic shoes. But she was a woman of great enthusiasms and not a half-bad golfer, either, though far from a favorite to win.

The match-play tournament of sixty-four began, and what a team we were: Eleanor Roosevelt and the club's lowliest caddie. But lo and behold, Mrs. Silverman was about to sustain the highest level of golf in her life. She was the epitome of confidence: crackerjack drives, precision iron play, uncanny putting. We soared into the final four; we pounced into the championship match.

The title match was tied after eighteen holes; we entered sudden death. On the first fairway, a brisk wind blowing over the course, I told Mrs. Silverman: "You can get home with a 6-iron. Hit it all out." She caught the shot perfectly but was short-snagged by a bunker. I cursed my misjudgment, the ill will of the loopy summer seemingly unending.

Then Mrs. Silverman bladed her sand wedge. The ball took off like a shot, struck the flagstick with a bang and careened miraculously into the hole. *Ker-plunk*. Club championship.

After the celebration, Mrs. Silverman handed me my tip: a thick stack of hundred-dollar bills. "For college," she said. I walked away from Acacia forever, that summer of '65, my existentialism jettisoned, my career as a caddie ended, my future bright as I thumbed a stack of fresh bills—a most delightful rub of the green.

Tommy Ehrbar

Slicker Sam

*Giving never moves in a straight line—it
always travels in circles.*

Robert Schuller

Twenty years ago, a car accident claimed the life of long-time Augusta National Golf Club Manager Phil Wahl. Janice, his widow, was left with nine children. Phil's friends wanted to help.

As the club's photographer, I had gotten to know Phil pretty well. The idea of a golf tournament to raise funds for his family seemed like a good one, so I made a few phone calls and was heartened by the overwhelming response.

The one-day benefit tournament was set for West Lake, a popular Augusta country club that donated use of its course. Fee was set at one thousand dollars per player. The first obstacle was that some of Phil's friends could not afford the fee; still they wanted to show their support. While agonizing over this dilemma, I received a phone call from a member of the National who wished to remain anonymous. He offered to put up the fee for those who could not afford it. We were off and running!

Fifty-five players came out, including such notables as Jack Nicklaus, Ken Venturi, David Graham, Chris Schenkel and Ed Sneed. One of the first guys to sign up was Slicker Sam of Chicago, an internationally known golfer who regularly played for large sums of money—and usually won. Anyone who knew Slicker agreed he should be deemed a national treasure. I say this because of his reputation for charity.

At the end of play, we gathered in the dining room for tournament awards. A substantial prize—a luxurious new Cadillac donated by a local dealer—stood out from the usual closest-to-pin and longest drive awards. All eyes were riveted on the shiny new set of keys that Master of Ceremonies Ken Venturi held up. After a long, dramatic pause, Ken finally smiled, and said: "Come on up, Slicker Sam, and claim your prize!"

Silence fell over the room as Slicker Sam moved to the podium. He was quite a champion. Ken handed him the keys.

Slicker Sam had broken 70 to claim the victory, but only at that moment were we to learn why he had played with so much determination.

"I already have a car!" Sam said to Venturi, returning the keys. "Please, give this Cadillac to Phil Wahl's family!"

The room responded with a standing ovation. That was class, Slicker-style.

The following day, Slicker and Doug Sanders had arranged to play for some serious money. Doug's playing partner was singer Andy Williams. I was the fourth. We played the match in Aiken, South Carolina, about fourteen miles east of Augusta, at the Houndslake Golf Club.

As we rode down the first fairway I remembered I had been given some raffle tickets to sell on behalf of my neighbors, the Adas Yeshurun Synagogue in Augusta. The one-hundred-dollar tickets were good for a chance at a new

Cadillac. As we putted out on the first hole, I pulled out the tickets. Doug and Andy bought the first two. By the time Sam walked up to us, we were exchanging money for tickets. When he heard what the prize was, Slicker's eyes flashed and he produced a roll of bills from his pocket.

A few weeks later I attended a dinner where the raffle tickets were pulled, eliminating contenders. As the night wore on, all names were eliminated except two, and Slicker Sam remained in the race. When someone else's name was called, my heart dropped. I thought they were declaring a winner. I was wrong. Slicker Sam was the winner!

I phoned him with the good news. "I knew I was going to win that car," he responded.

I guess some things are ordained by a higher power. There's one thing I know for sure: Sam had been rewarded for his wonderful generosity. As I went to bed that night I had a vision of Phil Wahl. In his own unique way that had endeared him to so many people, Phil turned his head to speak to Slicker Sam.

"Thanks, Pard," he said.

I slept happily.

Frank Christian

The Spirit of Harvey Penick

My father says to me, "Respect everybody, and
your life, it will be perfect." Then, even if you are
poor on the outside, on the inside you are rich.

                                        Costantino Rocca

It's funny how circumstances sometimes transpire to
lead us in unexpected directions. This tale recounts the
chain of events that led me to the legendary Harvey
Penick and the subsequent effects that encounter had on
my life.

I was visiting an uncle I had not seen in many years, a
golfer's kinship sort of thing. Uncle Norman introduced
me to the game of golf, starting as his caddie. A miserable
experience, thanks to weather and other circumstances; I
hated the game, and I didn't take it up in earnest until the
age of thirty-five. Immediately, the golf bug bit me. During
this visit, I picked up a book lying on the kitchen counter,
Harvey Penick's Little Green Book, *If You're a Golfer, You're*
My Friend. The book so impressed me, I read it cover to
cover that night and decided to meet Mr. Penick. Now was
as good a time as any.

From South Florida, I drove the following week to Austin, Texas. After checking into a motel on a Sunday night, I looked up his phone number and anxiously placed the call. I knew that Penick was old and frail, but I was shocked to learn his current condition. Helen Penick informed me that her dear husband was "released from the hospital that very day and he was not expected to make it." It was even more surprising that she said to call in the morning and if he felt up to it, "Mr. Penick would be happy to see you." I was given directions to the house and instructed to call around 10 A.M.

My emotions surged. At first, I felt sorry for myself. I had driven fifteen hundred miles, and I expected that effort would get me the audience I came for. I began to feel guilty, knowing how selfish that was. Saying a prayer, for Mr. Penick and myself, I retired early.

Arising at the crack of dawn the next morning, I restlessly waited for 10 o'clock to arrive. Precisely at 10, I began dialing, and for what seemed an eternity, I heard busy signals. The worst crossed my mind. *Was he even sicker? Did he die?* Paranoid that I am, I even thought that the phone was intentionally left off the hook to discourage my calling. At 11, I drove to the house.

Following precise directions, I arrived at the Penick home, situated in a beautiful part of town. Worried about coming before calling, I sheepishly knocked on the door. When a nurse answered, I asked for Mrs. Penick. She was out shopping, but the nurse asked if I would like to visit with Mr. Penick. After traveling such a long distance I was aching to say yes, but I declined. "I think I'd better wait to see if it's okay with Mrs. Penick first." The next several hours were awe-inspiring and would change the course of my personal and professional life.

Outside, in this pristine setting, I became aware of changes, faint at first, in my sensory perceptions. The colors of the flowers were distinctive and bright. A gentle breeze blowing, the air was crisp and clear. Rich, pleasant aromas abounded. I heard several birds and could distinguish the differences in each of their songs. My body tingling all over, I was captivated by a heightened sense of awareness, actually feeling a part of nature. For a cold, calculating, bottom-line guy like me, this experience was a first.

I remember seeing a squirrel on the opposite side of the street. I closed my eyes, believing the squirrel would come closer, and to my delight he did. Closing my eyes again, I knew he would come right beside me. Well, nobody's perfect. This trancelike state lasted for what seemed an eternity, yet in reality was only thirty minutes or so. Mrs. Penick arrived and asked me to come in.

The bedroom resembled a hospital ward with tubes and machines everywhere. Mr. Penick was glad that I had come, eager to talk golf and share his wisdom. His love for the game was obvious, and talking about golf seemed to lift his spirits. A glow enveloped him as he shared with me a lifetime of teaching, people and stories. He asked about my personal life, my game, and how he might help me. What we discussed is almost irrelevant, for I knew that I was in the presence of greatness.

His son Tinsley stopped by the house, and our session continued. From his deathbed—he would pass away the following week—Mr. Penick was giving me a golf lesson. Incredibly perceptive, from our conversation, he could detect my flaws. After a few hours, I could see how tired he had become, so I excused myself to see if I should go. Though Mr. Penick wanted to continue, Tinsley felt it was time for rest. I thanked them all and left. How remarkable this family is. At a time when most people would only think of themselves and their troubles, they welcomed me into their home as if I was a lifelong friend. I made a conscious decision to live my life and play the game of golf according to a higher principle, Harvey Penick's way. Meeting him altered my life.

To make a long story short, that encounter led to my writing *The Secrets to the Game of Golf & Life*, for which Tinsley agreed to write the foreword. I still get goose bumps every time I read it. Among other thoughts in his foreword, Tinsley wrote that his father and I became "kindred spirits and soul brothers" and that "Leonard has brought that special feeling to the pages of his new book." I am now firmly entrenched in the golf community, as a writer and consultant. Meeting Harvey Penick helped me to become a better golfer, but more importantly, a better person. I look at both golf and life from a different perspective, more aware and more appreciative.

Leonard Finkel

Through the Footsteps of Time

The men crouched behind low stone walls. Musket fire pierced the air above their heads, seeking randomly the warm flesh of the unlucky one who happened in its path. Worse yet were the sorry souls cut down by cannon fire, the evil spheres that succeeded in the demise of multiple patriots with every blast.

It is hard to imagine the angst, the fear and the nobility of the brave soldiers who squared off on this rocky slope.

I was flooded with emotion as I strode down the majestic fairways of the Carnegie Abbey Course in Portsmouth, Rhode Island. On a perfect New England spring day, I was playing golf with new friends Don, Patrick and Bill. We had just hit our drives on the tight, slightly dogleg left, par-4 6th hole. I was struck by a sight of a Colonial-era graveyard surrounded by massive stones, stones that for hundreds of years had silently stood as sentries to the confines of its occupants. While the inscriptions were moving, I found it even more fascinating that this noble sight must have sat in near obscurity for two centuries before its liberation from the scrub brush by the artistic stroke of the golf course architect.

Describing my emotions to Bill, he was quick to note that

directly beneath us, less than twenty yards off the tee, was the final resting place for forty former slaves who had lived and farmed the property during part of its long history.

Approaching our drives, I turned to Manny, my caddie, to express my reverence for this special place, when Manny informed me that far more was to come. On cue, Bill explained that this beautiful, rolling property on Narragansett Bay was the location of numerous confrontations during the American Revolution. Specifically, the hole we were playing was the very sight of the "Battle of Bloody Run," where estimates are that five hundred to two thousand men had lost their lives and were buried beneath the ground we strode.

I stood for a minute in awe, consumed by the thought that a place that was now so beautiful could have been the sight of such violence.

I can never remember feeling on a golf course the way I did that day. Part of me felt out of place, as if I was violating this land that still belonged to the hearts, sounds and emotions of its past. Another part of me felt a true reverence, a sense of common union with this spot and an appreciation for the people who had been there before me.

That's when it hit me.

How wonderful, how fantastic is this game of golf that by using this land as the canvas upon which a beautiful and challenging golf course would unfold, this distinguished land would be freed from its past and from the obscure pages of history. I will admit that I did not know a thing at that time about the "Battle of Bloody Run," much less the actual spot where the battle took place.

Now, thanks to Carnegie Abbey, the efforts and the sacrifices of these brave men would not be lost to obscurity, but would be remembered and forever celebrated because of numerous historical markings and environmental sensitivity.

I love the game of golf, not only for its dignity and camaraderie, but because every now and then the game becomes a vehicle to explore and appreciate something deeper, as on this day, a garden memorial to people who gave so much so that we may enjoy the moment.

Matt Adams

Dr. Scholl's Caddy

I spent many a Saturday and Sunday in my father's 1946 Chevy parked in the lot at the Ridgewood Country Club in New Jersey. My father would earn extra money as a caddy, and he would always tell me not to wander too far from the car. The pro at the time was George Jacobus who was also president of the PGA at one time. In the thirties he hired a young pro named Byron Nelson as his assistant. My dad showed him to me one day and said, "Make sure you are near the car if you see Mr. Jacobus around."

Well, after a few Saturdays and Sundays, I had my timing down to a T. I could run to the woods to watch the members play and shag some balls for fifty cents. All in all, I felt I wouldn't be seen away from post. I had an old 5-iron, and when I would see Mr. Jacobus pull away in his car, I would run over to the practice fairway and try my luck. I tried not to make divots because then I would have to waste too much time replacing them.

Once I began to make contact, the ball would sail so far that I was afraid to retrieve it. The members who I shagged for usually parted with a few old balls and kept me in supply. I stashed my old 5-iron and the balls in the rough off the practice fairway so if I was seen walking around, at least I was empty-handed. I soon noticed that every golfer wore the nicest shoes I had ever seen, just like the pros in the magazines and on the television. I worked extra hard that summer shagging balls and even washing some of the members' cars in the lot. The caddymaster took a liking to me and supplied the soap, pail and towels.

One day as I was sneaking toward my cache of club and balls, I noticed Mr. Jacobus leaving the clubhouse. I ducked behind a huge Buick that would have stopped an artillery shell and was sure I was not seen. As I watched his car round the bend I grabbed my 5-iron, chucked the balls onto the fairway and ran over to practice. For sure he had gone home—it was almost 5 o'clock. My dad should almost be done with his second round. As I approached the balls, my sneakers slipped as I was taking the biggest swing I could muster for a ten-year-old and landed on the seat of my pants. I didn't have a chance to get up when I heard a voice behind me say, "Son, I'd say that was a little overswing." It was Mr. Jacobus and was I ever speechless. "You need two good things to hit that ball, Son," he said. "A better swing and a pair of golf shoes."

I guess he knew how hard I was working to earn a pair of my own, and he took me into the locker room and told the attendant to find me a pair in the pile of old golf shoes slated to be tossed out by the members. After a few minutes of trying on shoe after shoe, the attendant came out with the neatest pair in the pile. Black-and-white wing tips. I saw Sam Snead and Arnold Palmer wearing them. The attendant said, "Try these on." I remember him saying over and over, "These are Dr. Scholl's, these are Dr. Scholl's, this is a great shoe."

They fit like a glove, and the attendant polished them and buffed them and even replaced a few spikes. After all, Mr. Jacobus put him on the case, and he was up to the task. My dad returned after his caddying and couldn't believe his eyes. He asked me where I got the shoes, and I told him the truth. "Some rich doctor was throwing them away, and Mr. Jacobus gave them to me." He had to pull over to the side of the road on the way home when I asked, "Hey, Dad, did you ever caddy for Dr. Scholls?"

Dennis Oricchio

Father's Day Arrives During Christmas

A few days before Christmas I got a Father's Day card from my dad, who passed away nearly three years ago. It arrived while my son and I were at the Palo Verde Golf Course in Phoenix. Palo Verde is a compact little course on Fifteenth Avenue north of Bethany Home Road. We started going there shortly after my mother died in 1997. My father was staying for a time in Phoenix, and his doctors told him he should try to get some exercise. He hadn't been well. Specialists described his condition as coronary artery disease. We knew it simply as a broken heart.

My boy and I own nine battered old golf clubs between us. My father had left his set back in Pittsburgh. So we only utilized Palo Verde's driving range. We'd bring along a few lawn chairs, and my dad and I would sit and talk while Sam teed off, hacking at each golf ball like a power hitter chasing a slider in the dirt.

"Why don't you teach him to swing the right way?" I asked my dad.

"As long as he's having a good time and hitting the ball, that is the right way," he answered.

He had been retired from the steel mill for fifteen years by then. When I was growing up, he coached baseball and bowled on a team from the mill's tin plate department. Only in retirement did he and his friends discover golf. It got so they'd go out several times a week in the summer.

Every once in a while during our trips to Palo Verde, my father would get up from his chair and hit a few balls. Years of practice had given him a fluid stroke. He'd send a tee shot arching high into the darkness beyond the range's big lights.

"That ball's going to outer space," my boy said one night. "Maybe all the way to Grandma."

When my father returned to Pennsylvania, he kept a photograph of himself and Sam in a homemade frame in his basement workshop. After he died, Sam and I took the picture home with us. We keep it in our golf bag and take it out each time we go to the driving range at Palo Verde, so my dad can watch us hit balls and evaluate our unorthodox swings.

The last time we were there over the holiday vacation, the frame my father made for the picture came apart and the photograph slipped out. While fixing it, I saw that the matting board on which the photograph had been mounted was actually an old greeting card. I had sent it to my dad years ago on Father's Day. This Christmas, he sent it back.

During my father's final days, my brother and I kept the conversation light. We knew he was dying. He knew he was dying. He had a stroke and couldn't speak, so we said and did things to try to make him smile. To make ourselves smile. It was all a blur, and afterward a part of you wonders if your true feelings came through. Then you get this gift, this greeting card addressed to your dad in your handwriting that you don't even recall having sent.

A person can be more sentimental in a card than in conversation. At least it was that way in our family. I wrote in the card about how I never doubted that my father would do anything for me and ended by saying that as a dad, "You're a helluva hard act to follow." The card is back in its frame now. Back in the golf bag.

When I was a kid, the first thing friends asked when we returned to school from Christmas vacation was, "What did you get?" It was a happy, hopeful way to start the new year.

This Christmas, among other things, I got a Father's Day card from my old man.

E. J. Montini

You May Be a Winner

My friend Tony gave a golf trip to his son one Christmas. And Tony's son gave a golf trip to his uncle. And the uncle gave a golf trip to Tony. As these gifts were revealed, one by one, over the course of Christmas morning, Tony's mother-in-law's astonishment grew. "I can't believe you all gave each other a vacation to the same place! And on the same weekend!"

Not all non-golfers are as easy to fool as Tony's mother-in-law was. A gambit like that would never work with my wife, for example, because she knows (and is appalled) that my brother and I long ago agreed to simplify our lives by never giving each other anything for any reason. Tony's wife wasn't fooled, either, but she said nothing, because the men of the family had (astutely) expressed their selfishness in a form that seemed to endorse a deeply cherished belief held by the women of the family: that major holidays are important occasions for loving, commitment and renewal, and so forth. The men got what they wanted by pretending to play the game by the women's rules.

Anyway, Tony's success at Christmas got me to thinking, and I'm pretty sure I've come up with an even better idea. My idea is so good, in fact, that I'm going to share it with you.

Here's what I've done. I've started a company called the International Golf Sweepstakes Foundation, Inc., of which I am the sole employee. Let's say that you and three buddies want to take a ten-day golf trip to Ireland, but you know that your wives would never in a million years let you go. You contact me by e-mail, and I send you an entry form for a contest in which the grand prize happens to be an all-expenses-paid ten-day golf trip to Ireland for four. You fill out the form and ask your wife to sign her name on the line marked "witness."

"What's this?" she asks.

"Oh, just some dumb animal-rights thing they made us contribute to at work."

Your wife happily signs, you send the form back to me with a check for five hundred dollars (my fee), and you never again mention the contest to your wife. Three or four months later, a fat, official-looking FedEx package arrives at your house. You open it in the presence of your wife, appear puzzled for a moment, then begin hooting, "Remember that dumb contest? I actually won!" you shout.

Non-playing wives view all golf trips as wasteful extravagances, but they can't help thinking of contest winnings as money in the bank. To fail to cash in a prize already won would be like throwing jewelry out in the trash, so of course you'll get to go—especially if you promptly offer to give your wife some sort of compensating goodie, like a new kitchen. You'll have to make all your travel arrangements yourself—and conceal your credit card charges as you do—because that's not part of what my foundation does, at least for the time being. All I do is get you out the door. The rest is up to you.

David Owen

My Course, My Rules

Did you hear about the guy in Chattanooga who won a Big Game lottery jackpot worth $60 million and went out and bought himself a golf course?

Damn right.

All my life I've wanted my own golf course. I dream of calling the starter and asking, "Any way you can squeeze me in for a round?" and having him answer, "All we got left is 6 A.M. until 7 P.M. Will that work?"

If I felt like playing 27, I could. If I felt like playing 54, I could. If I felt like playing from the 14th tee into the deep-fat fryer, stark naked on a unicycle, I could. Overnight, I guarantee you, my handicap would drop to a four. That's because I would turn par into a radio station, say, 103.5.

Not that there wouldn't be rules. Oh, there would be rules at Chop Acres.

- No collared shirts. They all look like an explosion at the Dutch Boy plant anyway. No kilties, either. And none of those ridiculous screw-you sunglasses.
- No men's locker room. That's what the trunk of your car's for, right? Or can't you get through your day

without Vitalis, Bay Rum and Old Tom Morris's comb soaking in blue formaldehyde?

- No tee times for women. No tee times for kids. No tee times for men. If you can play in less than three-and-a-half hours, get out there. If not, we've saved the midnight-to-2 A.M. window for you.

- Come to think of it, all you *get* is three-and-a-half hours. After that, the carts run out of juice and the caddies hop the fence—with your Pings over their shoulders.

- No mulligans, breakfast balls, Clintons or hit-till-you're-happys. You don't have to prove to us you can smother-blade a driver twice in a row. We believe you. Besides, the first hole is a twenty-three-yard, downhill par-3 from an elevated tee to a huge funnel green. We love seeing people make holes-in-one. We also love drinking free.

- No practice swings. We've seen your practice swing. It's slow, graceful and bears absolutely no resemblance to the hideous chop you end up using, so why bother?

- No cell phones, either. There's a $10 fine for incoming calls, $25 for outgoing. One thing we don't need on our backswing is you discussing the freaking Acme account.

- Take a caddie or a cart, but we think you'll like the caddies. They get a $20 bonus if they get you home in three hours, and they usually do. That's partly because they have you hitting from the women's tees.

- Mandatory betting. What do you think this is, the Walla Walla First Presbyterian Four-ball? As our head pro, Two Down, likes to say, "If you're not betting, you're just going on a very long walk in very ugly pants." And if you get a little upside down in your wagers, don't worry. Two Down gives fast and friendly auto appraisals.

- No duck-hooking into the adjacent fairway just to stop the beverage-cart girl. One comes with every foursome.
- No plumb-bobbing without a Ph.D. in physics. Like anybody knows how to do it anyway. If a caddie sees you plumb-bobbing, he'll confiscate your putter and make modern art out of it.
- No pacing off yardage. Does it really matter whether you're 230 or 231 yards from the hole? That's still three seven-irons and a canoe for you.
- No out-of-bounds. White stakes are for albino vampires. If you can find your ball, hit it. If you can't find it, hit it from where you think you would've found it. If you can't decide where you would've found it, return to the cart, reach into the glove box, pull out the complimentary copy of *Quilting for Fun and Profit* and begin reading.
- If it's within the leather, it's good. If it's within the Bertha, it's good. If it's something that a Bruneian slave would give the Sultan, it's good.

After the round, come on in for All You Can Pour Night. The hot-tub massages are free, the cigars are smuggled, and the mook who answers the phone never heard of you.

Oh, and if you don't feel up to driving home, stay the night next door at Courtyard by Hooters.

You might as well.

Two Down will have sold your car.

Rick Reilly

The Greatest Shot of My Life

Pressure is playing for ten dollars when you don't have a dime in your pocket.

Lee Trevino

Like most guys I know, I was introduced to the game of golf by my father. My dad was a pretty good golfer when he was younger (5 handicap). When my sisters and I came along, he couldn't play as much as he'd like, but he still stayed in touch with the game.

In the early sixties, dad bought a bar in Portage Lakes, a nice series of recreational lakes in Ohio. My dad was in his fifties by this time and still liked to play the game. The problem was that after practically giving up the game, he would still take sucker bets from the younger guys who frequented his tavern. One guy bet Dad one hundred dollars that he could give Dad five and use only three clubs. Dad lost one hundred dollars. Another guy bet Dad fifty dollars that he could throw out his worst two holes, and once again Dad lost.

I felt bad for Pop because he was such a nice guy, and although these guys spent lots of money at Dad's tavern, at the age of twelve, I felt people thought Dad was a joke around the golf course and everyone was making fun of him.

Several days later, Jimmy Ray Textur, a young "hot shot" golfer, told my dad he would give him ten strokes and do all his putting with a driver. The bet was one hundred dollars and, of course, Dad accepted.

The following morning we met at Turtlefoot Golf Course in Portage Lakes, a beautiful course surrounded by water. On the 1st hole, Jimmy Ray hit a sweet drive, high and long, and straight down the fairway. Dad's drive sliced OB. I cringed and thought, *Here we go again.*

After Dad's misfortune on the 1st hole, he settled down and played pretty well. Jimmy Ray didn't putt as well as he'd thought with his driver.

Dad had lost all of the shots Jimmy Ray gave him by the 15th hole. They tied on holes 16 and 17. The last hole was a par-4 straight away with an elevated green and trees lining both sides of the fairway. At this point in time, the match was tied. Jimmy Ray hit his drive left center and had a flip wedge to the pin. Dad hit an awful slice deep into the woods where it rested on a huge clump of dirt that was the remains of a tree that was removed. By this time a few of Jimmy Ray's friends had wandered onto the course to watch the match.

I stood at the edge of the woods where I saw my dad climb onto this mound of dirt and debris and address the ball. In my heart, I figured Dad was about to lose another one hundred bucks. I felt rotten, and even worse for my dad. Just then I heard a *crack* echo through the woods that sounded like a cherry bomb going off under a pop can. The leaves parted, and to my amazement, the ball came out of the woods like a bullet, hit the bank in front of the green, bounced twenty feet in the air and came to rest two feet from the pin. This might have shook Jimmy Ray up a bit, for he chili-dipped his next shot. Jimmy Ray then chipped up within five feet and made the putt for par.

Dad needed his two-footer to win the match. As I walked up to the green, beaming with pride, I handed Dad his Bull's Eye putter so he could finish off Jimmy Ray. Dad walked past me and gave me a wink. He went to his bag, pulled out his driver and proceeded to knock in the two-footer!

The drive home was one I'll always remember. We drove straight to Montgomery Ward where he bought me my first set of golf clubs and a cool green, yellow and black plaid golf bag.

I'm still playing golf and running a small driving range in Mount Vernon, Ohio. Dad passed away in '93, but sometimes when I visit family in Akron, I play Turtlefoot. Whenever I come to the last hole, regardless of my score, I always feel good; for on this hole, I witnessed the greatest shot of my life.

Del Madzay

Winnie's Barn

No one becomes a champion without help.

Johnny Miller

I was raking my yard on a warm autumn afternoon when Arnold Palmer phoned to say Winnie had passed away that morning (November 20, 1999). He said he wanted me to know before I heard the news on television or from someone else. I thanked him and asked if he was okay. He sighed, and his voice cracked. "I don't know," he said. "I feel like I just took 12 on the opening hole."

Golf, to say nothing of life, would never be the same for anyone who knew Winnie Palmer, least of all her husband, Arnold.

Being invited to help Arnold Palmer craft his memoirs was a dream come true for me, because like millions of you, decades before I actually met the man, Palmer was my sports hero, my personal god in golf shoes. As the mortals of Greek mythology learned the hard way, though, mingling with gods and heroes comes with certain perils. The private great man is seldom as engaging as the public one and, at least in my professional experience, rarely as nice. The good news in Arnold's case was that he turned out to be everything he appears to be and then some—as warm, thoughtful, open and honest as I dared to hope he might be, an autobiographer's ace. The best thing I can say about my golf hero is that I liked him even better after I got to know him.

The unexpected bonus of the three-year project, however, was Winnie Palmer.

Almost from the moment we met, we became good friends and devoted allies in the task of putting Arnold's oversized life on paper. It was really Winnie's book, as I came to think of it, something she understood the golf world needed but Arnold would never seriously undertake on his own, and I quickly learned that the best way to convince Arnold Palmer to do anything was to get Winnie Palmer behind the idea.

A marriage, someone said, is like a medieval morality play. There are things you see on one level, currents you feel on another. After spending nearly eight hundred days slipping in and out of Arnold's and Winnie's lives, being granted poignant proximity to the ordinary ups and downs of the extraordinary Palmer family life, I began to understand what a unique and powerful partnership Arnold and Winnie really were. Their marriage had been tested in almost unfathomable ways, and perhaps because they'd been through so much together—the trials of fame and the dangers of fortune—they often appeared to cling together like shipwreck survivors on a beach.

You could see it in the way they instinctively clasped hands while moving through large crowds or relaxing with intimate groups of friends, you could feel its currency when Arnold affectionately called her "Lover" and teased her about running his life and bossing him about. Whatever else was true, when Winnie spoke about a subject that mattered, Arnold truly listened. The truth is, he relied on her opinions on just about everything for the simple reason that he would have been crazy not to. She was a crack judge of character, a no-nonsense advisor with an Ivy League brain, an unfaltering follower of the heart.

Besides Arnold's memoir, the other great project Winnie had in mind, well over a year and a half before being diagnosed with cancer of the intestinal lining, was the restoration of an old barn adjacent to the golf course in Latrobe. She jokingly referred to it as her "mink coat" while Arnold simply called it "Winnie's barn."

One gorgeously flaring summer afternoon she drove me to the high hill above the barn, overlooking the golf course, and explained that someday she hoped to convince Arnie—that's what she called him—to build a cozy "retirement" cottage up there for just the two of them, if and when he ever agreed to retire. The night before at dinner, out of the blue, Arnold had revealed his latest brainstorm: He was thinking of planting a vineyard and starting a winery on the hill adjacent to the barn. This was news to Winnie. She had looked at me and rolled her eyes with deep amusement as if to say, "Arnold the Dreamer at work again."

Now, Arnold, who happened to be playing the par-5 14th with a group of visiting corporate bigwigs, spotted us and sped up the hill in a golf cart, grinning suspiciously. He asked what the devil we were doing up there, and she replied cheekily, "Why, just checking out the view from the living room of our retirement house."

"Winifred, I'm going to build that house for you," he bellowed good-naturedly at her. "Just you wait and see!"

"Right, Lover," she teased gently. "Will that be before or after the winery?"

With that, she laughed that great laugh of hers, sounding every bit like the smoky, polished, dark-haired, underage beauty who kept her father Shube Walzer's accounting books. She was studying to become an interior designer and dreamed of traveling the world when a handsome, smooth-talking, largely unsuccessful paint salesman from Cleveland, who happened to be the new National Amateur golf champion, reached beneath the dinner table at Shawnee-on-Delaware. He impulsively took her hand and audaciously suggested that she marry him, three days after their introduction.

Strong-willed as a spring colt, she said yes in a matter of hours, beginning golf's most durable love story, and spent the next four decades shaping the views and interior life of the modern game's most commanding figure.

By her own design, Winnie Palmer was one of golf's most private people. Even at the height of Arnold's fame, she walked outside the ropes and a few steps behind, never asking nor tolerating any special privilege, as comfortable among the caddies as the VIPs, often invisible but always watching. "Arnie's the people person," she would say. "I'm a person person."

That was true. One-on-one, Winnie had a way of making everyone feel unique and deeply valued in her sphere. Her home was simple and unpretentious but as gorgeously made and richly hued as an Amish quilt, always dressed immaculately for the season.

There were private times with Winnie I will cherish most. Sometimes, after Arnold and I finished up one of our productive early-morning research sessions, he would jet away to fulfill an obligation, to film a commercial or appear at a function or charity tournament, at which point Winnie would take me under her wing for the balance of the day.

Several times after lunch we slipped out and took long drives with Prince, their retriever, through the countryside. One afternoon she drove me to see Unity Chapel, a two-hundred-year-old Presbyterian chapel sitting on a hill outside Latrobe. She told me its history and explained how the chapel had once fallen in disrepair but thanks to a number of people who loved the place, Unity Chapel had been restored to its simple grandeur.

I realized later that Winnie was one of those special people, but she wouldn't have told me that in a million years. The fact is, she loved going to church—almost any church—and sometimes she took me with her. She enjoyed old hymns and a sermon that made you think. She worried about the world her grandchildren and yours and mine will inherit. She took her quiet faith very seriously but never herself overly so.

I took professional insight and personal wisdom from these moments of easy companionship when we roamed around, went to church, talked about everything—God, books, children, art, dogs, music, history, the passing scene or the passing landscape. Occasionally, we even talked about golf and Arnold. I learned she loved the paintings of Andrew Wyeth and David Armstrong, the piano of Doug Montgomery, Andy Rooney commentaries and a well-made Fitzgerald old-fashioned. The rest of the short list included her daughters and seven grandchildren, icebox cake, good manners, peonies, her brother Marty, London's West End, Augusta galleries, cozy hotels, museums of any kind, early suppers, British golf writers and phone conversations with her partner-in-crime, Barbara Nicklaus.

Speaking of crime, the woman seemed to have read every other book published in the English language, especially mysteries. She was keen for a foggy night, a door left ajar, a crime unsolved. Somehow, she also found time to read half a dozen or so magazines and regularly corresponded with friends by way of handwritten notes packed with clipped articles she thought they should read. I used to kid her that if golf failed to pan out for

Arnie, she could support them both by starting a journalism clipping service.

I loved her Moravian sense of economy and value. After my children and I lost our retrievers to old age, Winnie set out to help me find the right replacement. She introduced me to a woman she'd heard about who bred champion goldens. A month or so later the woman rang me up to say she had the "perfect" dog for us: a three-year-old spayed female, beautiful disposition, papers, the whole nine yards, and a real bargain at just eighteen hundred dollars. When I reported this news to Winnie, she thundered, "Don't you dare buy that dog or I'll reach into this phone and break your arm!"

Her funeral service at Unity Chapel, on a stunning Indian summer day, was a simple and beautiful affair. The music was Bach and Beethoven. A few prayers of thanksgiving were read, the navy hymn sung. Her granddaughter Emily read a few passages from Proverbs. There was no eulogy under Winnie's strict orders—but none was necessary because each of us sat there writing our own eulogies in our heads for the new patron saint of golf wives.

After a little while—Winnie hated services that went on too long—we all filed out and drove to Latrobe Country Club for lunch. In the din of conversation, I was pleased to see Arnold laughing again, gently needling Jack when he pulled out a cellular phone to see how Gary was doing at the PGA Tour Q School. A few minutes later, I saw him lead George and Barbara Bush out the grillroom door, and I knew exactly where he was taking them—to see Winnie's barn, now fully restored, sitting in the autumnal sunlight like a David Armstrong original.

The truth is, some of us stood there worrying about how Arnold Palmer will fare without his Pennsylvania original, Winnie. I was lost in these thoughts, I confess, selfishly thinking how I was going to miss Arnold and

Latrobe and most of all, my weekly phone conversations with Winnie, when a large, strong pair of hands suddenly settled on my shoulders. I turned around and it was Arnold, looking at me with what Winnie once called his "Deacon look."

We hadn't really spoken up to this point. Perhaps I'd even consciously evaded him a bit—and maybe him, me. He knew what I thought of his wife, how we were all a bit in awe and in love with pretty Winnie Walzer. He thanked me for coming, and I asked him for the second time in two days if he was okay. Arnold's look softened. His eyes began to glisten.

"I'm okay for now," golf's most public man said softly of his most private loss. We both knew it would be the early mornings and evenings to come that would be toughest for him to get through, when Winnie's presence filled their house with such warm abundance.

He cleared his throat and managed a smile. "The good news is, she left me good instructions on how to live the rest of my life," he said, still squeezing my arm with those huge blacksmith hands of his, perhaps picturing Winnie that gorgeous summer day on the hill above the barn. Remembering her as I always will.

"Very firm instructions," he said.

James Dodson

4

GOLFMANSHIP

Straight Down the Fairway

The game has such a hold on golfers because they compete not only against an opponent, but also against the course, against par, and most surely—against themselves.

Arnold Palmer

Alberta's Jasper Park Lodge in 1940 was a place for the rich. On my first day as a caddie, I was out with an old bird in cap and pipe, a pretty good golfer who, moreover, paid me $2.50 for eighteen holes. When I asked if I could caddie for him regularly, he agreed. I asked Vic, the young assistant pro, how long he thought my old bird would be a guest.

"All summer," Vic said. "His name is William D. Mitchell. He comes every year for the whole summer, and he plays seven days a week. He was a member of Herbert Hoover's cabinet, the attorney general, I think."

Boy oh boy, two-fifty a day, guaranteed, every day of the week for ten weeks equaled—my brain worked at high speed—$175 less, say, $25 for rainy days or the old codger being sick now and then. But he never got sick, and only the foulest weather kept him away.

I seldom caddied for anyone except Mr. Mitchell. He played deliberately and said almost nothing. He knew my first name, but didn't encourage me to impart any further information. One day when we were out on the course alone, I timidly asked about the senators from Vermont (my Quebec hometown borders on that state). "Give me the 5-iron, please, David," he said. And that was that.

Mr. Mitchell's summer was dedicated to breaking 80, and I got caught up in his silent campaign. He was easy to caddie for; he didn't hit the ball a great distance, was only rarely in the rough, and he putted well.

Once in a while he would top his drive and dribble the ball off the tee. He didn't complain and never had me retrieve the ball for another drive, even when he was playing alone. He walked the few feet to the ball in front of the tee and said. "Two-iron, please, David."

The summer wore on, and my man's score descended little by little. He was seldom worse than 85 or 86, and halfway through August he hit an 81, and then 80, twice.

One day he dropped a long birdie putt at the par-4 sixteenth, and I realized that par on the last two holes would give him a 79.

"There's a good chance, sir," I said.

"Don't say it. It's bad luck, like talking about a no-hitter in the eighth inning." But there was a gleam in his eye.

He was playing with another old bird who didn't talk much either. My man's drive on the par-4 seventeenth was straight down the center. The ball carried over a little crest and out of sight. His companion had a good tee shot too, carrying over the same ridge.

Mr. Mitchell stopped to relight his pipe, and I went ahead, saw the ball when I reached the top of the ridge, and parked the bag and myself beside it, waiting for him to select his iron. He took a 6-iron and dropped the ball on the green. Easy par, I said to myself, thinking of a huge tip.

His playing partner was also on the green in two, but away. He was close with his putt and tapped in immediately. Mr. Mitchell was a little strong, but came back nicely with a five-footer for his par 4. I went to retrieve his ball from the cup and put the flag back.

I soon realized that it wasn't his ball. It was the other guy's. I hadn't checked when I'd come over the ridge and had just assumed the first ball I saw was his. I wished the cup was a hundred feet deep and that I'd fall into it.

"I'll just wash the ball," I said, heading for the scrubber on the eighteenth tee and hoping I could switch the balls. I signaled the other caddie to come quick.

"No, David, don't wash it," Mr. Mitchell said. "That might break my string."

I handed him the ball as nonchalantly as I could, without looking at him. I prayed. But when he leaned over to tee up the ball, he saw.

"I'm afraid this isn't my ball," he said to the other golfer, looking stricken.

His companion looked at his. "You're right," he said.

"There's a two-stroke penalty for that," Mr. Mitchell said. "That gives me a 6."

"Don't be silly," his companion said. "We're just playing for fun."

"It wouldn't be right. Rules are rules." I knew he would have said the same thing even if he hadn't been attorney general of the United States.

He would have to shoot an eagle 2 on the last hole to break 80. I prayed hard he would make a bogey 5, so that, even without the disaster on the seventeenth, he still wouldn't have shot 79. He looked weary and drawn. But he shot a par 4.

"I'm sorry, sir," I said, nearly crying. "It was all my fault."

"No, David, it wasn't," he said. "I should have looked too. See you tomorrow."

He played another five rounds, but didn't do better than 82. He never mentioned the switched balls.

"Maybe next summer," he said when we parted for the last time.

"I hope so, sir."

Dave McIntosh

Payback

The measure of a man's real character is what he would do if he knew he would never be found out.

Thomas Macaulay

Bob stood on the first tee taking in the sunrise, enjoying a picture-perfect June morning. As the dew glistened on the neatly groomed grass, he wondered who his playing partner for the day would be. He had decided at the last minute to head out to the course without a tee time with the hope of being worked in with another group.

As luck would have it, there was a tournament going off that day. As such, no one was allowed to tee off until after 11:00 A.M., but the club pro let Bob sneak on ahead of the tournament as long as he pledged to keep up the pace. The only other disclaimer was that he was being paired with another "walk-on."

So there was Bob standing on the tee box, and enjoying the fine day waiting for his mystery partner to appear, when up walked Steve Henderson. *OH, NO!* Bob screamed to himself.

It just so happened that Bob and Steve had gone to high school together, with "together" meaning only that they were both in the same building every day. They lived in two different worlds—Bob in that of the socially awkward types; Steve in the realm of studly athletes. The only interaction Bob had with Steve was when Steve would give him a "wedgie" after gym class or administer some type of other public humiliation on him at any random moment.

Bob had spent four years constantly in fear of the sudden and cruel attacks inflicted upon him and his friends by the athletes hanging out in the hallway at the "Jock Wall."

Now here they were ten years later in a nightmarish reunion of the predator and the prey. *Only now,* Bob thought, *we are on a more level playing field,* as Bob was a pretty decent golfer. It also soon became apparent that Steve had absolutely no recollection of Bob.

Bob, sensing a chance to deliver a dose of retribution upon his tormentor from days gone by, started out with some small talk. Then knowing Steve's inherent competitive nature from his days as a star quarterback, quickly suggested putting a little wager on the round—of, say, one hundred dollars. In a flash Steve accepted and Bob was ready to deal some long overdue payback.

However, Bob had failed to factor in the fact that Steve was also a pretty decent golfer, and they were tied up as they headed to the eighteenth tee. Bob started to panic somewhat, not having much acquaintance with competitive arenas.

I can't let this guy beat me again. I can't live my whole life without sticking it to this guy at least once! Bob reached deep within to summon all of his remaining inner strength and will to finally defeat the wretched demon from his youth—and promptly shanked the ball into the woods.

Steve, being the calm, cool and collected athlete, drilled the ball down the middle of the fairway.

That's alright, thought Bob, *as long as I'm not behind a tree I'll be fine.*

Bob, of course, was behind a tree.

As he stood looking at his ball, he thought back to the day that Steve had humiliated him in the school cafeteria. Bob had finally worked up the courage to ask Nancy Lewis to the senior prom.

Steve had thwarted his effort at romance just to amuse himself and his Cro-Magnon friends who thought it would be a great stunt to dump a plate of food on Bob's head. Nancy had looked over at the commotion and saw Bob standing there with spaghetti hanging from his ears, and she had laughed.

Now, as Bob stared at his ball hopelessly pinned behind an old cottonwood tree, reliving the anguish, he felt a burning anger rising up inside him. He was not going to let Steve win again, no matter what the cost.

Glancing quickly to make sure Steve was not looking, Bob kicked the ball out into the fairway.

"Boy, I sure got a lucky bounce," Bob yelled over, trying to sound as convincing as he could, but deep down knowing that Steve would always have his doubts about the "lucky" bounce.

As it was, Bob went on to win the hole and the match, and collected his one hundred dollars. Most of the round Bob had been dreaming of the moment that he would take The Great Tormentor's cash and how he would dance around the green and joyously rub the payback in his face. Only now that the moment was here, he didn't feel like dancing. He quietly took the money and walked away.

On his way home in the car, Bob began to cry.

He was still upset when he arrived home. He tearfully recounted the entire tale to his puzzled and concerned wife, who had never before heard of the torment her husband was carrying inside.

After a while, they both decided that no matter what had happened in the past, exacting revenge in this manner was no way to behave. So together they drove over to Steve's house to apologize and return the ill-gotten wager.

As they sat in Steve's living room confessing, a curious transformation came over Steve, who had his wife at his side. At first he was visibly angry over being cheated, but as he slowly began to recall that he had in fact known Bob in the past, his face began to soften. By the time Bob had finished, both Steve and his wife were teary-eyed.

Steve had often looked back regretfully at his youth, wishing he could take back some of the mean-spirited things he had done during a time when he simply didn't know any better. Now here was an opportunity staring him in the face.

The men apologized, and the couples cried, laughed and recounted old tales late into the night. As Bob pulled out of Steve's driveway, he thought to himself that it would make a nice ending to the story if he and Steve would now become friends, and laugh about those "crazy high school days." But he knew that wasn't going to happen. Most likely he would never talk to Steve again unless they happened to have another chance encounter on the links.

But he also knew that did not matter. He knew that they both would from this day forward walk through life with a slightly lighter step, both of them having shed some heavy demons on a gorgeous day in June.

Scott Hipp

Playing It Down

*There can be no happiness if the things we
believe in are different from the things we do.*
Freya Stark

Like the vast majority of golfers, I was ruled by the concept of fairness. My self-worth was a reflection of my golf
score. When I first began playing, I would move my ball to
improve my lie or to eliminate an obstacle from its path.

As my game improved, I felt the need to move my ball
less frequently, except on occasions when the concept of
fairness came into play. When a ball is struck cleanly, soaring directly at its selected target, we deserve to be aptly
rewarded. This ball, dead center in the fairway, merits an
appropriate lie, not in a divot or another poor setting.

Good shots SHOULD be rewarded. So we move that
ball. Fairness calls for it. I, like most other golfers—winter-
rules players—moved it.

In time, guided by the wisdom of Harvey Penick, a profound change began to free me.

Golf was not about fairness. The ball was to be played
from where it sat. There are benefits to this approach,

Mr. Penick said, and I would seek to discover them. In golf, as in life, obstacles are placed in our path. In overcoming these roadblocks, our greatest triumphs occur. By improving our lie, we are only cheating ourselves of the opportunity to achieve.

There are no good or bad lies, only what is. When we see things as they are, without judgment, we provide ourselves an opportunity to come through with our best performances. This state of mind will not ensure success, only our best effort. For me, there was a gradual change in my outlook. At first, in situations when that concept of fairness came into play, the unfairness of my lie dominated my thoughts. Weak shots tended to follow. Over time, as I began to free my mind of judgments, better results occurred. I began to look at situations and make objective determinations that would give me the maximum chance for success.

One anecdote always comes to mind. I was paired with a stranger, playing a par-5 that often proved difficult. I hit two perfect shots. One hundred yards to the pin, MY perfect distance, but in a two-inch hole. My mind lapsed to a similar situation earlier that week. That divot had seized my clubhead and, as a result, I shanked my ball into the woods. I remembered that, although the result was poor, I was proud that I did what was right. My thoughts now returned to the present situation, and as I chose my course of action, I remember thinking to myself, "I'm going to stick it and make birdie." Just before I was ready to hit, I glanced at my playing partner. His look seemed to say, "What are you doing? Take the ball out of that hole."

I stuck that ball two feet from the pin and made birdie. I smiled, inside and out. As we left the green, he asked me why I didn't move my ball. After all, I WAS in a hole in the fairway. "Because that's not golf," I replied.

Leonard Finkel

We Play 'Em All

It was a typically pleasant early spring South Carolina day as our regular group of twelve prepared on the first tee for the normal Tuesday morning match. As usual, Henry's risqué jokes created enough confusion to raise Bob's dander a little as he pulled the balls from the hat to line up the foursomes to compete for the much sought-after two-dollar Nassau. . . . Nassau? Perhaps! Bragging rights? Absolutely!

As our last group teed off, the gentle breeze at our backs helped our drives travel a little further than usual down the first fairway. It was the beginning of a good game for all of us, with Dick's short game working very well, Rich knocking the cover off the ball, Henry playing his wide slice to perfection and my putter performing well enough to allow me to do better than my 24 handicap.

After about four holes we noticed a twosome creeping up close behind us. Before we could motion them through, they fell back again, only to close the gap again on holes 8 and 9. We thought that perhaps they would go through as we stopped for a snack at the turn, but they did not, only to get close again on No. 12. Being a true advocate of golf-course courtesy, I took advantage of

Henry's slice into the woods to go back and invite them to play through.

"Sorry to hold you up . . . would you like to play through?"

"Thank you for asking but we're doing just fine. We don't get in a hurry anymore. Just being out here and enjoying our friendship, this wonderful game and God's glorious universe is quite enough for both of us. . . . You see, Joel here is ninety-one and I'm eighty-nine years old, and we have enough aches and pains that we only play the downhill holes!"

William M. Bowen

A True Gentleman

If you think it's hard to meet people, try picking up the wrong golf ball.

Jack Lemmon

Several years ago, golfer William Reynders received a Christmas gift from his family: a dozen Titleist balls with the name "Billy Reynders" imprinted on them. Shortly after, while playing a muni course in Sacramento, one of his errant drives went onto an adjoining fairway. When he arrived at his ball, he found a lady preparing to hit. He explained to her that she might be playing his ball. She then picked up the ball, looked at it and coolly stated, "No. This is mine. I always play Billy Reynders balls." Being the gentleman that he is, Reynders did not argue.

Hugh Baldwin

The Day I Cheated

Golf is like solitaire. When you cheat, you cheat only yourself.

Tony Lema

Golf has always been the game I love. The physical challenge. The mental challenge. The ability to summon a shot from the depths of my being when double bogey is staring me down. Golf is pure, and that's the way I play it. Except for that time a few years ago.

For the first time, for the only time, I cheated in a golf match. It haunts me to this day. It was against my best golfing buddy, Frank, and it changed me as a person and as a golfer. Forever.

Until that heated match one Sunday afternoon, I had never intentionally broken or even bent a single rule of golf. Never.

Like so many of our duels, our match that day was all square going into the eighteenth hole, a par-5 where anything worse than par meant losing the hole. At stake was the normal whopping three dollars. I hooked badly into the woods off the tee. Frank, aka Steady Eddie, split the middle of the fairway as usual.

After a short search alone amongst the trees, I found my ball wedged between two roots. It was quite unplayable.

Through the leaves, I could see Frank striding toward his tee shot. I dropped within two club lengths and smacked a 3-iron through an opening in the trees. Frank was applauding as I emerged from the woods, and for good reason. My ball laid 175 yards down the fairway in perfect position for my approach.

A few minutes later, Frank tapped in to match my "par."

"Nice match," he said, extending his hand. "No blood."

I shook his hand and kept my mouth shut. I don't know why. I have thought about that day often, and I have no answers.

I remember throwing cold water on my face in the clubhouse restroom after the round. I stared at myself in the mirror and let the water drip back into the sink.

Frank had obviously not seen me take the drop in the woods. He assumed my tap-in was for par, when I knew very well that it was for bogey. So I kept my three dollars that day.

The next morning I took a long hard look at myself. I wondered who this cheating person was and how long he would be around. It pained me to have cheated, and it pained me to have dishonored a game I consider so noble.

I can't help but think about that afternoon as each new golf season begins. I remember how badly I felt, but mostly I remind myself how good it feels to walk off a green after having ground out a par, a real par, or maybe even a hard-fought bogey, from a situation that looked like a sure double. I tell myself that the shots that feel the best—the ones you remember in the nineteenth hole and in the car on the ride home—are those you pull off from horrendous lies with a clump of mud stuck to the ball. I remind myself that my playing partners—my friends—should never, ever, have to question my integrity on the course, no matter how miraculous my recovery shot.

A trip to Ireland last year emphasized to me the importance of the relationship between golf and integrity. "Lad," said an Irishman I played a round with, "over here we touch the ball just twice each hole: when we tee it up and when we pluck it from the bottom of the cup."

Perhaps more than anything, it is precisely such memories of the men and women whom I have had the honor of walking a round with over in Ireland and Scotland that compel me to be true to myself on the course. It seems every player over there has been somehow imbued with the spirit of Old Tom Morris. Just as they cannot comprehend why Americans would choose to ride around in a "buggy" when it is abundantly clear that golf is walking, neither can they understand why anyone would ever do something as foolish and demeaning as cheating on the course.

In the British Isles, golf is played by the rules, and never by "winter rules."

The majority of players in this country break the rules—or choose to ignore them—every weekend, never understanding that they are diminishing themselves every time they roll it in the fairway. Is there a truer adage than the one that says we can tell everything we need to know about a person's character by playing a round of golf with him or her? If your playing partners witness you bumping your ball in the fairway, do you think this doesn't influence their opinion of you?

I only wonder what Frank thinks of me.

John Meyers

The Clutch Putt

Pressure is part of golf. It shows up when a golfer fails to make a shot he would normally make because he tries too hard. A non-golfer doesn't understand this when he watches Freddie Couples nonchalantly knock in a fifteen-foot putt.

All golfers have experienced pressure, but what is perhaps more difficult to comprehend is the amount of additional pressure that is created when golf is played as a team sport, rather than an individual one. The fear of letting your teammates down is undoubtedly the big factor.

Whether golfers are playing in the Ryder Cup or the Border League, they have to contend with this extra pressure. In these parts, the Border League is a group of golf and country clubs along the New York State-Eastern Ontario border that play an annual team competition: eight-man teams from each club—total score to count—medal play.

One such competition was being played at the Prescott, Ontario, Club, a nice course overlooking the St. Lawrence River. I was a member of the Cornwall, Ontario, team. Most observers were saying if anybody was going to beat the home club, it would probably be us. As the day progressed, this analysis proved correct—Prescott and Cornwall well ahead of the other clubs. Seven of our eight players were in now, waiting and relaxing at the nineteenth hole, as golfers sometimes do, and our eighth man was now on the eighteenth tee. Our eighth man was Reggie Evans, an 8-handicapper, a school principal by profession, a keen but occasionally erratic golfer. We, of course, were tired, but anxious about the outcome. Somebody said, "Kenny, it's your turn—go over to the scoreboard and see how we stand." A quick trip over to the board revealed that all teams now had seven players finished and the scores were listed by teams. The scorekeeper, whoever he was, hadn't given us any subtotals, so I checked them out, did some quick mental additions and went back to where my teammates were sitting.

"Hey fellas, we got this thing in the bag—we are eleven shots up on Prescott and Reggie was one up on his man after nine; surely he can't blow a twelve-shot lead on the back nine."

The elation and excitement were rising; somebody suggested, "Hey, let's go over to the edge of the green and cheer Reggie in."

"Good idea."

By this time, Reggie had played his second shot onto the green—pin high about twenty feet to the right of the flag.

"Let's have some fun," I suggested. "Let's tell Reggie that he has to sink that putt."

"Wait," cautioned Alex. "Before you do that, you had better check out his lead—you wouldn't want to blow us out of first place."

"Okay."

We joined the small greenside gallery as the players approached the green. The Prescott player chipped up for what looked like a tap-in par, and the other two players had played onto the green when Reg came around to where I had strategically positioned myself.

"How are you doing, Reg?" I asked.

"Pretty good, Kenny, two putts here and I break 80."

"How is the Prescott player doing?"

"Well, let me see now, he'll get his par here and he will be one stroke ahead of me. How is the team doing?"

The stage was set and set perfectly.

"Look, Reg, listen now, we have a one-stroke lead over Prescott—you've got to sink that putt."

"A one-stroke lead?" Reg muttered, as he digested the situation. His facial muscles tightened. "That's not an easy putt."

"Give it a go, Reg. Knock it in and we win, but hell, don't three putt it."

Reg was on the green now, putter in hand, crouched behind the ball, studying the roll of the green.

"Don't be short, Reggie," chirped Joe from greenside.

"Shush, Joe, don't distract him," whispered Alex. But Reg wasn't going to be distracted; he was in full concentration like I have never seen him before. Things were working perfectly. He looked over the line from both directions, studied the surface to make sure there were no impediments, and now he was back behind the ball again.

My teammates were all watching intently, some with expectant grins on their faces. We were expecting anything, but inwardly hoping he might sink this putt.

Reggie took a couple of practice swings with his putter to ensure a smooth stroke and now took his position over the ball—pause—here it comes—the ball jumped off the putter face—bobbled a bit—lots of speed—a bit to the right of the cup—now a slowing down and breaking towards the cup.

"It's in!—way to go, Reggie—you did it! Boy!"

Loud cheers and high fives from the gang and then a

sudden shushed silence to allow the others to putt out; then handshakes all around and back to the lounge to celebrate our victory.

When Reg sank into his chair, his face reflected both relief and excitement from his achievement. About this time, Joe decided to let the cat out of the bag. "Reggie, you really didn't have to sink the putt. We won by eleven strokes—we were just putting you on."

"Aw, you guys," groaned Reg, "you don't know the pressure you put on me out there."

"We just wanted to see how good you really are," I ventured. The chatter continued, only to be interrupted by the public address system: "Ladies and gentlemen, here are the results of today's tournament.

"In first place, Cornwall, with a total of . . ."

"Yeaaaa."

"In second place, one stroke behind, Prescott with a total of . . ."

"One stroke behind?"

"One stroke behind. Hey, Kenny, where did you learn to add?" exclaimed Alex.

"Aw come on, fellas," I said, "I was only telling Reggie the truth out there. You didn't expect me to lie to him, did you?"

Ken Robertson

The Gentle Hustler

It was June 1952 when Hal Bruce was transferred to Boise, Idaho. He had no trouble finding an affordable apartment, but a golf course was a bit more difficult. When he looked in the phone book only two were listed, and because one was private, he called the municipal course to ask about a starting time Sunday morning.

"Come on down any time before nine," said a friendly voice, "before church lets out."

He showed up at 8:30 A.M. and sure enough, the place was deserted. The only soul in sight was a slight woman, maybe in her seventies, chipping balls onto the putting green. After Hal paid and made his way to the first tee, he looked over at the woman. She waved and began to walk—limp, actually—toward him.

"Well, son, no sense in us playin' alone on such a fine mornin'," she said with a peculiar, lilting accent. "How 'bout if I join you? I'm Mary O'Leary."

"Good morning. I'm Hal Bruce." They shook hands.

"Hal," she said, "what with lumbago and all, I'm only good for nine holes. By the way, what's your handicap?"

"Well, since this is my first time on the course, I don't have one here, but I normally carry about a 10."

"Fine. But seein' as you're new to the place, I'll spot you a couple of strokes to make the game more fun."

Hal couldn't take such an offer and protested. "Oh, I couldn't do that. After all, we're just here to enjoy the fresh air. No big stakes are involved."

Mary seemed disappointed. "Okay, but I always play better under a bit of pressure."

Her backswing had a little hitch and she didn't have much length, but everything was hit cleanly up the middle. Putting seemed to be her main weakness, but Mary also chipped in from the fringe a few times, which evened things out. Coming to the par-4 ninth, both players had totaled 38.

When Mary requested a short rest, they took a breather on the bench. After asking a few questions about his work and home life, she said, "You know, Hal, I don't usually gamble at golf, but this mornin' I feel lucky. I went off and left my purse on the kitchen table, but Mike let me put the greens fee on my tab. Just for the heck of it, I'll play the last hole for what's on my bill. If I lose, I'll pick up the tab for both of us another day."

Hal hated himself for taking advantage of the sweet, and now tired, old woman but he agreed. The ninth sported a frog-infested pond about 180 yards out; it was straight away, but Mary chose a 3-iron and hit her ball safely to the left, into the eighth fairway. Hal used a 3-wood, hit it fat and drowned the ball. Mary hit her second near the green, chipped close and made par, which was good enough against Hal's bogey. Just before departing, she shook his hand, "Hal, I really enjoyed this game. Can we do it again next Sunday?"

"Sure," he replied eagerly. "See you next week." Then she walked off toward the parking lot and Hal went into the modest golf shop.

Mike was behind the counter when Hal told him he was paying Mary O'Leary's bill. Mike smirked, opened a

file and said, "Well, Mary is in arrears for two greens fees
. . . balls . . . and a bag of tees. The total's $15.10. But an
even fifteen will be close enough."

On the way back to his apartment, Hal knew one thing:
He wasn't about to be skunked twice by a woman—especially one old enough to be his grandmother—so that
week he hit balls every day after work, sharpened up his
short game and even took a lesson.

On Sunday, as expected, Mary offered him a chance to
get even. "What say we play for the price of my tab from
last Sunday?" she asked on the first tee. "And I'll still spot
you two strokes."

"I'll take 'em," he said firmly.

Mary had him two down on the ninth tee, so they
played the last hole with nothing at stake. Hal thanked
her for the match and, after she left, he made his way to
the golf shop. After forking over fifteen bucks for the second straight weekend, Hal went to the bar for a beer and
sat down next to an elderly gentleman who was obviously a regular.

"Well, friend," the stranger said, "I see you played with
ol' Mary today. How much has she taken you for?"

"Only about a day's wages, but how did you know?"

He took a sip of his cocktail, re-lit a cold stogie and
explained, "Mary is sort of a fixture around here. I met up
with her a couple of years ago when I moved from
California. The experience led to a little research. I found
out that she came from Ireland, was a pretty famous golfer
in Europe before she turned pro over here and now sur-
vives by waiting tables at the country club. Once or twice
a week she comes out and plays with newcomers—anyone she doesn't know. During the winter she goes to
Arizona and does the same thing. Nothing illegal, mind
you, and she keeps her tab paid up, so they tolerate her."

It was about a month later when the doorbell rang, just

as Hal was sticking dinner into the oven. Upon opening the door he saw a young woman standing in the hallway. "Are you Hal Bruce?" she asked.

"Yes. Come in."

"Thanks, but I'm in a bit of a hurry. You're the last on my list. You were a friend of Mary O'Leary's?"

"Well, I met her a couple of times."

"I'm Megan O'Leary," she explained. "Mary was my grandmother. She passed away in the County Hospital two weeks ago and wanted you to have this." She handed Hal an envelope.

He couldn't begin to understand why a woman he had met only twice would send him something, but as soon as Hal opened the envelope he realized what it was—a bill from the golf course.

"Her bill began to add up," Megan said. "Just before she passed away she wrote down the names of all those who owed her a game."

As he stood there, staring at the little slip of paper, Hal realized what Megan—or more clearly, Mary—was saying. He was to pay for the outcome of a game never played.

Megan looked at him intently. "She said if anyone became angry, to take it back." She reached out her hand.

"No . . . no," Hal insisted. "I'll take care of it." Then he laughed. "Mary was absolutely right. This would no doubt have been the outcome."

Bob Brust

The Compassionate Golfer

Down south, where snowflakes are seldom seen, there lived an elderly gentleman who was an excellent golfer. Even in his seventies, he could beat the most self-assured of the younger golfers. It wasn't uncommon for him to shoot his age, and the year he turned seventy-two, he shot eight rounds that bettered his age. Over the years he was often asked why he didn't turn pro. His reply was always the same. With a mischievous grin he'd whisper, "I'll let you in on a little secret. With my job, I get to golf as much as the pros, and I probably enjoy the game more."

Many an ardent golfer would request a game with him, to which he happily obliged. Every now and then, he would get beat by a lesser golfer. For the forty-some years that he was a member of the club, no one could figure it out. How could he beat the club pro one day and lose to a mediocre guest the next? The consensus in the clubhouse was that he didn't know how to be a tough competitor. His wife knew better, however.

Whenever her husband would come home from a day at the golf course, she greeted him with a kiss and asked, "Did the guy you played against need a self-esteem booster?" If he answered "Yes," her next question was, "How bad did you let him beat you?"

Carla Muir

Victory for the Golf Rats

There are two games called golf, but the only thing the same about them is the little white balls. One game is club golf. The other game I call "golf-rat" golf.

In club golf the players arrive when they want, and play when they want. They walk or ride and rarely wait. They never have bad lies in the perfectly raked bunkers or on the triplex-cut fairways. They never get thirsty or hungry because there is something to eat or drink around the next dogleg. And after a four-hour round, their golf shoes barely hit the lockeroom carpet before an attendant scoops them up to be polished, bagged and returned. Hot showers, steam baths and a drink at the bar end a leisurely day of club golf.

In golf-rat golf, the players stagger out of bed before dawn, drive to the local public course so they can stand in a long line, drink bad coffee from a plastic cup and pray that they can get a starting time within the next three hours. When they do play they pray that the foursome ahead gets off the green before the foursome behind beans them with their drives. They blast out of bunkers that look like the lunar landscape and hit out of fairways with divots the size of craters. They eat the cold sandwiches and melted candy bars squashed into their tattered golf bags. But mostly they wait, and wait and wait. After five and a half or six hours the golf rats stagger back to their cars, stash their wet and dirty golf shoes in their trunk and head home to families who were beginning to wonder if they had been kidnapped.

Almost all the courses we see in televised golf tournaments are the guts of club golf, but the galleries that throng to those tournaments are the guts of golf-rat golf. When we gathered at Bethpage to announce the coming of the U.S. Open to the Black Course in 2002, the golf rats were there. They were the people standing behind the fence at the back of the first tee—watching and nodding silently and waiting for that day when the best golfers in the world would play their course. They knew that the decision to give the U.S. Open to a truly public course for the first time was not just a victory for the metropolitan area, for Long Island, for politicians or the businesses nearby. They knew that this decision was the greatest victory in the history of the game for public golfers—the golf rats.

It is a victory because it is a way to honor the public spaces that offer rare and precious shelter from the ugliness of urban life to those who do not have enough money to buy private shelter in places affluent people know.

It is a victory because it is a reminder that golf was first played on unmanicured farmer's fields with ruts and valleys, weeds and, yes, even cow dung. And although there will probably be precious little manure on the fairways of the Black Course during the Open, it will still, I hope, be at least a little raw, a little wild, a little public.

Most of all, however, it is a victory because, six years from now, there will be a dad who works hard and has little in material terms to show for it, a guy like my dad, who will be able to say to his son or daughter, "Oh yeah, the U.S. Open is at the Black Course this year. I've played it."

Rabbi Marc Gellman, Ph.D.

A Practice Round for Life

The ball soared forward, arching away from its perch on the ladies tee without a trace of slice or hook, and landed with a solid *"whump."* I was too far away to see it a foot or so from the cup on the eighteenth green. Grinning from ear to ear, my father said, "You'll be back next week."

When you're a kid, it seems like your parents utter the same mantras over and over, day after day—"wash your hands, eat your peas." For my father, playing golf with me was his venue for spouting forth a barrage of maxims gleaned from a lifetime of living. Often, by the time we'd reached the eighteenth hole, I'd heard, "Never up, never in" at least four times. I was never sure if this phrase related wholly to golf, or had some deeper meaning in the overall scheme of existence. Still, I was only thirty-four and had a lot of learning yet to do.

"No way, Dad," I told him. "I hate this game."

He'd heard that one a few times, too. He ignored it, even though he knew, perhaps, it was the truth.

It was, almost. As a busy, career-minded, up-and-coming investment trader who hustled and clawed her way to the top of a demanding, frenetic field, I thought golf was a pointless, boring way to spend an afternoon. It just happened to be my father's favorite pastime since he'd grown a little too old to play tennis the way he was used to as a teaching pro. So now he loved playing golf with his coterie of cronies, but he loved playing golf with me, just the two of us, probably more than anything else in the world.

I was, of course, a very busy person, but I loved my dad and squeezed a round with him into my schedule whenever possible.

I drove the cart past the palms and pines lining the fairway. It was a glorious Florida afternoon with a slight breeze off the ocean and the songs of birds in stereo. My father could not have been happier. His grin would just not go away. I think this was years before the phrase "quality time" was coined, but that's what we were spending together. Since the time I was born, my dad sequestered every spare minute to spend time with me in active pursuits—tennis, of course, but also surfing, basketball, skating, building sand castles, gardening and just hanging together. Even when we puttered around, not a minute had been wasted, because the memories that remained were like splashes of molten gold. At the very least, I owed him this.

When we approached my ball, he patted me on the back, acknowledging, "You're really good at this game."

"Yeah. What about the last seventeen holes?" I had played dismally, but a father's love for a daughter is beyond reason or logic. He always, without fail, looked for the good in people and in life, and every round of golf was a good one.

"Don't worry about the past," he'd say. "It's the hole that lies ahead that matters." Another gem of unmitigated common sense I ignored, but which had somehow stubbornly insinuated its way by osmotic repetition into the web of my life.

Even though my ball was only inches from the cup, I missed the putt. I was thinking about the beer I would be having in the clubhouse instead of focusing on the moment. I slammed the head of my putter into the green, fully aware displays of impatient annoyance irked him, the quintessential sportsman who never showed his emotions during play.

He ignored my outburst as though it never happened. His shot from the edge of the green rolled smoothly into the hole, landing with that satisfying plunk of a golf ball coming home. We tallied our scores, and he had beaten me by a mere fifteen strokes.

I had never once bested my father in anything, much less golf. He had innate athletic ability and his concentration and ability to focus were unmatched. Part of it was about being a female, about never being quite as good. When the frustration got to me at times, he would say patiently, "Don't ever let being a woman be an excuse." When he saw that one didn't work, he would fall back on the old standby, "Things will be better tomorrow." I loved that one. Never mind that he was right.

When my dad was diagnosed with cancer and the doctors said with grim finality that he would not recover, I took a leave of absence from my job. This was many years before the Family Medical Leave Act made this an acceptable and legal avenue. I didn't know how long he had to live and didn't care that I might lose my job and all the effort it had taken to get it. All of sudden, those gems of thought, those words of wisdom I'd shoved to the hinterlands of my psyche took on a crystal clarity. I wanted to immerse myself in his wisdom, understanding, patience and all the other stable qualities he had but I had been too busy to care about, before they would be lost forever. It appeared to others as though I was making a sacrifice for him. But the truth was I needed him now, even though he had been there for me every day of my life. We played golf as much as we could, until he couldn't play anymore, and I soaked up his insights like a woman lost in the desert of life without water.

When he died, all of his golfing friends, most of whom I'd never met, came to the funeral. It made me sadly aware of how little I knew of his life outside our time together. It also became apparent, as they paid their respects in various ways, that he had bragged to them about what a great golfer I was. It was a ruse I tried to stifle, but I knew that even in death, he had used his love of golf in yet another way to profess his love and confidence in me.

I don't mean to imply my dad was perfect. He could sometimes be a bit inconsistent. Nonetheless, today, ten years later, I would give up every car, every house, every everything I have ever had for one round of golf with him, just for the simple pleasure of absorbing each link in his chain of pithy expressions: "Relax, it's just a game!" which he alternated to suit the occasion with, "Golf is much more than a game, sweetheart. It's a practice round for life!"

Debra Moss

Snakes Alive!

Golf is temporary insanity practiced in a pasture.

Dave Kindred

Dave Harris, my roommate and golfing partner in college, was almost a scratch golfer. He would have been invited to play on the university team except for one frailty; he was an incorrigible practical joker. Sometimes it was the duck call he blew during somebody's back-swing, but mostly it came from the collection of rubber snakes in his golf bag. One afternoon, a burly freshman from Spokane lined up a putt on the 6th hole, but backed off when, out of the corner of his eye, he spied a nasty-looking articulated python lying on the green. "Harris," he said, "you pull this stuff again and I'll part that blond crew cut with a 5-iron and reduce your fat frame to blubber!" So Dave laid off for a while, but one afternoon while playing as a twosome at Green Hill Country Club, he caused a big black snake with yellow stripes to appear suddenly at my feet just as I was about to tee off.

Then in the spring of 1947, Dave and I parted company. I took a job with the Montana State Highway Department, but he stuck around at the University of Washington to go for his masters; I ended up on a sizable construction job working out of Shelby in northern Montana. Shelby's major claim to fame was having been the scene of the infamous Dempsey/Gibbons prize fight in 1923; a gigantic billboard on the road into town told the passing world about it. Its other notable feature was that it was one of the few prairie towns up along the High-Line to sport a real municipal golf course.

The course was singularly spartan in its configuration. The locals had simply mowed down a few acres of buffalograss for fairways, set the mower as low as it would go to make greens, dragged in an old granary for a starter's shack, and voila!—instant golf course. But they had to dig the cups about two feet deep so the wind wouldn't blow the flagsticks over, and most short putts were conceded because nobody relished the idea of reaching up to the elbow into those dark recesses for a ball. Also, a lot of the mowing and some of the fertilizing was accomplished by allowing a local rancher to graze a few scrawny old cows on the place. I had tried playing the course twice but gave up in disgust both times, once after nicking the dickens out of a brand-new 8-iron on a rock and the other because the tumbleweeds, running before a Wild West wind, sailed across my line of sight every time I set up to swing. But there was no waiting, since the course was always completely deserted until the weekends, when one of the cattle owner's kids kicked the cows out to another pasture and then opened up the starter's shack and accepted two-dollar green fees from a few hardy souls.

Dave and I had kept in touch, and one evening he called saying he was working at Glacier Park for the summer and invited me up for a round of golf whenever I was free. "Davey," I said, "I'd love to, but we're working seven-day weeks right now. But, heck, we've got a perfectly good course right here in Shelby; I can take off a little early one day and we can play some twilight golf. After all, it doesn't get dark up here until about ten during July, and you're only a two-hour drive away."

"Great! How about this Wednesday? Thursday's my day off."

"Fine. See you then, ol' buddy."

First I reserved a room for Dave at the hotel, then made a small purchase in the novelty section of the drugstore and dropped in for a short chat with Tom, proprietor of Tommy's Bar and Grill. Then I located Jimmy, the kid who insisted on riding shotgun whenever I went out of town because he loved to watch heavy equipment move earth.

"Jimmy," I said, "do you think you could find a couple of snakes somewhere by Wednesday afternoon? Any kind, as long as they are good-sized and not rattlers."

"Sure. How about gopher snakes? There's a bunch of 'em living under our chicken house."

"Beautiful," I said, and handed him a piece of paper with instructions along with a dollar bill. "And there's another buck in it if you do a good job."

Dave showed up at the hotel right on time, and on the way to the golf course he said, "Bob, I know I used to give you strokes back in Seattle, but here you have all the local knowledge, so how about playing this round even-steven and just for a couple of beers?"

I said okay, and while Dave surveyed the course from the 1st tee with a certain air of misgiving, I said, "Davey, you're a city guy and this is a country course, so I think I owe you some pointers. First of all, I notice the cattle are grazing out here this evening, so I'd suggest you either take off or cover up that red shirt. Also, if your ball comes to rest on or within six inches of a cow it can be lifted without penalty. And I should point out that this is rattlesnake country, and they start coming out this time of day, so please watch your step; the nearest antivenom clinic is ninety miles away."

So, although it was still about eighty degrees in the shade, Dave pulled a blue sweater out of his bag. Then, despite glancing over his shoulder at the cows every five seconds and scanning the grass for snakes, he managed to hit to within a couple feet off the green in three on the par-4 1st hole. He sank a twenty-foot chip. "Bobby," he said as he pulled out the pin, "I think I've already begun to figure out your little course." But when he reached for the ball and his fingers encountered the cool coils of a big snake moving around looking for daylight, he flung his 6-iron away, tried to run but stumbled, fell on his behind and lay there gasping for breath. "Bob," he whispered, "I think there's some kind of snake in there!"

I looked in the hole, reached down, grabbed the animal by the neck, turned him loose to the prairie and, as he slithered away, said, "Heck, Davey, he's just an ol' gopher snake. Wouldn't hurt a soul. In fact, folks like to have 'em around because they eat mice and rats."

On the next hole, another par-4, Dave regained composure, hit a lucky shot out of a clump of cactus and actually scored a birdie. Then on the 3rd, a 175-yard par-3, his tee shot landed in the only "sand trap" on the course, a natural alkali seep which had probably been there for a few thousand years, and Dave ended with a terrible lie. But he laid open a sand wedge, blasted out to within three feet of the pin, and was about to putt out when the handsome head of another gopher snake poked itself over the edge of the hole, stuck its tongue out at Dave, and then fell back. "Hey, Bob," he yelled, "there's another one of your pet snakes trapped in here!"

I trotted up to the hole, peered in and said, "Davey, this one happens to be a rattlesnake with six rattles on his tail, and I don't understand why he didn't buzz at you. But if you had come any closer, we might have been on our way to the clinic in Great Falls. So for the rest of the round, why don't we just concede any putts under four feet? And I hope that wasn't a new ball." Then while Dave shakily marked down the scores, I reminded myself to slip little Jimmy an extra buck. He had performed well.

After that, all the wheels came off Dave's game, and at the end of nine holes he flung away his sweater, gazed at his new white shoes covered with cow dung and said, "Well, Bobby, I've had it with your damned country golf course, and the beer is on me."

Later, sitting at the bar in Tommy's Bar and Grill, Dave lifted his first mug of cold suds, hesitated, looked again into the glass and then reeled back in disgust. There in the bottom rested a little rubber snake, coiled and ready to strike.

After a couple of deep breaths, he looked around the room at all the quiet, expectant faces, reached into the mug with two fingers and extracted the snake. Then he drained the beer and said loudly, "Tommy, would you put a head on this? But you don't need to be so fancy with the next one. I'll just have it plain without a snake." The regulars, primed ahead for this event, gave him an ovation. One anonymous patron must have been really impressed, because somebody picked up the dinner tab that night.

I said good-bye to Dave early while he was in deep conversation with Lucy, the waitress, because I had to get up at five in the morning. The next afternoon back at the hotel, Bill, the desk clerk/manager/owner, hailed me in the lobby and handed me a note from Dave:

"Dear ol' buddy—I got to know little Lucy pretty well last night, and she ratted on you. It was all nicely orchestrated, but did you really need to get half the town involved? Anyhow, you made your point. Looking forward to another round on a course as far away as possible from yours. —Dave."

I tucked the note in my shirt pocket and started for

the room and a shower, but Bill stopped me and said, "By the way, your friend must be into novelties or toys or something."

"Nope," I said. "He's a dumb engineer like myself."

"Well, it's strange. He didn't check out until just before noon, and when Hilda finally got in to make up his room, she came down all excited because he left a dozen rubber snakes in the wastebasket."

Bob Brust

Your Cheatin' Heart

If you think it's hard to meet new people, try picking up the wrong golf ball.

Jack Lemmon

The one thing to be said about my Uncle Steve was that he never let a rule stand in his way of winning. I first witnessed this behavior when I challenged him to a game of Snakes and Ladders. I was only a mere child of five, but that didn't keep him from using his warped logic to win. He argued that since he was not afraid of snakes, he should be allowed to climb the beasts as well as the ladders. This comment, of course, begged the question: If my uncle would go to that much effort to win a child's game, how far would he go for something important?

By the time Steve was in his early thirties, he had become an adequate golfer whose handicap was that he still hated to lose. Because of his attitude and temper he was often forced to play alone, which did not keep him from playing as though his life depended on a victory. Rules became suggestions for people with limited imaginations. He would take a one-foot gimme and then whirl around to see if I was going to argue. I, of course, had long since learned that reminding my uncle of the rules meant a small tip.

I turned fifteen the summer Pine Greens Golf Club held its fiftieth annual championship. Pine Greens was the oldest business or club in the area and therefore was viewed with reverence. The Golf Trophy, a truly unimaginative name for the award, was the most prestigious prize in the county, and my uncle was geared up for the victory.

"Al, my boy," he said, "this year the Golf Trophy is mine and you'll be my caddie."

I hesitated to remind him of his promise to never play in the tournament again. This oath had been made after calling the tournament officials fascists for refusing to allow him his multi-mulligan rule.

"Are you sure you want to play?" I asked cautiously. "After all, you did offend quite a few people last year."

"Water under the bridge," he assured me. "I'm a changed man."

This appeared to be true. As the tournament wore on, my uncle demonstrated levels of self-control that would have put a Zen master to shame. He followed, without the slightest complaint, every rule he had ever dismissed as archaic. What made the situation even more unbelievable was that he managed to keep his anger in check.

At the 8th hole, he missed a three-foot putt and smiled. Everybody in the group, myself included, had fallen to the ground in preparation for the ritual tossing of the putter. "What gives?" I asked as I placed the putter back in the bag. "You're acting like a good sport. You should have lost your temper back at the 1st hole."

"I told you I was prepared this year," whispered Steve. "I went and got myself hypnotized last night. According to the Amazing Freddie, every time I would normally get angry, I focus the energy on the next shot. Considering the quality of my last drive, my tee shot should be a beaut."

It was. The hole was a dogleg left, 350 yards. Steve was on the green after his first shot and sunk a long putt for eagle. He smiled politely as the rest of his party bogeyed.

At the end of the day, Steve was tied with Angus Popovitch, a man whose reputation for cheating made Steve look like an amateur. According to club rules, they would face off the following day in an eighteen-hole match.

It was a lovely fall day as the two golfers prepared to tee off. Word had spread as to who was in the final, and a huge crowd had assembled. They had not come to see a great round of golf, but rather to witness what had the potential to be the first brawl in the history of Pine Greens.

The first sign of animosity occurred at the 2nd green. Angus's shot was within three feet of the cup, and he bent down to pick up his ball. Steve asked his opponent what he was doing, and Angus replied that anything under three feet was a gimme.

"Anything under three feet is a pygmy," snarled Steve. "Now putt the ball."

Thus the floodgates were thrust open, and those who had come to watch flagrant breaking of the rules were not disappointed. Angus drew first blood when he swore the wind from his practice swing had knocked the ball off his tee. It was not until Angus and his caddie were prepared to sign a sworn affidavit that Steve dropped his complaint.

At No. 3, Angus's second shot bounced into the rough among some daisies. It was not a difficult shot to recover from as the weeds offered a minimum of difficulty. Angus, however, was not one to take chances. He plucked a handful of daisies and dropped them in front of Steve's face.

"Wind appears to be from the west," he laughed.

There was a murmuring of displeasure from the gallery at what was generally considered poor decorum. Steve surprised everyone by not saying anything.

My uncle's second shot at the 6th hole saw his 5-iron take him into the rough. It was not a totally bad shot except that his ball landed behind a small boulder. Steve surveyed the ball from all angles, as did Angus. The shot was difficult, if not impossible, as the ball was less than an inch away from the rock. Angus showed his usual compassion. "Drop the ball and take a stroke. It's getting late."

Steve was ready to comply when he was struck with an epiphany. He reached down and grabbed the boulder with two hands and slowly lifted the rock off the ground. The boulder must have weighed about two hundred pounds, and Steve only managed to lift it waist-high. Before Angus could utter a protest, Steve tossed the rock away from his ball.

"You're right, Angus. The wind is westerly," Steve said, and he proceeded to hit his ball onto the green.

This time the gallery gave a polite round of applause at what it deemed to be poetic justice. Steve doffed his cap, leaving Angus to complain to his caddie.

At last the combatants arrived at the 18th. Angus had the lead by one stroke, and the par-3 offered little hope for my uncle to mount a comeback. Still, he did his best as his tee shot landed twenty yards from the green. We waited as Angus prepared for his tee shot and were rewarded by a drive that trailed left, toward the woods.

"Keep an eye on him, Al," warned Uncle Steve. "Angus will try to drop a ball in play if he can't find his."

We walked toward the green and watched as Angus and his caddie searched for the ball. I joined in the search, but Steve wouldn't move from where he was standing. It was not easy to look for the ball and watch Angus and his caddie. I was about to suggest that Steve help when I heard a shout of joy as Angus found his ball. It was a feat just short of a miracle, I thought, as I had searched the same piece of ground just moments earlier. I rushed back to Steve.

"We got him," I whispered. "That's not his ball."

The prestige of winning the tournament and the trophy disappeared with Steve's sharp retort. "I know," he answered. "I'm standing on it."

Alan Broderick

Check Your Bag

My brother Maurice and three of his buddies—Sam, Renwick and Earl—have a regular golf game every Friday during the summer. In order to make the game interesting and even, they use handicaps. As a result of this, Maurice and Earl are partners, and Sam and Renwick play together.

Maurice never walks the golf course and is always trying to get one of the other guys to ride with him. This particular Friday in July, it was very warm, and he asked Renwick to ride with him.

It just so happens that Renwick had been on a health kick for a couple of months, so he told Maurice that he would prefer to walk. Renwick had lost about twenty pounds and had just purchased a carry bag from the pro shop, deciding that toting, rather than using a pull cart as he walked the course, would help him stay in shape.

Maurice candidly cautioned Renwick, "Remember, you are fifty-eight years old. Walking the course is one thing; carrying your bag for eighteen holes is something else."

Nevertheless, Renwick insisted on walking, and off they went.

After nine holes, Renwick said to one of the other guys

who was walking, "I think Maurice was right. Carrying this bag is wearing me out."

Naturally, the other guy suggested that Renwick ask Maurice for a ride in the cart, to which Renwick stubbornly replied, "Not a chance. If you think I will admit this to Maurice, you are crazy."

They continued on. Renwick struggled but refused to give Maurice the satisfaction of giving up.

At about the 12th hole, Sam confided in Maurice, "Renwick realizes carrying the golf bag was a bad idea, but will not admit it to you because he knows he will be in for a real good ribbing."

Shortly after hearing this, Maurice called Renwick over and said, "Are you getting tired of carrying that golf bag? Why don't you take a load off and put the bag on the cart?"

Renwick grimaced but replied, "No thanks. It's not bad at all."

With a sly grin, Maurice continued, "Then why don't you unzip that side pocket and lighten your load?"

Knowing he'd been had, Renwick unzipped the side pocket, where he discovered two rocks—slightly smaller than a couple of footballs—that he had been carrying for twelve holes!

Needless to say, Renwick had some choice words for Maurice, while Sam and Earl were rolling on the tee, laughing until they were crying.

And rest assured, Renwick now checks his bag for foreign objects before every golf game . . . particularly on Fridays.

Robert Lalonde

Play It As It Lays

When it comes to the game of life, I figure I've played the whole course.

Lee Trevino

When I turned fifty, I discovered three essential facts of middle age: periodontia, bifocals and golf.

Golf?

Let me explain. I once assumed that golf was a sport for elderly Country Club Republicans. The sort of men who wore green pants with whale belts and protected their clubs with fuzzy duck head covers.

Golf was Dwight David Eisenhower. My family was Adlai Stevenson.

In my twenties, I thought golf was God's way of telling you that you had too much time on your hands.

In my thirties, I decided that a low handicap was admissible evidence of child neglect in any custody dispute.

In my forties, as a fairly decent tennis and squash player, I couldn't imagine hitting a ball while it was standing still. Quite frankly, it seemed unfair.

But somewhere along the way, somewhere between Bill

Clinton and Big Bertha and Tiger Woods, between chiro-practors and knee surgery and Advil, I had an epiphany (that's something close to a muscle spasm) that said: Golf is my next sport. To wit: my last sport. I better learn it now.

This decision was aided and abetted by a quirky nine-hole golf course in Maine where people still stroll and stop to look at the view.

It was also aided and abetted by a quirky husband (more Bobby Kennedy than Adlai Stevenson) who enthu-siastically gave me all his clubs. This was an act of gen-erosity that I didn't immediately recognize for what it was—a ploy for him to get new equipment.

Now, as I approach Columbus Day weekend with a full set of clubs and big plans, I feel fully qualified at last to offer up my views on why golf begins at fifty.

Yes, I know that one sign of a new and erratic duffer is the penchant for turning golf into a good walk through midlife spoiled. For reasons that remain unclear, golf has spawned more philosophical rambles than fairways.

Nobody compares tennis to life. A love game? Ken Burns and several million fans talk about baseball as the collective field of youthful dreams, but there's no senior tour on the diamonds.

Today there are, I hasten to add, some 25 million golfers and 16,010 golf courses. There are speed golfers and net-working golfers and boring golfers. There is even, for rea-sons that escape me, a golf channel. All golf, all day long.

There is a business writer who actually correlated the handicaps of CEOs with their stock performance. And there are the very, very serious golf professionals who sit around discussing whether they should ban new improved clubs because they are making the game too easy. Say what? But from my perspective, golf is the midlife sport of choice for very different reasons. First of all, it's easier to reach your goals. In midlife, after all, it's a snap to have a handicap below your age and a score below your weight. And getting easier all the time.

Golf is like midlife because only now do you realize that the course you have set upon is governed by rules so vast, so arcane and so arbitrary that the average person—you—will never figure it all out.

Golf is like midlife because it is absolutely unfair. As a young person, you carry the illusion that if you do your homework, study and work overtime you'll get it all right. By middle age, you know that every time you've got it all together—work, family, putt, pitch—some piece is about to unravel. Promise.

Golf, like midlife, is played against only one opponent: yourself. By the time you reach fifty, you had better figure out that doing well doesn't depend on others doing badly. You don't have to wish them ill. They're not the reason you are shanking the ball.

Golf is like middle age, because—ah, you knew this was coming—in these years you really do have to play it as it lays. You don't get to start everything all over again. The most you get is a mulligan. If it's an unplayable lie, everybody sympathizes, but you still have to take a penalty.

Ellen Goodman

The Best Golfer Tantrum of All Time

*Golf is a game that creates emotions that some-
times cannot be sustained with a club in the
hand.*

Bobby Jones

Workers at the Riverside Golf and Country Club in
Portland, Oregon, were taking down some of the golf
course's towering poplars when they came upon evidence
of what appeared to be the enraged-golfer tantrum of all
time. Forty feet up in one tree was a 10-iron that looked as
though it had been thrown right through a ten-inch branch.

Closer examination, however, revealed that the club,
which is of the era when they first started making steel
shafts, was probably thrown about forty years ago. It
seems to have lodged in a high crotch in the tree, and
since that terrible moment, the branch has grown around
the club and the poplar itself has grown taller.

The cut section of tree—complete with club—will be
kept on display at the pro shop.

Rod Patterson

Character Building

I take the revolutionary view that all this talk about the virtues of practice, for the average club golfer at any rate, is a snare and a delusion. "Practice makes perfect," they say. Of course, it doesn't. For the vast majority of golfers it merely consolidates imperfection.

Henry Longhurst

I was playing golf at the local course in my hometown when I sent an errant approach shot into the parking lot adjacent the clubhouse. It took one hop and plowed right into the side of a pickup truck parked in the lot. To make matters even worse, the owner was sitting on the tailgate changing his shoes. Of course, my first reaction was to slink the other way and hope that nobody would know where it came from. But, I decided, I had to own up, take responsibility for my actions.

Taking a deep breath, I walked over to the truck and sheepishly apologized for what I had done. To my surprise and delight, the man smiled and told me he learned long ago that sometimes you get the better of the game, and other times the game gets the best of you.

With a heavy sigh of relief, the weight of the world off my shoulders, I reached down to retrieve my ball from its location near the front tire. However, as I bent over, the shift in weight caused my bag of golf clubs to swing around, smashing into the side of his truck. I looked up at the man, and with a smile that was beginning to flatten out he said, "Now I'm starting to get mad."

Enough character building for one day. I grabbed my ball and took off.

Jim King

Perfect Stroke—for the Car?

*Actually, the only time I ever took out a 1-iron
was to kill a tarantula. And I took a 7 to do that.*

Jim Murray

About twenty years ago, when we lived in Tulsa,
Oklahoma, my husband Harold bought a new car and
gave me his, a 1973 Ford LTD. It ran very well, and I had
no trouble with it until one day while out doing errands.

I came out of the grocery store, sat in the car and turned
the key. Nothing happened. I tried again. Silence. The car
had apparently died a quiet death while I was in the store.

I went back in the store to a telephone and, fortunately,
Harold was home.

"I need you," I said after telling him my plight.

"Where are you?"

I told him.

"I'll be right there."

He came, sat in the car and turned the key as if he had
to prove to himself that I was right, and I wouldn't have
been surprised if it had started for him. I'd had this experience before, you see. But the car remained inactive.

Next he popped the hood and puttered around a bit, then opened the trunk. After rummaging around, he pulled a club out of my golf bag and tapped on one of the battery cables.

"See if it'll start," he said, looking confident.

Sure enough the engine purred like a satisfied kitten.

"Well," I said, "in case this happens again, I guess I need to know what to do."

"If it does, use a 5-iron." He grinned and winked.

I've had golf lessons before, but never one on this particular use of a 5-iron.

All went well with the car until a week or so later when it stalled right in the middle of a busy intersection. I remained undaunted, knowing exactly what to do this time.

I popped the hood, opened the trunk, took out my 5-iron and tapped that battery cable just like a pro. I sat in the car, turned the key and the engine purred again. Several well-intentioned men had come to my aid and watched the procedure with obvious wonder. When the car started, one of the men came up to my window, grinned and asked, "Hey lady, I have to know—what club did you use?"

Marci Martin

5

GOLF LINKS A FAMILY TOGETHER

The Collection Basket

My mother was my dad's grand passion in life. One of my fondest childhood memories was watching my father flip on the radio each morning before he left for work, then whirl my mother around the kitchen floor in a joyous dance.

But second only to my mother in the love department was my father's adoration of golf. My dad, a Michigan dentist named Cy Collins, cherished the game. He was a deft player, regularly shooting in the low seventies for eighteen holes. He played whenever he could, at home and on vacation in Hawaii, Scotland, and other locales. Golf was truly his nectar of the gods.

In the early 1980s, we began noticing the early signs of the Alzheimer's disease that eventually took his life. Dad became confused and forgetful. Though he had paid the family bills for decades, numbers now mystified him. Once he took the family car out for a drive and became lost, stopping only when he ran out of gas many miles from home. But Dad's love of golf lived on. He couldn't remember many things, but he remembered perfectly how to play the game. His drives and his putts were as good as ever.

And this is the part of the story where Dad's love of golf and generosity of spirit converged in the most touching way. A few years before he died in the small northern Michigan town where they had a summer home, Mom and Dad went to Sunday Mass as usual. Dad smiled and shook hands with friends and neighbors, then listened attentively to the priest's sermon. And when the collection basket was passed down his pew, Dad very deliberately reached into his pocket and placed in the basket the most precious gift he could imagine: three golf balls.

Jan K. Collins

Remember When

"You know, Mom, a person's true character always comes out on the golf course. Since you never played golf, you really didn't know Dad—Pat Gardner, the golfer—now did you?" This was one of the toughest things I'd ever said to my mother. It was a calculated risk I had to take.

My eighty-five-year-old mother glared at me, slowly shaking her head, her stern look signaling me to stop. She wanted no part of this. We—my mother Goldie, sisters Evelyn and Marge, brother Don, and my daughter Jill—were sitting in the Schmitt Funeral Home in WaKeeney, Kansas, putting the final touches on my Dad's funeral, scheduled for the next day. Dad, who had suddenly died of a heart attack, was lying in an open casket about fifteen feet from us.

Because two other funerals were scheduled that weekend, the atmosphere was morbid to say the least. So I decided to lighten things up a bit.

I began telling a story about my dad's crazy antics on our golf course. He had taken up golf late in his life and never quite got the hang of it, playing to a 30-something handicap. "One day, Mom, when we were teenagers," I said, "Dad actually hit a drive in the fairway—it was the first one I'd ever seen. Huh, Don?" Don nodded, grinning, knowing what was coming.

"When we got to where his ball was supposed to be, we couldn't find it, which got Dad all riled up."

"Okay, where is it? I hit it right here!" he barked. Then he stopped dead in his tracks. He had spied his ball about two feet down a ten-inch-wide gopher hole, sitting on a dirt ledge. 'Shut up, you two, and don't move,' he scolded.

"Heck, Mom, we weren't talking or moving. Right, Don?"

"That's right, Mom," said Don, mischievousness dancing in his eyes. Mom narrowed her eyes, still glaring at me.

"Then, Dad got down on his knees and carefully reached for the ball with his 5-iron. Hope soared within him as he hooked the ball with the club face. Holding his breath, he gently lifted the ball upward, hand over hand, delicately holding the club by his thumbs and fingertips. Sweat beads appeared on his forehead. His hands were really shaking now, and he winced each time the ball nearly slipped off the club. It was painstaking work.

"'Keep quiet, you two,' he whispered. 'I've just about got it.' After what seemed like an eternity, he finally pinned the ball near the top of the hole and ever so tenderly reached down with his left hand to retrieve it. Just as his fingers approached the ball, two more balls fell out of his upper shirt pocket and slammed into the first ball, causing all three balls to disappear down the gopher hole, lost forever. Dad flew into a rage. He jumped up, kicked the hole a few times, then beat the hole half to death with his club. Don and I were dying laughing on the ground."

As Mom gave me that dreaded old schoolmarm look that she had perfected in one-room schoolhouses out on the prairie where she had taught for forty years, the family exploded into laughter. My plan was working, the gloom lifting.

Dad had demonstrated a great sense of humor all his life and loved a good belly laugh. I was banking on Mom understanding this, and I was looking for some help from the rest of the family. Just then, Don chimed in.

"Remember the time, Bud, when we were sitting on the bench behind the raised tee box on the third hole, and Dad was getting ready to hit his driver? Now, Mom, I'm not trying to degrade Dad in any way. You know he was a great baseball player, who played a mean first base and hit cleanup for the WaKeeney town team and even played against the great Satchel Paige once. Remember?"

Mom, warming up a bit, nodded at Don.

"Well," continued Don, "standing over his ball that day, he told us he really felt like clobbering a drive. Bud and I glanced at each other but kept quiet as Dad addressed the ball. Then he swung with all his might. He stared down the fairway, yelling at us. 'Did you guys see it? Where in the devil did it go?'

"The truth is, Mom, he had swung so hard he overshot the ball and just nicked it with the heel of his club, causing it to trickle between his feet and slowly meander off the tee box and down the hill behind him. Don and I couldn't hold back. We laughed so hard we fell off the bench into an anthill.

"Seeing our predicament, Dad bellowed, 'Serves you right, you galoots! Now where's my ball?' When he saw it still trickling down the hill, he realized how silly this all was and cracked up, too."

The whole family roared at that one, which brought a brief smile to Mom's face. She quickly regained her serious composure, but we were on a roll and couldn't stop now.

"Another time, Mom," I recalled, "Dad, Don and I played in an out-of-town golf tournament. When Dad's foursome was called to the first tee, Dad pulled the head cover off his wood driver and threw the club to the ground in disgust.

"'What's the matter, Pat?' asked one of his playing partners.

"'Would you look at that?' snapped Dad. 'See all those white marks on the top of my driver. Darn it, my kids have been using my clubs again.'

"His buddies all sympathized as he addressed the ball. Dad made a ferocious swing at the ball—which he had teed up way too high—and whipped the club head right under the ball, sending it straight up into the air. Then things got real serious as everybody scattered when the ball came crashing down in the middle of the tee box, leaving no doubt who had been putting the white marks on that driver."

The twinkle in Mom's eye told me I was doing the right thing. She had finally realized I was just trying my level best to help us cope with the loss of Dad. We then told a few more golf jokes about Dad, which seemed to lift the spirit of our family at this mournful time. A few minutes later, Don asked Jill and me to accompany him over to Dad's casket. Dad was dressed in his best gray suit with a matching tie. "Bud, take a close look at Dad's tie," urged Don. I couldn't believe it. It matched all right, but the words on it caught my eye. It had "Happy Anniversary," scrawled repeatedly on a diagonal its entire length.

"And watch this," said Don, as he reached for the tie. He pressed a small button on the back of the tie and out jumped a classic song. I couldn't believe it.

"Who chose this tie?" I asked when the last note had faded away.

"Mom did," said Don. "I gave Dad that tie as a joke years ago for one of their anniversaries. I guess Mom was too numb over Dad's passing to know what she had done."

Knowing my dad had a great sense of humor, I believe he would have gotten a big chuckle out of watching this scene unfold. Just then, I heard Mom laughing at something my sisters had said. It was music to my ears.

The next day during Dad's funeral, I was extremely nervous. I had agreed to do Dad's eulogy on behalf of the
family. I had done only one other eulogy for a dear friend,
which I had mishandled badly. I had lost control and
cried throughout my entire presentation. So, I wasn't sure
I could pull this one off; after all, it was my Dad's final
hour. The family was counting on me. The funeral home
was crowded with about seventy-five family members
and friends. I was so shook up, I asked my daughter, Jill,
to accompany me to the lectern—and to finish reading
my prepared statement if I began to cry and lose control.
She agreed.

Then it was time. The minister nodded, and Jill and I
moved to the pulpit. I thanked everyone for being with us
to honor Dad's life and then began to read my statement.
About a third of the way through, my voice cracked and
tears began streaming down my face. I paused, then
started reading again. I choked up again as tears spilled
onto my papers. I was about ready to have Jill continue
for me when she slipped something into my left hand. I
felt an old familiar friend—a golf ball. At that instant, an
overwhelming wave of relief washed over me, followed
by a serene peace. Just then I understood the depth of
Jill's unconditional love for me. I was thankful she had
made the long trip from California to Kansas to be with
me. That ball—a symbol of joy and love—and Jill's reas-
suring smile gave me the courage to finish one of my
greatest challenges.

Bud Gardner

Being There

*R*egard *the small as important;*
make much of the little.

Lao-tzu

The ninth hole at Caledonia Golf Course is a par-3 nestled in the mountains of south-central Pennsylvania. The tee is perched about seventy-five feet above a tiny green that is surrounded by a raised berm, with trees leaving only the narrowest of openings to the flagstick below: a donut in the middle of a forest clearing, 140 yards away, daring visitors to bite. I remember it well.

The last time I saw this hole was the first time I played golf with my father. I was fourteen. He swung a 9-iron, sailing the ball onto the rear edge of the green. The ball went into reverse and backed itself to within inches of the cup.

I stood amazed at the skill and power of my dad, hoping beyond hope that I could be just like him.

He handed me a 5-wood and said, "Okay, Don, just like that. Keep your head down and take a nice easy swing."

I obeyed his command but the ball did not obey mine.

It flew with a wicked hook into the woods. Dad didn't say a word and tossed me another ball. Then another, and another and . . . six Wilsons later, I finally managed to dribble the ball down the hill and bounced it next to the mounded barrier protecting the green.

We walked down the mountain together and all I could do was stare at the man for whom I had found yet another reason to worship. He was the best golfer I had ever seen. Better than Palmer or even that new guy on the tour, Jack Something-or-other.

I can't tell you how many strokes it took to finally sink that ball on No. 9 at Caledonia. I do remember, however, what my father said when it was finally over: "You're getting there, son, keep up the good work." He gave me assurance, not ridicule, and I loved him even more.

That was thirty years ago. Dad died six years later. We played many rounds of golf together in those six years, but I could never achieve his greatness. My mind was too occupied with girls, war protests, school dramas and more girls. Dad, though, was a patient and willing teacher who allowed my dalliance and led me to the links and through the passages of adolescence.

It was that hole at Caledonia, though, that burned a vision in my soul. I have often described that particular par-3 to others, without regard to a reciprocated interest. It was not only the memory of a perfect golf hole I described, but a perfect day, a perfect shot and a perfect dad.

Today, the first time in thirty years, I stood at that same tee box on the same mountain. Not much had changed. It was the same trees, the same hill, the same green below, but a different me. I thought not about people, politics or work. I thought only of Dad and how a hole-in-one would sanctify and honor his memory. I reached into my bag and withdrew the 9-iron.

His mentoring filled my ears as it had not done in many

years. Head down . . . feet shoulder-length apart . . . slow
backswing . . . eye on the ball . . . follow through . . . !

With his instructions I teed the ball up and prayed for
redemption. My life has not turned out the equal of my, or
most likely his, expectations. The trees, the hazards, the
traps along the way got the better of me so many times. I
have survived though, and I'm happy to report that my
life has found the fairway again. But with this shot, with
this ball, with his memory, I could atone for my sins.

I drew the club back slowly and reached for the heavens above, begging salvation and guidance. Head down,
eye on the ball, follow-through. The club struck squarely
and the ball soared into the crisp mountain air. I could
swear there was a halo around it.

"You da man!" my partner screamed as the ball headed
for the flag that was waving down below. I smiled and
kept my eyes peeled on the tiny white dot as it moved
away into the distance.

The mountain breezes and early morning mists play
tricks, not only with the flight of golf balls, but on the eyes
as well. What had looked to be a perfect shot suddenly
turned bad. I screamed, "Go baby! Go! Turn! Get there!"
The ball, which was out of earshot, did not heed my pleas.
It landed short and plugged itself in the right-hand berm.
It never had a chance.

Instead of agonizing over a shot of improbable propor-
tions, I laughed at myself as I recalled Dad's most important lesson. "It's the little things in life that matter the
most, Son."

Just being there was enough. I didn't need a hole-in-
one or even to land the ball on the dance floor to obtain
the peace and redemption I sought. He already gave that
to me. He gave me the fortitude, the perseverance and the
will to overcome difficulties many years ago. When I
needed him most he was always there. He still is.

Thanks, Dad.

Don Didio

Way Above Par

One afternoon I had the chance to meet a couple of friends on the course for a quick nine. We were paired together for a scramble at our church the next weekend and we admittedly needed the practice. As I was driving to meet them, I started reflecting on my marriage. After seven years, we had become too predictable. No itches mind you, but more than enough rashes and hives from the children. With the kids, the mortgage, the bills and, of course, the job to pay for all of the above, we had landed in a sandtrap.

In college, it seemed like everything enjoyable in life centered around our time together. People always said that we were the ones that lit the fires, but it seemed like we had forgotten the matches.

Golf was an escape for us. I'd chase that stupid white ball around a deep green golf course and would never get any better. My wife drove the electric golf cart, always wearing a shorts-and-tank-top set, dark sunglasses, and a white golf visor. For ten yards in either direction, you could smell the unmistakable scent of cocoa butter. The only reason she went was to get a suntan.

If the truth were known, the only reason I went was to watch *her*.

One afternoon, she studied my golf swing more intently than ever before. Finally, on the seventeenth hole, she came out with her notion.

"Let me try to hit one."

At first, I thought *what a novel idea*. Then I changed my mind. Golf was a man's sport, or so I thought. "You? You can't hit a golf ball. You're a girl."

"Thanks for noticing. Just the same, I think I can lose golf balls as well as you can."

A very true observation.

I handed over my 3-wood and dug the tee into the hard clay at the tee box. Without even a practice swing, she promptly knocked the ball straight down the middle of the fairway. When we got to our balls, her drive was five yards further than mine. From that day on, she started playing golf.

Some of the best times we shared early in our marriage were on the golf course. We'd go in the mid-morning before the temperature would climb. The time we spent together laughing and teasing under the sun cemented our relationship. As I pulled into the parking lot outside the clubhouse, I realized how much I missed seeing her on a golf course.

All the guys at church looked forward to playing our annual tournament. Mike and Danny, a couple of fellow church members, were going to play on my team along with a mystery partner. Hopefully someone who could drive and putt, our collective shortcomings.

Every team invited someone outside our church to play. Sort of a community involvement thing. What I always found amazing was how all these strangers could hit the cover off the ball and always straight down the middle! Let's face it, there are more ringers in a church golf tournament than in the children's bell choir.

When I got to the practice green, I saw Danny and his

wife, Beth, pulling out Danny's clubs. A second golf bag was resting on the side.

"Whose clubs are those, Danny?" I asked, expecting him to say that next week's mystery golfer was already inside the clubhouse, paying for our tickets.

"Why, they're mine," said Beth as she threw them across her shoulder.

"Yeah, she's my secret weapon today. She tees off from the women's tee box, you know. With her drives, we are guaranteed at least a good one."

I snickered at the thought of a woman playing golf, then I caught a whiff of cocoa butter.

The three of us spent the afternoon chasing balls, hitting horrible iron shots and missing almost every putt. Danny and Beth didn't care. They enjoyed playing golf together in a way that I suddenly recalled.

It's not the winning but the losing together that matters most.

As we were starting to leave, the conversation came to the tournament. Danny asked, "Well, do you think you can find a fourth player by Saturday?"

"Yeah. Playing this afternoon reminded me of the perfect partner."

I came home to find my wife in the kitchen. She smiled and asked, "Did you play well?"

"Nope. Just as hopeless as usual."

"How did the others play?"

"Hopeless as well. We need a fourth player for the tournament and I think I found one."

She looked up at me with those bright eyes and asked, "Really, who?"

"You."

Surprise grew across her face. "Me? I haven't played golf in years. I can't help you win."

"Can't help us lose either. But it sure would be nice to see you out there again."

That next Saturday, the four of us played golf on perhaps the most beautiful spring day that I can recall. We laughed and teased all over the course as shot after shot missed the mark. On the last hole, we finished with a score of 79, seven shots above par, buried deep in last place.

Afterward, the awards were handed out and we got the prize for having the roughest day, a kind way to say we lost. Each of us received a sleeve of shiny pink golf balls for our hard day's work. On our way back to our table, I put my arm around her shoulder and whispered, "These guys just haven't figured out who really won!"

Harrison Kelly

Divorce, of Course

We took a mulligan.

Cheryl Kratzert

As most public-course golfers know, it is not uncommon for a weekend round to take five or six hours, if you can even get a starting time on your favorite local course. The volume of people who cannot play mid-week, coupled with those looking for a respite from yard work or the spouse, causes a flood of players filling every available tee time. Slow play is inevitable because of the varying capability of weekend golfers. As a result, you will hear complaining, more-than-occasional cries of "Fore" and frustrated players waiting on every tee.

Marching into this fray one weekend, I joined a threesome following a group of older women. My playing companions were male, somewhat grayer than I, and seemed unusually anxious about playing behind the women. They muttered while the women teed off, they muttered while waiting for the fairway to clear and they muttered continuously until they reached the green. I could only make out a few words here and there, mostly about slow play.

After several holes, which seemed to take forever, one of the men asked me if I was married (I am), and if my wife played golf (she does not). I returned the conversation by asking the same questions.

The first gentleman waived a disdaining hand and said, "No more, and thank God." I was not certain which question he was answering.

The second man smiled and said, "Divorced, and she does." I just smiled back.

The third man looked intently down the fairway at the women ahead of us and then turned and spoke. "I was married to the woman in the blue pants, up there in the fairway. George was married to the woman in yellow, and Dave to the one in white. My wife hit the ball farther than I could, and she putted better. Asked her for a divorce last year, after thirty-seven years of marriage."

"Is it just a coincidence that they are in the group ahead?" I asked.

"No," the third man (I can't recall his name) replied, "we've been doing this every weekend for two years."

"You mean you arrange this, even though you are divorced because of golf? But why, if it frustrates you?"

"Frustrates us? What do you mean?" George asked.

"Well, you're muttering on every hole, complaining about how slow the round is. Why would you want to play behind them?"

They smiled at each other, then looked back to me. "Son," George started, "we're not frustrated. We've got new clubs, good health for our age and a regular game every Saturday."

"You see," the third man continued, "our playing golf left them home alone. So, after George's wife divorced him three years ago, and then Dave's, the women took up the game with my ex. They enjoyed it so much, it changed their attitude. In fact, they became like girls again, and

George and Dave have been dating them ever since."

"But you said you were divorced last year."

"Sure. It improved George and Dave's sex life, so I convinced my wife to divorce so we could have the same thing. And it worked. Couldn't be happier."

"But the complaining I hear, what's that?"

George and Dave smiled again. "Slow play!" Dave said. "The sooner we get done with this round, the sooner we get to date night."

Gordon W. Youngs

The Ace Man

I consider myself an incredibly lucky man, possessed of a wonderful, interesting and eclectic life. I have a remarkable wife and life partner, Ewa, a fantastic and truly unique stepdaughter, Nikki, a wonderful twin and mother, and, thanks to a truly mystical golfing adventure, a magical dog that enhances all of our lives.

The Charlotte Golf Links is an expertly crafted layout carved out of the rolling farmland outside of Charlotte, North Carolina. It has often been the scene of peaceful late afternoon walks, one of the few courses where you can still walk nine holes at dusk. That, as well as its obvious ties to the traditional roots of the game, has made it a place where we sometimes can feel a connection to the deeper, more spiritual side of things. We were, however, unprepared for what was to happen one eventful morning.

On a clear, beautiful Thursday, Ewa (who shares most everything in my life, including a passion for golf) and I had an early tee time. I felt completely at ease warming up, and had, surprisingly, become aware of and was able to repeat a simple swing thought that was allowing me to hit the ball better than I had in quite a while. I hoped the thought would stay with me.

The course was serenely uncrowded, rare nowadays,

especially on such a gorgeous golfing day. We began the round in a relaxed and unhurried mood, both grateful, as we often are, for the kind of lives that allow us to be out on the course together.

I was +1 after six holes (not bad for a 10 handicap), and Ewa and I were laughing as we went to the seventh hole, a long, uphill par-3 whose tee is surrounded by tall, heather-like grasses, waving in the breeze. As we turned to approach the tee, we cleared the tall grass, and there, standing at the tee, was a small dog staring straight at us. We all seemed to pause for a second, and then, being unabashed dog lovers, Ewa and I said our hellos to this funny, playful, reddish-coated pup. A mixture of long-haired dachshund and something resembling a fox (with no tail), he rolled around on the tee, licked us a few times and stood watching as we hit away.

We said, "See ya later," and proceeded up to the green. Before we got there, our little friend ran up to the green and picked up my ball in his mouth, looking child like and full of mischief. After we stopped laughing, Ewa and I bogeyed the hole, but before we could leave the green, there he was again, this time with his head entirely in the cup, looking, no doubt, for the deeper meaning of the game.

We proceeded to the next tee, followed of course by you-know-who, who jumped into our cart (sadly you must ride early in the day) and climbed into Ewa's lap. The eighth is a dogleg left (of course) par-5, and I snap-hooked my drive into the trees lining the fairway left, feeling my score slipping away a bit. I heard no contact with wood, so I presumed my drive was out of bounds. I re-teed and hit a provisional ball, trying not to think too much about losing a good round's score. On returning to the cart, I found our new friend asleep in my wife's lap, and chuckled at this strange new golfing partner.

After Ewa hit her tee shot, we drove out to the fairway, and lo and behold, about two hundred yards out, dead in the middle, was my first tee ball. *Incredible*, I thought, and turned to Ewa and said, "It has to be the pup. He's lucky. That ball never touched a tree." I proceeded to hit a flush 3-wood, then a really crisp 8-iron to about three feet, and made the putt for birdie. Back to +1, and really laughing now.

The ninth hole is an uphill par-3 that was playing 167 yards that day. I took a look at the still-asleep, gentle face of my good-luck charm and suddenly was reminded of the swing key I had used earlier in the round. I hit a pure 5-iron at the flag, the bottom of which was hidden by the elevated green. I watched the ball in flight, and, as we are wont to do after a feel-good strike on a par-3, yelled "Go in the hole," or some such brilliantly worded phrase. As I walked back to the cart, Ewa remarked on the seeming ease of my play that day, and we both looked again at the dog. I said, "If the ball is in the hole, we're keeping the dog."

Ewa hit her tee shot, and as we approached the green, there was only one ball visible. Still in a playful mood, I asked Ewa to go pick my ball out of the hole, and I sat with a now wide-awake, furry-faced pooch staring at me. I looked up in time to see Ewa jumping up and down, a beaming smile on her face, saying, "Yes, yes, yes...." I ran up to the green, followed by, you-guessed-it, and, somewhat in shock, picked the ball out of the hole, the first time in eighteen years I ever had that privilege.

It wasn't much of a choice after that. His name is, naturally, Ace, and along with our other two, Stella and Raquette, he is now an integral part of our home and lives, and is, I think, a symbol of all the reasons that golf is the greatest game—he gives us joy and constant surprise. Although he is often frustrating and difficult, when we pay attention and allow him to teach us, he rewards us with unending gifts.

Mitch Laurance

Early Retirement

My fiancée, Lauren, and I were in her hometown of Philadelphia, where her aunt was hosting Lauren's bridal shower. The plans for the day largely entailed my staying out of everyone's way until the end of the shower, when I would then be introduced to several of her parents' friends and family.

My prospective father-in-law, Milt, who had only recently taken up golf, naturally thought the best form of introduction would be a golf outing involving me, him and a family friend whose wife would be attending the shower.

Now I hadn't picked up a club in months, but not wanting to disappoint Milt (and not wanting to play a larger role in the bridal shower than absolutely necessary), I agreed.

As it turned out, we were running a little late in making our tee time and I didn't have any opportunity to warm up with a bucket of balls before the round, as I had hoped. There was also a slight backup on the first tee. To make room for the influx of golfers, Milt had pulled our cart a little further forward than safety would normally dictate. I thought about saying something to him but as he was to the left of the tee box, and I normally hit the ball so far right that golfers in the next fairway are occasionally sent ducking for cover, I assumed he would be in no danger. I was wrong.

I caught the ball off the heel of my driver, sending it directly into my future father-in-law's right hand. Now, my relationship with Milt had always been friendly, but formal. At this point, not only was I confident that was going to change, but I wasn't certain Milt was going to lend his blessing to my marrying his youngest daughter.

I was also convinced that I had, with that one blow, sent my future father-in-law heading toward an early retirement. Milt is an ear-nose-and-throat doctor and is required to perform certain types of surgery in order to continue his practice.

Horrified at what I had just done, I began to shake so badly that I couldn't even think about finishing out the hole. So I picked up my ball, got an ice pack for Milt, and took the wheel of the cart while Milt bravely attempted to continue playing. By the time we got to the second hole, Milt somehow had me laughing about the whole incident.

"Todd, you didn't hit me hard enough," he told me. He explained that if I'd done more significant damage, he'd have been able to retire (something it turned out he'd been contemplating anyway), while collecting on a nice insurance policy he'd taken out just in case of golfing accidents involving future sons-in-law.

I chuckled, then replied, "Well, we've got seventeen more holes. I'll see what I can do."

It was the first time I'd felt completely at ease with my future father-in-law, and perhaps more than anything else that took place during Lauren's and my engagement period, his gentle, good nature during the incident made me feel like a part of her family. After all, who else but a family member could have forgiven such an act?

Milt finished the round and made it to the bridal shower

before heading to the emergency room. It was determined that I had, indeed, broken a bone in his hand—a fact he kept hidden from me until well after the wedding as he didn't want me to feel any worse than I already did.

But now that I know, I feel even better.

Todd Behrendt

Mom Hits the Links

Age is not important unless you're a cheese.

Helen Hayes

I talked to my mother on the phone one night. She had just returned from her first golf school, which also happened to be her first golf game.

"I sure do love this game," she gushed.

You see, my brother and sister and girlfriend and myself had purchased a starter set of clubs for Mom last Christmas. She runs her own business, in the sports insurance and benefits arena, and over the years her travels to meetings had taken her to places like Doral and Pebble Beach. But she was the only member of the family that didn't play golf. So the rest of us would hear: "Well, I could have played a round there if I played golf. But I did enjoy riding around the course in a cart. You know how I love the sound of the ocean."

Naturally, there was only so much of this we muni hacks in the family could take. So we took a chance and surprised her with the clubs. We figured she'd be decent because we'd seen her take a few swings one time at a driving range. Although she's a southpaw she seemed comfortable swinging right-handed, and she had whacked the heck out of the ball. Plus, it seemed like a good mode of exercise for her as she moved into a different phase of her life.

She was very excited, but knew so little about the game and how to play it that she feared embarrassment.

"Just go to the range for a while, Mom. Then you can try playing a few holes, and gradually work your way up to a full round," I counseled.

Those first few months, she went to the range just a couple of times. But it was exciting to buy the clothes.

"I got myself a new golf outfit today. And I now have golf shoes."

"How about your swing—have you hit any balls lately?"

"No, but I'm going to be all ready when it's time for golf camp!"

We siblings conferred and separately advised her to start some simple stretching and exercises a few weeks before going to Pine Needles. Then we sat back and waited.

I didn't hear from her the entire week. The day I knew the school ended I called her not long after she arrived home.

"Oh, we had so much fun," she said again. "And you know what? Yesterday I played my first round."

"Wow, a full eighteen?"

"Well, it was a nine-hole round. And my team won! It was what they call 'best ball.' And on one hole I drove it all the way to the green and we used my ball."

"What do you mean—was it a par-3 or a par-4?"

"Oh, I don't know."

"I love that kind of attitude, Mom." I really did.

"All I know to do is try and get the ball into the hole in as few strokes as possible," she continued succinctly. "The other ladies' shots were back a ways, and one of them said, 'Oh my gosh, Sally's ball is on the green.'"

I could tell that this was one of those watershed conversations, the kind you only have once.

"So I played another nine holes later, and guess what? I shot a 46."

"Holy cow," I said, stunned, "you must have even had a par in there somewhere."

"Oh yes, I had a couple of those, and also did one of the holes under par."

"A birdie?" I said, sitting down. "That's incredible! What was it, a par-5?"

"I don't remember. When I told the bartender what I had shot, he was surprised, and said, 'Sally, do you realize that if you doubled that score for a full eighteen, you'd break 100? That's fantastic.' But I thought it wasn't that great, since it was over par."

I paused to let that settle in.

"Thank you again for the clubs, Adam. Oh, you know what? I need to find out where you got them, so I can get a sand wedge and pitching wedge."

"Oh yeah," I said sheepishly, "we only got you the starter set. I suppose you'll need some even-numbered clubs too."

"Oh, heavens no. Not yet. But I did learn about what to hit what distances. Of course, I'll probably fall back some now, but I sure love this game!"

It was a wry turning of the tables, as I, the son, pondered the wonderful, fleeting innocence of my mother's introduction to golf. There she was, discovering the pleasures of the game, apparently still whacking the heck out of the ball and enjoying the very act. The experiment had succeeded, and she was launched on a late-blooming golf career. Perhaps she will never pay attention to the score . . . until she reaches par that is.

For me, and anybody else who is unlearning the techniques and visualizations and just learning to hit the darned ball, it is a lesson in rediscovery. Chances are we sure do love this game too. And I, for the thousandth and not the final time, get to say . . . thanks, Mom.

Adam Bruns

Silent Swing

If it is a part of you, golf can heal. Without it, I couldn't withstand the challenge my life has become. It is God's plan, I guess, that my little girl live in a world of near silence. I just wish she could live with me.

Despite normal intelligence, at age seven Angela could read one word: her name. Boarding school was her best shot—perhaps her only shot—at a future.

So a few weeks after Angela's seventh birthday, I found myself printing her initials on socks, a dozen pairs of Pocahontas panties and the derrieres of her Barbies. Tying her bike to the station-wagon roof we drove her to a school for the deaf—a place I swore she'd never go.

Angela is adopted. So no matter how much I love her, she may someday wonder why her mother gave her up. When she came to us, I swore she would never be given up again. Yet, by sending her away to school, that's exactly what I felt I was doing.

I knew it was her best shot—perhaps her only shot—at a future. But as the reality of her leaving sank in, I ran from it. I had learned, while fending off cancer, that when you're doing all that can be done, and the rest is out of your control, denial can be a good thing. I knew only one place to escape the pain: the golf course. Golf is so much a part of me, it's hard to tell where it leaves off and I begin. It was a gift from my father. It brought me together (on a blind date) with my husband. And it provides a home for the part of me that needs to fight—and win.

When I faced the possibility of losing my own life, I practiced chipping and putting, with plastic tubes hanging out of my left armpit (a capital violation of the dress code). So it was natural that when it came to losing my daughter, I found myself at the golf course that wraps around our weather-beaten Kansas house like a mother's arms.

In a primal way, golf is my earth mother. It held me all that summer, many times past dusk.

It also held Angela. I hadn't expected my baby to be like me. Then one day when she was barely two, I walked into the playroom and found her plumb bobbing a plastic putter a friend had given me as a gag. My heart soared. That summer before she left, we spent hours together at the driving range and chipping greens. On her own, Angela would quietly tote her little bag to the front lawn, where she taught herself to smash a ball seventy-five yards into the woods. Golf spoke to her, in her silent world.

With all of that devotion came the gift of improvement. In July a woman friend and I won my club's member-guest tournament. I even won a longest-drive contest. Then, one steamy August day I did the unthinkable:

I broke 90.

This was golf as I'd only dreamed it. Surely it would sustain me through the darkest hours looming ahead. Three weeks later, Angela left, and so did my game. It was a full face-down collapse. I couldn't drive. I couldn't putt. I couldn't do anything. My scores skyrocketed back to where they had been ten years before.

Maybe I could have withstood the cruel, below-zero Kansas winter missing my daughter, if I could have looked forward to the golf season. But even that promised only the humiliation of revealing the flailing nincompoop I'd turned into. I cursed God for piling it on. There was no place for me to go. Then, finally one day it dawned on me: golf school. The school would restore my game. The game would restore my spirit. Then, before I'd know it, golf season would begin in April. Soon Angela would be home for the summer.

Many times during that monstrous winter I worried that Angela, born brave, would cope by gradually disconnecting from me. During an early visit home, she headed outside to play, layered and looking like a balloon in the Thanksgiving Day Parade. When I looked out the window to check on her, I couldn't believe what I saw. She was standing out front, hitting snowballs with her sawed-off 8-wood.

A revelation rushed through me: Angela has it, too. The love that won't die. The spiritual link. I felt as if I were looking at myself, and I knew we would survive intact.

Betty Cuniberti

One at a Time

My introduction to the game of golf came as a teenage caddie at an exclusive country club near our home. The $3.50 I was paid for eighteen holes of carrying singles and $5.75 for doubles was a welcome wage for my first job outside our home. My blue-collar family could never afford to belong to a club like this, so my duties were also my entry inside the gates that we so frequently passed. Every Monday was "caddie day," which meant we could play the course for free.

I had always been an above-average athlete. I expected I would do as well with golf. Never having taken even basic lessons, my transition from a baseball bat to a 5-iron was not pretty. My ability to deal with this fact was uglier still. My frequent shots hit out of bounds, whiffed at or drubbed thirty feet up the fairway generally led to a loud, blue stream of cursing. More than one golf club was left to decorate some elm tree, having been thrown and caught up too high to retrieve. At eighteen, even I was mature enough to realize that I needed to either get serious about my golf or give it up. Shortly thereafter, college pursuits gave me little time to play, and a new job meant I would have to pay real greens fees. The "pleasure" I derived from playing made not playing an easy decision.

At the age of thirty-five, I found myself the father of two boys—eight and ten years old. Their friends in our Iowa neighborhood all played golf. So one summer, our boys took group lessons at a public course near our home. They were both quickly hooked. The lessons they took and a "kids play all day for five dollars" program at a short course in town made for a great summer. About this time, my new job was requiring some very long hours, and my wife suggested that I take up golf as a way to spend time with the boys. I quickly confessed my "dark past" with golf and that I didn't think I would enjoy it any more now than I did then. In the end, her motherly instincts and wifely persuasion won out. "Free Lessons with Every Purchase of a New Set of Clubs" caught my eye, and armed with my credit card I trekked down to the discount golf store.

Much to my surprise, it was different this time. Same basic instruction . . . the grip . . . the setup and stance . . . backswing and follow through . . . all helped me focus more on the process than necessarily just the result. After many hours on the driving range, I was still not breaking 100 but I enjoyed the experience of learning something new. It propelled me out of the office and into the fresh air of the Iowa heartland. And it did give me more time with my boys. It was interesting, though, to see how their own impatience and lack of maturity caused problems on the course. The ebb and flow of good moods and bad determined what kind of an outing we had. Both boys had inherited my competitiveness. After each hole, they would argue about the accuracy of the score reported by the other sibling. While I was older and more patient than when I first took up the game, I still did my share of carping about lost balls and their slow play as other foursomes waited behind us. Back at home, I was usually greeted by my wife's insightful, "Well, how did it go this time?"

It bothered me that our time together on the course was not creating the father-son bonding experience that my wife and I had envisioned. In my earlier years, I might have become discouraged and vowed not to take the boys out anymore. But giving up is seldom the answer, and some of my favorite memories were of my own dad's love of sports and the way he taught me to play by playing with me. At times like this, if we can only discard discouragement and replace it with a search for new possibilities, we can often rekindle an earlier dream.

I decided to take the boys out one at a time. I also decided to relax and let them play their game at their pace without regard for the result. If they lose a ball, we'll buy another. When they say their score, I'll just write it down. After all, it is their score not mine. I would also take half-days away from the office so we could play during slow times and maintain our own pace. But above all, I remembered, be encouraging, no carping and no criticism. The time we spend together will be our goal and our reward. And it worked! I have great memories now of times on the course with the boys. My best Father's Day gift was when my oldest son took me for a free round of golf at a course where he worked.

I am forty-seven now. My scores are not much lower than they were in the past. But I can play all day and not care. So what has changed since my first set of clubs and the frustration of those early years? Golf has taught me much about life, even as life has taught me much about golf:

1. Relax—the easier you swing, the farther the ball will go. A white-knuckle grip and a harder swing will probably only increase the tension and reduce the joy—with poor results to follow.
2. Get some basic instruction from the experts . . . better

yet, find a mentor and vow to have a listening, teachable spirit.

3. Focus on people. Choose to play with people you enjoy, people who you've found that lift your spirit. Head out to the course on your own sometime and practice showing interest in whomever fate may place you with that day. Look for ways to be an encouraging and uplifting gift to their day.

4. Refresh yourself by learning something new. New experiences will help to keep you young, will rekindle your interest, your vitality and your love for life. Find a partner who shares your interest in learning and in experiencing new things.

5. Look for the positive possibilities in every challenging situation. Very seldom will you have no shot at all. Even when you do, you may be able to take your drop and scramble back into play. Go for it.

6. Realize that life, like golf, has its ups and downs ... its bunkers and fairways. Ride it out. Beyond each bunker is a well-groomed fairway or green. It only takes one shot to put it back in play.

7. Sharpen up your "inner game." A smooth, relaxed swing—like a smooth, relaxed life—begins in your mind and heart. Learn to stir and rekindle the human spirit by stopping to "smell the roses" along the way. Take a deep breath. Look around at the beauty of the course and get the most from the experience.

8. Tempo is important. Get in touch with your feelings. A good swing has a distinct and gratifying feel. Developing a feel for the game is as important as the mechanics.

9. Above all, have fun—enjoy the journey and the process and let the results take care of themselves.

Larry R. Pearson

The Substitute Caddie

An unusual experience occurred at the L.A. Open, where I came out of retirement from my previous job to caddie. My husband Tom Lehman's longtime caddie, Andrew Martinez, was injured the night before the tournament, and Tom asked me to fill in. I agreed under the condition that I did not have to carry Tom's Taylor Made tour bag, which is huge. We struck a deal, and they got me a much smaller bag.

My first duty as caddie was to meet Tom on the driving range so he could warm up before his round. Other players and caddies were stunned to see me. I proceeded with my job like any other caddie—marking balls, cleaning his clubs and getting the towel wet.

Things went smoothly, and Tom played okay, but the whispers and comments from the gallery as I passed by were amusing. The only rather tense moment came on Sunday on the sixteenth hole. Tom had been having a very, let's say, trying day as far as golf. But I was proud of him because his temper was under control.

When Tom three-putted for bogey, I noticed his putter

in mid-air, sailing into the middle of the pond. The crowd gasped and looked at me for my reaction. I just smiled and walked with Tom to the next tee.

As we walked, I whispered to him, "That's fine. At least you didn't swear. But now I get to pick which club you'll be putting with on the last two holes."

Tom went along with it.

The seventeenth hole started with a drive down the middle, and his second shot landed just over the green. He proceeded to hit a sand wedge and left the ball six inches from the cup. I told him to putt out with the same club, and the crowd loved it. Especially when he made it.

The eighteenth hole, a par-5, started with Tom's driver straight down the middle, and his second shot got him in position for an easy approach. I handed him the wedge that had just served as his putter. He almost holed it (that would have eliminated the putting problems), the ball rolling to six feet.

Just for effect, I handed him his driver. After the crowd figured out that he didn't have a putter anymore, they were all eagerly awaiting a birdie with the driver. He missed it. But ending on two pars was not such a difficult lesson to learn.

Melissa Lehman

Angel's Flight

"Fore!"

Instinctively I ducked, covering my head with my arms. A golf ball sizzled past me and landed no more than twenty feet from my quaking body. It careened off a hillock, rolled down a nearby cart path and, then, as if to punctuate its passing, neatly *plopped* into the water hazard beyond the green.

"What the . . . ?" I turned slowly, nostrils flaring, my eyes fixing upon the culprit. Marching up the fairway and smiling radiantly was a creature of such incredible beauty I have yet to recover. Her hair, blowing back from her temples, was fiery red. Her prancing gait ran a shock through my senses. It was the kind of shock any man would love to receive.

"Oh, I am sorry," she said, glancing at me and then peering beyond to the murky pond. Her enormous green eyes returned to me and she said, "Did I frighten you?"

I began to stammer my response. I was frightened, but more as a result of being intimidated by her ravishing beauty. She stood patiently, alternating her gaze between me and the pond. I finally emitted something audible.

"No, no, certainly it's a part of the game. Nothing

special about having a ball fly by."

She looked again at the pond and then said, "Well, I must say, I never will trust the yardage on this scorecard. I was sure I had at least a hundred yards to the pin." She frowned and then again looked directly into my eyes.

"Ah, well, this is a short hole," I offered. "The seventh has something of a reputation for being deceptive that way."

"The seventh?! Oh, I feel so foolish." She paused, and then began fumbling through the pockets of her neatly tailored windbreaker. Then, after examining a wrinkled scorecard, she said, "I thought I was playing the sixth."

She smiled and looked at me sheepishly, perhaps expecting me to be amused by her mistake. But I stood silently, my face expressionless. Finally, after a moment, she extended her hand.

"I'm so sorry. I have neglected to introduce myself."

Her soft hand, warm for so brisk an autumn morning, fell across my palm as gently as a feather. Her voice betrayed a Southern gentility. This beauty had so soundly smitten me, I was nearly catatonic.

"I'm Clarice McGraw," she said.

Fumbling with my golf bag, and feeling as if my cardigan sweater was starting to unravel, I mimicked her polite gestures and sputtered, "Ah yes, ah well . . . I'm Jimmy Olden."

As I shook her hand and looked into her eyes, I imagined I saw a growing discernment of my condition. *She must encounter fools like me often*, I thought. But in a comfortable way she gave my hand one last shake, surprisingly firm for so soft a hand, and released it. Somehow, I felt assured that I would not be so quickly dismissed.

I gradually loosened up, and we had something of a conversation. Since we were both playing alone we finished the front nine together. She had an appointment, so

I continued on alone, enjoying the back nine. But before we parted I did learn that she was new to the area, had opened up a ladies' dress shop along the boardwalk in town and liked to play golf in the early morning. I told her a little about myself and expressed the hope I would see her again soon. She smiled warmly.

That night I couldn't sleep, and it was still dark when I pulled my car into the club. As I rolled down the long sloping drive to the parking lot I could hear sprinklers clacking faintly somewhere in the distance. I parked and turned off my headlights. A lone light shone over the door of the golf shop.

I sat quietly, clutching a cup of decaffeinated coffee. As the rays of morning sun began to filter through the stand of eucalyptus at the edge of the course, I started wondering if I was doing the right thing. *What if we did hit it off? What if my dreams came true? Could I take all the pressure of being at my best every moment of the day? How could I survive with this beauty?*

The sunlight strengthened, and the warming glow of a new day filled my car. I stretched my arms out across the rim of the steering wheel, and cracked my neck with a sudden twist. After a while the assistant pro opened the shop and turned on the lights. Soon he would be brewing his own coffee, dark and strong, and setting up for the morning business. His name was Ted, and we called him "Go Ball." He was a young, strong man who could drive the ball prodigiously. When he really laid the wood on he'd shout out, "Go ball!" He had such exuberance—it was more natural than anything.

There it was. It struck me that I had the perfect medium through which I could speak to Clarice. It was the game of golf. There is nothing more natural or easy than the bond that grows between players enjoying a round. All I had to do was to play a round of golf with her. I thought of the many times I had teed off with three strangers who soon became three friends. In fact I had met many of my oldest and dearest friends playing golf.

Clarice drove her Volvo into the parking lot and pulled in right alongside my old Fiat Spider. I just happened to have arrived there a mere hour before, and so I casually dismounted my rusting steed.

"Oh, hello," I said in my best Gary Cooper voice.

"Oh, Jimmy, so nice to see you again."

"Are you about to go play?" she asked, looking at me with those beautiful eyes.

I was slightly dumbstruck but finally said, "Yeah sure, you bet. Would you like to join me?"

She smiled broadly and laughed. "I suppose you think it might be safer to play with me instead of ahead of me."

I had to laugh.

We teed off and walked down the fairway, speaking of the things golfers do.

By the time we had completed the front nine we knew each other well enough to say we were friends. We laughed and commiserated over errant shots and generously conceded putts. I was encouraged when she asked if I would play the back nine with her. By the time we came up the eighteenth fairway we each in our own way began to hatch plans. I asked if she would have dinner with me.

She feigned a moment of concentration, as if to envision her cluttered social calendar. Then, smiling impishly, she invited me to her house for meatloaf and mashed potatoes.

Our friendship was born, and we met regularly to play during the remaining fall days. We found new passion in the winter months as a snowy shroud covered the greens. She gave me a driver for Christmas. I gave her a putter. We became more than friends and traveled to a warmer climate to try them out. By spring, I had asked her for her hand.

We were married at the church on the road behind the tenth green, and as we walked out the front door a band of our golfing friends saluted us with golf clubs held high, splashing us with grass seed. At first, the game did all the talking, but soon our hearts were filled with love. It all was so natural and relaxed. And I grew to like being at my best all the time for Clarice.

In sharing our new life together we spent what time we could on the links. We vacationed by traveling across the country and playing all the finest courses.

One year I cheered as Clarice nearly won the ladies' championship at the club. I bought a bottle of champagne with which we celebrated her third-place finish and drowned her disappointment. Our heads clouded with the bubbles, I told her she had easily won the championship of my heart. She was my champion of all champions. She was the winner of the Angel's flight.

For twelve years the game gave us joy, and made it possible for us to see each other in ways that were otherwise probably impossible. Our lives together were filled with many rich experiences. The people and places and our love for the game that brought us together were all so interwoven. It was like a warm quilt, and my memories of it will never tarnish with time.

But one day my Clarice came home from a checkup with her doctor and told me that she had been diagnosed with breast cancer. We sat for an eternity, looking into each other's eyes, neither wanting to show weakness in the face of so daunting an ordeal. Her last days in the hospital came just after Christmas. At home for the last time, we had exchanged gifts beneath the tree. She gave me a new driver, one picked out by our head pro, Ted. I gave her a red sweater with a pattern of falling leaves. It reminded me of the day we met.

My Clarice passed away the first Tuesday of January.

I took a long trip, but I left my clubs at home. When I returned in early spring my first impulse was to go out to the club. When I arrived I was greeted by all our dear friends. I decided to go to the range and see if I could loosen my spine. After a while I found I was hitting the ball pretty good. I decided to go out and play a few holes alone. As I set my bag down aside the first tee, I realized that this would be my first opportunity to see how my new driver felt. It was a beauty. I laced a good drive straight up the fairway. From the golf shop window I heard Ted yell out, "Go ball!" I smiled and waved to him.

Of course, my mind was on Clarice. The first buds of spring were just beginning to open and the grass was a deep lush green. We always reveled in the beauty of springtime. I was playing well for so long a layoff; I hit a nice shot toward the seventh green. My ball lay at the edge of the green, so I used my surefire 7-iron and chipped it to the very lip of the cup.

As I walked toward the hole a gentle breeze gave my ball just a nudge and in it went. A warmth filled my senses as I looked skyward and whispered, "Are you with me, my Angel?"

As I collected my ball from the cup, I heard a distant voice. It spoke to me with urgency, and sounded almost like . . .

"Fore!"

A golf ball landed with a thud no more than twenty feet away. I raised one arm belatedly to protect my head. Then I turned and looked up the fairway. There, in half-gallop, was a young redheaded lad with a bag nearly equal his size draped over his back.

"Sorry, mister, I didn't think I could reach this green."

As he stood before me I smiled, thinking back to someone else who didn't think she could reach this green. I looked into this young boy's green eyes and said, "It's all right, boy. It's part of the game. Nothing special about having a ball fly by."

We walked in together and talked of the things golfers do.

That evening I sat near our fireplace in the company of a glass of red wine. As the embers cast an orange glow about the room, I looked back over the years and thought about how the game of golf had enriched my life. I thought of Clarice and how golf had introduced us, nurturing first our friendship and then our love. Somehow, I knew that every day I spent on the course Clarice would be with me, and perhaps occasionally, with the gentle breeze of her wing, would give my ball a nudge into the hole.

J. G. Nursall

Father and Son

Golf is the "only-est" sport. You're completely alone with every conceivable opportunity to defeat yourself. Golf brings out your assets and liabilities as a person. The longer you play, the more certain you are that a man's performance is the outward manifestation of who, in his heart, he really thinks he is.

Hale Irwin

Writing, painting or music can often capture the splendor of the best of life, but occasionally life mirrors art. An experience occurred recently that brought this home to me: Our student son Mark and I enjoyed a round of seaside golf near the Giant's Causeway in Northern Ireland—one of the most beautiful coastlines in the world.

I write not as a good golfer in the technical sense, but hopefully as a "good" player who enjoys a round in the company of family or friends, who tries hard to win but who doesn't mind losing to the better golfer. Sadly, "good golfers" in that sense are becoming harder to find in a competitive world.

Mark and I were intent on enjoying a day out together, one of those rare occasions where a father and son can share each other's company totally without interruption. Mark had just returned from a vacation job in Germany, where he had been shoveling curry powder in a spice factory. He was about to return to the University of Manchester in England, and I was due to go back to my busy desk at Queen's University in Belfast the next morning. So we settled for a sharing of seaside golf.

Those people who do not understand golf should still read on. I'm not sure that I understand golf myself, or why grown men and women spend so much time, money and energy—and suffer so much anguish—in trying to knock a small white ball into a tiny hole in the ground using a long awkward-looking stick, and trying to do so in as few strokes as possible. It is more than a game: It is a lesson in life. I have seen mature men pale at the prospect of knocking in a final three-foot putt to win a match. Even worse, I know men who have found it hard to lose gracefully to their close friends, or to their own sons. Sometimes such winners are really the losers.

Despite all such angst, there is a totally irrational surge of satisfaction—sometimes peaking into joy—when the golf swing works well and that little white ball zooms down the fairway as if Jack Nicklaus himself had hit it. It was one of those great days of unexpected golfing successes when Mark and I strode along the fairways, bounded on one side by the picturesque River Bush. I had played this course for more than twenty years, but on this particular morning I realized that Mark was coming of age and was beating his father for the first time, fair and square.

As we walked and talked, my mind lingered on the theme of life imitating art, and particularly the art of that great and much-loved English poet Sir John Betjeman, who captured the magic of "Seaside Golf":

How straight it flew, how long it flew,
It cleared the rutty track,
And soaring, disappeared from view
Beyond the bunker's back —
A glorious, sailing, bounding drive
That made me glad I was alive.

As our game progressed through the regulation eighteen holes, it was obvious that Dad, playing quite well by his standards, was hanging on for dear life. And at the very last hole, Mark, a gentle giant of a young man, strode forward none-too-confidently to try to sink a short putt that would win the match. As he stood there concentrating, I wanted him to sink the putt and win, but I was equally prepared to play on to a "sudden death" if necessary. Agonizingly he hit it, and the ball rolled gently—into the cup! A beam of joy lit up his face, and I felt deep in my heart: "That's my boy." I thought, too, of the lines of Betjeman:

It lay content
Two paces from the pin:
A steady putt and then it went
Oh, most securely in.
The very turf rejoiced to see
That quite unprecedented three.

Afterwards, in the clubhouse, we had a simple but splendid lunch overlooking the very green where Mark had clinched his memorable victory. We replayed every stroke, we talked about sport and we philosophized about life. I even pointed out, for the umpteenth time, the sparkling white hotel across the headlands where his mother and I had held our wedding reception a quarter century earlier, and I told him, yet again, of my early and troubled attempts to learn to play golf on this very same course. One day I became so frustrated that I put the ball in my pocket and walked on with my partner, rather than try to play a few holes. Later, my editor, when reading of this in my Belfast newspaper column, wrote the following headline: "The Day I Played Four Holes in None!"

Mark, for his part, listened intently and appreciatively to this family history. He too has an eye for beauty and an ear for poetry. He is (I'll say it) a treasured son, a partner and confidant in his own right, and his triumph on the golf course had underlined his maturity and growing sense of independence. With such a son I, technically the loser, knew that I was, happily, a long-term winner in a much deeper way.

That night, I read to Mark the last stanza of the Betjeman poem that recaptured so beautifully our feelings of privilege and joy.

> Ah! seaweed smells from sandy caves
> And thyme and mist in whiffs,
> In-coming tide, Atlantic waves
> Slapping the sunny cliffs,
> Lark song and sea sounds in the air,
> And splendor, splendor everywhere.

Indeed. There had been enough splendor on that fine day to warm the hearts of a father and a son for a lifetime.

Alf McCreary

Return to Inwood

What a beautiful place a golf course is. From the meanest country pasture to the Pebble Beaches and St. Andrews of the world, a golf course is to me a holy ground. I feel God in the trees and grass and flowers, in the rabbits and the birds and the squirrels, in the sky and the water. I feel that I am home.

Harvey Penick

We used to drive past a beautiful-looking golf course on the way to Rockaway Beach, touring about in our '57 Studebaker, and then after that, a '63 Dodge Dart. As we passed by, I would crane my neck and look out the back window. It turned out to be Inwood Country Club.

I had never seen a piece of land as beautiful. A wrought-iron fence surrounded the grounds, setting it off from a series of dilapidated single-family houses. Traffic breezed by, making the stately parkland site all the more intriguing. So one summer morning, I would guess when I was nine years old, I headed off on my bicycle and an hour later found myself at its gates.

It was something out of a movie, or better yet, the cover of one of those Hardy Boys books I had at home, with me standing there, looking up at this massive stone entrance-way, and deep inside the grounds was this spooky, old-fashioned clubhouse. Beneath the metal plate announcing "Inwood Country Club" was a warning about "Private: Members Only." All of this was too inviting for me to turn back now. My sole act of deference was to get off my bike and to walk it up the private road.

Various groups of people stood around in the distance—golfers, accompanied by caddies. Dense shades of green were everywhere, all of it framed by graceful trees and some lovely shrubbery and flower beds. It all seemed in such contrast to the world I had passed through to get here. I thought it best to avoid the clubhouse because there was no way I was going to be able to explain away my visit if any member confronted me. Just as the path climbed up to the clubhouse, I veered off to the right and headed down behind the parking lot. There I found a spot behind some bushes and left my bicycle unlocked.

On one side stretched the swamps of Jamaica Bay, and across the water were the main runways of Idlewild (later John F. Kennedy) Airport. To my right was a row of hedges, and just beyond it unfolded this huge expanse of lawn and trees. We had a black-and-white TV set at home, and the only other time I remember being overwhelmed like this was when I first watched a baseball game on a neighbor's color set. It wasn't just the size of the yard here, it was also the intensity of the green color and all the shades and varieties, and the way the branches draped so lovingly over everything. I walked down by a putting sur-face, headed across a little stone bridge that carried me over a lily pond, and then walked along one side of a fair-way back toward a group of golfers.

Way in the distance, I saw someone swing. The metal

shaft glinted, the ball rose against the blue sky, and then I heard a kind of "click" sound as the ball headed right at me, except that it gently climbed, then leveled off and floated, seemingly forever. By the time the ball butter-flied down to earth in front of me, I had fallen in love with the game.

More than twenty-five years later I returned to Inwood CC, this time with our eleven-year-old daughter, Cory, in hand, to show her the spot where my fascination with golf had started. Like my father, she had done a good job of playing along with my interest, at one point even tak-ing up the game as a way of spending time with me. She could even watch it on TV with me and began to register a certain familiarity with players. So I thought it a good idea one morning while we visited my parents to conjure yet another reason for an early morning escape.

She was always quick to join a conspiracy, and so we set off together in my '90 Toyota Tercel.

The ride didn't seem nearly as long this time. Strange, how age shrinks distance. The buildings along the way all looked a little smaller than they had been when I was growing up. The roads were more packed with chintzy businesses, neon signs and the general sense of nowhere that has become typical of strip-mall culture. But then I made the right turn off Sheridan Boulevard and it all came back to me just as it had been, replete with the empty sandlot in front of the country club and the sign remind-ing me that I didn't belong.

This time, though, there was nothing to hide. One key to American society, I have learned, is that if you act as if you belong, people will play along. It's just a matter of knowing how to look like you're part of what's going on. This time I parked close to the clubhouse, waved a friendly greeting to the doorman, and then headed off with Cory to the pro shop, where we introduced ourselves to the resident professional. Tommy Thomas, his name was, and I had known him tangentially from my caddie days on the PGA Tour several summers earlier. He had been one of the many journeyman golfers who tries his hand at the big life and then finds out for all sorts of reasons that he just can't quite compete or that life on the road is too demanding. In any case, I remembered him not for any success he enjoyed—on the contrary—but for his trademark use of a certain suspect golf ball: "the Molitor man," he had been called, and now, some twelve years later, he smiled when I recalled this nickname. There is no escaping a nickname on the Tour.

In brief compass, we divested ourselves of our limited supply of shared Tour memories. "Would it be okay if we headed off to the eighteenth hole? I want to show Cory where I . . . well, where I first discovered golf." "Sure," he said, "just make sure you stay out of the way of any play. We have a few early birds; they went off the back nine and may be finishing already."

This time, the grounds took on a meaning that had not been available to me in my youth. Inwood Country Club, after all, had been the site of two major golf championships, the 1921 PGA and the 1923 U.S. Open. That stone bridge fronting the green was copied from the famous original on the eighteenth hole at the Old Course at St. Andrews. I recounted this to Cory as we walked down the right side of the eighteenth fairway.

It was a lovely day, the air warming up, the sky clear, and none of those noisy airplanes disturbing the morning calm. And as we walked over and stood on the exact spot where so many years ago I had begun my affair with the game, I turned around and saw a historic marker that, I later found out, had only recently been placed there in the ground. "In 1923, Bobby Jones clinched the first of his four U.S. Open titles by hitting a two-iron from this spot to within six feet of the hole during a playoff with Bobby Cruickshank."

Cory read the marker aloud without really understanding it. She did, however, understand what the moment meant to me. This eleven-year-old, who usually talked for hours without coming up for air, stood quietly by my side for a few minutes while I relived all the emotions of my first visit.

Then she looked up at me, and with utter seriousness in her gray eyes, said, "Cool."

Bradley S. Klein

A Measure of Love

It was the afternoon of Christmas Eve, and I had just finished wrapping the last gift for my family when Greg, my sixteen-year-old son, came into the bedroom after returning from shopping with his dad.

"Mom, you are not going to believe what Dad got you for Christmas!" he announced. "It's a gift that shows how much he loves you."

My mind immediately envisioned a diamond ring or gorgeous tennis bracelet. Without giving away my idea of a "love" gift, I responded with the question, "Do you think I got Dad enough for Christmas?"

After a few moments of thoughtful consideration, Greg answered, "Gosh, Mom, I don't know. You might want to run down to the hardware store and buy him that tool chest he's been wanting. It's going to be hard to match what he got you though."

With a teaser like that, I found it as difficult to sleep on Christmas Eve as I had when I was a kid. Visions of rings and bracelets danced in my head and I was the first one up in the morning. I eagerly gathered Greg, my other son Jeff, and my husband Randy for the ritual of opening gifts. As each one took his turn opening, we oohed and aahed over the selections each had made to show our love. I opted to open my gifts last, saving the moment when I would see the gift that would be the measure of my husband's love.

Finally, it was my turn. The first gift I opened was a blender. Next, I opened a set of pots and pans. I took each one out of the box and carefully looked inside them, on the handles, and even in the packing for anything that resembled a piece of jewelry. My next gift was some cologne, my favorite kind. Still, I didn't see any evidence of the spectacular gift for which I had been preparing myself to be surprised and overwhelmed. My last gift from my husband was a pretty gold nightgown and robe (in the wrong size).

Hiding my disappointment, I good-naturedly thanked Randy for the gifts and planted a big kiss on his lips. Mentally, I was trying to determine which gift in a sixteen-year-old's mind had deserved the assessment that it showed how much he loved me. I decided probably the pots and pans!

We started to clean up the mountain of wrapping paper, bows and boxes. Randy came up behind me as I was stuffing them into the trash bag, put his arms around my waist and navigated me into the living room where we had another Christmas tree. My deflated spirits took wing, and I fully expected to find the ring or bracelet decorating one of the branches. Instead, he took me over to the tree and pointed behind it, where I saw a golf bag filled with shiny, new clubs.

My face fell as I tried to figure out how a new set of golf clubs for Randy was going to show how much he loved me. I already knew how much he loved golf, so he certainly didn't need to convince me on that point.

My boys said in unison, "She doesn't like them, Dad."

Randy, so secure in his choice, calmly reassured the boys, "Don't worry, guys. I knew she'd react like this. It's just going to take some time for her to learn the game and enjoy it like I do!"

"They're not yours?" I dumbly questioned. "They're for me?" I was now becoming indignant. "I can't believe that you think I would want to play golf alone!" Randy, an excellent golfer who consistently shoots in the 70s and always attracts a gallery of spectators even on the driving range, had often expressed his frustrations with women golfers who slowed the play down because they weren't very good. I, a woman with no athletic ability, had only swung a club once or twice. With a giant stretch of the imagination, I would not even fit into the category of "not very good."

Randy, undaunted by my less-than-enthusiastic reaction, said, "I thought this would be something we could do together. When the boys and I go out, we could have a foursome, and I know you'll grow to love the game like we do."

"You're serious, aren't you?" I asked incredulously. Things were starting to make sense. To take me on the golf course was a true measure of love to Randy. To allow me, a woman who was totally incompetent at golf, to play with him really was a sign of how much he loved me. And in the months that followed, his patience and perseverance in taking me to the driving range and enrolling me in lessons had proved that his gift was a gift of love and not a mere whimsy or desperate last-minute purchase for Christmas.

Because we are both teachers, we spend our summers at the beach in San Clemente, California, camping and now going to the golf course. With our sons grown and busy with their own lives, we have something that we can share as a couple that will keep us active and young. Randy still loves to play competitive golf and he is awesome, but he takes the time and patience to help and encourage me and keep me motivated to participate in what I have found to be a very challenging and alluring activity.

Greg, the sixteen-year-old who prepared me for the gift of love seven years ago on Christmas Eve, married recently. I gave him a little womanly advice on gift giving to take with him into his marriage. I looked him in the eyes and said, "Son, when you want to show Sarah how much you love her, go for the bracelet or the diamond ring in the first five years. Save the golf clubs for later when she can fully appreciate how much love that kind of a gift shows."

Judy Walker

Dad's Magic Clubs

My father died last month. He was eighty-six, in poor health, and his passing was not unexpected. His funeral was marked by an outpouring of affection and accolades. If novenas, Masses and prayers mean anything, then Dad is already a consultant to St. Peter. Ironically, this outpouring of adoration was not fully appreciated by his children.

My father was a medical doctor, and by all accounts, a good one. His specialty was bringing babies into the world, and he loved it. He came from a generation that believed that the doctor an expectant mother saw throughout her pregnancy was the one who should be there at the birth. Many a seashore excursion, vacation or special occasion was delayed, curtailed or postponed because Mrs. So-and-so's baby was due at any moment.

I was always amazed at how many parents named their sons Joseph, after my father. Patients loved him. He had a way of making each individual feel like the most important person in the world. He was also a man of the people outside the office and hospital. His Irish heritage, of which he was immensely proud, his love of poetry and his sense of humor made him a sought-after speaker for public and private affairs. In short, he was a charming man. Unfortunately, his children believed that wherever he parked his car each night was the same place he parked his charm.

Dad was a strict and demanding parent. He was the oldest of five in hard economic times, and his childhood was purposeful, tough and short. In turn, he expected his children to think and act like adults. Our dinner table was not always a happy place.

Having said that, it was my father who introduced me to golf. In the late 1940s and early 1950s, sports to a young male teen meant baseball, football and basketball. I did not know another teenager who played golf. My friend Frank Costello and I were recruited to caddie for Dad and his friends. The bags were heavy, the pay pitiful, and we were expected to find balls in places where no golf ball—much less human—should go. Frank and I soon discovered it was good sense to have something else planned for Wednesdays and Saturdays.

As a caddie, I learned about the quality of golf scores. I knew that anybody who could regularly break 100 was a good golfer. And if they could score in the 80s, they were great golfers. It never dawned on me that an amateur could shoot in the 70s.

Then my father joined a golf club—Upper Montclair Country Club, a quality 27-hole layout a dozen miles west of New York City. We had a family membership, and I was encouraged to play. I did so only as an activity of last resort. I usually played by myself and only nine holes. I rarely broke 50 and only did so with the help of mulligans, generous gimmes and a few should-have-beens.

Playing with my father made Latin seem easy. From him, I learned almost nothing about how to play golf, but everything about the game of golf. My first lesson was in the proper pace of golf. Slow play was sinful. To this day,

I am uncomfortable when groups behind us have to wait, even when we are not at fault.

A golfer never steps to the tee without at least two balls in his pocket. If you need to hit a second ball, it is bad manners to make everyone wait while you return to your bag. Dad was a stickler for preparation. Have enough tees and know where your ball marker is. He would be appalled at the condition of my sons' golf shoes. His were always clean and shining. I suspect, at age sixty-three, I am one of the few left who regularly take polish and brush to their golf shoes.

He disdained practice swings, and his view on winter rules was simple: They are for cheats. Through the years I have played with generals, admirals and politicians, many of whom can give great speeches on honor, duty and country but think nothing of moving the ball all over the course.

Dad was scrupulous about the accuracy of his scores. In later years, when he knew his memory was failing, he would ask his fellow golfers to help him keep track. To Dad, the difference between a seven and an eight was important. I learned that some of the most boring people in the world are those who have to relive every shot after the round. Dad said, "What was done was done, and since most golfers dwell on their bad shots, who cares?"

Dad always had a bet, if only a modest one, but to him competition and survival were synonymous. All of this I learned about golf long before I could play it.

After graduating from college, I went off to a career in the Air Force. Early on, I caught the golf bug, and thanks to Uncle Sam, I had the opportunity to play around the world and throughout the United States. Thanks to Dad, there was never a doubt about how to play the game. As my handicap drifted in the low teens, I put into practice every one of my father's rules of golf. During those years,

I rarely played with Dad. Until my last assignment, we were never closer than one thousand miles, and often our trips home to New Jersey were not compatible with golf weather.

At thirty-eight I gave up golf for nine years. My wife and I were blessed with seven healthy, active children, and their many activities left little room for golf. When, on his own, my oldest son Michael took up the game, I was lured to golf again. This time the bug hit hard. In 1984, I bought my first semi-custom-fit clubs—Ping woods and Ping Eye Two irons, the blue dot model. New clubs, a back operation and the resultant compact swing brought new vigor to my game and handicap. It also brought a return to playing golf with my father.

Residing in Virginia, I was able to make regular trips north to New Jersey. Dad was now in his mid-seventies and his golf game weak. In his prime, he was thrilled to break 100 and broke 90 only once in his life. But his zest for the game never diminished. We always played for a bet, but his 36 handicap drew a surplus of strokes and he always won. And despite the quality of my handicap, by now a 5, I never played Upper Montclair at my best. Losing to my father I accepted, but Upper Montclair was something else. No matter how well I played, I could not break 80. Shooting 80 or 81 was easy, but I could not get through the barrier.

In late summer of 1991, I headed north to play what turned out to be my last rounds at UMCC. On that glorious weekend I shot 76 and 74. I was pleased beyond measure, but what surprised me the most was the great pleasure my father took in my accomplishment. At age eighty, he made more of a to-do about it than I ever could.

For me, that weekend was the culmination of a forty-year golf odyssey—from a disinterested teenager to a competent amateur golfer. Shortly thereafter, my father fully retired from his medical practice and moved to Hilton Head, South Carolina. We played a number of times at his Moss Creek course, but because of his declining health, we could never relive the magic of that day at Upper Montclair. Through the years, I have come to realize that my father had an appreciation and love for golf that few ever realize.

To him, golf was not just playing eighteen holes; it was the whole experience: the preparation, the wager, the good holes and the bad, the occasional par, the traditional cold potato soup and beer afterward, the discussion of world events, the hot shower and clean clothes. All were integral parts of a golf day, with each segment to be enjoyed to its fullest. The score was important, but only briefly and a small part of the picture.

After that weekend in 1991, my game continued to improve. By late 1992, I was taking myself seriously. Modest success in several one-day senior events led me to believe my golden years would be spent collecting golf prizes.

And then I got greedy. Deciding that my 5 handicap needed to be further lowered, I fell prey to modern technology. Never mind that with my trusty Pings I was playing the best golf of my fifty-eight years. I needed to do better. I gave my clubs to my son John, who is now playing the best golf of his life.

Technology has done wonders for me. Five years and five sets of clubs left me with a 14 handicap and a mechanical hack of a swing.

And then my father died. After the funeral, I remained in Hilton Head for a few days to help Dad's wife settle his affairs. Our mother had died suddenly many years ago, and we had come to love Dad's second wife, Louise, dearly. She offered the love and care that few men receive once in a lifetime, much less twice.

One of my tasks was to do something with Dad's golf equipment. He had a garage full of odds and ends, unopened catalog-company packages containing "magic" putters and wedges. At age eighty-five, Dad was still looking for that par-saving club. All of those were given to junior golf, with one exception: Dad's final and little-used set of irons were Ping Eye Twos, the blue dot model.

I took them back to Virginia, having no idea what I would do with them. Shortly after my return, I participated in a local three-day tournament. My play was indifferent, and I failed to make the third-day cut.

During the ensuing week, discouraged with golf, I played with my father's clubs. What happened was mystical. In an eleven-day period I shot 76, 75, 73, 75, 74 and 75. Conventional wisdom says there is no way an honest 14 handicap can play that kind of golf. The next few rounds were not as impressive, but there is no doubt my game has taken an amazing turn. My handicap is plunging, and my swing is easier and more fluid than it has been in years.

Golf is fun again. Why? I only have a clue. For his entire life, my father was considered the consummate charmer. In his lifetime, I received little of that charm. In his clubs, he gave me my share.

John Keating

Her Mother's Presence

Friday, March 20, 1998, was a bright, sunny day in Phoenix, Arizona. I was preparing for my afternoon tee time at the Standard Register Ping LPGA Championship. My sister lived in nearby Scottsdale and my parents were in town. I was looking forward to having them there to follow and enjoy the day.

My mother especially enjoyed spending time in Phoenix with both of her daughters. However, what we didn't know was that this trip to Arizona would be her last. It also was going to be the final golf tournament she would watch me play.

Mom was one of my biggest supporters and loved being out on tour to watch and cheer me on. She never missed a shot; she saw everything from the first tee shot to the last putt. She was known for her high-pitched screams that followed every birdie I made. I always enjoyed looking into the crowd and seeing her beaming smile. Mom took advantage of any chance she had to spend time with me.

In September 1997 our entire family life changed drastically. Mom experienced a small stroke and the doctors found multiple brain tumors. Two brain surgeries followed, and the final diagnosis was cancer. Six months later, as the disease was destroying her body, Mom was confined to a scooter to navigate the golf course. Instead of her smile and high-pitched screams, I saw a weary, defeated, blank face. Only the hum of the motor came from her direction.

God blessed me with a fantastic round on that Friday in March. I shot a 64, one of my lowest scores of the year. The golf was enjoyable and the results great, but I felt more joy knowing Mom was able to watch me play. Throughout the day I found my attention focused not only on my golf, but on her as well. It seemed as though she had to concentrate hard on maneuvering the scooter so as not to hit anything. I wanted to understand how she felt having to rely on a machine to get from one point to another, but I couldn't. My heart was breaking as I saw how the deadly disease was consuming her body and her mind.

It was a day of overwhelming emotions. Joy, laughter, sadness and tears seemed to flood my heart all at the same time. This was a reality check for me on the perspective of life. Shooting a 64, having a chance to win a golf tournament and making a career out of walking a green fairway is not what life is all about. Remembering Mom as a part of my gallery is a much greater treasure than shooting a 64. God's word says to store up treasures in heaven—things that cannot be destroyed by the hands of humans, for "where your treasure is, there will your heart be also." Life is about enjoying time with family and friends. Life is about love—loving God and loving those around us!

Mom died from cancer on May 31, 1998, just two months later.

I will never forget that Tour stop, the last tournament Mom watched. Under the hum of that scooter, I knew in my heart she was screaming at each birdie. Mom is gone now and I miss her very much. But what gives me comfort is the fact that she is in heaven and I will see her again. As I continue through my life—both in and out of golf—Mom's presence will always be with me. I can still hear her sweet voice cheering me on.

Tracy Hanson

A Sudden End to a Love Story

All love stories should include a moment when the heroine sends out her 2-iron for repairs. This one does.

Renay White's 2-iron shots flew on a line not much higher than a wallaby's belly. So the Australian teenager decided the stick needed a new shaft. Her coach delivered it to another young player, Stuart Appleby, a country boy off an outback dairy farm who made ends meet by doing the odd club repair.

As it happens, Appleby earlier had admired a small, strong, smiling woman striding with wonderful cockiness through his field of vision. He asked, "Who's that?"

"Renay White," said Ross Herbert, her coach.

"Does she have a boyfriend?"

"No."

So in the summer of 1992, Appleby came to know White as smart, funny, cute—and altogether too much the flirt. She returned the favor by declaring him drop-dead gorgeous with those blue eyes—and what a snob.

Ah, young love, sweet love. She was nineteen, he was twenty-one, they were confused.

He knew certainly that he wanted to put his hands on her 2-iron. Within minutes, Appleby gave the club back to the coach, who later said, "Stuart was very keen to do a good job on it. Even then he and Renay were using golf to communicate."

Words had failed when they mistook voice for character. She was loud, laughing and sassy. He was quiet, reserved and serious.

But soon enough they understood each other. No flirt, she had been born vivacious. No snob, he came to work focused. They filled in the gaps of each other's personality. On the Australians' tour of U.S. college teams that fall, it was only natural Renay and Stuart were mixed-twosome partners.

And from then on they were always partners, first friends and lovers, then husband and wife who lived by one of life's coolest rules: *Dance as if no one's watching, love as if it's never going to hurt.*

The story really begins on a beach.

After the American matches, Appleby knew he wanted golf and Renay. He had the one but not the other. Then she asked, "Why don't you come visit my place?"

It's a five-hour drive from his home to hers on Australia's southeast coast.

Appleby made it in, oh, five minutes. They spent a day together before he went home. His mother soon said, "Stuart, you're moping, you're useless. Go back to Renay's."

This time around, Stuart and Renay swam, took the sun and sat on the beach, where by the end of a week he said words that came so easily they seemed inevitable.

He said, "I've always wanted to meet someone like you. I want to spend the rest of my life with you." She said, "I want to be with you." And she thought, *Oh, my God, this is it.*

She told her sister, Duean, she had met this guy, she adored him, they spoke each other's thoughts, he made her laugh and he laughed with her.

Renay had been a promising golfer since age twelve, a contemporary of Karrie Webb, who became a sensation on the American tour. But, however talented Renay might have been, she no longer cared. She knew her passion for golf ran a distant second to her passion for Stuart.

She would rather be with him than put in the work demanded of a Webb or an Appleby. She sat for hours on practice ranges from Melbourne to Orlando, watching her guy, waiting, talking, sometimes even curling up to sleep on the night's-coming grass. She often caddied for him.

They had great dreams together, and there came a day when he said, "These dreams were fulfilled to a very high extent right up to the time she left us."

From the road, she wrote letters to her parents. She carried a laptop computer and filled cyberspace with laughing emails. Any happenings, any new jokes, any sudden realizations would put her on the phone to Duean, determined to keep her sister within five seconds of all the news.

When Stuart drove to the golf course, Renay told him where to turn.

When he dawdled, she said, "Stuey, move your rear," and he did, laughing all the way, a two-hour tiff for some couples, for them two seconds.

When he groused, "I'm putting so bad," she brought light to his eyes by saying, "Bad? Bad? You're putting bloody *terrible!* And, by the way, I love you."

When Stuart played, she walked along by the gallery ropes, wearing a schoolgirl's shorts, T-shirt, sneakers, a funny little cap and a backpack.

When he missed seven cuts in nine tournaments early in 1998, she wrote an email to his coach, Steve Bann, saying, "Stuart's playing so very well. He's about to win." And he won the Kemper Open.

He had become a star at age twenty-seven. Through

two-and-a-half seasons on the PGA Tour, he had won twice and earned about $2 million. He and Renay bought a house in Isleworth, the Orlando development that is home to Tiger Woods, Mark O'Meara and tennis pro Todd Woodbridge, whose wife Natasha had become Renay's best friend.

Renay won Tash with laughter. Such a happy woman. Todd Woodbridge thought to teach the golfer tennis and heard Renay shout, "Why is it the ball's NOT STILL?"

One evening Tash needed a glass for red wine.

"The crystal," Renay said.

"But we're going out in the boat."

"So?"

So crystal stemware awarded to the winner of the 1997 Honda Classic found itself in use at a backyard picnic.

This June, Renay sat on her veranda. She had played golf with the Australian pro Jody Adams. Renay's first round in months, a 75, had been so remarkable Adams encouraged her to try the tour.

"No need, Jody," Renay said. "I couldn't possibly be happier with my life."

She and Stuart painted bedrooms, finished a television room and installed a twelve-seat dining-room table made of Australian wood. They hung aboriginal art and set out bowls carved from Australian trees. In the kitchen, after workmen cracked a kitchen countertop, Renay re-ordered it. She loved its look, loved to move her hand across its face. It is black Italian marble. They wanted children. "She'd have been an amazing mother, so loving, so patient," Stuart said. Tash Woodbridge once whispered to Renay, "I might be pregnant," and Renay punched her arm. "No, no, you can't be. We're getting pregnant at the same time!" When the pregnancy test came back negative, Tash said, "We jumped around together like two-year-olds," so happy were they to still have a chance at simultaneous maternity.

The last time they spoke, Tash heard happiness. Renay and Stuart were on a second honeymoon. From London they would take the next day's train to Paris. So Renay called to ask about Paris. Where to eat, which churches, which museums.

They spoke across the Atlantic for forty-five minutes. Then Tash's husband said the girls should get off the phone. He said they could talk another day.

The next day, she died. Struck by a car backing up as she waited with Stuart to leave their taxi at London's hectic Waterloo train station, Renay Appleby died before reaching a hospital. The watch she wore that day, Stuart carries in his pocket today, still on London time.

She wore a chain around her neck with her name on it. He wears it now. On his golf visor is her PGA Tour wife's badge. He touches her pajamas. He looks at the train tickets, London to Paris, and says, "They're the end of the story. Full stop."

The light of joy disappears, emptiness rushes in with its darkness. Stuart Appleby, empty, came to the PGA Championship four days after last taking flowers to Renay's grave. He asked to do a press conference. He came to the dais a haunted man, unshaven, stricken, weeping and brave as hell.

He called Renay "first prize of a raffle in life." He talked about her laughter, her friends. He'll mention her name, he'll talk about the memories.

One day when he needs her, she'll be there, a force of belief working for him.

It's the little things you miss, a kiss goodnight, orange juice in the morning, a half-hour's conversation. "They make up someone's life," he said.

Stuart asked that Renay's headstone be carved from the black Italian marble she loved in her kitchen. Her family and Stuart agreed on an epitaph, leaving the last lines to him . . .

> *In Happiest, Loving Memory of Renay Appleby*
> *We can only hope to pass on your qualities to*
> *those we meet*
> *We are blessed to have had you in our lives*
> *The memories you have given us will all remain*
> *Adored wife of Stuart*
> *"My best friend forever."*

Dave Kindred

Remembering My Father

Romance fails us and so do friendships, but the relationship of parent and child, less noisy than all others, remains indelible and indestructible, the strongest relationship on earth.

Theodor Reik

I never met anyone more competitive or more intense than my father. My eighth-grade basketball team was playing on the road in the regional finals. As usual he was sitting in the crowd, letting the official know exactly what he thought of every single call. I guess since he himself had refereed basketball games after graduating from college, he felt he had the authority. No doubt he had the voice. It was so loud you could hear him from any part of the arena, and he knew it.

Finally, one of the officials, tired of being abused by some obnoxious stranger in the stands—and who could blame him?—called a technical foul. My coach went berserk. "Who is that technical on?" he shouted. "That man up there in the orange sweater," the referee responded. *Thanks a lot, Dad,* I felt like shouting at him. I couldn't hide far enough away on that bench. How could he do that to me? I vowed right there and then that I would never do that to my children.

So much for the innocent vows of youth. I recently did exactly the same thing. I screamed at the umpire during my son's baseball game. As exasperated as the official twenty-five years ago, the umpire turned around and said, "Any more out of you and you're out of here." I laughed, flashing back immediately to eighth grade. Yes, I had become my father. You know what, I'm glad. Because that man, wiser than I ever realized, taught me how to compete and how to care passionately about whatever you're doing, which, in my profession, is absolutely essential.

I certainly brought a lot of passion to the golf course, probably because my father made me so mad. When I missed a short putt one time, he chuckled and said, "You got your right hand in there." The next hole, when I missed another short one, he started laughing even louder. Nobody got to me like that. Years later, I figured out that he was showing me that the game—and life itself—would always be filled with distractions. You either succumb to them or you survive them. He taught me how to survive them.

On the golf course Dad was more my friend than my instructor. A few years into my marriage, however, he handed my wife a sheet of paper filled with scribbled instructions, such as: "Watch Payne's head. Make sure his left foot is back and his right foot is up. Watch his address. Make sure he finishes high. Watch his speed on putting," and so forth. Soon afterward we found out he had cancer. Did he already know that at the time? Were the notes his parting gift to me? I don't know. I'll never know. I still have the sheet. My wife framed it for me one Christmas.

My dad hated golf carts, so we had plenty of time to talk on the course. One conversation I clearly remember is when I was preparing for my freshman year at SMU. He figured the moment had finally arrived to give me the famous father-son, birds-and-the-bees talk. So what if he was five years late? Maybe he needed the extra time to compose his thoughts.

I'm so much like him. I am also a traveling salesman of sorts, hopping from one town to another to do my job. I know how painful it is to be away from one's family for a long period of time. That's why I marvel at the way he was able to endure it. He left Monday mornings and returned Thursday evenings, sometimes Friday evenings, but he always devoted plenty of attention to us when he was home. What I experienced as a child has helped me be more sensitive to how my kids feel when I'm away for weeks at a time.

Money never meant that much to my dad. That's probably because he didn't have a tremendous amount of it. My father provided us with everything we needed, but the dollar never became an almighty object of adoration, as it is for so many people these days. He once looked at the new house I had built and said, "Why do you need something like that?" He couldn't understand excess. That was his generation. My generation is different. We swim in excess. But even though I've accumulated many toys—I think I've always understood, thanks to him, that money is not the answer in life.

Did my dad enjoy his work? I don't know. It's not the kind of question one thinks about as a kid. I hope he did. I know, like many others who grew up in the Depression, it was very important to him that his children go to college, and no child of Bill Stewart's was going to drop out of college to go to work. He never allowed me to downgrade education. I grew up knowing that if someday I couldn't hit 4-irons anymore, at least I would have a college degree to fall back on.

He prepared me for everything. Everything, that is, except his death. That, he neglected. The one memory that immediately pops out from his fight with cancer is the last day my father and I saw each other. My wife and I had just learned that she was pregnant with our first child. I was so excited, I couldn't wait to tell him. I also felt that the timing could not have been any better. I was sure it would cheer him up.

He was sleeping in his favorite chair when I walked up to him and whispered: "Dad, I got a secret to tell you. I'm going to be a daddy." His eyes opened up and he smiled. He was going to be a grandfather. I expected him to congratulate me, to express his joy, to say something poignant, perhaps even to break down. But, I swear to God, the first thing he said was, "Don't buy expensive baby furniture." That was such a typical Dad thing to say.

I probably should have been a little annoyed, but I wasn't. That was his way of expressing love. I gave him a big hug and kiss for the last time. Funny thing is, I never cried at the funeral, which no one could figure out. I'm a very emotional person. I suppose that as the new man of the family, I had to show strength. Six months later I took my baby daughter back home to Springfield. We went to the cemetery and sat down. I finally had my big cry.

Payne Stewart
as told to Michael Arkush

Fear of the Father-Son Tournament

It is in the blood of genius to love play for its own sake, and whether one uses one's skill on thrones or women, swords or pens, gold or fame, the game's the thing.

Gelett Burgess

No words strike greater fear in the occasional playing offspring of the inveterate golfer than these: father-son tournaments. For years, my father's mistaken assumption that I needed a valid handicap kept me off the hook. But when he learned otherwise, there was no escape. A date was set, a starting time inked.

Occasional playing is probably an overstatement, though years ago (fourth and fifth grades) I did live on the 15th hole of an Oklahoma City course. Consequently, I learned a lot: how to duck, and that some of the worst shankers in the world reside just east of the Texas panhandle. I had my first taste of the game then. Dad would take me out after dusk, and we'd play the closing holes. If I shot my age on a hole, I was thrilled.

My game peaked a few years later when I tagged along

on my neighbor's trips to South Carolina every summer. We played almost every day. There's no pressure to perform in front of someone else's dad. What do they care if you stink? It's not a reflection on their gene pool.

Outside of one glorious 94 in high school, my game has been in decline ever since. I play once or twice a year, three times if I'm lucky.

Dad, on the other hand, plays once or twice a week. He's a legit 12 or 13 handicap who's known for his long drives, despite a backswing that cannot be captured by time-lapse photography.

He assured me that we would get out on the course a few times before the tourney. And sure enough, two days before the big day, I set foot on the tee box for the first time.

It wasn't pretty. My scorecard sported more snowmen than a Minneapolis suburb in January. The putting display was the worst you'll see this side of a drunk on a miniature course at two in the morning. And, yes, despite using a driver half the size of my head, I whiffed, which, in terms of athletic ineptness, is surpassed only by striking out in kickball.

Still, there was hope. I didn't bean any deer. I found more balls than I lost. And off the tee, I wasn't looking too bad.

Have you ever tried to cram for the dentist? You brush, floss and gargle your brains out for two days trying to make up for six months of neglect. Well, this was me hours before the tournament. Poring over golf magazines, I'm putting in the basement and perusing the tube for tips—or at least a rerun of *Dead Solid Perfect, Tin Cup* or even *Caddyshack.*

Given my antics, you'd think my father was exerting a lot of pressure on me. Not at all. Sure, doing well would enhance the experience, but he just wants to have fun. Step onto that tee, though, and it's Little League all over again. You want to do well in front of Dad. Back when I was in high school we played tennis against two guys who together were about a century and a half old. They cleaned our clock as I sprayed balls everywhere but on the court. And tennis is my better sport.

D-day rolls around and the weather is beautiful. I discover that Dad has put me in for a 26 handicap, even though the last time I saw the 90s was, well, the '80s. Add his legit 13 handicap, multiply by 40 percent, and we get sixteen shots. It won't be enough.

While at the pro shop, he tries to buy me a new pair of golf shoes. My game doesn't deserve it, but one of the man's great joys in life is buying athletic footwear for family, so I relent. Without the old fifteen pounds of foot gear, the only thing left to keep my head down is a self-imposed burden of expectation.

We arrive at the 1st tee, and my fear of being paired with Johnny Miller and son disappears. It's a mother and son, and they're getting twenty shots. Maybe this will be okay after all.

The format: Both partners hit tee shots and then you alternate shots from the better of the two. After a spectator makes the requisite mulligan crack, I step up and pop up to short right. I half expect someone to invoke the infield fly rule, but no one does and the ball lands safely on the edge of the fairway. The mighty Casey has not whiffed!

We play my drive. Dad sticks it on the green; I almost drop the putt. Par! I crush the tee ball at the 2nd, and we make another par. We bogey the 3rd and then make a third par. Images of a net 54 and a club championship dance through my head. I am Tiger Woods!

Then reality rears its ugly head, and the train wreck begins: double bogey, bogey, triple, double, double. We briefly recover on the back nine and then fade. As the rain begins to fall, we struggle home with a 90, net 74. The mother-son combo takes us by two.

I have not led us to greatness. Nor have I let us down. I've simply been the mediocre golfer that I am, sharing a cart, a score and an all-too-rare afternoon with my old man. And that is plenty.

Besides, there's always next year. I might take lessons, hit the driving range and trade my running magazine subscription for golf. Maybe hit the course every Sunday and get that handicap. Then again, perhaps I'll just dust off my clubs (and those new shoes) in time for next year's tournament.

Mike Pennella

Corky's Wedge

*P*arents *lend children their experience and a*
vicarious memory; children endow their parents
with a vicarious immortality.

George Santayana

It was one of those moments that makes a golfer rejoice
in the fact that the game is a part of his life, a moment only
a golfer would be silly enough to get sentimental about.
The prelude to the moment occurred when I was with my
children at my parents' home, the house I grew up in,
which borders a public golf course. The course, in suburban Philadelphia, was built by two members of the famed
Whiz Kids, the 1950 Philadelphia Phillies. As a kid, the
owners were nice enough to let me go out onto the range
at twilight and hit all the balls I wanted, as long as I hit
them at the flag in the center of the range. That little spot
of land is where I learned how to strike a golf ball with
approximately the same lack of skill I do now.

I was in the house with my parents when I happened
by the kitchen window and saw the three children with
golf clubs in their hands. My parents are not golfers in the

sense that they play a lot. Typically, they play a few times a year, mostly when they go to Florida to visit my mother's sister and my uncle. Nevertheless, the garage of the house on Fairway Road still has a lot of clubs scattered about, remnants of the days when the five brothers who lived there claimed any club, ball or bag offered to us by someone at the club where we caddied. The kids had found a few rusted old weapons, grabbed a few muddy balls from an old bucket in the garage and were now giving those balls what-for in the backyard.

As you might imagine, the ground was getting it worse than the balls. With little two-handed chops at the ball, only the oldest, my ten-year-old daughter, was making occasional contact. The other two, a girl and a boy ages seven and five, were doing a proper job of tilling the soil. It was the first time I had ever seen them with clubs in their hands, though I suspected their actions were born more of boredom than genuine interest.

It was an admittedly odd moment for me. Because the game means so much to me, and because nearly every minute of my working life has involved the game in some manner—be it as caddie, editor or writer—I had long ago made the decision that I'd let my children decide for themselves if they wanted to play golf. I knew I couldn't be objective and feared I'd become one of those tennis or Little League fathers who becomes obsessed with his child's golf game. It's uncommon, but that type of person does exist in golf. I occasionally encountered them as a junior, and once saw a man bring tears to the eyes of his very talented son during a match in which the boy was whipping me handily. It just wasn't good enough for the father. You never forget things like that. Once in awhile, somebody will bring up that boy's name (although I suppose he's a man now) and mention that he is a very competitive amateur in the area around Philadelphia. I automatically think of his father. I realize now that he was probably a good man who just lost sight of the true purpose of the game. Back then he simply seemed like a mean guy.

"Why don't you go out there with them?" asked my mother, and so I did. I sat on the back porch and said things such as "Way to go" and "That's a great try, buddy." And that was it.

The moment happened the following way. We were at our home in rural Bucks County, Pennsylvania, and we were packing up our possessions to move to a bigger house just a mile or so away. My oldest daughter found an old wedge in a closet she was cleaning out, a wedge that had served me faithfully for years. Fact is, it wasn't actually a wedge. Years ago I discovered I was a lousy bunker player and decided it was because the flanges on sand wedges were too big for my liking. About that time, I stumbled upon an old 9-iron in my parents' garage. It was a Spalding Bobby Jones model, with a rather large, offset clubhead, and I noticed when I hit it full bore it only flew about 110 yards. It had a wonderfully thin sole, so I wandered out onto the course and hit a few bunker shots with it. Perfect—for me at least. So I went back to the garage, cut about an inch off the top of the shaft, put a new grip on it and had the wedge I'd been looking for.

As time passed the already dilapidated club became even more battered looking, but that just added to its appeal. The club was the one constant in my bag. I changed drivers, irons and putters every few years, but the wedge was with me wherever I traveled. It launched me out of the fearsome bunkers of Pine Valley, it (not I) executed the best recovery shot of my life from a steep hillside at Royal Dornoch, it bailed me out from desert lies in Phoenix and Palm Springs and the thick rough of Baltusrol and Westchester Country Club. Once in Florida, from the driveway in front of a clubhouse, it hit a beauty that landed two feet from the hole and stopped like a dart. I could even remember a shot from the fairway it played, to the 1st green at the Old Course. Even I couldn't miss that fairway. And then it ended up in the farthest reaches of a remote closet for a few years, an ignoble end to its career, no doubt initiated by one of my kids.

I was immersed in those moments as my daughter stood before me with the wedge. "Daddy, could you make this shorter so I could use it?" she said. *Could I make it shorter? Voluntarily destroy a link to my past, a landmark tool in my personal golf history? Are you insane, kid? Bad enough you lost it in the first place. Now, you want me to ruin it?* "Sure thing, kiddo," I said. "We'll do it tonight, right after dinner."

And so we did. In the last breaths of a late summer evening, when the only sound to be heard was the Delaware River on its slow but relentless march to the sea, Michelene Corcoran, with a little help from her old man, made her first golf club. Take care of it, I told her, and she assured me she would.

The next afternoon I saw the grip end of the club sticking out of the edge of our fish pond. I pulled it out and found a rope tied around the clubhead. It appeared someone had been trying to hook a big one with the club. *Oh well,* I thought, *as long as they were having fun.*

Mike Corcoran

A Matter of Course

Morning sun clearly defined the mountains, promising a pristine day, and luring him to answer the call of the links. He had left the house early, but not too early. Not before helping Mary through their daily routine.

Lionel wiped the dimpled ball, nestled it on the green of the 9th hole, and picked up his marker.

Not before gently lifting her in and out of the bathtub. Not before shepherding her back to the bedroom. Not before erasing the ravages of another sleepless night by combing her hair into place.

Lionel gazed at the lush grass as he bent his knees and gripped the putter.

Mary would love walking the course, listening to the hushed stillness. He could point out the geese gliding on the pond and the fragrant crabapple trees laced with blossoms. A love of the outdoors and God's creations. That was something they shared.

And they shared a lot. Six daughters. Twenty-two grandchildren. Allegiance to church. Devotion to each other. That hadn't changed, but other things had.

Lionel lowered his head and hunched his broad shoulders over the extra-long club.

Once, Mary's slender athletic body complemented his rugged six-foot-five-inch frame. Now, crutches supported her stooped shoulders.

Once, she agilely whirled with him on the dance floor. Now, the only spinning she did was a turn through the shopping mall in her wheelchair.

Once, her nimble fingers flew at the sewing machine, tucked a blanket around a slumbering child and tidied the house. Now, crooked and gnarled, they sat—idle—in her lap.

Lionel stiffened his wrists.

Rheumatoid arthritis invaded their union only nine years into their marriage. He watched it ravage his wife's body. The changes it made were both immediate and gradual, until—quite clearly—the disease determined their course in life.

Lionel closed his stance and shifted his weight forward.

Some people thought he carried quite a load. But as Mary was able to do less, he simply did more. He merely broadened his definition of husband, the job title he considered most sacred. After all, it was a pledge he had made to Mary before God. So he took upon himself new roles: cook, housekeeper, beautician and chauffeur. Even nurse.

He and Mary were good together. They should be. They had perfected their teamwork through twenty-four surgeries. He knew better than any health-care worker how to lift her, turn her, tend to her personal needs. That last hip replacement came at a high price for them both: a permanent infection that added a new element to their routine. Now his large hands tenderly applied fresh dressings twice daily to the draining wound.

Lionel drew the putter into a slow backward stroke.

He rarely glanced back at their old dreams. Instead, together they forged new ones. Like purchasing a self-contained motor home so he could assist her in the bathroom, something just not acceptable in public restrooms.

Lionel completed his putt with a firm follow-through.

And they could travel. They could visit their kids. They could attend the important family events most precious to them: baptisms, graduations, weddings, funerals.

Lionel watched the ball roll forward in a gentle arc and rim the cup. He listened to its satisfying drop and thonk. He made par.

Mary always said other husbands would have left long ago. She even called him "her good-hearted man." But he liked to remind her that those wedding vows some forty-five years past were sincere—and binding.

As his stubby shadow nudged the rich turf, Lionel glanced at the late morning sun. He leaned down and, with his thick fingers, plucked up the ball, brushed it on his pants and tucked it into his pocket.

There would be other days to play golf. But, for now, home beckoned. Home—and his Mary.

Carol McAdoo Rehme

Wake-Up Call

I was sitting in a bathtub full of moldy sheetrock when my thirteen-year-old son asked the question. "Can you take me golfing sometime?" he said.

I had a bathroom to remodel. It was fall, and the forecast for the next week was for 100 percent chance of Oregon's liquid sunshine. I wanted to say no. "Sure," I said. "What did you have in mind?"

"Well, maybe you could, like, pick up Jared and me after school on Friday and take us out to Oakway."

"Sounds good."

Friday came. The showers continued. Looking out the window, moldy sheetrock seemed the saner choice. But at the appointed hour, I changed from home-improvement garb to rain-protection garb and loaded the boys' clubs and mine in the back of the car. In front of the school, Ryan and Jared piled in. Ryan looked at me with a perplexed expression.

"What's with the golf hat, Dad?" he said.

It was, I thought, a silly question, like asking a scuba diver what's with the swim fins.

"Well, I thought we were going to play some golf."

A peculiar pause ensued, like a phone line temporarily gone dead.

"Uh, you're going, *too*?" he asked.

Suddenly, it struck me like a 3-iron to my gut: I hadn't been invited.

Thirteen years of parenting flashed before my eyes. The birth. The diapers. The late-night feedings. Helping with homework. Building forts. Fixing bikes. Going to games. Going camping. Going everywhere together—my son and I.

Now I hadn't been invited. This was it. This was the end of our relationship as I had always known it. This was *"Adios,* Old Man, thanks for the memories, but I'm old enough to swing my own clubs now, so go back to your rocking chair and crossword puzzles and—oh, yeah— here's a half-off coupon for your next bottle of Geritol."

All these memories sped by in about two seconds, leaving me about three seconds to respond before Ryan would get suspicious and think I had actually expected to be playing golf with him and his friend.

I had to say something. I wanted to say this: *How could you do this to me? Throw me overboard like unused crab bait?* We had always been a team. But this was abandonment. Adult abuse.

This was Lewis turning to Clark in 1805 and saying: "Later, Bill. I can make it the rest of the way to Oregon without you." John Glenn radioing Mission Control to say thanks, but he could take it from here. Simon bailing out on Garfunkel during "Bridge over Troubled Water."

Why did it all have to change?

Enough of this mind-wandering. I needed to level with him. I needed to express how hurt I was. Share my gut-level feelings. Muster all the courage I could find, bite the bullet and spill my soul.

So I said, "Me? Play? Naw. You know I'm up to my ears in the remodel project."

We drove on in silence for a few moments. "So, how are you planning to pay for this?" I asked, my wounded ego reaching for the dagger.

"Uh, could you loan me seven dollars?"

Oh, I get it. He doesn't want me, but he'll gladly take my money.

"No problem," I said.

I dropped him and Jared off, wished them luck and headed for home. My son was on his own now. Nobody there to tell him how to fade a 5-iron, how to play that tricky downhiller, how to hit the sand shot. And what if there's lightning? What about hypothermia? A runaway golf cart? A band of militant gophers? He's so small. Who would take care of him?

There I was, alone, driving away from him. Not just for now. Forever. This was it. The bond was broken. Life would never be the same.

I walked in the door. "What are you doing home?" my wife asked.

I knew it would sound like some thirteen-year-old who was the only one in the gang not invited to the slumber party, but maintaining my immature demur, I said it anyway.

"I wasn't invited," I replied, with a trace of snottiness.

Another one of those peculiar pauses ensued. Then my wife laughed. Out loud. At first I was hurt. Then I, too, laughed, the situation suddenly becoming much clearer.

I went back to the bathroom remodel and began realizing that this situation is what life is all about: change. Fathers and sons must ultimately change. I've been preparing him for this since he first looked at me and screamed in terror: not to play golf without me, but to take on the world without me. With his own set of clubs. His own game plan. His own faith.

God was remodeling my son. Adding some space here. Putting in a new feature there. In short, allowing him to become more than he could ever be if I continued to hover over him. Just like when I was a kid and, at Ryan's age, I would sling my plaid golf bag over my shoulder and ride my bike five miles across town to play golf at a small public course called Marysville that I imagined as Augusta National.

I remember how grown-up I felt, walking into that dark clubhouse, the smoke rising from the poker game off to the left, and proudly plunking down my two dollars for nine holes. Would I have wanted my father there with me that day? Naw. A boy's gotta do what a boy's gotta do: grow up.

I went back to the bathroom remodel project. A few hours later, I heard Ryan walk in the front door. I heard him complain to his mother that his putts wouldn't drop, that his drives were slicing and that the course was like a lake. He sounded like someone I knew. His tennis shoes squeaked with water as I heard him walk back to where I was working on the bathroom.

"Dad," he said, dripping on the floor, "my game stinks. Can you take me golfing sometime? I need some help."

I wanted to hug him. Rev my radial-arm saw in celebration. Shout: "I'm still needed!" I wanted to tell God, "Thanks for letting me be part of this kid's remodel job."

Instead, I plastered one of those serious-dad looks on my face and stoically said, "Sure, Ry, anytime."

Bob Welch
Previously appeared in Chicken Soup for the Father's Soul

The Miracle Ball

True miracles are created by men when they use the courage and intelligence that God gave them.

Jean Anouilh

There is no shortage of testimony to the power and magic of the Titleist golf ball, which is far and away the number-one choice on the PGA Tour. As guys like Phil Mickelson, Davis Love and Ernie Els relate in a current television commercial, the Titleist was present for all their special tournament moments.

None of their Titleist success stories, however, is as heartwarming as that of young Samuel Rachal. Sam would qualify as Titleist's youngest spokesman, except for the fact that at less than six months old he's still pretty much into baby babble.

So we'll tell the story for him.

Born five weeks premature on March 15, 2001, to a couple of Port Arthur, Texas, natives—Tom and Denise Rachal, who now live in Dallas, Texas—Sam started life with what in golf terminology would be an unplayable lie.

His heart arteries were crossed, meaning he would need something called an arterial switch to survive.

The surgery proved successful, but Sam's handicap was a heart so weak that he had to be put on a heart-lung machine. Then a kidney problem developed. Much agonizing followed for Tom, the son of Pat and Mary Helen Rachal, and Denise, the daughter of Sam and Billie Jo Henry.

Baby Sam, though, was not about to WD from this high-stakes game to which he'd just been introduced. Helped along by faith, prayer, hope and a Titleist 1 that remained in his bed throughout the entire ordeal, he overcame the life-threatening obstacles in his path and is expected to live a normal life.

Now about that Titleist 1.

Tom, an avid golfer, had spotted the ball in his car on the way to the hospital for Sam's delivery and thought he would stick it in his pocket for a good luck charm. Later, on a whim, he put the ball in Sam's bed at the hospital.

For the next eight weeks, while Sam was transferred from Presbyterian Hospital to the Children's Medical Center of Dallas, the Titleist 1 was his constant companion. Day after day, week after week, as he battled through a series of hazards tougher than Pete Dye could conceive, the Titleist 1 was always there.

"It's hard to explain but that golf ball kind of became a focal point for everybody," says Tom. "The doctors and nurses would always look for that ball when they came into his room. The ball was just sort of a symbol of hope."

Now that Sam is home, healthy and happy, the Titleist 1 sits on Tom's desk as a constant reminder to him and Denise of what they went through. One of these days, if Sam desires to give golf a try, Tom has already decided it will be the first ball he hits.

But it certainly won't be the last Titleist at his disposal.

Thanks to George Sine Jr., Titleist's vice president of golf ball marketing and strategic planning, Sam is well stocked. After receiving a letter from Tom relating how the Titleist 1 proved to be a positive symbol during his son's crisis, Sine responded with a heartfelt letter, 144 Titleist 1 balls personalized with Sam's name and birth date, and a pair of baby Footjoys.

"It was really a nice touch on his part," Tom says of Sine's letter. "We were so surprised when that care package arrived."

Sine, a father of four young children, was obviously touched by the story about Sam. He wrote, in part, ". . . While I am confident that it was your faith, prayer and hope that resulted in Sam's wellness, not to mention a dedicated medical team, the fact that a single Titleist 1 was along for the journey is indeed a proud moment for the brand.

"The round which you have described is unparalleled by any major championship, coveted trophy or record score, as it was not a game of honor but rather a game of life at stake. . . . So that you may permanently enshrine the now famous Titleist 1 which accompanied Sam on his journey, I am enclosing a supply of new No. 1s. . . .

"The enclosed are personally imprinted for that first occasion when you and Sam approach your first tee box, place the tee in the ground and cherish what is certain to be your first of many father-and-son moments sharing not merely a game but rather a milestone together that will not be forgotten."

Sounds like Titleist needs to get baby Sam and his dad under contract for what could be a powerful TV spot.

Bob West

Links Between Fathers and Sons

Dear Dad:

This year I won't be sending you expensive golf gear for Father's Day. I suspect you may be surprised. I suspect you may also be relieved.

Fact is, for purely selfish reasons I've spent a small fortune in recent years trying to prop up your ailing golf game. First I sent you a set of "super senior" graphite-shafted irons guaranteed to put the life back in your swing.

But they must have arrived DOA because when we played next you were still using the same beat-up irons. You said you were just too sentimental to let them go. I donated the space-age wonders to the church summer auction.

Next, after watching your drives grow shorter and shorter, I doled out for the latest high-tech metal woods that were supposed to forgive your fading strength. You sent them back with a polite thank-you note and scarcely a grass stain on them. Now they're in my bag, forgiving *my* erring ways.

The real kicker, though, came when I paid for private lessons with a crack young woman pro whose specialty is helping aging golf stags steal a few more years in the sun. It didn't hurt that she looks better than Helen Alfredsson—but geez, Dad, you never showed up for lesson one. What gives?

Actually, we both know what gives. You don't have to whack me over the head with Chairman Penick's Little Red Book.

After more than half a century, your once-splendid golf game is fading fast, heading for keeps into the clubhouse turn, finally going gently into that golf good night.

Though you clearly love the game, I get the distinct impression that the thing you desire most is to be left alone to play out the round at your own pace, without advice or meddling from me or anyone else, for however long the USGA official-in-the-sky grants you before darkness closes and the warning horn sounds a final time.

You're what, seventy-five . . . seventy-six? It's kind of embarrassing how you refuse to act your age. I know you still clock a fifty-hour workweek, go harder on the job than your twenty employees and think "retiree" is a four-letter word.

You're the only geezer I know who still cleans out his own gutters, mows his own lawn and would happily tee off at 6 A.M.—if the pro could just manage to haul his young backside out of bed.

Ironically, it's only in your golf game where your mortality is beginning to shine through like the seat of a worn-out suit. I suspect it's the thing that hurts you the most. If that's so, you should see what it's doing to me.

So, out of deference to your "advanced" age, I'll spare you the pro-shop sermon and declare a moratorium on further merchandise. After all, P. G. Wodehouse said, "No man can know the peace that passeth understanding until he giveth up golf."

So, how about if I give you a little peace and quiet and

the right to play golf—or give it up—according to your own internal clock?

This gift is conditional. I need to get a few things off my chest. We've been playing golf together for thirty years and I can't get it out of my head that when you decide it's finally time to toss in the towel for good, I won't just have lost my best friend and fiercest competitor.

I'll have lost my best golf. We hear a lot these days about golf being a family affair. Did you happen to catch the AT&T Pebble Beach National Pro-Am on the tube this year? You might have thought you were looking at a family reunion with a little golf thrown in for fun, what with all those Nicklauses, Floyds and Stocktons loitering about.

Mark O'Meara is on record as saying the happiest moment of his playing career occurred when he won at Pebble Beach with his dad as his amateur partner.

Payne Stewart has six Tour wins and two majors under his belt, but the tournament that means most to him was his first win at Quad Cities in 1982—because his father, Bill, who died of cancer a short time later, was there to witness it.

Every time Tom Watson reminds himself to hold his head still, he hears his father's voice.

Golf is a game about links—the kind made of grass and the kind made of blood. It's not just a game that binds fathers to sons, but also sons to mothers, and dads to daughters.

Was it simple coincidence or something fateful in the stars that Paul Azinger's mother carried him in her womb when she won a women's club title in western Massachusetts? Or that JoAnne Carner's father did odd jobs at a country club just so his daughter could have a good place to play to prepare for a national amateur title?

About the only thing Rush Limbaugh and Jesse Jackson

agree on is that a lot of what ails modern America could probably have been prevented if a caring father had been around somewhere when it counted.

Those of us who grew up with full-time dads should probably count our lucky stars they were around to scold us when necessary, to cheer us up when it was needed most.

People tell me I laugh just like you, Dad. Wish I had your short game and velvet touch around the greens. I know you developed that touch because the only club you owned as a teenager was a hickory-shafted 5-iron you paid a buck for.

You were caddying on the sly because your old man thought golf was a game for rich playboys. I think it was pretty ironic that your job in the Eighth Air Force during the war permitted you to play most of the great courses in Britain and that after winning a few tournaments here and there you came to believe that golf was anything but a game for rich playboys.

I grew up listening to you mouth all these corny platitudes about following the Rules, policing yourself and playing it as it lies. You were a field general about the basic courtesies of conduct, politeness, proper ball marking and so forth.

For years, I thought you were such a square. But I was a temperamental twit who had the benefit of starting out with a supportive father and a full set of clubs.

The first time I threw a club in anger, you simply walked off the course and told me to notify you when I was through being a jackass. When you caught me shaving my score, you explained that I better get used to playing alone because nobody liked a cheater.

The words stung. But they stuck. To this day, even playing mulligans makes me queasy.

I'll spare you a detailed regurgitation of all the good

times we had playing together as grown men—hacking balls and batting the breeze about everything from Nixon's tapes to Madonna's bloomers.

We were lucky, Dad, even charmed. We must have quit seriously competing sometime around Reagan's second term, but I somehow forgot to notice.

A few years ago came the news that your regular foursome of fifteen years was breaking up for good. Your partner, still smarting from a putter-thrashing you gave him in our last father-son match against him and his son, decided to start playing with "younger" men. Another moved to France with his new wife. The third suffered a coronary and wouldn't play on cool mornings.

That left you, your fading game and a lot of empty Saturday mornings. No wonder your enthusiasm plummeted.

I thought I was doing you a favor when I invited you to join me and two friends for a round at Pinehurst No. 2. It was a cold, blustery day. You topped your first drive and it got worse from there—a blur of double and triple bogeys.

Your once-invincible short game was gone. A wind gust almost blew you over in a sand trap. At one point I noticed both your hands trembling. On the drive home you apologized and I told you that was complete rubbish—that we all have lousy days.

We finally had a laugh about it, but I was scared. I'd seen the future of golf mortality, and I didn't like it. That's when I hauled out the checkbook and literally tried to buy us some more time.

That scheme, as we know, utterly flopped. So I have nothing left to give you this Father's Day except peace and quiet—and my heartfelt thanks.

I don't know if a son's gratitude counts for much these days, but I'm haunted by the fact that every time we play it could well be our last turn around the track. So I had better make it count—with sticks and words.

I once heard you say to a playing partner that when your allotted time was up you hoped you would just keel over cold as an alewife somewhere on a golf green—preferably after making a ninety-foot sidehill putt to close a tight match.

No lingering nurses and dehumanizing life-support systems for you. Just a neat, clean exit—stage left—with a birdie in hand. Real life, sudden death. Wouldn't even slow up play, probably.

I must admit, I was deeply shocked when you said that, but I was a kid of thirty who expected to live forever. Now, I'm forty and have my own kids who someday may realize that a golf club is something other than a useful tool for clocking an unsuspecting golden retriever over the head.

You'll probably be long gone by then, but if it's any comfort to know, your granddaughter shows flashes of being a genuine putting prodigy. No doubt in my mind where she gets it from. So, rest easy. The family tradition you started fifty years ago will far outlive us both.

Which gives me an idea, Dad. Let's make one final father-son pact. Whoever gets to heaven first has to book the tee time. Make it 6 A.M. on the Champion's Course.

You've earned it.

James Dodson

6

OUT OF
THE ROUGH

Just One More Time

Perhaps it comes to all men, or perhaps just to middle-aged former athletes. I'm talking about the Just One More Time Syndrome: Score one more touchdown, ride one more bull, hit one more home run. But when you're forty-five and your waist measurement has just passed your expanded chest measurement, then Just One More Times aren't easy to find.

I live in the little Texas town of Mason (population 2,153) and because we have no golf course, I play on the course in Brady, twenty-eight miles north. One day I was in Bill O'Banion's drugstore when he said, "The hospital fund drive is coming up soon."

"By all means put me down for a contribution."

"Had this idea that might raise a little extra money for the hospital. I thought we'd alternate our shots and hit a golf ball from the Mason courthouse to the hole on the ninth green of the Brady course. We'd get somebody to establish par, and then we'd get folks to contribute per stroke, as to how many strokes we'd finish under par."

"When y'all planning on doing this?"

Bill looked at me and said, "The date is June 11. And there ain't no *y'all* to it. It's *we*, as in you and me."

"Sorry, partner, I can't do it. Ain't no motels between here and Brady."

"We're not going to walk. Nobody would expect that. We'll figure out some kind of golf cart to ride."

"That aside," I said, "when I shoot my average 90 I'm exhausted. I'll be hitting the ball at least three hundred times before we make our way to Brady and *all* of them will be hard-swinging shots."

"It'll be all right. Just don't worry."

"Bill, we're talking about high weeds along the right of way. We're talking about pastures with cows and bulls. We're talking hills that go up and down."

That was in May when it was still cool, so finally I agreed. It looked as if I'd found my Just One More Time.

Then the local papers started running stories, and the Brady radio station wanted to follow us tee to green. Sure I wanted my Just One More Time, but not in front of a packed house.

June 11 and summer arrived at the same time. We were to tee off from the courthouse square at 10 A.M. By 9:30 the temperature was eighty-five degrees. Par had been determined at 688 strokes. Don't ask me how.

Bill got us past the Commercial Bank's window with his first swing, a beautiful 7-iron shot. Now it was my turn, and I hit a dribbler into a yard full of old farm machinery.

I left Bill a lie under a horse-drawn hayrack. From there he put it into the service bay of the Chevron station. It took us six strokes to get out.

From then on, things got worse.

Bill put one across the street and under a truck at Eckert Equipment. I got down on my belly to try to swipe the ball out so we wouldn't have to take a penalty shot. Half the people of Mason were following us, and I was lying there thinking that none of them knew that I once had held the interscholastic record for the hurdles or that

I had made my living riding bulls on the circuit for a year. I turned the putter on its side and swiped the ball fifteen yards.

Bill's next shot got us out of plate-glass territory at last, and we were approaching the edge of town when I knocked a 4-iron into the cemetery. By the time we got the ball headed back in the direction of Brady, we were at the foot of Mason Mountain and six strokes over the pace I felt we should have maintained coming out of town.

We call it Mason Mountain, though it actually rises no more than one thousand feet. But try hitting a golf ball up it.

Bill, using a 5-iron, made a shot straight up the middle that hit the pavement and bounced up and then rolled and rolled until it came to a stop. After that it started rolling backward until it was one hundred yards behind the spot where Bill had hit it. Now we had no choice but to keep the ball high in the grass beside the highway. So we hacked our way up that mountain, sometimes getting one hundred yards out of a shot, more often having to settle for less. When we finally got to the top, I estimated that we were twenty-six strokes over par.

Then it began to rain.

We had an extensive entourage in addition to the spectators who were following us. We had an ambulance with Dr. Jim Pettit in attendance; we had Mason policeman Jack Boring, who'd been empowered by the state to hold traffic; we had fore and aft trucks with signs warning that a "golfathon" was in progress. Most important, we had Brock Grosse, our caddie master. He had rigged up a trailer behind his three-wheeled motorcycle with a couch for Bill and me to ride in between shots.

It rained for almost an hour. Our gloves got wet as did the grips of our clubs. It was difficult enough to keep the club head square to the ball as we hit out of the grass. It was quite another matter with the club turning in your hand. Once I hit a shot that went right at a little better than a ninety-degree angle. I wouldn't have thought this was possible.

Our rules were that anything between the barbed-wire fences on either side of the road was fairway. Over the fence was considered the rough, and the ball had to be played as it lay, with the exception that we could take a drop and a one-stroke penalty. Thus we found ourselves in the rough when we hit one into a herd of cows.

We climbed over the fence and there they came, crowding around, shoving up against us, bawling and mooing and stepping on the golf ball.

Finally, our policeman jumped the fence and fired his revolver in the air. The cattle departed. But they'd buried the ball in the ground to the point where it was barely visible. Mayor Willard Aubrey of Mason, our course judge, calmly gave us a ruling: "This is rough. Play it as it is or take a stroke penalty."

Bill said, "Whaaat? Where in the PGA rules does it talk about cows stepping on a golf ball?"

The mayor was unmoved, and we took the one-stroke penalty.

By now we were gaining on par, but time was becoming a problem. To get to the Brady course we'd have to go directly through town, turn left at the courthouse and go another three miles out Highway 87. I had arranged with the Brady police to hold traffic up as we hit through. Otherwise we would be reduced to rolling 20- and 30-foot putts along the side of the road and there would go our chance to break par and make money for the hospital. I'd naively told the police we would reach the outskirts of Brady by 3 P.M., and they said they would meet us at the town limits.

At 3 P.M. we were fifteen miles from Brady. Seriously

tired, I went stumbling down the bank toward the spot where one of our caddies indicated the ball was. I suddenly heard a dry whir. I immediately executed a 180-degree turn and quit the area. There are several things I am more afraid of than a rattlesnake, but I forget what they are. After Jack Boring and a woman went down and trapped the snake, Bill took the next shot.

By the time we were five miles out of Brady I figured we were fifty strokes under; but we were so late, that so far as I knew, the cops had all gone to supper.

We went forward, but I was just going through the motions, hacking at the ball, hoping to move it forward a few yards so that Bill could then take us a couple of hundred yards farther. Dr. Pettit came over and said, "Rest in the ambulance. Let Bill hit it for a while."

I said, "After one or two more shots."

But I didn't rest, and soon we were at the outskirts of Brady. The police were still there to help us get through. Now we were seventy strokes under par.

A strange thing began to happen. The streets weren't exactly lined, but people were waiting for us. Folks who had been following our progress over the radio were driving to meet us, blowing their horns.

I don't know whether it was adrenaline or pride or some strange hormone, but my tiredness seemed to melt away. All of a sudden I realized that this was truly my Just One More Time.

We were using Bill's "chipper," a heavy weighted club faced like a 5-iron. And disregarding the plate-glass factor, I was hitting the best shots I'd hit all day, straight down the street, carrying one hundred yards and then rolling fifty more.

We got to the courthouse square in five shots and then took that left turn toward the golf course. We were within 150 yards of the ninth hole when Bill lifted a beautiful

9-iron shot that settled about ten feet off the green.

The green was ringed with maybe two hundred onlookers. I had never hit a golf ball in front of that many people. My chip up to the green was miserable. I left Bill a forty-foot putt. He lagged and left the ball three feet from the cup.

A knee-knocker. As I walked across the green I said to myself, "For once, don't choke." I knocked the ball dead in the center of the cup. Then I stepped across and shook hands with Bill.

They tell me there was a celebration. They tell me we went to dinner. I don't know. It became a blur after that putt went in. All I knew were three things:

We'd come in 108 strokes under par.

We'd raised fifty-five hundred dollars for the hospital.

And I'd accomplished my Just One More Time.

Giles Tippette

The Drive of a Champion

Having already accumulated a host of trophies since starting to play competitive golf at the age of ten, Larry Alford, at sixteen, had developed into one of the best young golf prospects in the country. Already shooting in the 70s, he was elected the most valuable player of the McCullough High School team during both his sophomore and junior years. Following his junior year, Alford matched against seventy-four of the nation's best junior golfers at the Mission Hills Desert Junior Tournament in Rancho Mirage, California. He was tied for the lead going into the final round after firing a 72 and a 71, but he dipped to a 78 in the final round, which tied him for second place, five strokes behind the winner—Tiger Woods.

Alford's performance drew the interest of coaches from some of the best college golf teams in the country, including Arizona, Arizona State, Stanford and Oklahoma State. Wanting to stay close to home, he accepted a scholarship at the University of Houston. "Just think, everything will be taken care of, and I'll be close to home, and it won't cost you anything while I'm going to college," Alford said to his mother, Missy, "and I'll be playing for one of the best college teams in the country."

Fighting back tears, Missy Alford hugged her son tightly, knowing that he had worked so hard to earn a scholarship to make it easier for her. "That's wonderful, Larry," she said. "I'm so happy for you."

That summer, Alford worked harder than ever on his golf game, hitting hundreds of balls daily while working at the golf cart barn at The Woodlands Country Club. At night, he and one of his best friends, Brendan, waded into water hazards at nearby golf courses to retrieve golf balls. Salvaging as many as 2,000 a night, they sold them for eighteen cents apiece, which enabled Larry to play more golf that summer. His paychecks from his golfing job went to his mother, an art teacher who also made and sold decorative wreaths and did wallpapering. "That's Larry," his father, Larry Alford Sr., said. "Finishing second in the biggest junior golf tournament of the year and then wading into water hazards to fish out golf balls. In no way was success going to change him."

Late that summer, a golf teammate asked if Larry could do him a favor and drive the teammate's father's Corvette to a relative's house. The teammate in turn would follow in his car and then drive Larry home. Larry said fine and off they went. Shortly after 6 P.M., while it was still broad daylight, Larry lost control of the Corvette on Interstate 45. The car flipped over three times, catapulting Alford through the open sun roof and onto the highway. Alford's friend braked his car to a halt and saw his teammate lying motionless and bleeding badly from the head, face and left arm.

In the emergency room at Hermann Hospital in Houston, a doctor emerged from behind a curtain and asked Larry's parents to come in. *Oh my God!* Mrs. Alford screamed to herself on seeing her son, who was the color of gray ice with a head as big as a basketball. Out of the corner of one eye, she saw what she perceived to be a look of horror on the face of one doctor.

"I got the feeling that they wanted us to see Larry once more, maybe for the last time," Missy recalled. Then, as she and Larry Sr. were led out, she pleaded to herself, *Dear God, please save him.*

From the moment Larry Alford arrived at Hermann Hospital, Dr. James "Red" Duke, the hospital's chief trauma surgeon, knew that his severed left arm could not be saved. Far more important was a life-threatening head injury. Then there were the lesser injuries: a fractured eye orbital bone that had jarred Larry's eye partially out of its socket, a broken jaw, ankle and shoulder blade, a collapsed lung and a badly injured right arm. "I'm sorry, but we had to amputate your son's arm below the elbow," Dr. John Burns, an orthopedic surgeon, told Larry's parents.

"Is he going to be all right?" Missy Alford asked.

"We don't know," Dr. Burns answered.

Standing alongside Missy was Jay Hall, a friend of hers who could not help but wonder about Larry's reaction to the loss of his left arm if he were indeed going to survive. *How would Larry ever get along without golf?* Hall thought to himself. But then, catching himself in mid-thought, Hall also realized there was a far more pressing matter than a golf career at stake. *They've got to save Larry's life,* he said to himself. *That's all that matters right now.*

For almost ninety days Larry Alford remained unconscious and in critical condition. Then, gradually, his condition improved and he was no longer in danger. But his parents knew that difficult days lay ahead. For one thing, he would eventually learn that he had lost his left hand.

One night Larry awakened and suddenly realized that his left hand was missing. He cried out for a nurse. One hurried into his room and said softly, "I'm sorry, Larry, but they had to amputate your hand." Meanwhile, his father, alerted, raced to the hospital.

"Dad, how am I ever going to play golf?" he asked.

"Don't worry, Larry," his father replied. "You'll play again, and you'll do fine."

Young Alford did not remain depressed for long. "Mom, I did it to myself," he said one day to his mother, "so I'm to blame. And God saved my life, so I'm lucky."

A few weeks later, while talking about golf, Larry turned to his father and asked, "Dad, do you have my clubs with you?"

"Yeah, I've got them in the trunk of the car, Larry."

"Good," Larry said excitedly. "Can you get my pitching wedge? Maybe we can chip some balls outside."

Within minutes Larry and his father were on the lawn outside the Del Oro Institute in Houston where Larry was recuperating. Although he had lost forty pounds and was weak, young Larry began to chip with his right arm. Ball after ball went soaring in beautiful arcs as both father and son looked on in delight.

"Dad, will you look at those shots," Larry said, ecstatic at swinging a golf club again.

"You're doing great, Son, just great," his father, replied heartened by Larry's joy.

A week later, at young Larry's suggestion, he and his father went out to play a round of golf at one of the four courses at The Woodlands Country Club. Understandably, Larry's father was both happy and apprehensive.

God, I hope he does all right, Mr. Alford said to himself. *Don't let him be upset.*

Larry Alford Sr. needn't have worried. Though still weak and lacking in stamina, his son hit his shots cleanly and accurately during his first outing as a one-handed golfer. His chipping and putting in particular were superb. "Boy, Dad this is great," he said at one point as he and his father walked down a fairway.

At the end of eighteen holes, Larry had shot an 86,

about ten strokes above his average before his accident, but an extraordinary score for a one-handed golfer. As they headed for the clubhouse, Larry, obviously elated at how he had played, turned to his father and said, "Dad, do you think that I can still make the PGA Tour?"

Larry Sr. was prepared for the question. "Yes, I do," he replied. "But I think we're going to have to take this one day at a time."

After that, and unbeknownst to Larry, Jay Hall began calling prosthetic manufacturers to find out if there was such a thing as an artificial golf hand on the market that would enable Larry to play competitive golf. Finding none, Hall decided that he, himself, would try to design a golf hand for Larry on his own. "First, I had to ask myself just what does the left hand do on a golf swing for a right-handed golfer," said Hall, a professional psychologist and a good golfer himself. "And the answer is quite simple. It holds the club with three fingers and it hinges or cocks the club. Essentially, it provides those two functions, and that's about all."

Of paramount importance, Hall knew, was that the hand had to grip the club firmly enough so that the handle wouldn't be twisted by the force of the swing. To ensure that, Hall designed the palm of the hand with pumped-up air cells. For the wrist, he came up with a ball and socket mechanism which, Hall felt, could perform the function of a human joint.

Hall then took his design to Ted Muilenburg, the owner of a prosthetics company in Houston. "Jay knew nothing about prosthetics, and I knew nothing about golf," Muilenburg said.

"But I must say I was impressed with his design—so much so that we went ahead and made 'The Halford Grip,'" as it came to be known, blending Larry and Jay's last names. Muilenburg used an aluminum child's knee prosthesis for the wrist and some air cells, which when inflated, fit tightly around the grip on the golfing hand like human fingers. Then a silicone suction sleeve, which slides over the elbow to hold the hand in place, was attached.

Seeing the mold the first time, Missy's eyes brimmed with tears, as she envisioned her son's reaction to the hand, which she was going to give to him on Christmas morning. "It'll work," Hall said, after looking over what Muilenburg had wrought. "I know it's going to work."

Unwrapping the last Christmas gift of the day, Larry peeked inside the box and, a look of amazement on his face, cried out. "It's a hand—my golf hand."

"It was Jay's idea," Missy said to her son. "He even designed it."

Overwhelmed with emotion, Larry threw his arms around Jay. "Thanks so much."

The Halford Grip has been a rousing success, although a number of adjustments have been made over the years. "Some golfers, seeing how well my golf hand works, have said they'd like to trade arms with me, but I tell them, 'No way.'"

Since receiving his golf hand, Alford has shot his lowest score ever—a 69. He also recorded his first hole-in-one and played three years of varsity golf at Sam Houston University. Since his graduation in 1997, Alford has worked as an assistant golf pro at his home course, The Woodlands Country Club, and has helped raise money for a number of charities by challenging golfers to try to get closer to the pin than he has on par-3 holes. "Not many people have," said Alford, who shoots in the 70s and booms his tee-shots more than 250 yards.

"My accident has been a blessing for me," said Alford who delivers inspirational talks to young people in schools and churches in the Houston area. "It happened for a reason. I thank God for saving my life, for giving me such a positive attitude and then giving me a second chance as a golfer. As for having to play with only one real arm, I tell people that golf is hard enough with two hands, so it can't be that much harder with one."

Jack Cavanaugh

On His Own Two Feet

One of the most fascinating things about golf is how it reflects the cycle of life. No matter what you shoot, the next day you have to go back to the first tee and begin all over again and make yourself into something.

Peter Jacobsen

Bob Hullender is telling the story of his life when he suddenly can't continue. The emotions flooding from the memories of what he went through, twice, are too traumatic. His voice breaks and his eyes well up, and a man who flew 221 combat missions in an F-4 Phantom jet over Vietnam as an Air Force general asks to be excused.

Like almost everything else about golf, senior amateur competition in America is thriving. Given the time, energy, dollars and sufficient game, golfers fifty-five and up can play a tournament a week, as Hullender almost does, most of them requiring gross scores of par or better to win. The memberships of the elite seniors' associations that operate the bulk of these highly formalized 54- and 72-hole events are full to bursting. Entries for the U.S.

Senior Amateur Championship have grown from a few hundred at its inception to more than two thousand— and rising. And perhaps twenty times that many gray-beards possess a good enough game to compete beyond the club level.

Hullender is at the top of this flourishing world. How he got there is a story of will over adversity.

Born in Ringgold, Georgia, in March 1937, Hullender grew up on a dairy farm loving any sport involving a ball. After high school he attended Georgia Tech as a coopera-tive student, alternating three months of classes with three working for the Tennessee Valley Authority. There wasn't much ball time then.

In 1959, about to be drafted, Hullender began an Air Force career through the Aviation Cadet Program, start-ing as a second lieutenant and ending as a general. Except for a thirteen-month tour of duty in Vietnam, ball time was sufficient for him to become a champion fast-pitch softball pitcher capable of under-arming at 105 miles an hour, close to the world record. He played some winter golf then, to a low handicap, but it remained secondary to his summer sport.

That changed as he got older, and since 1987, when he turned fifty, Hullender has played in three Senior Opens, making the cut twice. He's also qualified for every Senior Amateur since becoming eligible at age fifty-five, with a runner-up finish in 1994. His contemporaries swear it's only a matter of time before he wins the title. That's partly because of the astonishing distances he hits a golf ball, but mostly because of what getting to become the player he is says about his desire, determination and plain, unadulter-ated grit.

You see, both of his hips are artificial.

Newcomers to the senior-am fraternity don't learn this from the general himself because he never volunteers the information. But it's invariably the first thing they learn about him from his peers. Most of those who compete with and against Hullender still cannot believe a golfer so doctored can play the game so much, so powerfully and so successfully.

His hips began degenerating with osteoarthritis in his late forties. As they did, sport after sport became impossible, including his beloved softball, when pain and reduced mobility prevented him from taking the steps necessary to throw. The right hip went first, then the left.

Hip-joint replacement was pretty new in the early 1980s, but eventually Hullender found an orthopedic surgeon expert in what's known as the porous-coated procedure. This is done without cement, as the bone adheres to the porous coating of the prosthesis after it's press-fitted into the hip and leg bones.

He had the right hip replaced in 1986. Then came a wonderful surprise. Because of the way he swung the club—mostly with the hands and arms—as rehabilitation progressed, he discovered that the new hip wasn't a handicap to golf. That inspired him to work hard enough at the game to be shooting around par within a year.

By the fall of 1992, the left hip had degenerated to the extent that pain and impaired mobility prevented him even from tying his shoelaces. He went back on the operating table.

"Because I'd learned how to rehabilitate, that second time wasn't as traumatic as the first. And getting through it produced a big change in attitude. You know, when something's as bad as those hips were, getting worse every day, the hopelessness seems to increase. . . ." And here his eyes well up and he asks to be excused. This is tough to talk about.

"The rehab is the critical part. It's hard at first, but you have to do it religiously, no skimping. They get you up and moving the leg around isometrically the day after surgery. Then it's six weeks of progressively more strenuous flexibility and strengthening exercises, first in water, then in the gym. You walk on crutches until everything is fully weight-bearing, and they want you to walk as much as you can. I did miles and miles around my neighborhood and still do, every morning.

"The motivation is, if you do the work on your body you know it will steadily get better, stronger. Pretty soon after the second operation, I was exercising eight hours a day, for the hip and leg, but also, with golf in mind, on my hands and arms and upper body. The knowledge that I was going to play again inspired me. I wanted to make it the best playing I was capable of."

Back to swinging all his clubs to their full value in twelve weeks, a year later Hullender was one of America's top-ten senior amateurs. His first official number-one ranking came in 1995, followed by second in 1996, and top again in 1997. And he figures to get better yet, continuing to work at his game.

"But you know when they're wheeling you down to that operating room, you're not worrying about golf. What you're worrying about is whether you'll ever be able to put one foot in front of the other again, whether you'll be able to get around under your own steam. So, play well or poorly, win or lose, I'm a very happy guy just to be out there."

Ken Bowden

Close to Home

The kindness we extend to others in their hour of weakness will return to us at the time we most need.

Harriet Johns

For six years, Bob and Nancy Mills celebrated their favorite week of the year—the week of the FedEx St. Jude Classic—with a house full of friends and clients. Overlooking the Tournament Players Club at Southwind's eighteenth hole, the Mills's home was a hotbed of activity for this family of golf-lovers who'd participated in the tournament for fifteen years.

But a week after the 1997 Classic, Nancy Mills walked out her back door not to join a party but to capture a quiet moment alone as she grappled with a parent's worst nightmare. Doctors had told the Millses earlier that day that their five-year-old daughter, Ali, had cancer. Incredulous, Nancy stared at the tournament's scoreboard across the lake that now read "The St. Jude Kids Say Thanks" and realized that Ali was now one of those children. The tournament the Millses had loved and been involved in for years was now to affect their lives in a larger way than they ever imagined—by benefiting their Ali.

During the tournament the week before, Ali's leg had begun to ache, and she lost her appetite and grew very pale. Nancy instinctively knew something was amiss, and she was right: Ali's bloodwork looked wrong and the doctor could feel something in her abdomen. She was sent to St. Jude, and by that afternoon the Mills family knew they were dealing with cancer. A grueling series of tests the next day confirmed Ali had a very rare and potentially deadly solid tumor called neuroblastoma. The tumor stretched from her abdomen to her neck, and had already spread to her bone marrow, the most advanced stage of the disease. The Mills were completely shocked.

"I thought, 'How did I miss this?'" Nancy says. "We were just numb. We couldn't think. You know there are bad things that can happen to your children, but I never thought of cancer. There's no history of cancer in our family at all. For the first week, I couldn't even say the word 'cancer.'"

St. Jude doctors moved fast to begin treating Ali because her condition was so serious. She began chemotherapy treatments the same night as her battery of tests and the diagnosis. Groggy from sedation to get her through the tests, Ali awoke the morning of July 4 in the hospital and learned she had cancer.

"She was very quiet—which isn't like Ali," Nancy says. "We told her she had a tumor and were very up front with her. She took it all very well. Even though she had just gotten her hair long, she was okay when it started falling out from the chemo. On her second treatment, she pulled it out and saved it in a plastic bag to give to the birds to use in their nests."

The Millses lived through tough days as Ali's doctors at St. Jude Hospital attempted to put her cancer into remission so she could have a bone marrow transplant—

her only hope for a cure. Despite a year of various high-powered chemotherapy treatments and a surgery to remove the primary tumor, however, the cancer remained in Ali's bone marrow. At last, though, the Mills family received the wonderful news that for the first time Ali's bone marrow was free from cancer.

Ali had her bone marrow harvested the week of the FedEx St. Jude Classic.

"It's so hard to watch your child go through this, to know it's life-threatening," Nancy says. "You don't want to see them suffer, miss out on things, be stared at. We try to keep life normal."

Bravely soldiering through her treatments, Ali emerged from them with few outer signs of illness other than her bald head. A popular, bubbly presence at St. Jude, she entertains her nurses and doctors with songs and pranks. "She hasn't let her trials get her down," Nancy says.

In March, Ali went to see "The Lion King" on Broadway in New York. Her chemotherapy-induced baldness attracted the attention of another child in front of her. She heard the little girl say, "He doesn't have any hair!" Ali tapped her and told her, "A) I'm a SHE, B) it's called cancer, and C) it's the drugs." Then she leaned her smooth head toward the girl and said kindly, "Do you want to feel it?"

This is Ali's true spirit. She is known for bringing the St. Jude staff to tears with her favorite song, which says, "God doesn't see the same way people see. People see the outside of a person, but God looks at the heart."

It's Ali's beautiful, courageous heart that gives significance to the FedEx St. Jude Classic. This isn't lost on the Mills family, whose devotion to the tournament is ironically helping save their daughter's life.

Bob Phillips
Submitted by Phil Cannon

A New Perspective

*For today and its blessings, I owe the world an
attitude of gratitude.*

Clarence E. Hodges

The ball hooked right again. A loud cracking noise ripped
through the air like a gunshot, then a mesquite branch fell
and shattered on the fairway. My son beat the ground with
his driver and shouted, "That's why I hate golf!"

For weeks Trey, a left-handed golfer, had been knocking the limbs off trees on courses across three counties.
Now, just days away from the last high school tournament before the district championship, he still hadn't figured out what he was doing wrong.

I sat cross-armed in the cart, regretting the unguarded
moment when I'd offered to bring my son to this course
for a practice round. I resented his self-centered attitude.
Mentally, I tallied all the vacation days my husband and I
had used to drive him to out-of-town tournaments. All the
money we'd spent on custom clubs and private lessons.
All the efforts I'd made to time the delivery of "first-come,
first-served" applications to prestigious qualifying events.

I was beginning to hate golf myself. But I said nothing, afraid of what I might say.

Trey, a freshman on the varsity golf team, struggled to fit in with four seniors who shared a world in common. Unlike his teammates, my son had no driver's license, no girlfriend and no confidence that he could hit the ball as far from the blue tees as he had from the white ones. He'd gotten used to scoring in the 70s off the white tees, but since joining the team, his stroke average had jumped to 83.

My son was suffering his first slump.

Maybe, I thought, his snarly ways had everything to do with this misery. I tried to comfort him. I cast a bright light on his dark doubts. I promised an end to these desperate days.

But my son continued to wallow in his misgivings . . . until he overheard a comment at his next tournament.

The big world of boys' and girls' competitive golf is really a small community of players and parents who soon recognize each other at all the tournaments. So Trey knew immediately that the woman following his foursome was the mother of a player who had died a few months ago in a wreck on the way to practice. A teammate had lost control of the car on a steep, rain-slick hill. Everyone survived, except her child. This woman, despite her own crushing grief, worried about how devastated the team was, and came out to encourage her son's friends.

The mother didn't reserve her inspiring words just for that team, but offered them also to a competitor who complained that he was having a lousy round. "You're a talented golfer," Trey heard her tell him. "Be happy to play any golf."

Four days later, at the district championship, my son shot two great rounds in the 70s. The team won first place and Trey was named to First Team All-District. His coach told the newspaper reporter: "The kid really came through."

My son and I both know what really came through were the words of a grieving mother who is grateful for the time she had with her son and who now takes nothing for granted.

Melissa Russell

Taking a Swing at Stress

*The most wasted of all days is the one during
which you have not laughed.*

Nicolas Chamfort

In the world of business, golf is touted as a game that
relieves the stress of the job. It's where big deals are made
and friendships are won.

In a world exploding with information and change, trying to keep from being wired and tired is a major chore.
For far too many people, the stresses of life have zapped
their ability to do their best, be their best and enjoy their
daily activities.

Consider this for a moment: One million Americans
have heart attacks each year. Around thirteen billion
doses of tranquilizers, barbiturates and amphetamines
are prescribed yearly. Well over eight million Americans
have stomach ulcers. There are an estimated fifty thousand stress-related suicides each year. This is only the tip
of the iceberg. In fact, reports indicate that 80 percent of
the illnesses treated in this country are emotionally
induced illnesses.

I went golfing not long ago with some business friends who really like to have fun. We affectionately refer to our group as "the Golfing Angels" because we take ourselves lightly. One of the men has dubbed our particular brand of the game "flog" (golf backwards), and we've added some rules to the traditional game. One of the first rules is that everyone must laugh when something is funny. When somebody misses the ball while teeing off, laughter is mandatory. No offense is taken. In our game of flog, the only failure is the failure to have fun. One of the doctors on the flog team figured that if you live to be seventy years of age, you will spend 613,200 hours wandering the planet. That is far too much time to be stressed and not to have fun. Fun is a diversion from the norm that gets us out of the "dullness" rut that the stresses of life tend to create.

Another rule of the game is to never keep score. We've found that most people cheated anyway. If you do keep score, you must write it on the scorecard before you leave the cart to tee off. If you get close enough to the green, you can just throw the ball if you wish. The rule I like best is that you can tee the ball up regardless of where you are on the fairway. One flog angel loves to find someone's ball on the fairway and tee it up for them. He then hides in the trees to see their reaction. People look around in disbelief. Most just shrug it off and hit it off the tee. When we let people play through, everyone claps for them. Our group of hackers just has fun.

One day when we were just about ready to tee off, a foursome drove up behind us. We knew that they were serious about this game as we noticed they had their own golf carts with names boldly printed on the sides. This bunch had no smiles but lots of Zantac. Hole after hole, we could hear them yelling at each other and their putters. Sand flew and divots were dug. At the last hole, which was surrounded by water, one particularly intense

OUT OF THE ROUGH

fellow blew his final putt by inches. He grabbed his golf bag with all the clubs in it. He was so frustrated that he took the bag and tossed it as far into the water as he could and headed for his car. There he felt in his pocket for the keys. He threw his hat to the ground in disgust as he remembered where he had left his keys. He headed back to the water's edge and waded out to his sinking bag. He opened the zipper and grabbed his keys and threw the bag further into the abyss. By this time, we were laughing so hard that we just threw our golf balls onto the green. The team does get a lot of strange looks on the golfing fairways, but we sure have a good time.

One day late in the spring, someone complained to the course pro about the team's unorthodox conduct. The pro looked at the man, smiled and said, "Don't worry, they're on a hospital release program."

Steve Densley
Submitted by Pam Jones

An Embrace in the Bittersweet Middle

I first thought to write all this down so I wouldn't forget. As I look back, I realize there's no way I could forget. It was a handful of time . . . an experience out of plain sight. I was witness to a moment or two I don't know if I can adequately describe.

Mark O'Meara and I had just sat down for what has become a ritual since Paul Azinger won the PGA in 1993: SportsCenter's "Sunday Conversation" with the winner of a major golf tournament. As the cameramen were making the final lighting adjustments, the door flew open and in walked Ian Baker-Finch.

Baker-Finch had been something of a story himself during the tournament week. He had won the British Open when it was last played at Royal Birkdale in 1991 with weekend rounds of 64 and 66. He had seized that Sunday as if by birthright. A few years later though, his game mysteriously began to disappear. He went through a two-year period where he didn't make a single cut, routinely shooting in the 80s. He said at one point that his driving was so erratic he would stand on the tee with no idea where his ball was going to go. In the first round of the Open at Troon last summer, he shot 92 and withdrew. He had decided it was time to take a break and sort things out. He retired from competitive golf.

Baker-Finch had returned to Royal Birkdale as a commentator for ABC and ESPN.

I don't know if I could have done it if I were in his shoes. His trip back to the scene of his greatest triumph was not only a reminder of how skilled he had once been, but of how much it had all slipped away. Here were his colleagues, his peers, his mates having a go at a tournament and a course he once ruled. There he was, at age thirty-seven, holding a microphone instead of a golf club.

And now there he was, standing in the doorway. He had earlier asked me to convey his congratulations to O'Meara and his wife Alicia. When Baker-Finch won at Royal Birkdale in 1991, he had been paired the final Sunday with O'Meara. They both lived in Orlando and had become friends.

Now, before anybody could say a word, there were these two men, locked in a silent embrace. The room was full of officials and producers and technicians and family, yet these two men shamelessly hugged each other and cried, sharing a meaningful, wordless moment as if they were alone. One player was at the top of his game, filled with confidence and accomplishment, the other at the bottom of his, consumed by bewilderment and resignation. They met in the bittersweet middle, where the line between joy and sadness was impossible to find.

Later, Baker-Finch and I walked back to the SportsCenter set for our final segment of the night. As we made our way across the now-deserted eighteenth green, he stopped and looked at the empty stands, as the sun sank into the Irish Sea.

"Where was the cup?" I asked, not exactly recalling the details of 1991, but knowing he would.

"There," he said softly, pointing to a flat area on the back right of the putting surface.

"Where was the last putt?" I said, already knowing the answer.

He said nothing, but walked to the spot and pantomimed the winning stroke. Suddenly, the stands were full, the crowd was cheering and Baker-Finch was once again "the champion golfer for the year," as the R&A Secretary annually proclaims at the awards ceremony.

He smiled for a moment, but then his face turned blank. He said nothing, but it was clear what he saw: The vast distance between where he had once been and where he stood now. He looked frightened.

"I've held it in all week. Stuffed it, and I just can't do it anymore," he said. His eyes were now red, and the tears were streaming down his cheeks.

I stammered something about how they could never take that great tournament away from him, but I knew it was lame. We walked down the fairway in silence for a moment before I offered that maybe he might like to spend a moment alone.

As I walked away, I looked back. There was a once-great champion taking one long, last taste, drinking in how good it had all once been, before turning and walking into his new life.

Jimmy Roberts

A Wing Grew Back

So much has been given me, I have no time to ponder over that which has been denied.

Helen Keller

At any golf course, it's usually respectfully quiet around the first tee.

But when Bob Cox prepares for his opening drive, he can hear the whispers and low-voiced comments from the onlookers.

"Look, that guy's got only one arm."

And after Cox cracks a long shot straight down the middle of the fairway, he'll often hear, "Wow, I can't hit it that far with two arms."

Cox, who lost his left arm in a motorcycle accident twenty-two years ago, has a remarkable golf game. In a sport where the majority of fully able-bodied players can't break 90 for eighteen holes, he can do it.

"I'm very competitive," said Cox during a recent round. "I actually like the challenge of hitting the ball while people are watching."

In his weekly men's golf league, played at the Winchendon

Country Club in Winchendon, Massachusetts, he'll consistently shoot a 45 or less for nine holes.

His record for eighteen holes is an 88 (44-44) at the par-71 Gardner Municipal Golf Course.

"It's fun going out to play with friends and actually beating them," Cox said. "I love this game."

Cox, forty-one, wasn't always an avid golfer. When he was a teen, hockey was his game. That was, of course, before the accident.

In one fateful instant on June 9, 1976, around noontime, Bob Cox's life changed forever.

While riding his Suzuki 250 motorcycle on Elm Street in Gardner, he collided with a car. In the accident, Cox's left arm, from just inches below his shoulder, was completely severed. Cox and his motorcycle crashed to the road, while his entire left arm lay on the street twenty yards from his body.

"They told me later that there wasn't a lot of blood," Cox said. "I really don't remember anything. I was in a state of shock."

Rushed to a local hospital and then quickly transferred to Boston, Cox remembers waking up in Massachusetts General and asking the doctors how badly his arm was broken.

Just eighteen years old, Cox was given the terrible news. A reattachment operation would not have been successful.

Readjusting his life with only one arm took patience and acceptance. Said Cox, "It was the little things that were tough, like putting toothpaste on your toothbrush, tying a necktie or tying your shoes. And hockey, that's the one thing I really miss. I just couldn't shoot the puck anymore."

But there was never a sense of self-pity or "Why me?" attitude in Bob Cox. "It doesn't do any good," he said.

"Obviously I wish it had never happened, but you just have to go on."

So Cox, never looking back for too long, went on, staying active in sports by playing golf.

He's even quick to joke about his situation.

When asked by a playing partner, "What's your handicap?" Cox will often let the question float in the air for a few seconds. When asked why he doesn't wear a golf glove, he responds, "How will I put it on?"

Cox, who had played golf occasionally before the accident, decided to take the game seriously in his early twenties.

A few teaching pros advised him to swing from the left side, or backhanded, using his right arm to pull through the ball.

"I just couldn't hit from that side," Cox recalled. "I didn't have enough power."

Still, Cox developed a solid swing from the right side, a swing he could rely on.

He sets up with the ball in the middle of his stance, grips down almost to the metal part of the shaft with his muscular right arm and concentrates on hitting down on the ball.

"The hardest thing to learn was to keep my head still," Cox explained.

"I probably hit my irons better than my woods," Cox added. "I take big divots."

The best part of his game occurs on the greens where he displays a smooth putting stroke, keeping the club on line with an accurate follow-through stroke.

In years of practice, Cox has crafted a solid game using his right arm to draw back the club. He then shifts his weight and moves into a powerful downswing at the ball.

For twenty-one years Cox has worked as a customer service representative for Bell Atlantic. And he's very active in the Bell Atlantic Pioneers, a volunteer organization in which he has served as president.

Cox works closely in the administration and organization of the Special Olympics of Massachusetts.

During weekends and vacations, Cox and his wife, Becky, enjoy their thirty-six-foot boat on Lake Winnipesaukee, their summer haven.

In the winter Cox loves to ride his snowmobile.

When June 9 rolls around every year, Cox pauses and thinks about the accident.

"When it comes up on the calendar, I look at the date and remember," he said. "I think about the time of day when it happened. It sticks in my mind."

But most of the time Bob Cox looks ahead, to days of helping people during his job or his volunteer efforts with the Bell Atlantic Pioneers or to the time spent relaxing at the lake or golfing with friends.

His life brings to mind a poem by Nina Cassian, a writer from Romania. In her poem, "A Man," she writes about a soldier who lost an arm while fighting for his country. After a brief period of grief, the soldier moves on in life with an outlook of hope.

Cassian ends her poem with the following:

"From that moment on, he set himself to do everything with twice as much enthusiasm.

And where the arm had been torn away a wing grew."

Jay Gearan

The Healer

When someone asks you, "What's your handicap?" you probably respond with a variety of numbers, depending on if you are trying to impress or win a bet.

"I'm a nine," you might say to a new business associate, or "On a good day? Fourteen," to your weekend $5 Nassau buddies. For most golfers, "handicap" is a measure of how much the game of golf has gotten the better of them.

For Gus Bernardoni, a PGA Teaching Professional from Deerfield, Illinois, "handicap" is an expression of how much in golf—and life—can be overcome. In 1944, serving as a paratrooper with the 101st Airborne, Gus Bernardoni jumped out of a plane over Holland. His chute did not open properly, causing him to fall 300 feet onto a hostile bit of the Netherlands. Plummeting toward earth, he had what he describes as "a talk with God," during which time he asked him to bless all the friends and loved ones he would never see again.

Instantaneously, Bernardoni's body went limp as wet newsprint. He lived—and, understandably, became a life-long Christian. But for seventy-eight days on the front line, trapped under heavy fire, Bernardoni went without proper medical treatment, leaving his spine twisted and his right leg paralyzed.

After corrective spinal surgery, which restored movement to the young paratrooper's lower body, doctors at the Mayo Clinic suggested Gus swing golf clubs as part of his recuperative therapy. Employing all the tenets of a "correct" stroke—stiff left arm, keep the head down, rotate the hips, etc.—Bernardoni suffered excruciating pain.

But he didn't quit. He adapted.

"I found a way to hit the golf ball within my physical limits," Bernardoni explains, introducing himself to a small group of golfers at a Moline, Illinois driving range. "You can, too," he says.

The golfers at this instructional clinic, sponsored by United Cerebral Palsy, are not looking to shave strokes off their score. They're not trying to cure a troublesome slice. They don't want to play golf better—they just want to play golf.

And Gus Bernardoni wants to help them. "I know therapy can be difficult. I know the fear of working toward health and not being sure you'll ever get better," Gus says, pacing before the group, limping slightly. "But I also know there's somebody out there in worse shape than you. So you better start counting your blessings."

Telling someone like Mark De Vrieze, a parapalegic, or Don Smith, who lost the use of his left side to a stroke, to count their blessings might seem insensitive to some. Not Gus. "Let's not pretend we can do everything exactly like other people can. You may be 'less abled.' Maybe you can't walk or run too well. And maybe certain activities are hard for you. But you manage. So I don't want to hear about 'disabled,'" he tells the group of nascent golfers. "'Disabled' is someone who quits."

Gus tells the group he could have laid in a V.A. hospital and collected a pension, or convalesced at home. Or done nothing. Instead, he taught himself to play golf— not traditionally, but well. In 1974, still enduring chronic back pain thirty years after his parachuting mishap, Gus Bernardoni won the Illinois PGA Senior Championship. In 1978 he wrote a book, *Golf God's Way*, outlining his peculiarly effective methods. In 1993, he was inducted into the Illinois PGA Hall of Fame.

Bernardoni is a staff consultant to the Tommy Armour Golf company, whose eponym, coincidentally, also overcame a host of physical ailments en route to golfing greatness. Now seventy-four, Gus still plays out of the Pine Meadows Golf Club in Mundelein, Illinois, and coaches several Senior PGA Tour players, including the remarkable Joe Jiminez, who regularly shoots his age. But much of Bernardoni's life is devoted to work with the Special Olympics and hospitals around the country, coaching people with debilitating illnesses like multiple sclerosis, muscular dystrophy, and arthritis, to develop self-esteem, confidence and willpower through a game that normally inspires none of those qualities in its practitioners.

Today, on an autumn morning in the heartland, Gus Bernardoni is teaching this group of "less abled" athletes that, despite their various infirmities, they, too, can hit a golf ball. "If you can do that, you can do just about anything. Just ask anyone with the use of all their arms and legs, they'll tell you the same thing," he jokes, flashing the kind of smile you tend to see on those who really like their work.

Gus tells his audience that golf is really a lot simpler than most people think. "You've got to get balanced, you have to swing the club, and you have to hit the ball: That's it," he says, shrugging. Most of the game is mental, he explains, so someone's coordination, or lack thereof, is hardly an impediment to making contact with the ball. "There's no such thing as 'mechanical positioning,' no individual can copy anyone else successfully," Bernardoni says, growing impassioned. "Would you tell a blind man he 'looked up'? Would you tell a man with one leg he needs to 'shift-and-pivot' his weight on the backswing?"

To demonstrate, Gus hits golf balls from one foot, on his knees and facing backwards. And when I say "hit" I don't mean "makes contact with," I mean powders. "You've only got one hand to work with? You can't see? Can't use your legs?" Gus laughs. "You've got this," he says, pointing to his head. Bernardoni calls up John Irwin, who, since a massive stroke, can only move his left side. Gus has Irwin tuck his right hand into a pocket. "Get that thing out of the way," he says. Then he adjusts Irwin's left hand grip, turning all his knuckles on top of the club. Shifting Irwin's torso closed to the target line to "redefine his center of gravity," Bernardoni asks his student to pick up the club and chop at the ball while exclaiming "Pow!" at impact. "Pow. . ." Irwin whispers, as the ball dribbles off the tee. Gus stands with his hands on hips, in mock disbelief.

"Not pow," Gus says weakly. "POW!!"

His student laughs. But now he's all business. After a few emphatic practice swings, John Irwin addresses his ball, makes a mighty wallop and says "POW!" The ball sails into the distance.

Everyone applauds heartily. But John Irwin doesn't notice. Holding his golf club out like a sword, he's too busy savoring every wondrous yard of the ball's flight, a journey that he, a massive stroke victim, authored. When the ball finally comes to rest many glorious yards from where it started, Irwin shuffles, six inches per step, over to his chair. For the remainder of the morning, that golf club never leaves his hand.

The next time you are playing badly and want to throw a club or let loose a string of curses or behave with anything but dignified grace, imagine trying to play golf from a chair. Or with one arm. Or without sight. And then be profoundly thankful you have the limbs and faculties and ability to hit a golf ball, no matter how wretchedly.

Eric Black, eleven, has spina bifida. From his chest down he has no sensation, and must be strapped into a chair. His pal Mark DeDecker, twelve, has cerebral palsy, epilepsy and is deaf in one ear. Like most young boys these two love to watch sports on television, especially Mark, whose mom says he is crazy-nuts for golf. Mark dreams, as we all do, of one day making slam dunks like Michael Jordan or hitting home runs like Ken Griffey Jr. or blasting drives like Phil Mickelson. But unlike other eager boys his age, they are dreams that will come true only in his imagination.

Mark DeDecker and Eric Black can only watch the Masters broadcast every year. They will never play golf at Augusta National. They will never know the thrill of making par on a championship golf course.

That is why, after a dozen earnest whiffs and much cajoling and coaching and encouragement from Gus Bernardoni, when Mark DeDecker makes a bold one-handed swing with his 9-iron and sends his ball airborne, flying free and clear from all his earthly despairs, I am not the only one watching who has a tear in his eye. With a shot of maybe forty-five yards, Mark DeDecker has just eagled the Amen Corner of his dreams.

Michael Konik

Happy

I remember golf when it was played B.C. (before carts). Caddying was a great way to earn money. It also taught me a lesson or two about human nature, and how an act of kindness can change a man's life.

I was caddiemaster at a busy club. One morning, a gentleman asked me if I could use another caddie. He said he had a nineteen-year-old mentally retarded son who was strong and healthy. "The boy knows nothing about golf," the gentleman said, "but I'm sure he can be taught how to caddie."

The man's son, named Happy, had never been to school nor had any training. (Back then, there were no special education programs.) Despite a speech impediment, he could communicate fairly well. He quickly learned the fundamentals. The other caddies readily accepted him.

Happy was well-named, with a pleasant disposition. From time to time, though, I observed him sitting by himself in the caddieshack, with a pensive look. It almost seemed as though he were contemplating his condition and wondering why he was not like other people.

As expected, some people did not want Happy to

caddie for them. Many days, he could not get out. I explained this to his father as tactfully as possible, but his dad was just grateful that Happy could be part of a normal activity and make a few dollars each week. Still, I did not want to give up on him.

Then, a group of ladies who played regularly invited a newcomer as their guest. Mrs. Wentworth was her name. She appeared to be in her forties and was an excellent golfer.

Because it was a busy day, only four caddies were left, including Happy. He was assigned to Mrs. Wentworth. When the ladies finished their round, the newcomer reported that she had been very pleased with Happy. His manner was pleasant. He kept his eye on the ball, kept his mouth shut and generally did what a good caddie should do. She added that she planned to play more often and requested that I reserve Happy for her.

When I explained this to Happy, he was more than happy!

Every day he would wait in the caddie yard next to the parking lot. He eagerly watched as each car arrived at the club. When he would recognize Mrs. Wentworth's car, he became as excited as a child. "Here comes my lady!" he would proudly tell the other caddies.

As long as I was caddiemaster there, only Happy caddied for Mrs. Wentworth. She routinely tipped him twenty-five cents, a hefty sum in those days.

I often wondered why Mrs. Wentworth so wholeheartedly accepted this young man. She made him feel that he was important; he could do as fine a job as the other caddies. I think she saw something in him that so many others had missed.

I went into the service in mid-summer, losing touch with Happy, Mrs. Wentworth and others at the club. After four years in the Army, I returned to my hometown and visited the club. The pro was still there. When I inquired about Happy, he said that the young man had continued to caddie for Mrs. Wentworth regularly, never losing his enthusiasm. "But," he said sadly, "there is something I have to tell you."

Happy did not live to reach twenty-one. He died of a respiratory illness. His particular form of retardation carried genetic risks, untreatable at that time.

The pro told me that Happy was not only mourned by his father; his absence left a void in the lives of Mrs. Wentworth and others at the club.

The pro added that although Mrs. Wentworth continued to play golf, she often remarked that there would never be another Happy.

Though it was a long time ago, I'll always remember Happy and his lady. I think about how he put his heart and soul into that job. Perhaps Mrs. Wentworth was just being kind. Or maybe she saw in him that part of the human spirit that cannot help but soar, when given the chance.

David Field

The Benefits of Being King

King Hassan II of Morocco loved the game of golf and had his own private course built. The 9-hole course had forty-three bunkers, and the king could never seem to avoid landing in most of them. He called in golf pros who were experts at sand play to help him improve his game. After this failed, he did what any king would do. He ordered the course changed and all forty-three bunkers filled in with sod, proving once again, it's good to be the king.

Rich Mintzer and Peter Grossman
Excerpted from The Everything Golf Book

A Humble Beginning

I played in my first golf tournament—the Minneapolis Ladies Championship—in 1933. I was fifteen and had qualified for the tenth and very last flight with a score of 122, which for me at the time wasn't too bad, my usual score being about 140. My opponent in the first round of the tournament was an older woman who had qualified with a score of 121, so obviously the course record was in no danger of being equaled or surpassed by either one of us. Even so, my opponent beat me like the proverbial drum; I lost every hole and lost the match 10-and-8.

When I got home my father asked how I'd made out, and I said, "Not very good. I got beat 10-and-8.

"Oh," he said, "you played thirty-six holes."

"No," I had to admit, "just eighteen."

"You really weren't very good, then, were you?" he said. "Did you do anything right?"

"Yes," I replied, "I paid the caddie."

That defeat, humiliating at the time, made me determined to work—and work hard—on my game, the result being that the very next year I qualified in the championship flight and won the tournament.

Patty Berg

The Luckiest Golfer Alive

*Whenever I play with Gerald Ford, I try to
make it a foursome—the president, myself, a
paramedic and a faith healer.*

Bob Hope

No golfer worthy of his titanium driver would dare complete a round without complaining. The greens are always
too hard, the pin positions too difficult, the rough too high
and the sand traps too deep. The unwritten code of behavior dictates that every golfer must voice such complaints.

Either that, or admit the real reason for lack of success
on the golf course: your own ineptitude.

But even while joining the griping session, I know deep
down I am the luckiest golfer alive. I haven't holed a chip
shot to win the Masters on extra holes. I haven't canned a
sand shot to win the PGA. But I am lucky.

Just how lucky I am was brought home by an item in
the Golf Plus edition of *Sports Illustrated,* which read:

"A golf course is the fifth most likely place to suffer a
heart attack, but one of the least likely places to survive
one—about 5 percent of stricken golfers survive."

But here I am. I twice beat the statistics. And on the same course. I had what was described as a cardiac arrest on the 3rd hole in February and on the 5th hole in November. Improved, huh?

I survived, I am convinced, because of having good friends. In the foursome immediately behind me when I keeled over in February was Dr. Bob Bullington, a retired cardiologist. Behind that group were Cotton Fitzsimmons, former coach of the Phoenix Suns, and two of the Suns' current players, Joe Kleine and Dan Majerle. They called 9-1-1.

Bullington used chest compressions to revive me. I remember coming to, laying on the apron in front of the 3rd green and hearing another doctor tell Bullington he couldn't get a pulse.

"Isn't that nice?" I said.

I then suggested we let Cotton's group play through. I was too late. They already had skipped around me. I was lucky they didn't give me a two-stroke penalty for slow play.

In November, I holed a fifty-foot putt on the 5th hole. I was short of breath, possibly from the excitement of the putt, but made my way to the golf cart and passed out. My cartmate, Paul McCoy, immediately recognized my problem and raced to the group ahead of us, which, get this, included the same Dr. Bullington.

This episode was more serious. Bullington thought he had cracked a couple of ribs pounding on my chest. I didn't regain consciousness until reaching the intensive care ward. My problem apparently has been remedied by a new drug and a pacemaker.

One problem: Bullington won't play golf with me now. Says he wants to finish eighteen.

Bob Hurt

The Power of Charity Golf

When our little hero Ryan Dant speaks, he sounds like a chirping bird—only happier. "Yes, sir, we had a game today," he says.

He's thirteen years old, a baseball player, four feet, seven inches tall, eighty-five pounds of excitement.

"I hit a ball out into center field, and I got on base."

He plays second base and left field for . . .

"The Bombers."

Maybe because he lives near Dallas, Ryan's favorite team is the Texas Rangers. His favorite player is . . .

"Alex Rodriguez. He's a good shortstop and hits the ball really hard."

Behind Ryan's house there's an open field that runs toward a small creek in front of tennis courts. Back there he plays catch with his father, Mark, a police lieutenant in Carrollton, Texas.

"I hit golf balls out there, too."

The first time Ryan had a golf club in his hands, he went behind his house and thought it would be neat to hit a golf ball so far it flew over the field and over the creek and into the tennis courts maybe 120 yards away.

"Golf, it's easy," he says.

The ball just sits there.

"Easier than baseball."

Try as he might, though, his longest golf shots stayed on this side of the creek.

In October 1992, the Adams Golf Company was three people and one telephone with nobody calling except wrong numbers and insurance salesmen.

For staying-in-business money, Barney Adams, the boss, left the shop every afternoon to do club-fittings and repairs. On his door Adams hung a sign: NO SOLICITATIONS.

Mark Dant walked past the sign. The year before, at a routine physical checkup, a pediatrician thought Ryan Dant's head and liver were abnormally large. So he sent the boy, then three, to a geneticist whose tests showed Ryan had a genetic disease, mucopolysaccharidosis, known as MPS 1.

Because his body lacks an enzyme that breaks down sugar, his cells were overwhelmed by deposits of sugar molecules. MPS 1's damage is progressive and complete. Joints lock up. Organs fail, including the brain. By age six, Ryan suffered headaches so severe he would throw up until he fell asleep, exhausted. He was small; he ran with a stiff-legged gait; he couldn't raise his arms to take off a T-shirt; he couldn't hold a baseball bat, because his fingers were fixed in a curl toward his palms. All the while, Ryan's parents knew it would only get worse. "We were told Ryan would not live past ten," Mark Dant says.

The day they heard those words, Dant and his wife Jeanne went home and began a period of sorrow and grieving that lasted months. "We didn't do anything," he says, "but close the door and cry."

By October 1992, grief had been supplanted by the Dants' determination to give their son a chance to survive a disease that seldom allowed any child to live past his or her teens.

The Dants had done enough homework to know that such a chance would come only if science found a cure for MPS 1. They also knew that scientists rarely find a cure unless someone else first finds money for research.

That's why, despite the NO SOLICITATIONS sign on the door, Mark Dant walked into the storefront shop of Adams Golf. Not that he expected much. He'd been playing golf for only a year; he knew nothing about some company working out of a shopping complex. Dant had turned to the Yellow Pages and looked up "golf" because he'd heard that golf tournaments were a good source of charity money. Certainly, the Dants needed to do better than the $342 raised at their first event, a bake sale.

Barney Adams remembers: "I was walking a box of clubs to the front of the building when this young guy came in. Mark had been going door-to-door trying to raise money. He told me Ryan's story, but at that time I probably had less money than he did; our annual sales may have been $150,000. So I said, 'Why don't you auction off some clubs and make some money?' We gave him three or four clubs."

The Dants' first weekend golf event raised $25,000. That's small change in the high-dollar world of scientific research. But to the Ryan Foundation for MPS Children— established by the Dants after a visit to a conference of MPS children and their families—the $25,000 was huge.

It meant hope.

Golf tournaments became the Ryan Foundation's primary source of money, the proceeds rising from $25,000 to $75,000 to $150,000. Early on, the money went to the National MPS Society. "Every year Mark would come by," Adams says, "and we'd give him more clubs."

It was always a struggle. In 1994, because he had used

all his vacation time going door-to-door, Dant wrote letters to ninety golf companies.

"All 'no's,'" he says. "I was about to give up."

Worn out, dispirited, Dant came home from work one
evening and on his porch he saw some boxes. "They were
Tommy Armour irons and 288 sleeves of Wilson Staff
balls," he says.

"It was a sign. It was stunning. It said, 'Do not give up.'"

Soon he heard about work done by a California scien-
tist, Emil Kakkis, a Ph.D. in biological chemistry with post-
doctoral training in genetics. "Dr. Kakkis had found a way
to make the enzyme that's missing in MPS children," Dant
says. "But he was running out of money. He was two
months from closing his lab."

Life's moments are rich with coincidence so wonderful
as to seem ordered up. How else do we explain the inter-
secting lives of Emil Kakkis, Mark Dant and Barney
Adams? Consider . . .

Just when he needed big money quickly, Dant again
turned to the boss of Adams Golf—only by then Barney
Adams was no small-timer. He'd become a golf industry
sensation by creating and marketing Tight Lies fairway
woods. And he was eager to help Ryan.

"I asked Mark how much it would take to accelerate the
research process," Adams says. With the figure $200,000 in
hand, Adams called a friend, Tom Fazio, the golf course
architect. "I told him Ryan's story and said, 'I need X dollars from you to help me underwrite this.'"

That day, right then, Fazio wrote a check. "I had a big
lump in my throat," Fazio says. "I have six kids myself, and
I thought, 'What would I do if a doctor told me what that
doctor told Mark Dant?'"

Without the Adams/Fazio contribution, Dr. Kakkis's
research likely would have ended. Instead, as Kakkis's
work gained greater notice, the biotechnology company

BioMarin Pharmaceutical gave him $5 million, in hopes of bringing a treatment to market.

"Not to be melodramatic about it," Mark Dant says, "but if not for Mr. Adams, Mr. Fazio and the entire golf industry, my son would be deceased. Golf's a game, I know that. But golf has given my family life."

On February 13, 1998, Ryan Dant was the third of ten MPS children to receive Dr. Kakkis's enzyme-replacement treatment. A week later, standing in front of a mirror, his shirt pulled up, Ryan shouted, "Wow! Mom, Dad! Look how much smaller it is." His stomach was no longer grossly swollen.

Three years of four-hour weekly infusions haven't cured Ryan; what they have done is give him his body back. With the treatment, he has grown five and a half inches, gained thirty-five pounds and is again an athlete. He spent a week in June participating in a baseball camp.

"We're halfway now, and it's been a miracle," Mark Dant says. "But what the doctors tell us now is that what's happened to the body also has happened to the brain. There's the possibility of mental regression. The next step has to be gene-replacement therapy."

Barney Adams is aboard. "They say the gene-replacement research will cost $2 million. I told Mark, 'Okay, let's do it again.' I've never talked about my company's involvement, nor has Tom Fazio talked about his, but now we have this ulterior motive. We want to raise $2 million for Ryan Dant."

On February 13, 2001, the third anniversary of his first enzyme treatment, Ryan Dant went into his backyard with a new Tight Lies 5-wood that bore his name on its sole plate.

He teed up a ball, took a look at the creek way out there,

took a look at the tennis courts way farther out there and he whaled away.

The ball bounced off the tennis court fence.

"Wow, it really went," Ryan says.

Did he hit another?

"No, sir. I took my club to my room. I want to save that power."

Dave Kindred

A Profile in Courage

Pete Farricker never played in a U.S. Open or won a state amateur, although he was a scratch handicapper who could get up and down from a bird feeder when he had to. Before arteriolateral sclerosis (Lou Gehrig's disease) began wrecking his body years ago, he was a terrific golfer and twice as good a person, a master of humor and compassion who changed the lives of everyone who knew him. And hopefully, the lives of a few who never will.

His death at the age of forty-five was, of course, a tragedy—this wonderful man cut down in his prime by an illness as mysterious as it is vicious. That Pete left behind a wife and three-year-old son is sad enough. That two of his life's greatest accomplishments—starting a family, becoming the equipment editor at *Golf Digest*—occurred after he turned forty is snarled fate. Pete's time atop the mountain was far shorter than the climb.

It would be nice to say something remarkably profound about Pete, except the eulogies delivered at his funeral were beautiful and simple, reflective of a guy who didn't ask for nearly as much from this world as he gave it. Long after being diagnosed with ALS, Pete played every horrible lie without a complaint, made us laugh and made us cry, made us live and wonder why. Sitting in an office next door to his for six months was one of the best things that ever happened to me.

Employed as a carrier pigeon in the affluent suburb of reality known as the PGA Tour, I'm reminded that courage isn't the guy who makes a five-footer on the seventy-first hole or knocks it stiff to a back-left pin on Sunday afternoon. Courage is coming to work four days a week after your arms have taken the rest of your life off. Courage is letting somebody stick a spoonful of tuna salad in your mouth, then looking your little boy in the eye and telling him it's good to be alive.

Courage is asking somebody to follow you into the men's room so they can pull up your underpants after you've used the toilet. Just the other day, I was watching NBC's telecast of the U.S. Senior Open, where the word "patience" was used to describe men who make long strings of pars or hit their ball into the center of a three-tiered green. Excuse me for getting a bit oversemantical, but I've seen patience. It looks nothing like that.

Patience is needing fifteen minutes to go from your bed to your wheelchair, another ten minutes to get from your wheelchair to the van, then wondering if you can't talk because your throat is dry or because your vocal cords have permanently shut down. Patience is needing forty-five minutes to leave work at the end of the day, twenty of which you spend hoping your ankle will stop quivering. Patience is waiting for someone to turn the corner so they can help you off the floor.

One of the worst things about ALS is that your body turns into a puddle of applesauce while your mind stays totally functional. Driving Pete home one evening, I asked him what he felt like inside. "Like a 110-year-old man," he gasped, not sounding a day over 90. Near the end, his speech had become so slurred that when he said something, you'd have to ask him three or four times to repeat himself. Believe me, it was always worth it.

The last time I saw Pete he was so weak that his toes were curled up and frozen in different directions. He couldn't lift his head, couldn't eat, sleep or drink. Someone had to feed him ice chips to keep him hydrated. You knew the end was near, and so did he, but inside that ravaged body, there was a hearty, healthy, bulletproof soul.

"How's life on the tour?" he asked me five or six times before I understood him.

Not half as good as life with you, Pete. Not half as good as life with you.

John Hawkins

Making Contact

Driving back to New Orleans with his cousin Bill Kyle after attending a wedding in Baton Rouge, Louisiana, Pat Browne's thoughts drifted to a round of golf he planned to play the next day. It was late afternoon on Saturday, February 26, 1966, and Kyle was driving, so the thirty-two-year-old Browne, who had played on the golf and basketball teams at Tulane University in his hometown of New Orleans, did not have to concentrate on the road.

Suddenly, though, he saw a car driving at a high rate of speed from the opposite direction. As it got closer, it swerved out of control, crossing a small median divider.

"Look out, Bill!" Pat Browne screamed. As he did, the other car slammed into the auto Bill Kyle was driving. The force of the impact drove the hood of Kyle's car through the windshield, sending shards of glass into Browne's eyes and severing his optic nerve.

The teenage driver of the speeding car, which had been stolen, was killed instantly. But both Browne and Kyle survived with serious injuries. "Seeing that car jump the divider was the last thing I ever saw," Browne recalled thirty-five years after the accident which left him blind along with a fractured collarbone, jaw and knee cap and cost him several front teeth.

How in the world am I ever going to play golf again? Browne thought to himself when doctors told him that he would never see again. *And how can I bear not seeing my three daughters again?*

At the time of the accident, Pat Browne was married with three young daughters, aged eleven, nine and seven, who were the joy of his life. He also was a lawyer with a large law firm in New Orleans and a well-known athlete. When he was able to find time, Browne also excelled on the golf course, shooting in the 70s and holding a 3 handicap, which was 2 less than the one he possessed while playing on the varsity golf team at Louisiana State University. Occasionally, the six-foot, four-inch 210-pound Browne also played some pickup basketball. As a player at Tulane, he had gone up against such Half-of-Fame players as Bob Pettit of Louisiana State and Sam and K. C. Jones while they were winning back-to-back national championships at the University of San Francisco in the mid 1950s.

Indeed, Pat Browne had a lot going for him until, suddenly, the lights went out forever on that winter afternoon in 1966.

"Depressed? I guess I was for a while," said Browne, whose weight dropped from 210 pounds to 165 during his convalescence. "But I knew I had to get on with my life and was convinced that, even though I had lost my sight, I would still be able to do most of the things I did before the accident, including maybe even play golf."

Following months of hospitalization and a long convalescence, along with learning how to get along in a world that had suddenly gone dark, Browne returned to work with the law firm of Jones and Walker on a part time basis in June of 1966, four months after the accident. "In September, when I was back working fulltime, I tried my first case," he said, "and realized that I could still practice law effectively."

The following spring two friends, Bobby Monsted and Doc Schneider, convinced Browne to try to hit a few golf balls at the New Orleans Country Club to which the three men belonged.

"Come on, Pat, let's give it a try," Monsted said.

"Bobby, how in the world am I going to hit the ball when I can't see it?," Browne said.

"Don't worry, you'll do fine," Schneider said. "You're still going to be a good golfer."

At the club, after Browne had taken a few practice swings, Monsted placed a ball on a tee, set Browne in position, handed him a driver and set the club back on the ground directly back of the ball. "You're all set, Pat," he said. "Now all you've got to do is swing and hit it."

Browne, apprehensive and unsure of himself, swung easily and lofted a drive about 150 yards down the middle, about 100 yards shorter that he would normally hit his two shots before his accident. "That impact felt good," he told Monsted and Schneider. "Where did it go?"

"Right down the middle," Schneider responded. "Not bad for the first time out."

"Let's hit some more," an enthused Browne said.

For the next fifteen minutes or so, with Monsted and Schneider lining him up for every shot, Pat Browne struggled. Most of his wood shots went straight, some as far as 200 yards. But most of his iron shots sailed wide to the right—shanks, as they're known in golf.

As they left the driving range, Monsted said, "Pat, that was great for the first time. I think you ought to keep at it. After all, you were practically a scratch golfer before the accident, and you still have a great swing, good coordination and excellent reflexes."

"Maybe you're right, Bobby, and thanks a lot to you and Doe for your help today," Browne said to his friends as they walked towards the clubhouse. "Maybe if I really work at my game, I can still play reasonably well."

As it developed, Browne played more than reasonably well. Henry Sarpy, a member of the same law firm, volunteered to be Browne's coach, as the people who line up blind golfers for their shots and lead them around the golf course are known. Together, along with other friends, they played scores of rounds of golf together over the next two years. Then one day, Sarpy said, "Pat, I think you ought to consider playing in the national blind golfers tournament.

"A golf tournament for blind golfers?" Browne asked incredulously,

"Yes, they have it every year," Sarpy said. "Charlie Boswell is the head of the Blind Golfers Association, and the way you're playing, I'm sure you would do well."

Browne knew about Boswell. He had been an outstanding football and baseball player at the University of Alabama before losing his sight in World War II. After taking up golf following his blindness, Boswell had written a book entitled, *Now I See.*

With Sarpy as his coach, Browne played in his first blind tournament in Chattanooga, Tennessee, in 1969. At the time, the blind golfers' field was dominated by Boswell and Joe Lazaro, who, like Boswell, had been blinded during World War II, Browne finished fourth, shooting between 100 and 108, which is excellent in blind golf competition. "I know I can do better," he told Sarpy after the tournament ended. And he did, winning his first national tournament in 1975, and then, from 1978 through 1997, winning it a phenomenal twenty years in a row with Gerry Baraousse, a former All-America golfer at Washington & Lee, as his coach.

During that period, and into his sixties, Browne established himself as the best blind golfer in the world. Playing under U.S. Golf Association rules, he performed better than most sighted golfers, even very good ones. He carded an 80 at the very difficult Pinehurst course in North Carolina, a 76 at his home course, the New Orleans Country Club, and then, incredibly, put together four consecutive rounds in the 70s, including two in which he shot 74, in 1982 at the very challenging Mission Hills Country Club in California. By the 1990s, as the blind golf circuit expanded internationally, Browne was winning scores of other tournaments, both in the U.S. and abroad. At times during the mid-1990s, his "coach" often was his teenage son, Patrick, who had developed into one of the best junior golfers in Louisiana.

Numerous honors have been bestowed on Browne who served as president of the U.S. Blind Golfers Association from 1976 to 1992, when he was succeeded by Bob Andrews, who lost his sight in Vietnam. Browne has received the Ben Hogan Award from the Golf Writers Association of America and been inducted into the Tulane Hall of Fame and the Louisiana Sports Hall of Fame.

"I think I've been blessed," said Browne, who for the last twenty-five years has been president and chief executive officer of a savings and loan association in New Orleans. "I've played at some of the world's greatest golf courses in England, Ireland, Scotland, Australia and New Zealand, which I may never have played if I hadn't lost my sight. And I've met some wonderful people along the way, particularly the other blinded golfers. I've also been to the Masters six or seven times since the accident and played the Augusta National Course. Now that's golfing heaven. And to think I've played it twice. I imagine that some people wonder why blind golfers play. But they don't understand that the thrill of hitting the golf ball is what counts. And you don't have to be able to see it to enjoy doing it."

Jack Cavanaugh

A Thoughtful Gift

My husband, Richard, is an avid golfer and likes to practice his golf swing on our lawn. Often, during the summer, he breaks a window or two. "Oh, well," we always say, "at least it was our own window." And we have the glass replaced.

One year when he had trouble with his slice, he broke a grand total of four windows. The following spring, a parcel arrived, addressed to him. It was a box of a dozen golf balls, and the enclosed note read, "Have a good season. From Mike, your Window Guy."

Kay B. Tucker

A Childhood Passion Strikes a Chord

I waited until my mother had driven away. Then, after opening the front door, peeking down the road and seeing her white Ford Falcon disappear, I lined up my 8-iron shot. Standing smack in the middle of the living room, with a plastic golf ball sitting on the carpet, I took dead aim through the small opening that skirted the chandelier and led through the back door to my target, a square of screen at the back of the porch.

At thirteen, I had been hitting balls inside for well over a year. Eight-iron shots were my favorite—even plastic practice balls zipped off the club face at an ideal trajectory. I loved the unique contour of that particular club, its braveness as it stood distinguished from the rest of the set. It had none of the angular assertiveness of the 7-iron (which reminded me of a proud slice of pie), or even the bulbous, bloated roundness of the wedges. No, the 8-iron, viewed at address, appeared to be exactly what it was: a jewel-like machine of measurement.

Over the past year, a small worn spot had begun to appear on the carpet, and while the blemish didn't please my mom, perhaps some thought that one day I would make millions on tour and buy her a dream house had made her overlook it.

My next swing, however, would prove a swipe no one could ignore. The backswing seemed ordinary enough, a decent little turn. And the transition was good, too. Other kids had dogs; my swing was my faithful servant. The club dropped into the slot just as it was supposed to, and with a well-timed release, I squared the blade forged out of steel.

Next to my living-room practice tee sat the family piano. Now, a plastic practice golf ball yields a soft, light sensation when struck reminiscent of patting a balloon. On that fateful swing, I felt that little whiff, alright, which was followed by a most unexpected *thud*. I had caught the side of the piano solidly with my 8-iron, which had gone on to bury itself deep within the instrument's chamber, leaving only the silver shaft exposed. With my grip horrifically frozen in place, the image must have resembled a tableau in a French farce.

I didn't like to think of myself as a delinquent child. I was a good student, a good athlete. I ate my vegetables, didn't smoke and felt compassion for kids less fortunate than myself. But knowing that I had done something wrong, the criminal instinct took over.

Off I went on my bicycle to the candy store, then the art supply shop across the street. I saw my mom's car parked in the supermarket lot, and recalled her saying she was going to stop by her friend Phylis's house after shopping. So I figured I had an hour and a half to carry out my plan.

Back home there wasn't time to lose. I chewed a wad of gum and stuck it in the vertical "divot" slashed in the piano. Then, with the ecstatic freedom of Van Gogh, I painted the pink gum brown, hoping to match the hue of the instrument.

The end of this unfortunate escapade came swiftly.

Mom walked in, groceries in hand, spotted the oozing gum dripping cheap watercolor paint on the side of the family treasure and threw a fit. My dad, who on the golf course crooned over every great golf shot I hit like a tenor warbling "Sonny Boy" with a pint of Guinness in his hand, suddenly rejected the idea that golf encompassed spiritual values. My backside made the abrasion on the piano seem like the surface of a mountain lake at dawn. The scar in the piano never healed, but mine did, and I grew up to be a golfer. I even played scratch for many years while teaching school in Memphis.

My passion for golf, though, goes beyond the mere enjoyment of the game. It penetrates to the root of the word *passion* itself, with its base in the idea of suffering. From the recognition of the pain of others, we develop compassion. Every time I play golf, I see my own frustration mirrored in the exasperation of my partners, and I remember what I learned when I was a kid swinging in the living room—that the world is not a stage but a golf course.

Andy Brumer

Start of a Love-Hate Relationship

I'd like to see the fairways more narrow. Then everybody would have to play from the rough, not just me.

Seve Ballesteros

Apologies to the property owner on South Mountain, the one who must've wondered if a comet had crashed through the drywall. Honestly, I didn't know a little white ball made so much noise when hitting a house.

Apologies to the man who came into view just after I made contact, the one who suddenly appeared in my fairway and came within inches of not finishing his life, much less his round. I really must learn to say "Fore" a little earlier.

And sincere empathy goes out to a certain female, the one currently wondering about the return policy on husbands.

Yes, I did a very bad thing on vacation. I learned how to play golf.

I'm not sure what precipitated such madness, but one day, I was scanning the Internet, printing out pages on how to swing a golf club. The next few days were spent in a ridiculous cocoon: Trips to the cash machine, trips to the driving range, midnight swing sessions in the driveway. And then, the binge.

Eleven rounds, nine different courses and, oh, the things I've seen.

I have tasted the euphoria, the intensely satisfying moment when the swing is true and the ball sails forever. I have been slightly alarmed by my shortcomings, especially when the result lies somewhere past a warning sign regarding rattlesnakes in the immediate vicinity.

I have seen a woman stand aghast in her backyard, resentful of the ball that just plunked her tile roof, as if a golf course had suddenly sprouted around her home.

I have barged onto a hidden green, unaware that a foursome hadn't completed the hole. After apologizing profusely, I proceeded to hit one of their balls.

I have played a round in two hours and five minutes. Alone. An exhilarating day when it seemed like the course was empty and I was the only person alive. Naturally, on this day the planets were aligned, the clubs were wands and I was the maestro—a day I craved for witnesses.

Another time, I made the turn after nine holes in three and a half hours, stuck behind a legion of slow-playing foursomes. A tortoise parade that would qualify as golf purgatory.

I have seen men examine long-distance putts for five minutes, only to hit the ball six inches.

I have seen a friend hit the ball sideways, nearly decapitating another friend sitting in the cart. I have willingly raked sand.

And just when you think you're the biggest and only doofus on the planet . . .

One afternoon, while I walked to my ball, which teetered on the last blade of grass separating land from lake, a diver emerged from the black. In full scuba gear. Carrying about six thousand errant shots.

Yes, misery loves company.

And yes, golf is a lot like life. Humbling beyond reason. Laced with a rich bouquet of hope. And in the end, it gives you just enough to keep going.

To be honest, the intent of this experiment was born from curiosity and a desire to become socially equipped. Living in Arizona and not learning to play golf is like living in Paris and not speaking French. I still maintain that any endeavor requiring a collared shirt is not a sport, but for a recreational skill, golf is addictive. Much better than Ping-Pong, and much more than a good cart ride spoiled.

Fascinating game, really. Intoxicating in its solitude, decadent in its consumption of time, a wonderful reminder of how nice it is to walk on grass.

Granted, I still don't get the extensive volumes of etiquette, and I'll never forget the look on my friend's face when I arrived for our initial golf date in a T-shirt. But I quickly learned to love the game, and now I'm ready for the next step.

Because I'm starting to hate the game.

On Friday, I hit three excellent shots in succession, leading to a six-inch putt and the first birdie of my life.

On Saturday, I stepped up to the tee, swung at a ball and missed.

And now I get the joke.

Why do they call it golf? Because @!#@ was already taken.

Dan Bickley

7

THE NINETEENTH HOLE

Maybe I Need a Crystal Ball

Until I started playing golf, I thought that wine tasting had to be the most confusing thing I'd ever done. People with names like Higgins rambling on about residual sugar and tannin, describing each quarter-ounce sample in terms like "full-bodied, yet unpretentious." And I could never remember whether I was supposed to age it, chill it or drink it with fresh fish during a full moon. Just when I thought I was a genius for knowing the difference between a cabernet and cabaret, I went to the pro shop for golf balls.

"What kind?" the pro asked.

"I dunno, white, I guess."

He rubbed his hands together as he scanned the tri-level ball display. "Do you want a two-piece ball?"

I though this was a joke, of course. "No," I said. "I like to start off with them whole. They'll break when I wallop them with my driver."

"Oh," he said without as much as a smile. "A big hitter. Then you want distance."

He handed me a shiny box with gold lettering. The price tag on the end was more than I'd paid for dinner for my wife and I the previous evening.

"These have computer-generated dimple patterns and use a complex two-piece injection molding system. They offer blistering distance."

"Perfect," I said. "Course I'll probably overshoot the green now on any hole less than four hundred yards."

He still didn't laugh. He just removed the box of balls from my hand and said, "Aahhh . . . stopping power."

He slid another brightly colored box across the counter, looked me in the eye and said, "Lithium Surlyn."

I offered my hand. "Ernie Witham," I said.

"No," he said. "The cover. It's made of Lithium Surlyn. You know what that means."

"It's radioactive?"

"It's soft. And it's been reformulated for more feel. Plus the aerodynamics have been modified for lower trajectory. . . . Did you want lower trajectory?"

"Well, sure. I guess. If that means it'll go straighter."

"Oh, oh. Accuracy problem, huh? Slice? Hook?"

"Yes. Yes."

He walked down to the end of the ball display and came back with yet another package.

"These offer less sidespin. Plus they're 2 percent larger than a regular ball."

"Wow. Two percent. Guess I'll need a bigger bag." I looked at my watch. "Oh, oh. Tee-time."

He apparently didn't hear me. He grabbed more boxes from the shelf. "How about a balata ball? This one spins at more than eleven thousand RPMs and maintains consistent compressions. This other balata carries 266 yards and is an evolutionary achievement in balata ball performance."

"I—aahhh—"

"Don't want a balata? This brand precisely blends five different dimple depths for raw length and pinpoint control. Or one designed for swing speeds in excess of ninety-five miles per hour."

"I—aahhh—"

"And here we have one that rockets off the club face, with an earlier peak and shallow descent. . . . This one penetrates the wind. . . . This one rolls longer. . . . This one has Trilyn. . . . This one has Zylin. . . . This one . . ."

"I—aahhh . . . I think I'll just take a few of these." I picked two yellow balls and one orange one from the used ball jar and threw a five-dollar bill on the counter. I felt bad, but my foursome had already finished the first hole.

He sighed, took a deep breath and started putting all the bright shiny boxes away. Then the little bell above the door jingled.

"I need some golf balls," the young woman said. "But I'm not sure what kind. Do you have any suggestions?"

"Do you want a two-piece ball?" I heard him ask, as I ran for the second tee.

Ernie Witham

Riders

Preparing to tee off at our municipal golf course, I overheard two women discussing their games. "I had eight riders!" one woman exclaimed happily.

"That's wonderful!" her friend said.

Never having heard of a "rider," I interrupted to ask what it was. The women looked at me in surprise.

"It's when you hit the ball a long distance," one finally said. "Instead of walking that far for your next shot, you ride in the golf cart."

Arthur Berk

The Man Whose Secret Was a Secret

He was born in a small cow town that didn't have a golf course.

His parents didn't play golf and discouraged him from playing.

He was so small the other kids made fun of him, and the only club he had was left-handed even though he played right-handed.

At age nine, his father killed himself with a .38 revolver.

He never finished high school and never won a single amateur tournament.

He turned pro at seventeen and joined the tour, but ran out of money and had to return home a failure.

At twenty-three, he played in his first U.S. Open and missed the cut.

At twenty-six, he was down to his last $8 when a thief stole all four tires off his car and left him stranded on the road.

Through his first four U.S. Open attempts, his best was a tie for 62nd.

Through almost nine years as a pro, he didn't win a single tournament.

At thirty, when most golfers are in their prime, he was drafted into the service.

At thirty-six, he fractured his pelvis and broke his collarbone in a car accident and the doctors told him he'd never play golf again.

He never became a television commentator or played the senior tour or wore a logo on his hat. He never had a teacher, a manager or a sports psychologist. And his total career earnings amounted to less than $210,000.

Despite all these failures, by the time he retired, Ben Hogan had won sixty-four tournaments and established a reputation for pure ball striking unapproached by anyone before or since.

He wrote a series of articles for *Life* magazine in 1954 that purported to explain "The Secret." Ever since, there have been rumors that Hogan had held back a key element of The Secret, which he allegedly intimated to various friends and acquaintances over the years. Several professionals have claimed to know it, but they say Hogan put them under a seal of silence. A visitor was once pulled into a kitchen at Shady Oaks Country Club in Fort Worth by Hogan, who started to whisper that the secret was in the "weight transfer" until a busboy came by with a tray of dirty dishes and the moment was gone.

Shortly before his death in 1997, the former president of the Hogan Company arranged for this writer to meet with Hogan himself, because himself said he was finally ready to reveal The Real Secret. But within hours of the appointed meeting Hogan abruptly canceled.

Tom Kite, who wore Hogan's name on his visor, says he doesn't think Hogan ever held back any secret, or at least he had never revealed any secret to Tom.

"He had nothing to gain," said Kite. "He's not trying to beat anybody now."

Kite thought that Hogan's secret was simply that he

never stopped learning and improving.

"Mr. Hogan felt a constant desire to gain information, knowing that whatever he found would be improved upon by the players who came after him, who are constantly finding a better way to do it," said Kite. "He was always willing to admit that today's golfers are better than they were twenty years ago.

"His whole life was devoted to learning about golf. While winning tournaments is what everybody tries to do, it was the learning that he sought. He believed the journey was better than getting there."

The lesson of Hogan's success is a rare but familiar one in sports. Duffy Daugherty, the old Michigan State football coach may have put it best. In trying to explain what it took to be successful, Daugherty said you needed only three bones: A wish bone, to dream on; a back bone, for strength and courage to get through the tough times; and a funny bone, to laugh at silly things that happen along the way.

No one ever doubted Hogan's ability to dream, and certainly no one ever questioned his strength and courage.

As for a sense of humor, that was always his secret.

Jerry Tarde

Brush, Brush

I like golf because you can be really terrible at it and still not look much dorkier than anybody else.

Dave Barry

Seven years ago, at the age of forty-three, I was a novice golfer in a vendor-sponsored best-ball tournament. A friend had signed me up a month earlier, and I had spent that month getting lessons from a local pro. The vendor had brought in Johnny Miller as their celebrity photo-op for the attendees, and as I approached the par-3 where Mr. Miller and his entourage lounged, I was more than a little nervous. I had played just three holes of "real" golf that day prior to coming to this tee and hadn't been entirely impressive (I think only one shot of mine had been used at that point).

I stood next to Johnny Miller and had the photo taken, then he asked me how my game was going. "Not bad for a beginner," I answered, and he motioned with his arm for me to take the tee. The tee box was elevated and the postage-stamp green below the hill of Utah sagebrush looked ten miles away. I dragged out a 4-iron and started toward the box.

"Hold it," Johnny said. He stepped up next to me and *sotto-voce* said, "Try an 8-iron." I schlepped back to my cart and retrieved the 8-iron. I spent roughly forty-five queasy seconds over the ball then, finally rushing at the swing, topping a one-hopper three feet into the sagebrush below.

I moved quickly away, hoping to get out of sight of the small gallery as quickly as possible. Johnny Miller had hopped down from his perch, and taking my club from my hand said to the group, "Now here's an example of what I was saying," and he proceeded to discuss fundamentals of the swing. As he finished he said, "Now remember, brush, brush, just brush the grass." He hit my 8-iron to within five feet of the hole.

He handed me my club and said, "Try another one. I think you can beat me."

I was shaking so badly I couldn't tee up the ball for an eternity. Finally, it stayed put. I stepped back to survey a green I'd never forget in a million years and Johnny stepped up and said, "Forget everything, just brush, brush." He turned and walked away.

I felt a calmness I'd never known descend over me. I was in a sort of weird watery realm where sounds were altered and light had a quality akin to sunlight filtered through seaweed. I could hear the breeze but nothing else. When I pulled the club head away from my address, I felt a strange new strength coursing through my entire body, yet I was so fluid, so relaxed, I could have wrapped myself into a golf bag.

The club head descended and "brush, brush" perfectly swept the ball away from the tee. As the ball began to rise, I realized that in my haste I had teed it up behind the silver iron ball denoting the tee-box boundary. No one had said a word.

My shot struck the iron ball—*klongggg*—and rebounded into the cart carrying Johnny Miller and the tournament organizer, who both managed to dive clear. By the time they'd been helped to their feet and dusted off, I was far below, disappearing on to the next hole.

Since that day, I've introduced a number of people I like and admire to the sport of golf. I never teach, only suggest that they begin with lessons from a pro. Well, occasionally I will share the concept of "brush, brush," then I'll duck and watch what happens next.

Steve Minnick

Zen and the Art of Getting Over the Water Hazard

Golf is a spiritual game. It's like Zen. You have to let your mind take over.

Amy Alcott

I have a brother-in-law who could have made it on the Tour if fate and fortune had nudged him in that direction. Instead, he married my sister and became a weekend golfer, playing Saturdays and Sundays at a club called Paradise in Fayetteville, Arkansas.

Heaven Paradise is not. It's a modest course designed by someone whose imagination was not taxed. Unpossessed of an oak-paneled Men's Grill to help brace the athlete both at the turn and at the end of the 18-hole campaign, members are allowed to sign for a hot dog and a beer at the snack bar. Nevertheless, Raul is a man who wakes each morning convinced it's the best of all possible days in the best of all possible places on Earth; and if work lets out early enough he might get to play three holes in Paradise before dark.

He's a cheery optimist. One of those people whose eyes

twinkle all the time except when closed for sleep; and who knows, maybe even then. Raul tells jokes. Jokes he makes up, and most of them are pretty funny. He likes to sing, but not as a soloist. Instead, he encourages all family members to sing along, apparently deriving great pleasure from this musical communion.

Something happened a couple of years ago that took the light out of Raul's eyes. The jokes flew out the window and the music stopped. He was at a crisis point. My sister couldn't figure it, couldn't drag out of him what was wrong. The moping around went on for a couple of weeks. If the attitude hadn't been so contrary to his nature, hadn't been 180 degrees away from the Raul we knew and loved, the condition might have lingered indefinitely. We decided to confront him as a family: to find out what was wrong, then immediately offer him our individual and communal support.

Surrounded, he felt compelled to answer, "I'm off my game," he said. It took some probing, but we learned more. "I've gotten in the habit of throwing my clubs in the water hazard." Apparently it was true, because my sister went in disguise and undercover to observe for herself the murderous drownings of golf clubs. "He behaved like a poor sport," she said, near tears.

Playing, as he always did, in a foursome, the threesome who stood watching her husband's out-of-control fit of temper did not come forward to offer use of their woods, irons or putters. Instead, each of the three took to riding in their carts with golf bags set between their knees. It was an ugly sight. And sad, said my sister.

Later that same day, Raul admitted he'd become addicted to throwing clubs in the water. He no longer even needed to be angry. He just threw them willy-nilly. It was as if he'd lost the power to govern not only his game but his reason.

He was a broken man. A broken man with a total of two clubs left in his bag.

It happens that we count among our family members a few persons of mystic leanings who have leaned so far over into spiritual revelation that they view the world reposed on their sides, propped up by elbows and revealed truth. One of these is a practitioner of Zen. Smiling benignly, which I'm given to understand is one of the requisites of the discipline, our Zen cousin gently took Raul aside and spoke with him for an hour and a half. At the end of the consultation, Raul returned into the warmth of the family circle, and we were amazed to see upon his face a smile of balanced alignment and peace.

Of course she had to crawl on her stomach into the rough to keep herself from view, but my sister did go out the following day to observe Raul's behavior on the golf course. At the first water hazard, she held her breath.

Even from a distance, she sensed a calmness in her husband. She saw him turn his head and say something to his golfing buddies. She saw the threesome laugh. Without apprehension, they laughed. They threw back their heads and laughed, prompting a party of four who were putting on the opposite green to chorus "Shhhhh!"

My sister then exhaled and sat up in the rough. Raul had obviously said something funny. Was he cured of the golf depression that had lapped over into real life, sinking his sunny disposition? Hope rode high.

Then she gasped again, for her husband had entered the lake. Dressed in golf shoes, Bermuda shorts, regulation golf shirt and souvenir cap that proved he'd once played St. Andrews, Raul strode into the snake-infested water. As this was northwest Arkansas and the season summer, snakes were not only proliferate but bold, lying in tangles upon the shore, wriggling into the pond at will.

Suddenly Raul dove beneath the water's surface and

disappeared. My sister ran screaming from the rough onto the fairway. Kicking coiled vipers aside, she stood wringing her hands at lake's edge. Up he popped. Arising triumphant from the baptismal waters, Raul held aloft his 9-iron.

Whenever she tells this story, my sister dramatizes the moment. "It was like Arthur emerging with Excalibur," she says.

We've never been privy to the exact words our Zen cousin said to Raul. One of the more prosaic among us speculates our mystical cousin merely suggested Raul get a grip, get in there and retrieve his clubs. Whatever happened to turn the tide, to this day his clubs remain sacrosanct, polished, hooded, safe and bagged.

Micki McClelland

The Clown Prince of Golf

A *man without a sense of humor is like a wagon without springs—he is jolted disagreeably by every little pebble in the road.*

Henry Ward Beecher

Pro-ams take two basic forms: the normal week-to-week events populated by local businessmen who fork over the fee to play with Greg Norman or Nick Price—or players far less famous but, they often find, just as much fun. Then there are the celebrity pro-ams that mix business people with actors, politicians and athletes. These tend to be major yuck-fests, personified in recent years by Bill Murray, who has become the dominant figure at Pebble Beach.

Several years ago, Jeff Sluman found himself in Murray's foursome. A big Murray fan, Sluman was looking forward to the experience. It was a memorable week for Sluman but, he admits, he had some trying moments. "On the first day I three-putted three holes on the front nine," he says. "I just kept missing short ones. We get to the eleventh hole (at Poppy Hills), and I hit my tee shot about forty feet above the pin. As we're walking off the tee, I hear Bill say to [partner] Scott Simpson, 'Now we're really going to find out about him.' I knew I was in trouble."

Sluman left his first putt about six feet short and could feel the yips coming on as he lined up his second putt. He got over the ball and was about to draw the putter back when he heard Murray say, "Ladies and gentlemen, I need some love for this man. Right now, can you all say 'love!'"

Sluman stepped back while the crowd, coached by Murray, yelled, "We love you, Jeff!" several times. Sluman put his hand over his heart to show how touched he was, then began lining the putt up again. Sure enough, just as he was about to start his stroke, he heard Murray's voice again. "This man needs more love. More! Can I hear you, now!"

By now, Simpson had all but dissolved into a puddle of laughter near the edge of the green. This time, as all the love washed down on him, Sluman pretended to cry. The third time, much to his surprise, Murray let him putt. And, even more to Sluman's surprise, the putt went in. "I think I got a bigger roar than on the eighteenth hole when I won the PGA [Championship]," he says.

He deserved it.

John Feinstein

Golf Carts Do Not
Have Four-Wheel Drive

The revelation that golf carts do not have four-wheel drive came to me one morning as I tried to find my ball in the mud, which I found out later was actually not part of the golf course at all but rather the site of a pending condo project, half a block away. I must have missed the out-of-bounds marker when I was crossing the freeway. It was just one more lesson in the complex world of golf.

I remember the first time I played. My twosome was paired up with another twosome. After my tee-off on the first hole went somewhat awry, landing on the clubhouse roof, one of the other players asked if I had a handicap. I thought his joke in poor taste and threatened him with my 9-iron. Now, of course, I realize that having a handicap is a good thing, even if it is 52.

Learning the rules and language of golf is crucial. It separates the obvious beginner from someone just having another bad day. Therefore, I have from experience compiled a few lessons that may help other novices.

If the instructor tells you to address the ball, do not take out a pen and write "to green" on the ball.

Try not to stand on asphalt in the summer while wearing golf shoes, unless you are with a very strong friend.

The easiest way to find a lost golf ball is to ask the guy limping in the next fairway.

Never insist that your spouse golf. It can lead to only two results. One, she/he plays really badly, complains for four hours and ruins your whole day. Or, he/she plays really well, offers four hours of suggestions on how you might do better and ruins your whole day.

A double bogey is not a strong drink from the movie *Casablanca*. It means two over par. And not a bad score at all. If they have a name for it it's a good score. There is no name for a fifteen.

A chip is not something left behind by a foraging cow. That's a flap. A chip is a carefully choreographed half-swing that often goes further than your original drive.

A divot is a lump of grass that flies up from where the golf ball used to be. A damnit is a lump of grass that flies up in your face as you hit two feet behind the ball.

A slice is a ball that curves to the right. A bad slice is a ball that lands behind you.

A tough lie has double meanings. It's when you have to come up with an excuse—for the umpteenth time—as to why it took six hours to play nine holes and why your breath smells like nacho chips and beer. It also refers to a difficult spot to have to hit your ball from. For instance, the base of a tree, the crook of a tree or the upper branches of a tree.

Heavy rough is the area along the edge of the fairway just before your ball is legally out of bounds. A good rule of thumb—if the guy beside you is barbecuing, you're probably out of bounds.

And finally, Club Rules imply that you are not penalized by foreign objects on the fairway. Therefore, if you knock out a tourist with your drive, you are allowed to move your ball one club's length from the body.

Now that you understand some of the basics, you should be able to better appreciate the game. And, you can focus on some of the more intriguing idiosyncrasies of golf, like if it's completely made out of metal, why do they call it a 3-wood?

Ernie Witham

De Profundis, Homo
(About Some Deep Stuff, Man)

It is not a matter of life and death. It is not that important. But it is a reflection of life, and so the game is an enigma wrapped in a mystery impaled on a conundrum.

Peter Alliss

Philosophers down through the ages have produced the concepts that have shaped all of our present governments, our societies and our very way of life. So, isn't it curious that the Yellow Pages list hundreds of golf instructors, golf stores and golf courses, but not one single philosopher? Absolutely none, zero, zilch, nada ... a totality of nothingness manifested in a positive universal absence, as a philosopher might say. I believe there would be more call for philosophers today if only more were known about their past statements and questions on the metaphysics of golf. I researched the subject (without a government grant) and unearthed a veritable strip mine of wisdom. Most basic perhaps was philosopher Ronnie Da Cart's famous pronouncement, "I golf, therefore I am."

Da Cart was trying to establish a starting point, a foundation of irrefutable truth upon which he could build a philosophy to cover all existence. His starting premise collapsed when it was challenged by the Mexican philosopher and publinks player Manuel Cant. Cant said that if golf were the basic truth about existence, then poor golf would prove a poor existence. Cant knew that was wrong because he had caddied for many rich Gringos who played very poor golf but had a very nice existence.

During the months when one can't be out on the course personally struggling with the existential mysteries of golf, it is a good time to exercise the mind with some of the following classic golf/philosophy conundrums:

"If a tree falls over in the middle of a forest and no one is around, does it count as a free drop if it comes down on top of a ball?" Yes, but nobody will hear about it.

"When an irresistible force meets an immovable obstruction, do you get line-of-sight relief?" No, because Einstein proved that light bends; golf rules do not. And since light bends, the line of sight must curve around the obstruction.

"Is heredity or environment more responsible for the development of a slice?" A predisposition to slicing is in the genes, although it becomes most pronounced when there is an environment of trees, water or out of bounds in the direction of the slice.

"How many angels can dance on the head of a pin?" Angels don't dance on the pin; they just hover over the green and keep track of bad language. There are other winged creatures that waddle around on some greens and are the cause of some of the bad language. In this vein it was India's great naturalist/philosopher, Washadurtee Ultrabalata, who stated, "Animal rights should be extended only to animals who are toilet trained."

"What is the sound of one hand clapping?" My friend Al

Van Dine solved this Zen puzzle when he said the sound of one hand clapping is the sudden joyous outburst of silence that comes from your opponent when you miss a short putt. Al has also written at length about dimpleness. Writes Al, "Dimples have perplexed philosophers because they represent intervals of non-ball and yet are presumed to be part of the ball whose absence defines their existence." How true. In closing, the question all children ask, and the appropriate answer: "Why is the sky blue?" Because it can't play golf even on the nicest days. Go in peace.

Frank J. Haller

The Secret

It is a thousand pities that neither Aristotle nor Shakespeare was a golfer. There is no game that strips the soul so naked.

Horace Hutchinson

It was a glorious May day and the air was filled with the fragrance of a thousand magnificent blossoms. I was over-whelmed by the sights and sounds of spring as I slowly walked the path to the practice range.

I stood on the practice range to prepare for my usual Saturday match, but of more importance to me was find-ing a remedy for a snarling slice that had recently infected my game.

I began as usual, lofting a few gentle sand wedges to the red flag. Gradually, I worked my way down to the 7-iron, striking fairly even-tempered shots to another flag. Even with my particular collection of neurosynaptic connec-tions I was able to play a fairly decent game—that is, until I was pressed to hit the ball more than 150 yards. Then suddenly it was a question of how far left I should aim.

I hit several passable shots with the 7-iron before it

happened. Then as quickly as it came, it slipped out of my consciousness and drifted away. What was I just thinking? I began to reconstruct my last five minutes of conscious thought. It wasn't easy. But there was something, and suddenly I felt an exhilarating impulse traveling up my right forearm as I neatly crushed another shot. My, that felt good. What did I do?

A voice inside spoke to me softly, very faintly. My thoughts played back again and again and I heard a faint sound over and over. Supinaaaaation. Supinaaaaation. Supinaaaaation.

Huh? Then I realized what it was. It seemed so hard to believe, but echoing in my head was Ben Hogan's famous word. This was particularly annoying since I, for one, had given up on supination a long time ago. Here I was, plagued all my life with a shot pattern that moved right to right, and I certainly didn't need to know how to supinate my left wrist. What I really wanted was a way to square the blade.

I smashed another 7-iron and watched with amazement as the ball flew high and landed well beyond the white flag. I began to sense that my body was reacting differently to the club. Something had changed, but what?

From the pile of balls I pulled another toward me. Then I noticed what, for me, was an amazing revelation: I was standing there like a duck. My right foot was not square to the line, but instead was pointed away from the ball. Taking the club back a few times, I could feel a difference in my right hip—that I felt coiled and poised behind the ball. As I swung down into the ball I sensed a tremendous leverage to hit down and through. I felt as though I could hit the ball as hard as I wanted. Finally, there it was—my secret.

I hit several dozen more balls. I turned and looked behind me and two smiling faces, old-lined faces, set a steady gaze on me. "You've got something there, son," one man finally said. "Lightning in a bottle. Better enjoy it."

I did. But at the same time I was frightened—afraid to let the 7-iron out of my hands.

I needed to know if the magic would work with other clubs in the bag, so I drew out a 4-iron. As I rehearsed my swing, the club sweetly sweeping across the top of the turf, I also rehearsed my disappointment, anticipating the return of my errant ways. I realized my objective—to feel a complete follow-through, with the right hand really delivering the blow—so I decided to just let it rip. The ball flew well beyond any I'd ever struck with the club. I hit another, and another; and after twenty more I swear they all could have been covered with a picnic blanket.

I pulled out the 3-iron, then the 2-, and suddenly I was in uncharted territory—knocking balls to the fence at the back of the range. I finished the practice session by hitting 9-irons to within ten feet of the sign marked 135; I think I hit the sign five or six times.

I met Ted in the locker room a few minutes before our Saturday match, where I said I was going to try some new strategies on the course today. "You really should try something new," he said, his sardonic smile meeting my confident grin.

Ted played first on the opening hole and cut his drive to the right edge of the fairway. Reiterating my intent to try something different, I announced my selection of a 3-iron. Instead, I drew a 5-iron and laced a beautiful shot that landed a mere fifteen yards behind Ted's drive. He acknowledged my effort with a quiet "good shot."

I hit a wedge to within eight feet and Ted again remarked, "Good shot." He hit up and matched my two-putt par.

We were both about 235 yards from the front edge of the green at No. 2, a medium-length par-5. I drew a 2-iron from my bag, set up, aiming slightly left of the flag, and fired. The ball soared down the fairway, landed softly at the front of the green, and rolled up neatly about twelve feet away for eagle.

Ted said nothing. I missed the putt but tapped in for a birdie and went to the third tee 1-up. Ted's play from that point on became decidedly lackluster, so for the rest of the day I was chiefly pitted against the golf course.

But everything was distorted. I was hitting the ball so far, my biggest problem became choosing the right club. Finally I resolved to hit two or three clubs less than usual, and that seemed to do the trick as I came home with a sizzling 30. Together with the 33 I shot on the front, I was suddenly the holder of the course record, a shocking feat considering my previous best score was a dozen strokes higher.

I was beside myself. I didn't know what to think. I played several rounds that week and shot in the 60s each time. In my locker someone placed a white Hogan cap with a note that read, "Enjoy it while you've got it." That was puzzling, but not as much as my new golf game was.

About two weeks later I hit my first slice. Three weeks after that I was shooting in the mid-80s again. Ted began taunting me, calling me "the greatest golfer that never was." I was powerless to respond. As quickly as the magic had come, it was gone.

In September the letter arrived. It was a simple white envelope with a return address that read, "The Hogan Company, Fort Worth, Texas." As I opened it I was amazed to find a handwritten note from the man himself. "I want to congratulate you for your recent success in breaking my course record," Mr. Hogan wrote. "I will always remember the round I played there in 1953. My score of 64 stood for all these years as one of my finest achievements, and I know just how well you must have played to break it. Best wishes, and enjoy it while you've got it."

I was shattered. The man who knew what it was like to

possess "the secret" knew also of its mercurial flight. He knew that I would lose it. He knew it was only temporary. My wife is just taking up the game. I've toyed with teaching her for several years, but I never wanted to push it. I wasn't sure, but I thought her recent enthusiasm may have been out of a desire to empathize with my shattering devolution as a player. She invited me out to the practice range to see her progress. She said she'd really enjoyed hitting balls lately, and attributed her success to a videotape she used to learn the swing. I was intrigued and questioned her about it. As she hammered a middle iron she slyly said, "Oh, it was just something I recorded one day when you were hitting balls on the range."

J. G. Nursall

Thank God I Have a Day Job

Standing on the 2nd tee at St. Andrews Old Course, my playing partner and touring professional, Paul McGinley, turned to me with a wink and said, "Congratulations, you just managed to miss the two biggest fairways in golf." I laughed. Strange as it sounds, I had! OB to the right on number 18 and a shanked 3-iron off the 1st tee at the Old Course. Ouch!

We started the day playing off of number 10, and now as a team, were 10 under par after twenty-eight holes. (Yesterday we played Kingsbarns and Paul had gone around in 6 under.) Today, he was on his way to a course record–tying 64. So shank or missed fairway, whatever, nothing could break my humor. I was in heaven.

It was Friday, second round of the four-day Dunhill Links Championship Pro-Am in Scotland. Paul and I, along with Sven Struver and his amateur partner, legendary downhiller Franz Klammer, were playing the Old Course at St. Andrews. Tomorrow we would be heading to Carnoustie, with a fourth and final round to be played back at the Old Course on Sunday—if our team made the cut.

I was here because I had played in Michael Douglas's charity golf event in Los Angeles earlier in the year. There

I met Iain Banner, part of the Dunhill team who sponsored the event in Scotland. He had promised an invitation to all celebrity players involved in Michael's tournament and true to his word, a few months later, I received the invite in the mail for a week of golf on three of the sport's most hallowed tracks. *Are you kidding,* I thought, *I'm in!* I sent the signed application back that same day.

I arrived Monday afternoon from New York, determined to squeeze in as much golf as possible during the practice rounds before the tournament officially got under way on Thursday. The drawing for playing partners was Tuesday night. There were a lot of pros playing, but most were from the European tour. Very few pros had come from America in the wake of September 11. The list of actors from America was comparably short: Michael Douglas, Samuel Jackson, Hugh Grant (from Los Angeles) and myself.

Johann Rupert, chairman of the tournament and a bois-terous and generous host, read the names of the pairings. Kyle MacLachlan with Paul McGinley . . . people near me nodded their approval. Great golfer, Ryder Cup, competi-tive but with an easygoing manner. I just hoped I wouldn't get in his way because we're talking about an $800,000 purse for the winner.

My concern, naturally, was about my golf swing. I was a skillful enough player, having grown up playing golf from an early age. Tutored by my dad and his various golf-ing buddies, I had developed a pretty good-looking swing in the Tom Weiskopf mode. Upright, with a strong motion down and under the ball. I played on my high school golf team, usually sixth or seventh on the squad, occasionally putting together a decent round of 4 or 5 over. The prob-lem now was playing time. I usually managed about a dozen rounds a year. Enough to remember what I used to be able to do, but not enough to have much of a chance of carrying it off. Visions of a televised disaster on the week-end began dancing through my head. So Friday afternoon, after struggling through my first round at Kingsbarns and a disastrous second round at the Old Course, I threw myself at the mercy of golf wizard Robert Baker and his teaching partner Grant Hepburn.

The tournament sponsors, in their infinite wisdom, had set up a teaching facility next to the practice range for those unfortunate amateurs, like myself, who had lost (or maybe never really had) a swing. Well, after watching my swing and putting it on video, they dismantled me and then proceeded to put me back together in the image of Ernie Els. (He was the swing image on the computer that I attempted to emulate and one of the many pros Robert works with on a consistent basis.) When I say dismantled, I'm not kidding. New grip, new address at the ball, new body position at the top of my backswing—a complete overhaul—and it worked. I began to hit the ball. I mean, I began to crunch the ball. And it was straight! Years of hearing "from the inside out" but never really getting it finally occurred because my new position at address allowed it to happen naturally. Robert and Grant had saved me in one afternoon. I was reinvigorated and deter-mined to put this new swing into practice.

The following morning we drove north to Carnoustie. It was raining sideways. The tournament had been plagued by fog and rain all week. Today we were getting the worst of it, and playing the toughest course of the three. Our team managed to get around in 3 under, Paul playing bril-liantly in brutal conditions, seventeen pars and one birdie. I had a moment of brilliance as well, hitting out of the infa-mous Spectacles bunker on number 14, and making the putt for a legit birdie. The new swing was still a work in progress (what did I expect?) and I was anything but con-sistent, but I sure felt more confident.

That afternoon I was back at the practice range for more work. I began to dream about golf shots. The world and its troubles faded away. Outside contact with the real world was limited to a good-night call to my fiancée, who was incredibly supportive of my experience, and my father halfway around the world. I called him each day during my round, and on one occasion, as the cameras rolled, handed Paul the phone to say hello. My father, watching the Golf Channel at 4:00 A.M. in Yakima, Washington, saw himself talking to Paul McGinley on the 12th tee at Carnoustie with his son in the background. That moment alone was worth the trip.

My father had played over in Scotland about ten years ago on a golfing pilgrimage. He spoke to me about "links golf," about the wind, the quixotic weather, about the rugged nature of the Scots and their love of golf. These people really know the game. There is no wasted applause simply because you managed to land the ball on the green, no. You'd better have knocked the ball inside of twelve feet from the rough over some gorse with a 5-iron. Now that's a shot that would get you some well-deserved appreciation.

I had a few of those, but many more of the other variety. Not quite as bad as the shanked 3-iron, mind you, but enough to be grateful I had a day job that wasn't dependent on driving the ball three hundred yards or hitting greens in regulation.

Perhaps the greatest lesson I took away from that week of close observation is this: there is just no way for the amateur golfer at home to appreciate the professional golfer's process during their round. Every shot is executed with the conviction that the ball will do exactly what the pro wants it to do.

And it's not the galleries that create the pressure. It's the elusive dance between the physical and the mental inside the golfer. The continual shedding of tension, moment by moment. The unshakable conviction that you are holding the right club in your hand for the shot, and that the body will perform with the precision that the mind demands. Add your livelihood to that, and the pressure seems unbearable. I watched as Paul McGinley methodically did this over four days of tournament golf, and it has forever changed the way I play, practice and watch the game.

It's the last day and Paul and I have made the team cut, by one stroke. Even more exciting (and nerve-wracking), Paul is tied for the lead with Paul Lawrie at 14 under. This means I will be in the foursome teeing off in the final position from the 1st tee on the Old Course. (My hands are sweating at the computer just thinking about it.)

First tee. 11:27 A.M. I'm standing there with the coleaders of the tournament . . . breathe. No one expects anything from me, right? *Bang!* A good (not great) drive with a little draw down the left side of the fairway, and we're off. Paul McGinley hits an iron to the right and the ball takes an unlucky hop into the burn (creek). He starts with a bogey 5, Lawrie birdies and just like that Paul's dropped two strokes off the lead. I manage a par and would have been content to head back to the clubhouse and bask in that accomplishment. As it turns out, I redeem myself fairly well over the day, hanging in at 2 over after fifteen holes, before the wheels come off. I proceed to knock the ball OB on number 16, take a triple bogey 7 on the Road Hole, and on my old nemesis number 18—you guessed it —OB on the right. A bittersweet finish to a round of golf I would never have thought myself capable of at the beginning of the week.

McGinley struggled during the final round as his putter went cold, watching Lawrie knock in long putt after long putt. I could feel his frustration. It was not to be

McGinley's day, yet he always had a supportive word to say to me as he recognized I was putting up some pretty good numbers. Lawrie played a solid round of golf, holding off a late charge from Ernie Els by sinking a fifty-foot putt from the Valley of Sin on the 18th for a birdie and sole possession of first place. The crowd roared its approval as the putt dropped and Lawrie skipped sideways in triumph. In that moment, it all seemed quite surreal, standing just off to the side of the green, witnessing a great finish by a great player, feeling like I was included in this elite brotherhood.

And just like that, it was over, and a kind of emptiness descended over the course. I didn't want to let go yet; I wasn't ready to return to my world. I said good-bye to my partner and new friend Paul McGinley, wanting to say something encouraging and knowing it would sound ridiculous, so I thanked him for his company and for his words of support that had meant so much to me.

I walked back down number 18. There's something haunting about an empty golf course at the end of the day, with the echoes of the little truths it has revealed to each competitor. I began to think about tomorrow, my trip back home and how my experience in Scotland might resonate in me. New friends, a new appreciation for the game and the men who play it well, and just maybe a new swing that would carry me back to my world and the solitude of the practice range, where believe me, I will be imagining a hundred perfect drives straight down the 18th fairway on the Old Course at St. Andrews.

Kyle MacLachlan

Thursday Is Men's Day

A state judge has put a Massachusetts country club under direct court supervision, saying compelling evidence at trial showed systematic sex discrimination that warranted judicial oversight in the public interest. The judge will personally oversee putting new policies into effect at Haverhill Golf and Country Club.

—News item, January 2000

Owing to a harsh winter and business overload in the spring, it had been close to four months since I'd been out to my country club, so you can imagine my surprise when I drove up and saw all the surreys with the fringe on top. They were lined up where the golf carts used to be.

I parked under an oak and immediately went over to speak to the cart boy, who was now a girl. "Do you work here, miss?" I asked.

"I'm the cart person, yes," she said, eating yogurt out of a cup and leaning on a carousel horse that was attached to a surrey. "I'm Ellen."

"You're new, Ellen."

"Yeah. I was hired after James got karate chopped."

"James got what?"

"He called Francesca 'honey,' or 'babe' or something like

that, so she gave him a karate chop in the neck and fired him."

"Who's Francesca?"

"You don't know Francesca? She's the head pro."

"She is? What happened to Dutch?"

"Dutch who?"

"Dutch Miller. He's been the pro here for fifteen years."

"There's a Dutch who works in the kitchen."

"Dutch is the chef now?"

"I'm not sure you'd call a dishwasher a chef."

As calmly as possible, I said, "Tell me, Ellen. By what set of, shall I say, bizarre circumstances did somebody named Francesca get to be our head pro?"

"I don't know. You'd have to ask Juliette."

"Juliette . . . ?"

"Boy, you haven't been around here in a while, have you? Juliette's the director of golf."

I stormed into the golf shop and went over to a young woman behind the counter. "Are you Francesca?"

"I'm Samantha. Francesca's playing in a tournament this week."

"Where's Juliette?"

"She's playing in the same tournament."

I looked around. The shop was mostly stocked with women's clubs and women's apparel.

Heavy on the sarcasm, I said, "Do you have any fuchsia Titleists?"

"No, but we have egg yolk and lime," she said seriously.

I decided I needed a drink, a double Junior, and went around to the men's grill. Only the large sign above the door said it was now called Emily's Cafe.

"Hi, I'm a member," I said to the woman who greeted me. "I see the room has a new name, but I assume I can still get a cocktail."

"Only on Thursdays, I'm afraid," the woman said.

I countered, "You're telling me I can only come in here on Thursdays?"

"Thursday is men's day on the golf course. Naturally, you can drink and dine in here on Thursdays. You're not familiar with the new club rules? They've been in the monthly club bulletins."

"I guess I should have been reading them."

"Yes, I dare say you should have."

"Are you Emily?"

"No, I'm Dorothy. Emily's playing in a tournament this week."

"What if I hit your palm with a little whip-out, Dorothy? Do you suppose that would help me get a drink?"

"Tipping is not allowed, sir."

"What about begging? Is that permissible?"

"Sir, I will be happy to send a drink around to you in the men's locker room. It's where the women's used to be, of course."

"Of course."

I had my drink in what was now the small and cramped men's locker room, where an attendant told me he could bring me a zucchini and beet sandwich if I was hungry. I declined limply.

When I went outside to leave I found two female security guards standing by my car. One of them said, "You parked in Francesca's spot."

"Sorry," I said. "I didn't know."

"You'll know next time," she said.

I drove home on four punctured tires and desperately started looking in storage closets for my old croquet set.

Dan Jenkins

The Old-Guy Game

I went to the golf course alone the other day. There were four carts parked beside the 1st tee, and a young guy in a Greg Norman hat was taking gigantic practice swings in preparation for slicing his drive into the 18th fairway.

The pro offered to run me out to the 2nd tee so I could jump ahead. A group on the 3rd waved me through. I ran into another group on five, so I ducked behind the snack shack and went to No. 7. I had clear sailing for one shot.

That caught me up to a threesome of old-timers, who were moving down the fairway as slowly as if they were worried about land mines. They invited me to play through—many clear holes lay ahead—but I asked if could join them.

I like playing with old guys. My tempo drops out of the red zone, and I stop trying to hit the ball farther than I can—the opposite of what happens when I play with twenty-five-year-olds. I enjoy hearing stories about what the course or the club or the members were like forty years ago, when everything was better than it is now. Every so often, an old guy who can no longer reach the fairway with a driver will turn out to be a former hotshot—as I'll discover later, when I recognize his name on one of the plaques on the grillroom walls.

I like looking into old guys' bags: mismatched irons, woods made of wood, grips resurfaced with electrical tape, chippers, Gintys, Samurais, 23-woods, putters with punch marks on their faces and ball retrievers that extend so far you could use them to rescue your glasses from the Mariana Trench. The guy in the Greg Norman hat would sneer, but to me those golf bags prove that with good luck and the right equipment you can keep playing until the day you drop.

You also need the right swing, of course. Two of my companions the other day had one that I've been studying: a short, turnless lunge—the move you make when you throw dirt with a shovel. It's the old-guy swing, and it's the product of a compromise worked out by old bones, stiff muscles and osteoarthritis. I've been studying it because I suspect that someday it will be my swing. I want to be prepared.

Both players aimed left and hit right. They took their clubs back belt-high, then leaned forward and swatted. Their shots didn't go very far, but we never had to look for a ball except mine. After three 3-woods apiece, they were each close enough to the green to hit pitching wedge, just about the only iron that either of them still used. They drilled their putts, got two strokes and took the hole with net birdies, while I three-putted for a 5.

I still nurse a fantasy that I will wake up one morning and be Ernie Els, or even Morris Hatalsky. But it pays to be realistic, and time is running out. There's a lot to be said for the old-guy game. If my regular foursome wouldn't make fun of me, I would almost be tempted to switch right now.

David Owen

When You Wish upon a Par

Golf is a game in which one endeavors to control a ball with implements ill adapted for the purpose.

Woodrow Wilson

One defibrillator exhibit was okay, but two? I have enough reminders of where my physical health might be heading every morning when I have to suck it up—and in—to button my pants. The thought of emergency resuscitation is not something I particularly like to be reminded of at a merchandise show. Although with what they were feeding us in the media room, knowing at least one of those machines was close by did offer some comfort when stepping back in the chicken Parmesan line a second time.

I've known for some time that what my golf game truly lacks is more gizmos, gadgets, swing aids and nonconforming equipment, so my attendance at golf's version of Disney World—the annual PGA Merchandise Show in Orlando, Florida—was to determine just what it would take to get me closer to the hole and farther away from those defibrillators.

There was a golf glove touted to increase distance ten to twenty yards and prevent a slice. I tried it on, and it immediately slapped me upside the head. Since I've always believed that I could cure my slice and play better if someone would just slap me upside the head once in a while, I have to say the product lived up to its billing. I found another glove called the "Knuckle Glove" that helps you maintain a consistent grip on the club, presumably giving you a nice tasty knuckle sandwich every time you regrip at the top of your backswing.

I next strolled past an exhibit featuring miniature golf consultants. I tried to imagine what one of their sales pitches might sound like. ("Well, the clown's nose and windmill are certainly rich in the traditions of miniature golf, but our research has shown that dinosaurs, action heroes and dragons are trending strong in the market right now.")

Software is big, of course. One program took your golf score, analyzed it and then gave you tips based on what that analysis suggested. In my case, the tip was to buy one of those gloves that slapped me upside the head to cure my slice. I decided not to buy.

Oh, you can now buy antitheft devices for your clubs. I guess with the price of clubs approaching what you used to be able to buy a car for a generation or so ago, I suppose this is a worthwhile investment. Expect one day to see "The Club" in use at bag drops all across the country, but primarily near urban areas.

You can now earn a degree in professional golf management, from an accredited university no less. The B.G. program (bachelor of golf) probably includes concentrations in such critical areas as how to say "$150, walk or ride" with a straight face. "Optimizing the Routing of the Beverage Cart" and "The 400 Percent Pro Shop Markup: Theory and Practice" no doubt round out the curriculum.

A product will tee the ball up for you on the practice tee, thereby avoiding all that pesky bending and reaching when attempting to get a little recreation and exercise. (Note: See "defibrillators" above.) Another product for the practice tee promises to provide up to twenty-six degrees of cooling in the practice area. Oh, and air-conditioned golf carts are available in selected markets as well. It's always been a bit of a struggle to work up a sweat in our chosen sport. Soon, apparently, it will be next to impossible.

Myrtle Beach alert: You will no longer have to set the oven in your efficiency on "broil" in order to dry your shoes after a rain-soaked round. A product available now will not only dry your shoes but remove odor as well. That means Big Al no longer has to keep his shoes out on the balcony or windowsill during your annual hajj to the golf Mecca of the universe. And with wet, smelly shoes a thing of the past, figuring out how to stuff four sets of clubs into that Ford Aspire you rented just became easier with a trunk organizer called the Golf Butler. Figure one day the Golf Butler to be equipped with software that will make tee times for you, as well as change twenties into nice crisp ones for the evening's silicon fantasies at those gentleman's clubs.

And just what I needed: another swing-training gizmo, this one with two laser beams emitting from the bottom and top of the shaft. The theory is to keep the laser beam on a straight line (represented by a piece of tape stuck to the floor) on the takeaway (the bottom beam at the end of the shaft) and at the top of your swing (the top beam emitting from the top of the grip area). A proper swing will show the laser beams from both positions to remain on the tape. In my own experience, that didn't happen, but the salesman did say that with my reverse pivot, outside in, flying-elbow swing plane, I probably inadvertently performed a laser eye surgical procedure on myself.

One outfit extolled the virtues of its strengths in financial planning by claiming its goal was to eliminate income taxes, capital gains taxes and wealth-transfer taxes. Utilizing "offshore strategies" was also one of its boasts. I bit my tongue and chose not to ask if they also knew where Hoffa was buried, lest that also entail me to carry an unidentified package through the Miami airport on their behalf.

Back at the Orlando airport, instead, I was having a brew and trying to digest the product and services overload I had experienced the past four days. I felt completely wrung out, head spinning and thoughts reeling over how much golf stuff is out there driving our economy. What if everyone got as upset as me over rotten play and just quit? Hackers, or former hackers, might just bring down the whole global economy. It was a chilling thought.

I looked up from my ruminations and saw a young mom pushing a stroller with a child awash in Disney stuff. I looked at the mom's face and saw she was the one with the pacifier in her mouth.

I knew exactly how she felt.

Reid Champagne

Humor at Its Best

I had a wonderful experience on the golf course today. I had a hole in nothing. Missed the ball and sank the divot.

Don Adams

Hartman was a big man. Physically, he was a solid 280 pounds and stood around six-foot-two. He had a presence about him that demanded attention when he entered a room, and he had a twinkle in his eye. Oh that twinkle! Hartman was the kind of man who could talk a half dozen men into walking outside in the snow in their bare feet, and still be in position to close the door and lock it, before he actually had to go out himself.

Hartman was the person who introduced me to golf. He loved the game. On one occasion, when we were younger, a group of us rented a farmhouse for the summer. It was a place where we could go at the end of the week and just do whatever comes to mind. Hartman suggested one evening that we go to the local golf course the following day and play a round. Eight of us agreed immediately and went off to bed at a reasonable hour, which at the time was not the norm, so we could get an early start.

The next morning we arrived at the golf course early enough to be the first two groups off. Being a small "farmers field" type of golf course we fit right in. The skill level of all the participants varied from just above beginner to really struggling for a bogey round. Hartman was one of the more accomplished players out that day, but it was obvious that he was struggling along with the rest of us.

Finally, after the increasing frustration seemed to win out, Hartman snapped! He stood up on the tee of the par-3, 157-yard 8th hole and pulled his driver from his bag. With a great deal of drama, for which Hartman was known, he pulled back on that club and pasted that poor ball with every ounce of his 280 pounds. The ball took off as if it knew it was no longer wanted and headed straight for the trees and the river just to the left of the hole. By this time the other group had already joined us on the tee and the seven of us were howling with laughter. No one really tracked the ball except Hartman, who cringed as we all heard the ball hit a tree to the left of the green. What none of us were ready for was the look on his face as he excitedly asked us, "Did you see that?"

"See what?" was the common reply.

"My ball. It came off that tree, bounced off that rock in front of the green and rolled towards the pin. I think I'm close!"

"Yeah, right. That ball was so far gone you'll never find it," I said with a note of finality.

Fully convinced that there was no way in the world Hartman's ball was even on the golf course any more, let alone anywhere near the hole, we watched as Hartman teed up what we considered to be his serious ball. He hit it fat with his 8-iron, and we all started to walk toward the green disregarding everything he had to say about it being a provisional ball.

As we approached the green we were giving Hartman a pretty hard time. It was becoming more and more obvious his ball wasn't on the green. Hartman couldn't believe it.

"I know I saw it head in this direction." he said with absolute conviction.

"Maybe it's in the hole!" suggested Pete in a sarcastic tone.

Pete walked up to the hole, looked down and yelled back to Hartman.

"What are you hitting?"

"Top Flite number 4" was Hartman's reply.

You could have knocked Pete over with a feather as he leaned over and picked the ball out of the hole.

"It's in the hole," was all he was able to stammer.

Hartman was the last one of us to arrive at the hole to authenticate the ball.

"That's it. I don't believe it! A hole-in-one!" he exclaimed excitedly.

The rest of us just stood there with our mouths open and looks of utter disbelief on our faces. It wasn't possible, yet seven of us witnessed it. The most incredible shot in history.

We finished our round in a state of excited numbness, anxiously waiting to tell someone, anyone, what we had witnessed.

Back at the clubhouse we were indulging in a few beers and regaling the story among ourselves and anyone else who would listen. That's when someone suggested we call the local newspaper and maybe get our pictures taken and enjoy our fifteen minutes of fame. While we were planning all the TV appearances and endorsement contracts, Hartman sat at the end of the table with that twinkle in his eye. Oh that twinkle! It was the unmistakable tone of his laugh at that point that removed all doubt. We had been duped!

Being the first group off that morning put us in the unique position of being the first to each hole. Hartman took advantage of that fact when playing the 6th hole, which paralleled the 8th.

Having hit his ball in the narrow stretch of woods between the two holes, no one thought anything of his activities while he was looking for his ball. While wandering around in this no-man's-land he meandered over to the 8th green, casually dropped his ball in the hole and then wandered back to the 6th fairway as if he had just played his ball out of the rough. The rest of that hole and the next one leading up to the 8th was a display of acting on a Shakespearean level, to bring his apparent frustration level to a peak on the 8th tee.

The number of people with the imagination and savvy to pull off a prank of this magnitude and make all his victims feel good about being had are few and far between. This was the case with most of his pranks, the ones who laughed hardest were the ones at the center of the prank. We lost Hartman to cancer at the young age of forty-three, but he left behind a legacy of good-natured humor, a zest for life and a true appreciation of the good friends he had.

I miss the big man.

John Spielbergs

The Ten Inevitabilities of Hacker Golf

It took me seventeen years to get three thousand hits in baseball. I did it in one afternoon on the golf course.

Hank Aaron

It never fails. . . .

1) You're standing in the fairway 220 yards from the green. The group in front of you is still on the green. You know that if you hit the ball you will fly it to the green, send that group scattering, and once again have four angry golfers waiting for you at the bar. So, you wait until they completely clear, then you duff the shot and end up 75 yards short.

2) You're wearing your lucky hat, your lucky socks and your lucky underwear. Things are in your favor. And even though you typically shoot 90, you've had a really good back nine and you are at 76 with only two par-4s to go for your best score all year. Correspondingly, you triple bogey both holes, your only triple bogeys of the day, to end up shooting—you guessed it—90.

3) After careful consideration you decide to hit a high

soft lob shot onto the elevated green just like Tiger might do, but you hit it flat with your wedge and line drive it over the green. On the next hole, faced with a similar shot, you decide to bounce it on with a 9-iron like Sergio might do, but instead hit it straight up into the air and leave it three feet short of the green.

4) After muffing the tee shot, sculling the approach, pitching it into the sand trap and taking three shots to barely get it out and onto the green, you make a forty-five-foot, double-breaking, downhill putt that you couldn't make again if your life depended on it.

5) You place your tee shot right behind a tree so large that it should be named after a president. By some miracle not only do you get your iron shot around the thing, but it hooks right back into the middle of the fairway. On the next tee shot you land fifty yards behind a three-foot-tall sapling no bigger around than your finger. Using a lofted fairway wood, you hit the little tree dead on, the ball pops up into the air and lands five yards behind you.

6) You are playing really well and, therefore, decide to dole out a "bit of advice" on someone else's game. Instantly, your game goes south faster than a Canadian goose in late November.

7) You decide to wear your brand-new, birthday-gift golf shoes to a course you've never played even though they are not broken in yet. Upon arrival, you find out the club has a cart-path-only rule and, subsequently, you end up walking more miles than Lewis and Clark did exploring the Dakotas.

8) You are on the driving range and your buddy lets you try out his five-hundred-dollar driver. You have never, ever hit the ball as far or as straight. So you buy one for yourself. The first time you play with it, your cogolfers nickname you Water Boy, because you shank drives into the lake, the creek and a resort swimming pool next to the

course, before you put the thing away and go back to your fifty-dollar garage-sale driver.

9) After tossing some grass into the air to check the wind, you see that it's blowing left-to-right, so you alter your grip, play the ball back in your stance to keep it low, aim a little left to be safe. Then, after two great practice swings, you hit a wicked slice way up into the wind that lands two fairways to the right.

10) The course is busy, and they are backed up at the 195-yard par-3. The group on the green waves you up. You know the odds of hitting that green with everyone watching are slim-to-nil. So you decide to lay it up. Then you proceed to hit a wicked worm-burner that just keeps going and going, finally rolling up onto the green and stopping just inches from the hole. A dead bug and several blades of grass fall off the ball. The crowd cheers—and, of course, laughs.

What's the good news about these inevitabilities? You get asked to play often, because you are just so darned entertaining!

Ernie Witham

The Life and Times of a Golf Ball

I have talked to golf balls all my golfing life. I accept that a golf ball is inanimate; I understand that a golf ball does not have ears or a brain or even a nervous system. But it is, nonetheless, pleasing to see a golf ball pop right out of a bunker at the exact moment you've yelled, "Skip, golf ball, skip!" So, yes, I talk to golf balls; I admit to that. If I had to guess, I'd say we talkers are in the majority.

Michael Bamberger

There is nothing surprising about it—ending up in this trash can behind the golf shop. I suppose it was inevitable from the day they put me in a package back at the factory. Still it's deeply disappointing: Nobody or nothing in the world likes to admit that the end is near. Not even a golf ball.

A golf ball? That's right. So no golf ball has spoken out until now. Well, I'm going to tell my story. It needs telling—too many of us have been sliced, hooked, topped, scuffed and thrown to oblivion without a backward glance from the people we have served so loyally.

My life hasn't been typical, because for one splendid day I had the kind of life few golf balls enjoy—a chance to perform on the professional tour. But, other than that I've been the same as my brothers. Now, battered, bruised and severely cut I have been tossed out—worthless.

My last few weeks were spent on the practice range. A horrid kind of existence. You're poured into a bucket, then dumped onto the ground and clubbed down-range by golfers with talents ranging from lots of it to none at all.

But I was surviving all right until this morning. A lady beginner talked briefly with the pro before picking up the bucket of balls where I was resting. "I never have played golf before, but my husband insists that I give it a try," the lady explained to the pro. I winced.

She was dangerous, the kind who could deliver a fatal blow with one disjointed swing. My only hope was that she would hit the ground behind me so I could dribble along the grass and avoid serious damage. There wasn't a prayer that she would hit me square.

I watched painfully as she chopped away, missing some balls two or three times.

Finally my turn came, and she flailed at me with a 7-iron. It might as well have been an axe. The clubhead hit into my topside, and I would have screamed in agony if the golf ball code of ethics had permitted.

Instead, I needed all my strength and determination to hold my tightly wound innards in place as I skittered along the ground. The pain was almost unbearable, but I turned numb as I rolled to a stop less than thirty yards from the tee.

I took a hurried inventory and learned the worst—I had a mortal wound, a deep and ugly gash that laid bare my wrappings and assured the end of even my driving range days.

Less than an hour later I was picked up by the range boy. He took one look at me and, without hesitation, dumped me in a sack with other discards. A little later he tossed me into this trash can.

But that's only the end of the story, the saddest chapter. I would like to tell the whole thing, including the part about my close relationship with Sandy Douglas, the famous touring pro.

By some kind of a lucky break, I was given to Sandy by the sporting goods salesman. Sandy uses only balls with the number 3 on them, and that's my number. So into his bag I went just two days before the $200,000 Dorado Classic.

Several new balls were in the bag, but not so many that I couldn't be sure to see action. Sandy, like most of the pros, uses a ball for only six holes or so before switching it to his practice bag. I was delighted. I would compete in a major tournament, and then I would serve out my life with Sandy Douglas, traveling in a shag bag from city to city on the Tour.

Well, things started out just as I expected. Actually, they started even better, because Sandy picked me out as one of the first three balls he would use in the Classic. I got in on the preliminary action, too—he used me for his tuneup on the putting green.

Sandy Douglas is all the things everybody says about him. He's colorful, humorous, and he has the kind of charm that draws big galleries: there must have been five thousand people crammed around the 1st tee to watch him. Sandy placed me carefully on a tee and then took his address position. I was tingling all over.

"Okay, little ball, let's just send you out there nice and easy," Sandy said quietly, and then he swung smoothly. The driver came into me perfectly, and suddenly the green color below me was a blur. I reached my peak height and started down. I could feel myself being drawn to the middle of the fairway, and finally, I bumped down and rolled to a stop.

The spectators were applauding, and I could see that we were in perfect position, about 275 yards out and with a clear shot to the green. Sandy and his caddie strolled up, held a brief conference on distance and club selection, and then I was on my way again, this time with a 9-iron. Again the swing was good and I climbed into a high arc before dropping toward the flagstick. Sandy had been a little firm with me, but I managed to dig into the green and curl back to within eight feet of the hole.

A small coin was placed behind me and the caddie gave me a bath before Sandy placed me back on the green and prepared to putt. He wanted a birdie for a fast start, and I wanted to help him get it.

"It looks as if it will break about an inch to the left," Sandy said to the caddie.

"A little more than that, about an inch and a half," the caddie replied.

Sandy didn't say any more. He carefully lined me up and a hush settled all around. Finally, he tapped me, and I rolled gingerly towards the cup. Two feet away I began to break to the left, and I was dead on line. *Plunk!* In I went, and a huge roar arose from the spectators. Sandy picked me out of the cup and held me up to acknowledge the cheers. It was the supreme moment for me.

The 2nd hole was another par-4, and Sandy gave me another good ride off the tee, but with a bit more hook than he wanted. I ended up in the rough, but I managed to crawl into a good lie and there was no problem. A solid 8-iron put me six feet from the hole on a flat portion of the green. It was a straight-in putt and Sandy sank me for another birdie.

Two holes and 2 under par! I could hardly believe it! It was an exquisite experience; I had to be the luckiest ball in the world—or so I thought.

Little did I know that heartbreak was just ahead. What

hurts most is that it really wasn't the fault of either of us.

The 3rd hole is a par-3 of 180 yards with a pond right in front of the green.

"Give me the 6-iron," Sandy said.

"I think a 7-iron is enough," the caddie replied.

Then Sandy and the caddie huddled and I couldn't hear what they said, but when Sandy addressed me I could see he was using the 7-iron. The caddie had convinced him.

The next few seconds turned into sheer horror. Sandy hit me well, but from the moment I left the tee I could see that flying over that pond would be touch and go. If only he had stuck with that 6-iron.

I sailed through the air and started my descent. Everywhere I looked was water! Suddenly I was sick; I wasn't going to make it over the pond. With a knifing dive, I splashed into slimy weeds about three feet from the edge of the pond. I can't describe the agony I felt as I settled into the mud two feet under water.

A few minutes later I saw the head of a wedge poking about near me. Sandy was trying to find me, and I wanted desperately to reach out for that wedge, but of course I couldn't. Moments later, the wedge disappeared. I had been given up for lost.

Such was the end of the exciting part of my life. It was so brief, but so memorable.

What followed was almost predictable. About a week later a young boy was wading in the pond looking for balls. He found me along with a lot of others, sold some of the balls at the golf shop, but kept me. I still looked as good as new.

For the next month I served the boy's father, about a 12-handicapper who beat me up a bit but didn't give me any of those dreaded cuts. Finally he lost me in long grass behind a green. The next time I was found was by a greenskeeper who narrowly missed running over me with his mower. He turned me over to the golf shop, and that started my tour of duty on the driving range.

That's about all there is to tell. I lived dangerously but made it by okay until the other day.

Now I'm buried deep in this trash can, and I can hear the garbage truck coming. I recognize the sound because I've heard it many times in the last few weeks.

It's just a matter of minutes now until they haul me away to the dump. I wonder how Sandy Douglas finished in the Dorado Classic. I wonder how my life might have gone if it hadn't been for that pond. I wonder if that lady beginner ever will learn to hit a ball.

Bob Robinson

More Chicken Soup?

Many of the stories and poems you have read in this book were submitted by readers like you who had read earlier *Chicken Soup for the Soul* books. We publish at least five or six *Chicken Soup for the Soul* books every year. We invite you to contribute a story to one of these future volumes.

Stories may be up to twelve hundred words and must uplift or inspire. You may submit an original piece, something you have read or your favorite quotation on your refrigerator door.

To obtain a copy of our submission guidelines and a listing of upcoming *Chicken Soup* books, please write, fax or check one of our Web sites.

Please send your submissions to:

Chicken Soup for the Soul
P.O. Box 30880
Santa Barbara, CA 93130
fax: 805-563-2945
Web sites: *www.chickensoup.com*
www.clubchickensoup.com

We will be sure that both you and the author are credited for your submission.

For information about speaking engagements, other books, audiotapes, workshops and training programs, please contact any of our authors directly.

In Support of Others

We hope that the stories in this book have shown readers the positive impact they can make on the lives of others. To that end, a portion of the proceeds from every *Chicken Soup for the Soul* book, go to a worthy charity.

A portion of the proceeds from *Chicken Soup for the Golfer's Soul: The 2nd Round*, will go to the Payne Stewart Family Foundation. Established in 1988, the purpose of the foundation is to primarily assist with programs that allow children and youth to have new opportunities to experience the joy of the Christian life.

The Payne Stewart Family Foundation
c/o Ronald Blue & Company
450 South Orange Avenue
Suite #250
Orlando, FL 32801

Who Is Jack Canfield?

Jack Canfield is one of America's leading experts in the development of human potential and personal effectiveness. He is both a dynamic, entertaining speaker and a highly sought-after trainer. Jack has a wonderful ability to inform and inspire audiences toward increased levels of self-esteem and peak performance.

He is the author and narrator of several bestselling audio- and videocassette programs, including *Self-Esteem and Peak Performance, How to Build High Self-Esteem, Self-Esteem in the Classroom* and *Chicken Soup for the Soul—Live.* He is regularly seen on television shows such as *Good Morning America, 20/20* and *NBC Nightly News.* Jack has co-authored numerous books, including the *Chicken Soup for the Soul* series, *Dare to Win, The Aladdin Factor, 100 Ways to Build Self-Concept in the Classroom, Heart at Work* and *The Power of Focus.*

Jack is a regularly featured speaker for professional associations, school districts, government agencies, churches, hospitals, sales organizations and corporations. His clients have included the American Dental Association, the American Management Association, AT&T, Campbell's Soup, Clairol, Domino's Pizza, GE, ITT, Hartford Insurance, Johnson & Johnson, the Million Dollar Roundtable, NCR, New England Telephone, Re/Max, Scott Paper, TRW and Virgin Records.

Jack conducts an annual eight-day Training of Trainers program in the areas of self-esteem and peak performance. It attracts educators, counselors, parenting trainers, corporate trainers, professional speakers, ministers and others interested in developing their speaking and seminar-leading skills.

For further information about Jack's books, tapes and training programs, or to schedule him for a presentation, please contact:

Self-Esteem Seminars
P.O. Box 30880
Santa Barbara, CA 93130
phone: 805-563-2935 • fax: 805-563-2945
Web site: *www.chickensoup.com*

Who Is Mark Victor Hansen?

Mark Victor Hansen is a professional speaker who in the last twenty years has made over 4,000 presentations to more than 2 million people in thirty-two countries. His presentations cover sales excellence and strategies; personal empowerment and development; and how to triple your income and double your time off.

Mark has spent a lifetime dedicated to his mission of making a profound and positive difference in people's lives. Throughout his career, he has inspired hundreds of thousands of people to create a more powerful and purposeful future for themselves while stimulating the sale of billions of dollars worth of goods and services.

Mark is a prolific writer and has authored *Future Diary, How to Achieve Total Prosperity* and *The Miracle of Tithing*. He is coauthor of the *Chicken Soup for the Soul* series, *Dare to Win* and *The Aladdin Factor* (all with Jack Canfield), and *The Master Motivator* (with Joe Batten).

Mark has also produced a complete library of personal-empowerment audio- and videocassette programs that have enabled his listeners to recognize and use their innate abilities in their business and personal lives. His message has made him a popular television and radio personality, with appearances on ABC, NBC, CBS, HBO, PBS and CNN. He has also appeared on the cover of numerous magazines, including *Success, Entrepreneur* and *Changes*.

Mark is a big man with a heart and spirit to match—an inspiration to all who seek to better themselves.

For further information about Mark, write:

MVH & Associates
P.O. Box 7665
Newport Beach, CA 92658
phone: 714-759-9304 or 800-433-2314
fax: 714-722-6912
Web site: *www.chickensoup.com*

Who Is Jeff Aubery?

Introduced to the golf industry at an early age, Jeff was mentored personally and professionally by Nat C. Rosasco, owner of Northwestern Golf Co. Now an entrepreneur in his own right, Jeff founded and is the president of Golf Sales West, Inc./Tornado Golf, the world's largest original equipment golf bag manufacturer.

Jeff has been committed to golf as a lifetime passion and has traveled the world extensively in pursuit of the game and the industry that surrounds it. Jeff is most proud of his tireless work to help bring millions of people to the game of golf by developing programs and products that are accessible and affordable for everyone.

Jeff is an active sponsor of junior golf programs and charity golf tournaments all over the world. Jeff makes time for a round of golf whenever possible and has enjoyed playing with some of the greatest names in the sport at many of the world's most famous courses.

Jeff is a two-time *New York Times* #1 bestselling author in addition to a *USA Today* and *Publishers Weekly* bestselling author. Jeff's books have sold millions of copies worldwide, and he is a veteran of hundreds of radio and television interviews.

Coauthor of *Chicken Soup for the Golfer's Soul, Chicken Soup for the Father's Soul* and *Chicken Soup for the Golfer's Soul: The Second Round,* Jeff is no stranger to the *Chicken Soup* phenomenon. Jeff is married to Patty Aubery, coauthor of *Chicken Soup for the Christian Soul, Chicken Soup for the Christian Family Soul, Chicken Soup for the Surviving Soul* and *Chicken Soup for the Expectant Mother's Soul.*

The couple and their two sons, Jeffrey Terrance and Chandler Scott, make their home in Santa Barbara, California. Jeff is a dynamic and enthusiastic speaker and is available for personal appearances. He can be reached at:

Golf Sales West, Inc./Tornado Golf
2100 Eastman Ave., Suite A
Oxnard, CA 93030
phone: 800-GOLF-BAG
E-mail: *SoupStory@aol.com*

Who Are Mark and Chrissy Donnelly?

Avid golfers Mark and Chrissy Donnelly are a dynamic married couple working closely together as coauthors, marketers and speakers.

They are the coauthors of the #1 *New York Times* bestsellers *Chicken Soup for the Couple's Soul, Chicken Soup for the Golfer's Soul, Chicken Soup for the Sports Fan's Soul, Chicken Soup for the Father's Soul* and *Chicken Soup for the Baseball Fan's Soul*. They are also at work on several other upcoming books, among them *Chicken Soup for the Romantic Soul* and *Chicken Soup for the Friend's Soul*.

As cofounders of the Donnelly Marketing Group, they develop and implement innovative marketing and promotional strategies that help elevate and expand the *Chicken Soup for the Soul* message to millions of people around the world.

Mark was introduced to golf at the age of three. He remembers following his father to the golf course and finding a four-leaf clover that he believes enabled his father to win a prominent local amateur tournament. As a result of this and other golfing experiences with his father, Mark developed an appreciation for the game, along with a respectable golf game. Mark grew up in Portland, Oregon, and un-beknownst to him, attended the same high school as Chrissy. He went on to graduate from the University of Arizona, where he was president of his fraternity, Alpha Tau Omega. He served as vice president of marketing for his family's business, Contact Lumber, and after eleven years resigned from day-to-day responsibilities to focus on his current endeavors.

Chrissy, COO of the Donnelly Marketing Group, also grew up in Portland, Oregon, and graduated from Portland State University. As a CPA, she embarked on a six-year career with Price Waterhouse.

Mark and Chrissy enjoy many hobbies together, including golf, hiking, skiing, traveling, hip-hop aerobics and spending time with friends. Mark and Chrissy live in Paradise Valley, Arizona, and can be reached at:

Donnelly Marketing Group, LLC
2425 E. Camelback Road, Suite 515
Phoenix, AZ 85016
phone: 602-508-8956 fax: 602-508-8912
E-mail: *chickensoup@cox.net*

What Is Golf Digest?

Golf Digest is America's oldest and most widely read golf monthly with a circulation of 1.55 million and six million readers. Since 1950, *Golf Digest* has advised golfers on how to play, what to play and where to play. It has won every major golf-writing award and twice in the last decade has been named finalist in the prestigious National Magazine Awards.

Its contributing editors include the best writers and teachers in the country, including writers Dan Jenkins, Dave Kindred, Nick Seitz and Tom Callahan and teachers David Leadbetter, Jack Lumkin, Hank Haney, Butch Harmon and Jim McLean, among many others. *Golf Digest* Schools, which serve as a laboratory to the magazine's highly respected instruction content, are recognized as the leading golf schools in the country. *Golf Digest* has twenty-five affiliated publications around the world, offering the magazine's editorial content to some one million golfers in more than fifty-one countries in fifteen languages.

Golf Digest assisted *Chicken Soup for the Golfer's Soul* in the solicitation and the selection of stories and cartoons for this book. Several of the stories will be excerpted in the magazine and its writers are well represented in these pages.

Contributors

Several of the stories in this book were taken from previously published sources, such as books, magazines and newspapers. These sources are acknowledged in the permissions section. If you would like to contact any of the contributors for information about their writing, or would like to invite them to speak in your community, look for their contact information included in their biography.

The remainder of the stories were submitted by readers of our previous *Chicken Soup for the Soul* books who responded to our requests for stories. We have also included information about them.

Matt Adams is a veteran of the golf industry and a regular contributor to business reports on The Golf Channel. Matt is also a writer and coauthor of *Chicken Soup for the Soul of America*. Matt can be reached at *mattadams422@aol.com*.

Ahmed Tharwat Abdelaal is married to a Minnesota native, Caren, who teaches at the University of Minnesota. Together they came up with a lovely daughter whose name is Sara. Ahmed runs a marketing consulting firm in the Twin Cities that develops customer satisfaction programs for small business. He has been teaching business and marketing at the University of St. Thomas and abroad for the last twenty years. Another sidelight of his career is his involvement in producing and hosting the only local Arab-American TV program in the Midwest as an alternative medium for the Arab-American community. This weekly TV program offers the audience a new perspective on current events and a vehicle to strengthen the relationships among the many cultures in the community.

Michael Arkush is an associate editor for *Golf World* magazine. He has also worked for the *Los Angeles Times* and *People* magazine. Arkush has written three books: *Rush!*, a *New York Times* bestselling biography of Rush Limbaugh; *Tim Allen Laid Bare*; and *60 Years of USC-UCLA Football*, cowritten with Steve Springer. Arkush lives in Connecticut with his wife, actress Pauletta Walsh, and daughter Jade.

Paul Azinger won his first professional golf tournament in Phoenix, Arizona, in 1987. An eleven-time PGA Tournament winner, he was the 1993 PGA Champion and cocaptain of the U.S. golf team's entry for the 1994 President's Cup. He lives in Bradenton, Florida, with his wife, Toni, and two daughters.

Aaron Bacall has worked as a research chemist, college instructor and teacher. All the while he created cartoons on a freelance basis in the evenings and out they went to magazines. As sales started to come in he built up his business, adding advertising and illustration work. He is a full-time cartoonist now, specializing in magazine cartoons, spot art and advertising illustration. His work has appeared in *The New Yorker, Barron's, Reader's Digest, Wall Street Journal* and corporate projects. A book of his cartoons will be published in 2002. He can be reached at *abacall@msn.com.*

Todd Behrendt knows all too well the allure golf has for so many. He witnesses it almost daily during his duties as the golf writer for the *North Country Times* in Escondido, California. Perhaps that's why the traumatic event described in this passage hasn't kept him from teeing it up with his father-in-law again—thankfully, without further incident.

Patty Berg took up golf when she was thirteen and is known as one of the leading female golfers during the 1950s and 1960s. She won fifteen Majors and was a founding member of the LPGA in 1948. She became the LPGA's first president (1949-1952) and is one of the original inductees into the LPGA Hall of Fame. In all, Patty won fifty-seven tournaments on the LPGA tour. The LPGA honored her by establishing the Patty Berg Award in 1978 which is given to the female golfer who has made the greatest contribution to women's golf during the year. Her career sets an example to sportsmen and sportswomen everywhere. She is known for her great talent and lifelong dedication to the game.

Arthur Berk is a writer who has contributed to *Reader's Digest, Newsday* and *The Hampton Chronicle News.* At present, Arthur is preparing a one-man show in his hometown library in East Meadow, New York. He has taught writing and art at Westhampton Beach. At present, he is retired . . . on the golf course!

Greg R. Bernard, when not hacking his way around a golf course, is a college writing instructor, having taught at a small community college in Illinois before returning this past summer to his native northern Minnesota. He holds both a B.A. and an M.A. in English literature from Bemidji State University, and is currently teaching there on adjunct status. Susan, Greg's wife and life partner, provides him with encouragement, inspiration, and most recently, his latest muse—their daughter Madison.

Dan Bickely is currently a sports columnist for *The Arizona Republic* and is the author of *No Bull: The Unauthorized Biography of Dennis Rodman.* He was a syndicated columnist for the Copley News Service from 1997 to 98 and worked at the *Chicago Sun-Times* from 1987 to 1997.

Ken Bowden is currently president of Golden Bear Publishing, Inc., a division of Golden Bear International, Inc. Prior to his more than twenty-five-year association with Jack Nicklaus, Bowden was for three years editorial director of the world's leading golf periodical, *Golf Digest,* and prior to that the founding editor of the leading English-language golf magazine in London, *Golf World.* He has coauthored ten books with Jack Nicklaus that have sold over two million copies around the world. He has also coauthored bestselling books with John Jacobs, including *Practical Golf.* He has produced and co-produced more than 150 golf programs. His video productions include Nicklaus's top-selling "Golf

My Way" series. He resides in Westport, Connecticut and Jupiter, Florida.

William M. Bowen, a retiree, has added anecdotal writing to his list of hobbies which include grandchildren, traveling with his wife June, working with the elderly, golf and fishing. The writing, which of course complements all of the above, quickly became his favorite of those activities. He motivates the "old folks" with whom he works to join in telling the stories from the past that will die if they are not passed on through their writing or recording. He says he can tell golf stories better than he can play the wonderful game!

Susan D. Brandenburg, born in Hollywood, California, the daughter of an Air Force Officer, has lived in Germany, Japan, California, Texas, Montana, Nebraska, New York and Florida. She now resides in Sawgrass, Ponte Vedra Beach, Florida. Her job as a coordinator at Blue Cross Blue Shield of Florida keeps her busy during the day, and her evenings are filled with interviewing exciting people and writing weekly feature articles for the *Beaches Leader* newspaper. The most exciting adventure of her life is a continuing one—being a mother of a fine son and daughter, and grandmother to two healthy, beautiful grandsons.

Gina Bridgeman is a regular contributor to the devotional book *Daily Guideposts*. Her work has also appeared in several *Guideposts* publications and *A Second Chicken Soup for the Woman's Soul*. Her most memorable writing experience was collaborating with her father, broadcaster Joe Garagiola on his best-selling book *It's Anybody's Ballgame*. Gina lives in Scottsdale, Arizona, with her husband and two children.

Alan Broderick is a freelance writer living in Alberton, Prince Edward Island, Canada. His story originally appeared in *Golf Journal*, a publication of the United States Golf Association. Proceeds from the reprinting of this story will be donated to the USGA Foundation.

Adam Bruns is a freelance writer and poet from Lexington, Kentucky. His work has appeared in *Golfweek, Golf Journal, Central Kentucky Golf* and *Greater Louisville Golf*. His features have also appeared in *American Libraries* and *The Lane Report*. Adam is a member of the Golf Writers Association of America.

Andy Brumer is a freelance writer who writes on golf, art, literature and other subjects. He is a published poet and a 2-handicap golfer. Andy holds a bachelor of arts degree in English literature from the University of Wisconsin-Madison and a masters degree from San Francisco State University, where he studied creative writing. He lives in the Los Angeles area. Please reach him at: *abrumer@aol.com.*

Bob Brust, a native of Montana, worked as an engineer for Chevron U.S.A. for thirty-two years. After retiring, he pursued two of his greatest passions, writing and golf. His works have appeared in *Golf Journal, Chicken Soup for the Golfer's Soul*, several magazines and periodicals. He has also authored two books, *Idaho in June* and *I Thought I Heard a Rooster Crow*. The latter is about his life and his family on a ranch in Montana and is in the process of being published. Bob passed away in June 1999. Further information concerning his writing is available from Harriett Brust, *hebrust@iowatelecom.net.*

Tom Callahan is married with two children. He is a former *Time Magazine* senior writer, *Washington Post* sports columnist and a *Golf Digest* contributing editor. He coauthored *Around the World in 18 Holes* with Dave Kindred (Doubleday). He is recently back from seventeen months in Belfast and is at work on a book about "the Troubles," entitled *An Irish Thing.*

Jack Cavanaugh covers sports and writes feature stories for the *New York Times.* He has also written for *Sports Illustrated, Reader's Digest* and a number of other national magazines. Cavanaugh is also an adjunct writing professor at Fairfield and Quinnipiac Universities in Connecticut. He has contributed several previous stories for *Chicken Soup for the Soul* books. He is also the author of *Damn the Disabilities: Full Speed Ahead!,* which recounts the stories of athletes who have overcome handicaps to excel in sports. He lives in Wilton, Connecticut.

Reid Champagne has been playing golf with no noticeable improvement for over forty years. He not only believes in gadgetry, but also magic, sorcery, incantations, smoke, mirrors and a rare Asian ointment as the ultimate solutions to his swing problems. Reach him at *reid4bar@aol.com.*

Frank Christian and his family of photographers have been providing the official photos of the Masters Tournament for nearly sixty-five years. His recent book, *Augusta National and the Masters: A Photographer's Scrapbook* is one of the top-selling sports books. He lives in Augusta with his family.

Christine Clifford is CEO and president of The Cancer Club, a company that markets humorous and helpful products for people with cancer on an international basis. She is the author of two award-winning books, including *Not Now, I'm Having a No Hair Day: Humor and Healing for People with Cancer* and *Our Family Has Cancer, Too!,* especially for children. Christine is a professional speaker on how to use humor and exercise to recover from chronic illness. Her work has appeared in such publications as *Better Homes and Gardens, Coping* magazine, *MORE, American Health for Women, The Hindu in India* and *The Singapore Women's Weekly.* Recently she was featured on CNN Live as "one of the world's leading authorities on the use of therapeutic humor." Christine is also the host of the Christine Clifford Celebrity Golf Invitational, an event to raise money for breast cancer detection, research and awareness. Christine and The Cancer Club can be reached at 800-586-9062; fax 612-941-1229; 6533 Limerick Dr., Edina, MN 55439; e-mail at *canclub@primenet.com* or her Web site at *www.cancerclub.com*

Jan K. Collins is an editor at the University of South Carolina's business school and is also a freelance writer and columnist. A former award-winning newspaper reporter in Michigan, North Carolina and South Carolina, Jan was awarded a Nieman Fellowship at Harvard University. She coauthors two weekly columns, "Flying Solo"—on divorce and separation issues—and "Next Steps"—on issues involving the elderly—that are distributed nationally to more than 225 newspapers. She is a southern correspondent for *The Economist,* has been published in numerous national newspapers and magazines, and has contributed chapters to three books. She can be reached at 803-777-2510.

Mike Corcoran is a writer and former editor of *Golf Illustrated* based in Pennsylvania. His story originally appeared in *Golf Journal*, a publication of the United States Golf Association. Proceeds from the reprinting of this story will be donated to the USGA Foundation.

Betty Cuniberti is an award-winning journalist with a career spanning more than twenty years. She has covered collegiate and professional sports, profiled political figures in Washington, authored a humor column for the *Kansas City Star*, guest lectured at the University of Kansas journalism school and combined her twin passions of golf and writing for *Golf Digest* magazine. She became a fan of *Chicken Soup* books during her second bout with breast cancer in 1997, reading *Chicken Soup for the Surviving Soul*. She resides in St. Louis with her two golf partners/children, ten-year-old Angela and eight-year-old Oscar (originator of the left-handed, 360-degree, fall-on-your-face swing).

Gary D'Amato is an award-winning sportswriter for the *Milwaukee Journal Sentinel*. He has written two books—*Mudbaths and Bloodbaths: The Inside Story of the Bears-Packers Rivalry* and *The Packer Tapes: My 32 Years with the Green Bay Packers*—with Domenic Gentile. D'Amato's work has also appeared in *Chicken Soup for the Golfer's Soul* and *Chicken Soup for the Sports Fan's Soul*. Contact him at *gdamato@onwis.com*.

A. J. Daulerio is from Ambler, Pennsylvania, and is a staff writer for Great Media Newspapers in East Brunswick, New Jersey, and a freelance journalist. He would like to thank his parents, Colleen, and his friend, Ernie.

Steve Densley is president and CEO of the Provo/Oren Chamber of Commerce in Provo, Utah. After working on the East Coast and in Chicago, he and his wife, Colleen, settled in Utah. He has written articles for several magazines and currently writes a weekly column for three Utah papers. He spends his free time doing amateur photography and playing with his six grandchildren.

Don Didio is a forty-five-year-old father of four, recently transplanted from Baltimore to the scenic mountains and valleys of central Pennsylvania. He has been writing since college as both a hobby and as a means of release. Most of his stories are taken from life's experiences, dreams, hopes, failures and successes. He believes that success is measured by what we overcome, not by what we acquire. He can be reached at 31 Winter Trail, Fairfield, Pennsylvania, or by calling 717-642-8598 or via e-mail *didiod@mail.cvn.net*.

Paula DiPerna is a freelance writer based in Chicago. Her story originally appeared in *Golf Journal*, a publication of the United States Golf Association. Proceeds from the reprinting of this story will be donated to the USGA Foundation.

James Dodson is an award-winning golf writer and author of the bestselling book, *Final Rounds*. James always felt closest to his father while they were on the links. So it seemed only appropriate when his father learned he had two months to live that they would set off on the golf journey of their dreams to play the most famous courses in the world. *Final Rounds* is a book never to be forgotten, a book about fathers and sons, long-held secrets, and the lessons a middle-aged man can still learn from his dad about life, love and family.

Tommy Ehrbar works at the University of Pittsburgh when not golfing. He is director of feature services, speech writer and steadfast contributor to university publications. He previously held a similar position at Kenyon College. He is a graduate of Notre Dame University, former congressional reporter for *The New Republic,* former TV weather forecaster, and freelance writer of pluck and vim.

Darlene Daniels Eisenhuth lives in rural South Newfane, Vermont, with her husband and their two teenage sons. She is a firm believer that the finer things in life are the simple ones. Most of her inspirations for her writing come from her family and their experiences together.

Jolee Edmondson writes about golf and many other subjects for national magazines. She is the only woman ever to have won a first-place award from the Golf Writers Association of America. A resident of Savannah, Georgia, she can be reached at *wordworx1@aol.com.*

Sondra Sue Ward Elder is a freelance writer and artist who claims she is a former West Virginia divot champion. "Can't hit a lick with a golf club," she says. However, she couldn't miss the wit and self-reliance of the parachutist she has dubbed the "world's greatest play-through champion."

John Feinstein spent eleven years on the staff of the *Washington Post* as well as writing for *Sports Illustrated* and the *National Sports Daily.* He is a commentator on NPR's "Morning Edition," a regular on ESPN's *The Sports Reporters,* and a visiting professor of journalism at Duke University. John's first book, *A Season on the Brink,* is the bestselling sports book of all time. *A Good Walk Spoiled* was a #1 *New York Times* bestseller.

David Field is the author of The Story of Happy. He has an A.B. from Colgate University and an M.A. from Ohio University. He retired as lieutenant colonel in 1962 after serving twenty years in the U.S. Army, service in Europe during WW II, service in Korea during the Korean War and on special mission in Vietnam. He has spent thirty years in education as a psychology professor at Emeritus Thomas Nelson Community College in Hampton, Virginia. He is currently a freelance writer with 277 articles published in regional and national periodicals on golf, religion, psychology, travel, history and military topics.

Leonard Finkel, together with artist Gary Max Collins, produced *The Secrets to the Game of Golf & Life,* which contains fifty original oil painting by Collins. He is a freelance writer and editor of *Golf Journeys Magazine.* Leonard has had articles published in more than twenty magazines including *Golf Illustrated, Affluent Golfer* and almost a dozen cover stories for *Golf Today Magazine.* Leonard can be reached at *glfgd@aol.com* or visit the Web site at *www.golfandlife.com.*

Deisy Flood is originally from Cuba. She is married and has a son. She has contributed to *Golf Journal*. She resides in Lakeland, Florida, with her three dogs and owns a business. She loves golf, reading and writing. She is sorry her father didn't live to see her work, although not exactly professional, published. She can be reached at: *deisy_f@hotmail.com*.

Andrew Galanopulos is a fifteen-year-old sophmore at Daphne High School in Daphne, Alabama. In addition to being an avid writer and golfer, he is the editor of his school newspaper, a straight-A student and a member of the cross-country track team. He plans to become a doctor when he gets out of school.

Dan Galbraith is a fifty-six-time state and four-time national award-winner in sports journalism. The sports editor for *The Holton Recorder* and *The Sabetha Herald* newspapers, his first book *Sports Column Writing Is Life* is expected soon at bookstores. His e-mail address is *baberuthfan@hotmail.com*.

Bud Gardner has been playing golf for fifty years. He was a member of the Fort Hays Kansas State University golf team in the mid-1950s, and later won many open tournaments in western Kansas. He won his hometown tournament in WaKeeney, Kansas, shooting a 92 for 27 holes on the old sand-green course. In the mid-sixties, he coached golf at American River College in Sacramento, California, guiding his team to a conference championship. He now lives in Del Web's Sun City in Roseville, California, where he plays Sun City's Billy Casper-designed courses. He is the coauthor of *Chicken Soup for the Writer's Soul*.

Jay Gearan is a freelance writer and a sports correspondent for the *Worcester Telegram and Gazette* in Worcester, Massachusetts. Jay also teaches English at Gardner High School and Mount Wachusett Community College in Gardner, Massachusetts. A member of the Golf Writers' Association of America for several years, Jay has published several sports stories in New England newspapers and golf magazines. He is currently working with Bordalice Publishing in Delmar, New York on a book about the upcoming 1999 Ryder Cup Matches. Bordalice (*www.bordalicepublishing.com*) specializes in sports psychology books. Jay, his wife, Janice, and their two sons Jack and Mike, live in Massachusetts. You can e-mail him at: *jgearan@massed.net*.

Marc Gellman is the senior rabbi of Temple Beth Torah in Melville, New York. He holds a doctorate in philosophy from Northwestern University and a pretty decent handicap from the Metropolitan Golf Association. He has written for *Golf Digest* and the *Met Golfer* along with other important theological publications. He is the author of *Does God Have a Big Toe?*, *God's Mailbox* and *Always Wear Clean Underwear*. With his friend and golfing buddy Monsignor Thomas Hartman, he has written *Where Does God Live? How Do You Spell God?*, and most recently, *Lost and Found*, a kids book for living through loss. He appears regularly with Monsignor Hartman on ABC's *Good Morning America*, the "Imus in the Morning" radio program, and they have their own cable television program, *The God Squad*. He is the recipient of many awards, and is an honorary member of Old Westbury Golf and Country Club.

Rhonda Glenn, a freelance writer living in Atlantis, Florida, is the author of *The*

Illustrated History of Women's Golf and a contributor to *The Junior Golf Book* and *Golf for Women*. Her story originally appeared in *Golf Journal*, a publication of the United States Golf Association. Proceeds from the reprinting of this story will be donated to the USGA Foundation.

Jay Golden, PGA member, performs his golf comedy clinic entitled "THE FUN-damentals of Golf" across the U.S. He writes for several golf magazines, has appeared on TV hundreds of times, is a two-time quarter-finalist in the National Long Drive Contest and has produced a comedy and instruction video. For more information e-mail at *rjjjg1@aol.com*.

Ellen Goodman has been with the *Boston Globe*, where she is an associate editor as well as a columnist, since 1967. In 1980, she won the Pulitzer Prize for distinguished commentary. Her book on social change, *Turning Points*, was published in 1979. Five collections of her columns have also been published: *Close to Home, At Large, Keeping in Touch, Making Sense* and *Value Judgments*. Born in 1941, she lives with her husband in Brookline.

Frank J. Haller and his wife Julie reside in Scott Township, Pittsburgh, with their cat Max. They have four children: Jane, Nancy, Bob and Jim. Frank's main accomplishments are being a private to first lieutenant, U.S. Infantry, and working thirty-nine years in the ad agency business. The four most important things in his life are: God; family; friends; and his job—and not necessarily in that order.

Tracy Hanson has been playing golf on the Ladies Professional Golf Tour since 1995. She enjoys writing as a hobby. She can be reached through the LPGA Tour office at 100 International Golf Drive, Daytona Beach, FL 32124.

Johnny Hawkins's cartoons have appeared in over 250 publications, including *Reader's Digest, Woman's World, Barron's, Saturday Evening Post* and many others. His nationally syndicated comic, "Hi and Jinx," runs in newspapers around the country. He can be reached at P.O. Box 188, Sherwood, MI 49089, (616) 432-8071 or at *cartoonist@anthill.com*.

Scott Hipp resides in Mission, Kansas. He is a single accountant whose hobbies include: golf, Korean War history, and UFO and paranormal studies. He can golf both left- and right-handed and has broken 80 from both sides.

Bob Hope is an avid golfer and is one of the foremost proponents of the game and has contributed immensely to the popularity of golf as a participant, a spectator and as an author. His book, *Confessions of a Hooker*, spotlights the memorable moments of his more than fifty years of golfing. Probably his greatest achievement in golf is the development and hosting of the Bob Hope/Chrysler Desert Classic, a pro-am tournament held annually in Palm Springs, California. Now in its forty-second year, the Classic draws the most famous pros and celebrity amateurs. A total charity effort, the Classic has raised over 35 million dollars for the Eisenhower Medical Center and seventy other deserving desert charities.

Bob Hurt, a sportswriter for more than a half century, served as lead sports columnist on the leading newspapers in Topeka, Kansas, Oklahoma City and Phoenix. He is the author of a recently published book, *Return of the Football Fossils*.

Dan Jenkins, *Golf Digest* writer-at-large, is the author of seventeen novels and works of nonfiction, including two classic golf books, *The Dogged Victims of Inexorable Fate* and *Dead Solid Perfect*. He lives in his hometown of Fort Worth, Texas.

Jeff Kahler is president and CEO of Kahler & Company, a marketing communications agency located in Omaha, Nebraska. As a copywriter and creative director, he has won more than 150 creative awards on the local, regional, national and international level. A two-time club champion, he currently holds a 1 handicap.

Bil Keane created "The Family Circus," based on his own family, in 1960. It now appears in well over 1,500 newspapers and is read daily by 188 million people. The award-winning feature is the most widely spread syndicated cartoon in America. Check out The Family Circus website: *www.familycircus.com*.

John Keating is currently a wine consultant with a major interest in food, wine, travel and golf. He has a B.S. in political science from Georgetown University, Washington, D.C., and an M.A. in education from George Washington University, Washington, D.C. He was a fighter pilot in the U.S. Air Force for twenty years, a wine educator for eighteen years and a restaurant sales manager for a wine distributor for sixteen years.

Harrison Kelly is a freelance writer living in Memphis, Tennessee, with his wife, Lucretia, and their two children, Brad and Kristina. Some of his works have been published in *A Second Chicken Soup for the Woman's Soul* and *Stories for a Man's Heart*. He can be reached via e-mail at *dhk@sprynet.com*.

Dave Kindred has eaten breakfast with Julie Krone, lunch with Muhammad Ali and dinner with Robert Redford. Between meals, he has written six thousand columns and six books. The 1997 National Sportswriter of the Year, he is a winner of sport's journalism's highest prize, the Red Smith Award. He lives in Virginia with his wife, Cheryl.

Jim King received his bachelor of science from Purdue University. He currently works in the information technology field. Although he aspires to do more golfing and writing, most of his time is spent with wife Peg and their children, Tyler, Sydney, Ryleigh and Mykaela. He can be reached at *jimking_x4@yahoo.com*.

Bradley S. Klein, born in New York City in 1954, got his start in golf as a caddie, first at private clubs on his native Long Island then on the PGA Tour. He has caddied in half a dozen U.S. Opens. He is architecture editor/columnist for *Golfweek* for whom he also runs "America's Best," a national golf course ranking system of the top 100 classical and top 100 modern golf courses. He is also contributing editor to America Online's *GOLF*. His essays have appeared in nearly every major golf publication. He is a design consultant and frequent lecturer in the golf industry. Today, with a Ph.D. in hand, he teaches political theory and international relations at Clark University in Worcester, Massachusetts.

Michael Konik is well-known to frequent fliers as the west coast editor of Delta Air Lines' *Sky* magazine, where his monthly column "Tee Time" has been honored by the Golf Writers Association of America. Michael is also the gambling columnist for *Cigar Aficionado* and has been published in over 100 magazines and newspapers. He is the author of *The Man with $100,000 Breasts and Other Gambling Stories* (Huntington Press). Currently, he is working on his next book, *Good Shot, Mr. Nicklaus: Stories About the Game of Golf.*

Robert Lalonde retired from sales at the end of October 1999 and has spent most of his time traveling and playing golf. The adjustment came very easily and what little spare time he has left he enjoys visiting his two boys, Brendon in Toronto and Jeffrey in Montreal. "An author I am not and will never be, but playing a bit of golf with the guys in this story is very entertaining and adds a little laughter to my life."

Mitch Laurance is a passionate golfer, sports commentor (ESPN Championship 9-ball), television host ("On the Green" Golf Video Magazine, Myrtle Beach, South Carolina, and Infomercials), golf writer (*On the Green* magazine, *Golf Range* magazine), and actor ("Not Necessarily the News," "Matlock," "Dawson's Creek"). He can be contacted at 704-364-4864 or at *mitchewa@aol.com.*

Stephen Leacock (1869-1944), humorist, essayist, teacher, political economist and historian, was the recipient of numerous honorary degrees, awards and distinctions. He received The Lorne Pierce Medal, a postage stamp issued in his honor and the Leacock Medal for Humor established in his honor. Leacock was the world's best-known English-speaking humorist from 1915 to 1925.

Dr. Jerry P. Lightner served eighteen years as executive director of the National Association of Biology Teachers followed by sixteen years as senior consultant with Xerox Corporation. Author of several books, his most recent is *I Remember Jack,* a biography of his fighter pilot brother killed in the Korean War. He now resides in Spain and the United States.

Davis Love III has been on the PGA tour since 1985. He has won eleven Tour titles, including the 1997 PGA Championship and the 1992 Players Championship. He was a member of the last two United States Ryder Cup and Presidents Cup teams, and teamed with Fed Couples to win four consecutive World Cup titles. He lives in St. Simons Island, Georgia, with his wife, Robin, their daughter, Alexia, and their son, Davis IV.

Harvey Mackay is the author of *Pushing The Envelope* and four *New York Times* bestsellers, including *Swim with the Sharks*. The nationally syndicated business columnist is CEO of the $85 million Mackay Envelope Corporation based in Minneapolis. Toastmasters International named him one of the top five speakers in the world.

Kyle MacLachlan is currently guest starring on HBO's "Sex and the City" as Trey, Charlotte's (Kristin Davis) husband. He is perhaps best known for his performance in David Lynch's 1986 hit "Blue Velvet" and for his starring role as FBI Agent Dale Cooper in Lynch's television series "Twin Peaks," for which MacLachlan received two Emmy nominations and a Golden Globe Award.

Del Madzay teaches art at Centerburg High School. He runs a mini-golf and driving range in the summer. He collects antique golf memorabilia, photographs it and sells state-of-the-art golf prints, 22x28 available for purchase @ $5.00 each. (View at E-bay store, Sycamore golf prints). 740-393-0017. E-mail him at *sycamoregolf@axom.com*.

Carol Mann won thirty-eight LPGA victories in her twenty-one years on the tour, including a U.S. Open Championship. She is a member of the LPGA Hall of Fame, the International Women's Sports Hall of Fame, and was named one of the 100 heroes of the first 100 years of golf in America. Carol was the first female reporter for NBC's coverage of men's golf; she has also been the color analyst for ABC, PBS, ESPN and syndicated women's golf telecasts. Carol has served as president of the LPGA, and of the Women's Sports Foundation. She has written numerous articles for *Golf Magazine* and *Golf Illustrated*, and is an award-winning golf columnist for the *Houston Post*.

Marci Martin has been published in magazines and newspapers, winning many awards. Published books: *Go to Hell and Make A U-Turn, Muse on My Shoulder*, two series mysteries: *Secrets and Lies* and *License to Steal*. Her fourth mystery is a work in progress. She is coordinator for Arizona Mystery Writers.

Micki McClelland has her fingers in an assortment of pies. A published poet and fiction writer, she is also a produced playwright of comedies and one musical. In recent years Micki has been a freelance writer for magazines, newspapers and for individual clients. In her spare time, she paints, although not formally trained in the art of knowing what to do with color, canvas and brush, Micki's style can be described as primitive and she tends to paint off the page. Currently senior editor of *MY Table: Houston's Dining* magazine, Micki pens essays on food and spirits for the publication, and her paintings have appeared as cover design for four issues.

Clint McCown, author of the golf novel, *The Member-Guest*, has twice won the American Fiction Prize. His stories, poems and essays have appeared widely. He is a professor of creative writing at Beloit College, where he also edits the *Beloit Fiction Journal*.

Alf McCreary is an award-winning journalist, author and broadcaster who lives and works in Northern Ireland, home to some of the best golf courses in the world.

Scott Medlock is one of America's foremost artists. His work is becoming legendary in the world of fine art, particularly through his fine art reproductions. Although he has recently concentrated on the world of golf, his past successes include portrayals of great athletes, abstract painting, children's book illustrations, magazine covers, book covers and paintings for major advertising campaigns. He was commissioned to be one of the official artists for the 1996 Olympic Games in Atlanta. Medlock has also created and "sold out" numerous limited edition reproductions. His paintings involve what art historians refer to as the "psychological moment," the inner world of a golfer setting up an important putt, the one-on-one competitiveness of Bill Russell and Wilt Chamberlain, the emotionally charged environment of Yankee Stadium as Babe Ruth bids farewell to his fans. Medlock's talent surfaced early; a graduate of the Art Center of Design at Pasadena, now just twenty-nine years of age, he has already received awards of excellence from the New York Society of Illustrators, Society of Illustrators of Los Angeles and the European Illustrators Society.

John Meyers is a writer of film screenplays and feature articles who lives and golfs to an 8 handicap in Maryland with his wife and two children ages six and nine. As a regular contributor to *The Washington Golf Monthly*, his essays span the whole spectrum of what makes the game of golf so unique in the grand scheme of the universe. At least he gives it a shot.

Steve Minnick has been involved in designing and managing computer systems for over twenty years. He divides his spare time writing the occasional screenplay and traveling with his wife Leanna, a composer and music teacher. How's his game today? "Much improved since his brush with Mr. Miller."

Rich Mintzer is the author of thirteen books including four golf books. In the past ten years he has also penned over 300 articles on a wide range of subjects for national magazines. Rich lives with his wife and two children in New York City where he doesn't get to play golf as often as he would like, but loves the serenity of the course when he gets out there.

E. J. Montini has been asking annoying questions since his days at St. Titus Roman Catholic grade school outside of Pittsburgh, Pennsylvania, where the sisters of St. Joseph declared him a hopeless sinner whose persistent inquiries caused his guardian angel to weep constantly and who therefore would do little in life but disrupt the natural order of things. Naturally, the nuns were correct. Montini was born on Thanksgiving Day, 1954, the fortieth birthday of the great Joe DiMaggio. He grew up in the same steel town as Mike Ditka and Henry Mancini. After graduating from Penn State, he worked for newspapers in the East before going to *The Arizona Republic* in 1980. He saw the Doors perform when he was thirteen years old and when not quite six was taken by his mother to a speech by John F. Kennedy. He remembers that Kennedy's microphone didn't work correctly, and it didn't bother his mother a bit. Montini is married and the father of two children. From the moment they could talk, the children have been asking annoying questions. This pleases him very much.

Debra Moss combines a professional resume as a litigation paralegal and investment trader with a lifelong career as a freelance writer and photographer. During eight years living aboard a sailboat in Florida and the U.S. Virgin Islands, Debra wrote for fifteen boating publications, reporting on Florida,

Bahamian and Caribbean yacht racing, as well as technical articles on maintenance and chartering for *Cruising World, Yacht Vacations* and *Yachting.* Her book credits include coauthoring a full-length biography on the life of rhythm-and-blues singer Jackie Wilson, and a novel in progress, *A Suspicion of Destiny.*

Carla Muir is a freelance writer of poetry and stories published in *More Stories for the Heart, Keepsakes for the Heart, Do Not Lose Heart* and *A Second Chicken Soup for the Woman's Soul.* Contact Carla through her agent, Susan Yates, at Yates & Yates, LLP at 714-835-3742.

Sam Murphy was born in Carlisle, Pennsylvania. He is sixty-two years old and is married to Marita. He has three children and six grandchildren. Sam is a retired insurance company general manager. Nowadays, he tinkers with making golf clubs and enjoys playing golf with his cronies at Bogie Lake Golf Club in White Lake, Michigan.

Bruce Nash of Studio City, California, produces reality-based television shows for the major networks.

J. G. Nursall is a forty-nine-year-old attorney/teacher living and working in Southern California. Formerly an avid golfer, he writes to relax and to record some of the valuable lessons he learned while playing the game. Mr. Nursall anticipates publishing a collection of short stories in the near future and invites your further inquiry. Please contact him at: *JGNursall@yahoo.com.*

Hugh O'Neill has been writing and performing commentary on fatherhood for several years, including work for National Public Radio's *Morning Edition.* He is the author of *Daddy Cool* and *Here's Looking at You, Kids.* He has also written for several magazines as well as for television's *The Cosby Show, Thirtysomething* and *Sisters.* He lives in Princeton, New Jersey.

Dennis Oricchio is a member of the United States Professional Tennis Association and is a full-time tennis teaching professional for twenty-five years.

David Owen is a contributing editor of *Golf Digest* and a staff writer for *The New Yorker.* His books about golf are *My Usual Game, Lure of the Links* and *The Making of the Masters.* Contact him at *david.owen@sent.net.*

Rod Patterson has worked at *The Oregonian* for thirty years, covering news and features and is presently a features copyeditor. He was raised in Hawaii, graduated from Portland State University with a degree in English literature.

Larry R. Pearson has held a variety of sales, marketing and management positions in the information-technology industry, is a high-handicap golfer and sports lover of all kinds. He and his wife Carolyn have been married for twenty-five years and live in Marietta, Georgia. Their two sons, Benjamin and Gabriel, are now twenty-one and eighteen years old, respectively. Until now, his poems and short stories have been used as gifts and expressions of love to family and friends.

Bill Pelham played on the PGA Tour from 1976 to 1980. Today, he owns a golf marketing company, specializing in promoting corporate golf events nationwide. He can be reached at Doubleagle, 8702 Stone Village Ln., Houston, TX 77040, by phone at 713-937-3866 or at *www.doubleaglegolf.com*.

Mike Pennella is a runner, freelance writer and very occasional golfer residing in Maplewood, New Jersey. This story first appeared in *Golf Journal*, a magazine of the United States Golf Association. Proceeds from the reprinting of this story will be donated to the USGA Foundation.

Bob Phillips, who is now a local public relations executive in Memphis, Tennessee, was executive sports editor of the *Memphis Press Scimitar* and the *Nashville Banner*. The fifty-four-year-old native Memphian does extensive freelance sports writing in the southeast. Ironically, Bob does not golf, but loves to write about the sport and its participants.

Nick Price was born in South Africa, but moved to Rhodesia (Zimbabwe) at a young age. Growing up he enjoyed sports of all kinds including cricket, water-skiing and golf. He spent two years in the Rhodesian Air Force and obtained his pilot's license. As a family man, he believes in the importance of spending time together. His wife, Sue, and their three children often accompany him to his tournaments. Nick has been very generous supporting charities that benefit children and help protect wildlife. Because of his strong belief in giving back to his home country's youth, he actively supports Zimbabwe Junior Golf. For more information about Nick Price, please contact him at: 900 South U.S. Hwy. 1, #105, Jupiter, FL 33477. Phone: 561-575-6588; fax: 561-575-5420.

Rich Radford lives in Norfolk, Virginia, where he is a sports writer for *The Virginian-Pilot*, covering among other subjects, golf. He is a semi-regular contributor to *Washington Golf Monthly* and *The New York Mets Inside Pitch* magazine. He and his wife, Laurie, have two sons, Kevin and Alex.

Carol McAdoo Rehme, a frequent contributor to *Chicken Soup for the Soul* and other inspirational books, is a full-time storyteller, speaker and author. Her latest passion is a pilot program, "Silver Linings for Golden Agers." It is the recipient of several grants and provides highly interactive, multisensory presentations at eldercare facilities. Contact her at: *carol@rehme.com* or *www.rehme.com*.

Stan Reynolds is a freelance writer and security consultant. Now at work on his second novel, his articles have appeared in newspapers and journals. A former marine, Pinkerton detective, and president/owner of a security company, he also served as chairman of the Georgia State Board, Private Detectives and Security Agencies. He can be reached at River Plantation, 8566 Sawyer Brown Rd., Nashville, TN 37221 or call 615-673-1207.

Jimmy Roberts is an Emmy-Award-winning correspondent for ESPN and ABC Sports. He is also a contributor to ABC News, where his work has appeared on *World News Tonight* and *Good Morning America*. On the print side, Roberts writes for *ESPN Magazine*. He also has a regular column on *ESPN.com* from which "An Embrace in the Bittersweet Middle" was taken.

Ken Robertson considers himself a rookie author and a veteran golfer. He began golfing in the Ottawa area in the 1930s. Since that time, he has gained quite a reputation as well as a low handicap, and earned himself a place in history in the local Cornwall Sports Hall of Fame. He is retired and lives with his wife, Anne. He has three sons, Bruce, Gordon and Mark.

Bob Robinson a 1956 graduate of the University of Oregon, retired in 1999 after thirty-seven-and-a-half years as a sportswriter at *The Oregonian* in Portland, Oregon. He continues to do freelance writing, mostly on golf. He was named Oregon's Sportswriter of the Year in 1977 after covering the Portland Trail Blazers in their NBA championship season.

Lorne Rubenstein is one of the world's best known and most respected golf writers. The author of half-a-dozen books, he has been the golf columnist for the *Toronto Globe* and *Mail* for more than fifteen years. He's won three first place awards in Golf Writer's Association of America writing contest, and one National Magazine Award in Canada. Lorne still carries a 3.1 handicap, and won the Golf Writers Association championship in 1984. He continues to maintain that his best days as a player are ahead of him.

Melissa Russell is the wife and mother of golfers, and an award-winning writer in her own right. Having her story published in *Chicken Soup for the Golfer's Soul* is her idea of a double eagle! Her essays have been published as back-page features in *Smithsonian* magazine and *ByLine*. One of her children's stories will appear in an upcoming issue of *The Flicker Magazine*. She can be contacted at 909 Country Club Circle, Grand Prairie, TX 75052, or *wedoma@aol.com*.

Steve Schokett's story originally appeared in *Golf Journal*, a publication of the United States Golf Association. Proceeds from the reprinting of this story will be donated to the USGA Foundation.

Nick Seitz resides in Rowayton, Connecticut, with his wife, Velma. He graduated from the University of Oklahoma, where he majored in philosophy. Before joining *Golf Digest* magazine, he was sports editor of the *Oklahoma Journal*, where he won several distinguished writing awards. In 1967, he became editor of *Golf Digest*, and in 1982 was named editorial director of *Golf Digest* and *Tennis Magazine*. He is presently editor-in-chief of *The New York Times* Company Magazine Group. Nick has authored many articles and several books on golf, and was coauthor on Tom Watson's *Strategic Golf with Watson*. His work has been included in the annual anthology *Best Sports Stories* numerous times.

Bruce Selcraig, an Austin-based journalist, is a former U.S. Senate investigator and *Sports Illustrated* staff writer whose work has appeared in the *New York Times Magazine, Harper's* and *Sierra*, among others. He writes on topics as varied as corporate crime and baseball gloves, worships Irish golf and New Mexican food, and can be reached at *selcraig@swbell.net*.

Dave Sheinin, twenty-nine, loves chicken soup, golf and soul (music), which makes him feel peculiarly connected to this book. In addition to covering baseball for *The Miami Herald*, the Carrollton, Georgia, native and Vanderbilt University alumnus sings part-time for the Florida Grand Opera, which he thinks must be some sort of dubious first.

Alan Shepard was the first American launched in space in 1961. Ten years later, he commanded *Apollo 14* and became the fifth man to walk on the moon—and the first to play golf there. Alan passed away on July 21, 1998, following a battle with leukemia, at the age of seventy-four. His inspiration to many will not be forgotten.

Bob Shyrock has been a newspaper columnist for fifty-two years, writing about ten thousand columns, some of them golf humor. He also works for Pitman Golf Course as assistant manager/starter, and has been director of numerous golf tournaments, including the Gloucester County (New Jersey) Amateur for twenty years. A lefthander, he is a frustrated 14-handicapper.

John Spielbergs was born and raised in Toronto, Ontario. He currently is a custom homebuilder in Muskoka, a tourist area north of Toronto. He lives with his wife and two daughters and, in addition to golf, likes to play hockey. His story was written as a way of coming to terms with the loss of a life-long friend.

Payne Stewart was at the top of his game on every level when his life came to a sudden and tragic end on October 25, 1999. In June of 1999, he enjoyed the signature triumph of his career and solidified himself as one of the exemplary personalities in his profession with a victory at the U.S. Open and a place on the coveted winning U.S. Ryder Cup team. However, satisfying his professional accomplishments were, it was his personal triumphs that made him stand out.

Tracey Stewart was born in Queensland, Australia, where she also attended school. She met Payne Stewart in March 1980 during the Malaysian Open, in a meeting she describes as love at first sight. After romancing each other around the world, Payne and Tracey were engaged one year later in Singapore and married November 10, 1981, in Southport, on Australia's Gold Coast. As Payne's PGA career took off, the Stewarts moved to Orlando, Florida, where Tracey lives with their two children, Chelsea and Aaron.

Jerry Tarde, editorial director and vice president of *Golf Digest*, has been editor of the magazine for more than two decades. A graduate of Northwestern University, he started as an intern at the magazine in 1977 and since then has written hundreds of instruction and feature articles on golf. He is the co-author with Sam Snead of *Pigeons, Marks, Hustlers (and Other Golf Bettors You Can Beat)*. He now writes a monthly column for *Golf Digest*.

Giles Tippette the former rodeo cowboy, played college football, was a mercenary pilot in Africa, a venture pilot, has published fifty-four books with six major publishers and over 500 articles for major magazines. He has earned his living as a professional writer for thirty-four years. The most tired he has ever been in his life was when they got through hitting that golf ball for thirty-four miles.

Terry Todd is a professor in the kinesiology department at the University of Texas at Austin. He has published five books and over 500 articles in such magazines as *Sports Illustrated* and *Reader's Digest*. He is a former national champion in power-lifting and he has the world's largest collection of books and magazines about physical fitness.

Kay B. Tucker counts on her family and friends for inspiration for anecdotes and stories. She has been published in *Writer's Digest, Reader's Digest, Catholic Digest* and several upstate New York publications. Her e-mail is *Kaytuckerb@aol.com.*

Tom Turley is a former newsman, now retired on Cape Cod.

Don Wade, a former senior editor at *Golf Digest*, is the author of six bestselling collections of golf anecdotes. Covering professional golf since the 1970s, he has worked as a feature reporter for CBS Sports and NBC Sports and as a golf analyst for the USA Network. His writing has appeared in a variety of publications, including the *New York Times* and the *Boston Globe*. He has also written books with Ken Venturi, Sam Snead, Amy Alcott and Nancy Lopez.

Judy Walker is currently teaching seventh-grade language arts and has twenty-five years of teaching experience, which includes first through seventh grades. Her family includes her husband, Randy, and two sons, Greg and Jeff. She enjoys camping, golfing, cooking, reading, traveling, writing and scrap-booking. She would love to write a novel and be published.

Bob Welch is a columnist at *The Register-Guard* newspaper in Eugene, Oregon, and author of six books, including *The Things That Matter Most* and the Gold Medallion award-winning *A Father for All Seasons*. He can be contacted at *bwelch1@concentric.net.*

Bob West has been sports editor of the *Port Arthur* (Texas) *News* since 1972. A single-digit handicapper, West is a past president of the Texas Golf Writers Association. His most memorable golfing experience was playing Cypress Point for the first time. He can be reached at *rdwest@usa.net.*

Ernie Witham writes advertising copy for a living in Santa Barbara, California, but his real love is writing humor based on that ongoing adventure known as everyday life. His humorous essays have been published in the *Los Angeles Times*, the *Santa Barbara News Press*, *Santa Barbara Families* magazine and others. The moment he first stepped foot on a golf course, he knew he had discovered a new wealth of humor-writing opportunities.

Gordon W. Youngs has been playing golf for thirty-seven years, competitively in high school and college, and occasionally competitively (and always for pleasure) ever since. Golf has given him many enjoyable hours, and many alle-gorical lessons in life. He will always be thankful his father introduced him to the game. Gordon is a California native who is a human resources director for a local government; currently a single-digit handicap index, which varies with frequency of play; married to a non-golfer, but their eight-year-old son has shown some interest in the game. He enjoys trying new courses whenever and wherever they have the opportunity to travel.

Allan Zullo of Fairview, North Carolina, has written over seventy nonfiction books on a variety of subjects.

Permissions *(continued from page ii)*

A Day at The Tradition. Reprinted by permission of Christine Clifford. ©1998 Christine Clifford.

I Hate Golf—I Love Golf. Reprinted by permission of George Bush. ©1998 George Bush.

A Candle in the Wind. Reprinted by permission of Jack Sheehan. ©1998 Jack Sheehan and Peter Jacobsen.

Turning Back the Clock. Reprinted by permission of Betty Cuniberti. ©1998 Betty Cuniberti. Originally appeared in *Golf Digest Woman.*

The Promise Keeper, A Change of Heart, and *My Course, My Rules.* Reprinted courtesy of *SPORTS ILLUSTRATED:* "The Promise Keeper" by Rick Reilly, *SPORTS ILLUSTRATED,* February 21, 2000. ©2000 Time Inc. "A Change of Heart" by Rick Reilly, *SPORTS ILLUSTRATED,* October 4, 1999, ©1999. Time Inc. "My Course, My Rules" by Rick Reilly, *SPORTS ILLUSTRATED,* April 10, 2000, ©2000. All Rights Reserved.

The One Hundred Greatest Golf Courses. Reprinted by permission of Bruce Nash and Allan Zullo. From *Golf's Most Outrageous Quotes* by Bruce Nash and Allan Zullo. ©1995 Nash & Zullo Productions, Inc.

Daddy Tees Off. From *A Man Called Daddy,* ©1996 by Hugh O'Neill and published by Rutledge Hill Press, Nashville, Tennessee.

The Man with the Perfect Swing. Reprinted by permission of Bruce Selcraig. ©2000 Bruce Selcraig.

Common Ground. Reprinted by permission of Ahmed Tharwat Abdelaal. ©2000 Ahmed Tharwat Abdelaal. Appeared in *Golf Journal,* October 2000.

Ladies, Is Golf for You? Reprinted by permission of Deisy M. Flood. ©1998 Deisy M. Flood. Appeared in *Golf Journal,* November/December 1998.

Like Father, Like Son. Reprinted by permission of Michael Konick. ©2000 Michael Konick.

The Dying Light and *Wake-Up Call.* Reprinted by permission of Robert S. Welch. ©2000 Robert S. Welch.

Plimpton to the Fore. Reprinted by permission of George Plimpton. ©1998 George Plimpton.

There Is No "I" in Team. Reprinted by permission of Dave Sheinin. ©1998 Dave Sheinin. Originally appeared in *Golf Journal.*

The Magoo Caper. Reprinted by permission of Harvey Mackay. ©1998 Harvey Mackay.